Inquiry in Music Education

Inquiry in Music Education: Concepts and Methods for the Beginning Researcher, Second Edition, introduces research and scholarship in music education as an ongoing *spiral of inquiry*. Exploring research conventions that are applicable beyond music to the other arts and humanities as well, it offers a sequential approach to topic formulation, information literacy, reading and evaluating research studies, and planning and conducting original studies within accepted guidelines.

Following the legacy begun by Edward Rainbow and Hildegard C. Froehlich, this book expands what is meant by music education and research, teaching tangible skills for music educators with diverse instructional goals and career aspirations. The second edition addresses the changes in methods due to technological advances, a proliferation of new scholarship, and an awareness of the impact of place and culture on researchers and research participants.

This edition features:

- the most current information on research tools, strategies to remain up-to-date, and expanded supplemental online materials (see inquiryinmusiceducation.com)
- case studies that reflect recent research and discuss issues of gender, race, and culture previously absent from mainstream scholarship
- an acknowledgment of the assessment demands of contemporary K–12 schooling
- a chapter devoted to mixed methods, arts-based, and practitioner inquiry
- assignments and other resources designed to be friendly for online course delivery
- chapters from contributing authors Debbie Rohwer and Marie McCarthy, bringing additional depth and perspective.

Inquiry in Music Education provides students with the language, skills, and protocols necessary to succeed in today's competitive markets of grant writing, arts advocacy, and public outreach as contributing members of the community of music educators.

Carol Frierson-Campbell is Professor at William Paterson University.

Hildegard C. Froehlich is Professor Emeritus at the University of North Texas.

Inquiry in Music Education

Concepts and Methods for the Beginning Researcher

SECOND EDITION

Carol Frierson-Campbell and Hildegard C. Froehlich

with contributions by Debbie Rohwer and Marie McCarthy

Routledge
Taylor & Francis Group

NEW YORK AND LONDON

Cover image: DaniLana/Shutterstock.com

Second edition published 2022
by Routledge
605 Third Avenue, New York, NY 10158

and by Routledge
4 Park Square, Milton Park, Abingdon, Oxon, OX14 4RN

Routledge is an imprint of the Taylor & Francis Group, an informa business

First edition published by Routledge 2013

Library of Congress Cataloging-in-Publication Data
Names: Frierson-Campbell, Carol, 1961– author. | Froehlich, Hildegard C., author. |
   Rohwer, Debbie Ann, 1966– contributor. | McCarthy, Marie, 1956– contributor.
Title: Inquiry in music education : concepts and methods for the beginning
   researcher / Carol Frierson-Campbell, Hildegard C. Froehlich ; with contributions by
   Debbie Rohwer, Marie McCarthy.
Description: Second edition. | New York : Routledge, 2022. | Includes bibliographical
   references and index.
Identifiers: LCCN 2021041438 (print) | LCCN 2021041439 (ebook) |
   ISBN 9780367523947 (hardback) | ISBN 9780367523930 (paperback) |
   ISBN 9781003057703 (ebook)
Subjects: LCSH: Music—Instruction and study—Research.
Classification: LCC MT1 .R26 2022 (print) | LCC MT1 (ebook) | DDC 780.71—dc23
LC record available at https://lccn.loc.gov/2021041438
LC ebook record available at https://lccn.loc.gov/2021041439

ISBN: 978-0-367-52394-7 (hbk)
ISBN: 978-0-367-52393-0 (pbk)
ISBN: 978-1-003-05770-3 (ebk)

DOI: 10.4324/9781003057703

Typeset in Bembo
by Apex CoVantage, LLC

Access the Support Material: inquiryinmusiceducation.com

Dedication

Carol Frierson-Campbell dedicates this book to . . . her students who taught her to teach, her mother who taught her to sing, and to Bob, who (still) makes her heart sing!

Hildegard C. Froehlich dedicates this second edition in loving memory to her late husband Edward L. Rainbow.

Contents

Figures

Tables

Preface

The second edition of *Inquiry in Music Education: Concepts and Methods for the Beginning Researcher*, like the first, has its origins in a previous work, namely *Research in Music Education: An Introduction to Disciplined Inquiry*, which was written by co-author Hildegard C. Froehlich and her late husband Edward Rainbow and published in 1987 by Schirmer.

As excerpted from that Preface:

> This book is a reflection of our collective experiences in teaching research to both begin-ning and advanced graduate students. These experiences included introducing master-level students to basic concepts of research, developing skills of critical analysis in doctoral students, and guiding doctoral candidates in dissertation work. In all these situations it appeared that the main problem in bringing research close to the students' minds is anchored in their diverse views of what music education is.
>
> For many, the content of music education consists of the methodologies and skills employed in teaching music to people from 5 to 18 years of age. For others, the content is found in the acquisition of knowledge about appropriate music and teaching literature. A third group tends to equate music education with any form of music teaching wherever it occurs—in schools, universities, church programs, camp activities, or private studies.
>
> Because of the diverse goals most music education students have set for themselves, a research book in music education should have a two-fold aim: to train the future researcher and to make those who do not wish to conduct research comfortable with the role of disciplined thinking in music education. The book should be general and specific at the same time.
>
> (p. xiii)

This second edition of *Inquiry in Music Education* proudly follows the legacy begun by Rainbow and Froehlich of integrating the notion of research as disciplined inquiry into a description of the field of music education. The thought processes inherent in that inquiry are balanced with basic techniques for conducting research. In all instances, emphasis is placed on using questions about professional concerns to guide chosen methods and processes.

PURPOSE AND OBJECTIVES

Since the publication of *Research in Music Education* nearly 35 years ago, and the first edition of *Inquiry in Music Education* 9 years ago, many changes have impacted university requirements for graduate student research in music education. These include the technologies used for research; institutional assessment demands for practicing K-12 teachers; the proliferation of scholarly publications in the fields of music, education, and music education; and in particular the rise of online teaching and learning—especially since the advent of the Covid-19 pandemic—resulting in a large increase in the number of graduate courses and degrees offered online. Many of those programs have eliminated or cut back on thesis requirements, offering only a five to six week summer research course to fulfill the requirements mandated for the degree. As a result, even some doctoral students enter degree programs without ever having undertaken an original research project.

In the *Coda* to *Research in Music Education*, Rainbow and Froehlich (1987) stated: "Not all persons should be expected to become professional researchers any more than all music students should be expected to become professional musicians" (p. 281). We still subscribe to that statement, but also believe, as did Rainbow and Froehlich, that the field of music education needs for educators as well as researchers to develop investigative skills that go beyond finding useful sources for writing term papers or completing required reading assignments.

Many graduate music students begin their respective degree programs questioning the utility of scholarly work for becoming better musicians and teachers. We believe, however, that skills in research and scholarship serve a larger purpose than simply completing a graduate degree. They should introduce graduate students to the critical thinking and information literacy necessary to navigate, evaluate, and use the bounty of online information about teaching and learning, as well as the language, and protocols by which to succeed in the competitive market of grant writing, arts advocacy, and public outreach as a contributing member of the community of music educators.

Mindful of this purpose, the objectives of the second edition of *Inquiry in Music Education: Concepts and Methods for the Beginning Researcher* remain to:

1)   expand what is meant by music education and by research,
2)   help students find their niche in those definitions, and
3)   teach tangible skills that are useful for music educators with diverse instructional goals and career aspirations.

APPROACH

Accomplishing those objectives calls for an even more student-centered approach than Rainbow and Froehlich followed in 1987. To accomplish that task we:

*   use language and examples throughout the textbook, updated in the second edition of *Inquiry in Music Education*, to include recently published research, often done by graduate students, to meet novice researchers at the place where they likely begin doing research—in the classroom.
*   weave case stories from members of a fictitious introductory research class throughout the text to help novice scholars see students (un)like themselves experience the struggles and rewards of learning to do research. Updated for the second edition, these stories reflect current concerns about the impact of place and culture on both teaching and research, and a new chapter brings mixed methods, practitioner, and arts-based inquiry into the conversation. Created from a combination of ethnographic research and informal experiences over many years of teaching research to music students in the United States, any resemblance to actual persons is unintentional.

- offer guidance, new in the second edition, for crafting a research proposal, completing a required research report, and continuing with the spiral of inquiry by presenting or publishing their findings.
- bring perspectives from a variety of experts in music education research, namely our contributing authors Drs. Marie McCarthy (Chapter 6), and Debbie Rohwer (Chapters 10–12). We believe their voices bring additional depth to and expand the scope of the book beyond what two authors alone could have done. Their voices also demonstrate how form and content in various modes of inquiry might be reflected in a researcher's style, language, and tone of presentation.

This second edition of *Inquiry in Music Education* had just gotten underway when the Covid-19 pandemic compelled the closure of many schools and universities, consequently forcing most research courses (and numerous research projects) to migrate into an online format. Mindful of how this change impacted the delivery of instruction, the second edition has updated within-chapter and end-of-chapter questions and assignments designed to be friendly to online course delivery and available as supplemental online materials (see inquiryinmusiceducation.com).

ORGANIZATION

The first four chapters (from the Introduction through Chapter 3) in combination with recommended reading and some written work, are intended to teach the basic processes of scholarly thinking: Asking questions, accessing, reading, and critically examining appropriate literature. Chapter 4 (the first of two chapters on philosophical inquiry) introduces the kind of philosophical thinking (you might call it critical thinking) that underlies all music education scholarship while Chapter 5 is geared toward students who will pursue philosophical inquiry as a degree project. Chapter 6 offers a comprehensive view of historical inquiry, from asking historical questions to conceiving of a project and designing a proposal. Chapters 7 and 8 address a selection of qualitative research traditions with conceptual elements covered in Chapter 7 and more technical aspects featured in Chapter 8. Chapter 9 introduces the measurement theories that underlie quantitative research, while Chapters 10–12 provide direction for descriptive, correlational, and ex post facto/experimental research, respectively. Chapter 13 features three traditions that utilize both qualitative and quantitative procedures as tools: Mixed methods, practitioner inquiry/action research, and arts-based and arts practice research. Chapter 14, dedicated to the use of research tools suitable in both quantitative and qualitative research approaches, is recommended for those students who want to "dig deeper." Chapter 15 offers steps for completing a course or degree project and invites readers to share their research with additional audiences via scholarly or general-interest articles, grant proposals, and workshops. A final "Recapitulation" chapter guides readers to continue the spiral of inquiry by thinking about their research in the bigger picture of music education.

TO THE INSTRUCTOR

This book is designed for a one-semester course or two-semester sequence; it would be difficult to teach in its entirety in one course. The instructor, therefore, should make a judgment as to what to use. Some chapters are lengthy; however, in many instances the subsections were written to stand by themselves and allow for specific reading assignments of manageable proportions. The recommended reading lists at the end of each chapter are intended as invitations to become familiar with important scholarship in the field rather than mandatory reading. Many of the sources not only are pertinent to the topic but also represent good examples of how to look at the usual in an unusual way.

Should you direct or teach in a graduate program with a two-semester research sequence, we recommend that the first semester focus mostly on the chapters in the first section, accompanied by those methods chapters that are most pertinent to your students' research needs. Each methods chapter, from Chapter 5 through 13, concludes with an outline and description for completing a research proposal.

During the second semester, a "deep dive," possibly with some repetition, into methods chapters would work well, combined with recommended reading and discussion of students' original research.

As is customary, we present a series of questions at the end of each chapter for review. These are intended simply as guidelines, since the students themselves usually generate better questions than the authors. Second, the kind of questions being asked depends entirely on the focus the instructor has chosen for the overall course. Because the book seeks to be useful for a variety of teaching situations, we have listed a few topics from which questions might be developed. But even these topics are only suggestions. It is our opinion that the instructor should teach "around" the book, not "by" the book.

ACKNOWLEDGEMENTS

Indebted to anonymous peers who critiqued the original manuscript and made constructive criticisms and contributions, we incorporated into the present version of the text many of their comments and suggestions. Any remaining errors and misrepresentations remain our responsibility. Some accommodations had to be made to address the different needs of upper-level undergraduates, master's students, doctoral students and possibly others: How comprehensive should the coverage be? How deep? If we were to go further in-depth on certain topics, would it overwhelm those who would not use that information (and also inflate the price of the book)? If we omitted such concerns would the book cease to be useful for more advanced instruction? Believing that research skills at every level develop on a continuum, we decided on a compromise between depth and breadth.

Special thanks are due to many past and present colleagues and students who used and critiqued preliminary drafts of the text, making many excellent points along the way. From the first edition of *Inquiry in Music Education* we gratefully acknowledge Drs. Dale Bazan, Wayne Bowman, Richard Colwell, Susan Conkling, Terry Gates, Adria Hoffman, Kathryn Roulston, and Craig Resta. For the second edition we add research interviewees Cara Bernard and Joyce McCall, philosophers Elizabeth Victor (Carol's colleague) and Matteo Ravasio, members of the William Paterson University Professional Writers Group. Very special acknowledgements are due to UNT doctoral candidate Kelsey Nussbaum (now Dr. Nussbaum) who served as research assistant for the second edition, and Brad Haefner for his expert assistance with illustrations in both editions. Our most sincere thank-yous go to Routledge Senior Editor Constance Ditzel for the first edition and start of the second; and Routledge Music Editor Genevieve Aoki and Senior Editorial Assistant Peter Sheehy for their patient guidance and encouragement as we completed the second edition.

Research is an ongoing process and so is writing: This edition is not anymore "final" than one would consider the performance of a musical composition in recital to be the final product in one's career as a musician. As soon as one steps off the stage, thoughts about improving the next performance come up. So it is with this textbook: Plans for further work immediately arise.

Carol Frierson-Campbell and Hildegard C. Froehlich

June 2021

Introduction

Learning about the Book and Getting Involved

As its title suggests, this Introduction:

- states the objectives of *Inquiry in Music Education* (2nd Edition) and describes its layout, and
- gets you started with the research process.

Involving yourself in the task of asking questions is one of the most important attributes of a good researcher. That task is aided when you keenly observe what goes on around you and document those observations.

PURPOSE OF THE BOOK AND ITS OBJECTIVES

This textbook portrays scholarship in music education as a cycle of thinking, reading, observing, and publicly sharing the results of those efforts. Each activity is supported by the other, building toward what we call an ongoing *spiral of inquiry*. Thus, the second edition of *Inquiry in Music Education: Concepts and Methods for the Beginning Researcher* has three objectives:

1) expanding what is meant by music education and by research,
2) helping students find their niche in those definitions, and
3) teaching tangible skills that are useful for musicians, music educators, community musicians and others with diverse instructional goals and career aspirations.

To that end, the chapters in this textbook focus on the following skills:

- critical reading of research articles and books,
- scholarly writing as a tool for professional communication, and
- basic skills for conducting research on the learning and teaching of music.

Those skills are most useful when applied to professional interests in a sequential way. We describe that sequence as:

- thinking about *areas of professional concern*,
- *framing* those concerns into *research ideas* based on perspective, mode of inquiry, and professional focus,

DOI: 10.4324/9781003057703-1

- narrowing research ideas into a researchable *topic* through engagement with scholarly literature, and
- discerning from that topic a *research purpose, purpose specifications*, and *rationale* for the purpose of crafting a final research project (i.e., literature review, research proposal for a course, or research project as a degree requirement).

We retain the description of the characteristics and skills that define a scholarly mindset used in our predecessor publication, Rainbow and Froehlich's 1987 *Research in Music Education*:

- having a basic inquisitiveness and intellectual curiosity about the learning and teaching processes wherever they occur,
- turning basic curiosity into detailed questions, and addressing them in appropriate ways,
- being aware of and open to creative thoughts and ideas in fields other than your own,
- thinking about and systematically planning approaches and perspectives by which to study an issue, and
- sharing (in the written word, in public speaking, or in both) newly discovered insights with members of the field.

The shorter version of those characteristics is: (1) asking questions, (2) turning any one of them into a finite research purpose, (3) applying specific methods of data gathering and analysis to your purpose, and (4) reporting the findings through speech and publication. These activities are what the spiral of inquiry portrays: think, read, observe, share, and think again . . . in any order. It is a short description for a life-long process.

When registering for an introductory research class at the graduate level, many students doubt that research is "for them." Far more pressing matters—practicing their instruments, playing in or conducting ensembles, and "having a life"—occupy their minds and time. Perhaps you feel similarly. But because of a general sense of curiosity and interest in your chosen career path, you likely will soon discover the excitement inherent in learning how researchers in the field of music, education, music education, and many other fields have addressed important questions about learning and teaching. Learning to do research connects you with those researchers as your future peers. This is the hope that guides this book.

Exploration: A Round Table Discussion

- Why have you enrolled in this class?
- What do you know about research?
- What are your plans after you complete the degree?
- What has been your greatest experience as a Musician? Teacher? Student?
- Which of the students described later in the introduction do you most relate to, and why?

CONSIDERING PERSPECTIVE: AN ONLINE EXCURSION

The *Times Square Earthcam* website displays several "webcams" that overlook New York City's Times Square, enabling viewers to get different real-time views of this famous setting. The camera can be accessed by going to www.earthcam.com and choosing the Times Square camera or by entering "Times Square Earthcam" into a search engine.

With the lens zoomed in (4K or Street Cam views), you have only a limited view but you can see a lot of detail in that view. It is a perspective that does not allow for easy comparisons. With the lens zoomed out (Crossroads or North View or South View), you give up detail for "the bigger picture." You can see many more people and objects, thereby gaining in numbers but losing in detail.

The lesson to be learned from this example is this: Perspective impacts what you see. When you take an overview, you miss details; when you zoom in on details, their place within the larger scheme of things gets lost. So it is with research: Taking a macro-perspective of the learning and teaching of music can obscure the details of how individual learners learn or how particular teachers teach. The opposite is true as well: Being concerned with a micro-view of the teaching-learning process in music can prevent you from seeing how your own actions or that of a few colleagues fit into the bigger picture of music education as it is practiced in the country or even the world.

Now imagine that you decided to devote an entire semester to a study of Times Square. What would it take to expand the webcam observations into an extended project that would interest a musician/educator? The best and fastest way to start any observation project would be to ask "who, what, where, when, why, and how." Given your interest in music performance and teaching, focus first on music-related questions:

- *Who* are the musicians that work in Times Square?
- *How* do they find employment?
- *What* music do they play?
- *Where* do Times Square musicians get their training?
- *When* did Times Square become an icon of U.S. popular culture?
- *Why* is Times Square so famous?
- *Why* is Times Square so commercial?
- *How* has the music performed in Times Square changed over time?
- *How well* does the music performed in Times Square represent music across the United States?

Any one of these questions catapults you into a myriad of further questions by which to try to answer the first one. To illustrate, consider the question about Times Square seemingly being very commercial. Before seeking answers to that question, however, consider: Why might you ask the question in the first place? Two possibilities come to mind: One, as a classically trained performer, you find the commercialism of Times Square unnerving and view the glamour associated with it as a cultural centerpiece overstated. Your intent is to document this point of view by identifying what you consider to be the most flagrantly commercial characteristics of Times Square. Two, as a budding music entrepreneur, you are interested in learning whether Times Square might be a model for other cities. You look to replicate in your hometown what you consider the main reasons for Times Square's success as a tourist attraction: its buzzing commercialism.

What would you need to do to study either of these two scenarios and derive questions from them that suggest the need for more research? In both cases, you would need to clearly define the term "commercial" as it relates to your questions. Only once that is accomplished can you look for and catalogue the characteristics mentioned in any definition of "commercialism." Such cataloguing however triggers new questions:

- When would the observations take place?
- Do all observations address the criteria of the term "commercial" as originally formulated? Are there some that do not? If so, what needs to be done to account for those things that confound the issue—things that are not readily observable but likely present?

- How could you set up the observations to assure agreement among several observers? Where might disagreement occur, and why might it exist?

After all observations are collected, catalogued, and analyzed, equating the classical musician's findings to those compiled by the music entrepreneur would be like comparing apples and oranges. Therefore, good scholarship mandates that perspectives chosen and actions taken be articulated, justified, and documented. This means (1) stating your reasons for asking specific questions before making particular observations, (2) defining the key terms in your question, and (3) documenting each and every step taken in zooming in on certain details and zooming out of others.

Exploration: A Writing Exercise

For the purpose of comparing what you and your classmates saw when engaging in the webcam exercise, select ONE of the three tasks as your first writing exercise:

1) Put into words what you see with the lens zoomed in. Make your description as detailed as possible and document the time of day when you made this observation. Write your observations down and share them with your classmates.
2) Look for and discuss agreements and disagreements between your descriptions and those of your classmates.
3) Given who you are and what you do, create your own questions for a *Times Square Observation Study* or a comparable study in your own neighborhood. Then carry this one step forward and apply it to what you do professionally or as a student.

VIEWING MUSIC EDUCATION FROM A PERSONAL ANGLE

The Times Square EarthCams enabled you to zoom in and out of a geographical location to obtain either a bird's eye view of its overall character or obtain details about specific buildings, roads, street corners. A similar process can be applied to examining yourself with the above "who, what, where, when, why and how" questions: How have you become who you believe you are? What events, persons, and experiences have contributed to where you stand on an issue at any given time? When and where did those events shape your own private and professional self the most?

Comparing your answers and life story to that of others around you, it probably comes as no surprise that each biography is unique. Variances in lifestyles, acquired knowledge and skills, upbringing, age, race, nationality, gender, and other factors—too many to list here—contribute to how you see the world and yourself in it. Call it your worldview—the source for and reason why answers to "who, what, where, when, why, and how" questions differ from person to person and groups to groups. A good researcher becomes aware of those differences and accounts for them in the way answers to any given questions come about. To illustrate, we begin with you and other students (un)like you.

OTHER STUDENTS (UN)LIKE YOU

Who you are impacts not only the topics you are interested in; it also impacts *how* you approach their study. Take, for instance, *Carlos, Chi -Hui, Christy, Dale, Greg, Isaac, Jeannette, Keisha, Liam, Marguerite, Michelle,* and *Muna*, students in a research class (RC 533) like the one you are enrolled in. Their instructor was Professor Edwards (known to most students as Prof. E.), an experienced college teacher and researcher with 10 years of public school and 7 years of college teaching experience.

Prof. E. allowed his students the freedom to explore many different topics before settling in on any one project. Responding to the fact that each adult learner brings to the class unique life experiences, varying personal and professional histories, motivations, and aspirations, Prof. E.'s instructional plans included a high degree of individualization for class assignments and projects.

Carlos pursued an MME degree during the summers. Teaching band in a small rural high school in the Midwest, he was motivated by two things: his district's require-ments that he develop standards-based methods for assessing the students in his ensembles, and the raise he would get once he completed his degree. He hoped the research class would help him find "a foolproof system" of assessment.

Chi -Hui, a last semester senior in music education, received special permission to enroll in the research class because of her intention of continuing with her master's degree at the same university. She was already certified as an elementary music teacher in Taiwan, with two years of teaching experience to her credit. Fearing that what she learned in the United States might not be applicable to what was going on back home, she occasionally expressed that concern to her peers. She pur-sued the U.S. degree believing it would open doors for her at home.

Christy pursued a DMA in Performance with Music Education as a related field. She was an experienced private voice teacher who freelanced at night and on weekends. She came back to school because she felt her life to be in a rut. Always a challenge-seeker, she wanted to get excited about research but was hesitant to think about teaching in new ways.

Dale, a PhD student in music education with a background as a teacher of jazz, modern band and concert band ensembles, also played the guitar and composed music for his own band. His master's thesis, completed a year earlier, involved a survey of all of his concert band students and their parents about their views con-cerning scheduling, trips, uniforms, and instructional content. Valuing the exper-tise gained by doing that study, he now was motivated to expand that knowledge. But he was a bit impatient about the "hoops" of the degree program that at times seemed unrelated to his own interests.

Greg was in the early stage of the PhD Program in music education after nearly 15 years of teaching strings in the Midwest and after a divorce had upset his life goals. He came back to school to get away from his "former life." Still somewhat unclear as to the purpose of the degree in his career plans, the idea of teaching at the college level appealed to him. He was concerned, however, about the pay cut he would likely face as a beginning college instructor.

Isaac, pursuing a Master of Music (MM) with conducting as his major field, was a high school band director with three years of teaching experience. His primary objective was to improve his performance and conducting skills. Although he found the courses for the degree valuable, he sometimes felt that they did not really tell him what it took to become a better teacher-conductor. A good student academically, he mostly focused on finding conducting opportunities and on score study.

Jeannette, a PhD student in music education with a minor in education administration, was also a seasoned choir director who continued to conduct a very successful church choir in her own community. She also had some teaching awards to her credit and was highly motivated to complete the doctorate. Her experience teaching in underserved settings spurred a particular interest in the education of minority students. She hoped to find a position at an HBCU (Historically Black College or University) or other institution of higher education that prioritizes the success of students from traditionally underserved communities, especially Black, Indigenous, and students of color. She actively tried to direct all course assignments toward that interest.

Keisha, an MM student with aspirations of getting a PhD in the future, was an elementary general music teacher on leave from her school after 10 years of experience. She was interested in issues concerning child development with special emphasis on early childhood. Holding endorsements by Kodaly, Gordon, and Orff Associations, she was married and had two small children.

Liam, an MM jazz studies major who worked on the side as a teaching artist, was interested in scat singing and liked to listen to such artists as Louis Armstrong, Ella Fitzgerald, Sara Vaughn, and Billie Holiday. Liam was especially intrigued by what he considered Armstrong's invention of scat singing and was excited about the research class because he planned to document Armstrong's leadership role in the development of scat singing.

With a master's degree in music education and a bachelor's in English to her credit, *Marguerite* came to music education later in life. She had developed an interest in philosophy and the arts in general and wanted to pursue a PhD with emphasis in those areas. A quiet yet inquisitive person, she preferred writing to talking. She thought a great deal about music-making and learning outside of the confines of school and had already started seeking reading sources on that subject prior to taking the research class.

Michelle pursued a Master of Music Education degree (MME). With more than 20 years' experience teaching music in the inner city, she had learned how to reach students through a well-balanced, sequentially structured, culturally relevant music program. But the advent of online music learning, especially during the recent pandemic, led her to think she needed to update her approach. She looked to the research component of the master's program to help her find direction, and looked forward to what she would learn from taking the class.

Muna, seeking a PhD in Music Education, was most interested in what is known as Community Music. A recent immigrant from a country with a history of political upheaval, she wanted her research to be more than just "an academic exercise." She definitely preferred facilitating community music experiences over bookwork.

Is there any person in RC 533 with whom you identify more closely than with others in that class? If so, what are the commonalities? Asked differently, what do you bring to the research process in terms of your own biography, professional background, and life experiences that could impact your work as a teacher? Write down your answer(s) and keep what you wrote; you might need it later.

THE RESEARCH PROCESS PERSONALIZED

Once or twice a month during class time, Prof. E. would meet students in a coffee shop on campus for what they called "coffee talk." It was a time for students to share and ask questions in a setting less formal than the classroom. Some students might talk about putting research plans into practice while others would point out what might stand in their way. At times, the conversations centered on similarities and differences between expectations for a musician, a teacher/educator, and a researcher. Usually, however, the students talked more about parallels between music-making and teaching rather than the place of research in their lives. In fact, the subject of "research" only came up when prompted by Prof. E. A patient teacher, he knew that the students would need time to accept research and scholarship as important complements to becoming well-informed musicians and teachers.

Similar to what it has taken you to become a fine musician and a successful teacher, adding scholarship to your professional skills takes ongoing and engaged practice, patience, a good dose of self-discipline, imagination and creativity, and a zest for wanting to be the best you can be. Once you couple those characteristics with an inquisitive mind, you have the ingredients that make a musician-teacher-scholar/researcher. An inquisitive mind of that caliber not only asks questions but also tries to answer them. Both the asking of questions and efforts to address them are learned skills. They consist of reading, documenting your reading, examining evidence in support of specific answers in a variety of ways, and sharing those answers with others.

Throughout the book, the process is visualized as a spiral of ever more focused inquiries and actions. Figure I.1 shows that spiral in its most basic form, suggesting that research should begin with your own professionally pressing concerns and experiences. Those, in turn, undergo a continuing regime of thinking, reading, observing, and sharing with others (ultimately in writing) what it is that you have thought, read, and observed and how it all fits together.

Each of us engages daily in the activities of thinking, reading, observing, and sharing—the latter in conversation or when writing; but we may not always knowingly combine all four

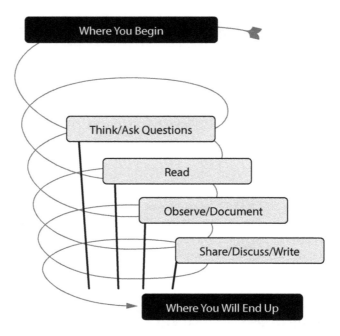

FIGURE I.1 The Spiral of Inquiry in Its Most Basic Form

actions for the purpose of addressing a specific research problem or question. This is because as teachers we are held to respond through immediate actions to what we see, hear, or otherwise experience around us. We generally do not have the time to reflect on the experiences themselves as springboards for examining ourselves, how and why things are done the way they are, or questioning what lies behind those experiences. Research, however, allows us to do just that.

Actively engaging in the scholarly process undoubtedly takes you out of the relative comfort zone of the practice room, the studio, or the rehearsal hall into the perhaps less familiar environments of the university library (be it in person or online), the computer lab, or a *bona fide* research lab (if your school or department has such a space). You may also spend more time than usual with your peers discussing and examining accepted traditions of teaching, and you may begin to test old assumptions or new ideas about how you think learning might take place. Furthermore, extra time may be dedicated to documenting your own thinking on particular topics and, eventually, to planning out a research study of your own. In addition to time, however, you also need perspective about yourself as a musician-teacher as well as musician-performer, how you see the field of music education, and what has traditionally been done in the name of research and scholarship. Finally, as in studio class, be ready to accept criticism from others for the purpose of improving your own work.

DEVELOPING A SCHOLARLY MIND

What follows are three student examples from RC 533 about the connection between disciplined inquiry and thinking, reading, observing, and sharing.

Isaac's expressed interest in wanting to become a "better conductor" required a definition of what he meant by "better." What experiences or what role models did he have in mind that suggested what a "good" or "better" conductor/band director was? How well did his definition of "better" fit with other definitions in the worlds of music and music education? Thinking through those questions, it became inevitable for him to consult the literature on how the term "good conducting" was used, if not defined. The combination of thinking, talking to experts, and reading launched Isaac's work for the semester.

Christy—no stranger to the library—spent hours browsing through books and articles about vocal pedagogy to document and compare different approaches with each other. She did this to get a sense of how her own teaching differed or was similar to methods "out there." She hoped that such documentation would help her in identifying a researchable question, a task she hesitated to execute because she did not want to commit to one finite question too soon.

Marguerite's interest in outside-of-school learning processes had led her to the work of Christopher Small (e.g., 1977/1996, 1987/1998a, 1998b). She particularly liked his term "musicking" (with a "k" purposefully inserted by Small) because the invented gerund suggested active engagement in making and listening to music rather than learning about music as a non-participant. She used the term loosely until some friends challenged her to define what she meant by the term they thought she over-used. In pondering their challenge, Marguerite wondered about studying situations in which students controlled their own musical learning. Perhaps she could observe such students in action? She also located and examined publications that described so-called community music processes and informal learning among teenagers and young adults. As she began pondering the notion of informal learning, she began to realize how many questions could arise from just one area of concern.

Driven by personal inquisitiveness at first, each of the three students directed their thinking and reading activities on different issues and zoomed in on them in ways unique to their own perspective of what was important to them individually. However, each of them also connected their personal perspective to the thinking and work by others in music education and related fields.

Because you are now embarking on a similar journey to the students in RC 533, we remind you that a researcher and scholar not only thinks about their own professional interests and concerns but also addresses them in the larger context of the field of music education. Taking that step requires discipline and resolve. Just as making music without practicing takes you nowhere fast, simply being inquisitive without having the research discipline to examine what you are inquisitive about can easily become stale rhetoric.

THINKING ABOUT AREAS OF PROFESSIONAL CONCERN

Undoubtedly, there have been moments in your professional life when you wondered in exasperation why your students reacted in seemingly unpredictable ways and "just did not get it." Indeed,

"When will they ever learn?" or "Isn't there anything that interests them?" has been voiced aloud in many faculty lounges. You may also have said to yourself at times: "If I only had more time, I would like to learn . . ." or "I would love to know why my colleagues/my boss/my students/my students' parents react that way."

The scholarly process described in this textbook offers you a chance to respond to any of those concerns in a productive and proactive way. You turn general expressions of exasperation or curiosity into articulated *areas of concern* by:

* Recalling situations in which you sighed in frustration or got excited about good things happening,
* Describing the situations with many active verbs, and
* Turning your descriptions into actual questions.

Recalling and Describing Teaching and Learning Situations or Moments

The more vividly you can recall critical teaching situations in your recent past and describe them, the more specific your follow-up work can become. If you have not had any professional teaching experience, think of moments where you (as a student) said to yourself, "If I were the teacher, I would do it differently." What is the "it" in this statement and what did the teacher do that prompted you to imagine change?

When you describe those moments, use *descriptive* rather than *judgmental* terms. For instance, saying that a colleague is an *efficient* or even *great* teacher delivers a judgment rather than a description of that teacher's actions. What does your colleague say, do, or stand for that warrants the interpretation of efficient or great teaching? Does your colleague engage all students during rehearsal? Are her lectures full of real-life examples? Does she know all students by name? Allow for unsolicited questions? Have a recognizable instructional plan—visible for all to see? Summarize the contents of the lesson at the end and tell students what she expects for the next lesson? Grade fairly? With all of these attributes present, the conclusion might be that "great" is an apt summary of your colleague's instructional style. However, missing in this assessment would still be how her students assess her teaching: Do all of them feel equally spoken to? Could they understand the points she wanted to make and recall them after the lesson? Clearly, much descriptive evidence is needed before a statement about "great teaching" is more than an assertion. This means that questions, too, should be descriptive rather than judgmental.

Turning Recalled Situations into Actual Questions

Greg brought up a question many teachers ask: "Why are some of my methods class students hesitant to take risks?" Further examination, however, revealed his question to be a lament: "Some of my students are not willing to take risks!" Prof. E. asked Greg to re-word his lament into a question that could be answered by focusing on what the students did that suggested an avoidance of risk. Aided by others in class, Greg came up with this list:

* Did "risk avoidance" involve the same behaviors and actions for all the students in the methods class?

- Did the absence of such behaviors and actions in other students suggest that they were, indeed, willing to take risks in their teaching?
- When did students act in the way that Greg saw as risk-averse? When did they not act in that way?
- How did risk-averse students explain their hesitancy? What reasons did they give?

Greg now had posed "real" (i.e., non-rhetorical) questions that asked for "real" (i.e., information-providing) responses.

Chi- Hui chose to focus on the differences between her experiences in Taiwan and the United States because they impacted her the most in a personal way as a performer and musician. She therefore came up first with "Why are things so different in the U.S. from how they are in Taiwan?" but soon turned that question into "How does the music teacher training in Taiwan differ from that in the United States?" and "Who determines teacher training curricula in both countries?"

Muna and *Christy* found it difficult to turn real life experiences into truly descriptive rather than judgmental questions because both had a strong sense of right and wrong. Muna had taught for several years in a conservatory in her home country and felt that this environment left out the students who most needed music. Christy, on the other hand, was a longtime studio teacher who had highly developed instructional routines that she did not feel needed questioning. Although coming from very different vantage points, both needed some extra time for thinking and browsing before they managed to turn their somewhat emotional sentiments into specific questions. Prompted by Prof. E., Muna came up with these questions: "Were there things about the conservatory experience that excluded traumatized students?" "How might I determine what kinds of music can best reach students who have experienced political unrest?" "Are certain activities better for certain groups?" "Is gender a consideration when providing community music to refugee communities?" "Which members of the refugee community might benefit most from community music?"

Christy began to ask herself: "What are my teaching routines? Did they work equally well for all of my students?" "To what extent does my own teaching approach resemble that of my teacher?" "Were there routines imposed on me by my teacher? If I disliked them then, have I changed them in my own studio routines?" "How do I know that they work(ed)?"

Whether you think of yourself more as a student or as a teacher, your own questions, too, should articulate moments that bothered or pleased you. When you write them down, describe those moments in active verbs without using judgmental words. For instance, instead of saying that something or someone was really good, happy, or successful, describe actions you saw that were "good," "happy," or "successful." Once you have done that, turn those descriptions into "why-what-how-when" questions and share them with your classmates. Then you are on your way to becoming a researcher.

But words as well as actions can be the source for "why-what-how-when" questions. If, for instance, you find ideas in your reading that contradict each other, or find that two historical accounts of the same event describe different occurrences, you have reason to examine why inconsistencies exist, what caused the authors to see the events differently, and how or whether the differences have a bearing on current practices in thought and/or action.

OUTLOOK FOR WHAT IS TO COME

This chapter has introduced you to two premises that permeate the research process in general: (1) The ways you look at objects, actions, experiences, and ideas tend to influence what you focus on and ask questions about; and (2) the experiences that made you into the professional you are or want to be also contribute to defining your researcher-self. Both themes reappear throughout the book because they impact everything that follows.

Like the two themes, two metaphors will resurface as well: the spiral of inquiry visualized above, and the image of research as a journey with markers that guide the way. The markers are the steps you take from the initial literature search to the writing of a proposal (and possibly an entire study). Those steps are reflected by the book chapters, divided into two parts.

Part I (Chapters 1–4) takes you from identifying several areas of concern to exploring a number of research ideas from which a research topic gets selected for detailed study. You learn to turn the topic into a purpose statement and are guided in how to reason out why—in the light of extant literature—your research purpose is important for you to examine and for the profession to know about.

The second part of the book (Chapters 5–13) is organized according to what is referred to as modes of inquiry: The philosophical mode (Chapter 5), defined as the study of *ideas, past and present*; the historical mode (Chapter 6) as the study of *past events, documented actions, behaviors, and experiences*; and the empirical mode (Chapters 7 through 13) as the study of *present events, actions, behaviors, and experiences*. How those events, actions, behaviors, and experiences are expressed, documented, and analyzed as *data* determines whether a study might be called *qualitative* (Chapters 7 and 8) or *quantitative* (Chapters 9–12). Both qualitative and quantitative approaches are used in *mixed approaches, practitioner inquiry, and arts-based research* across a continuum from more to less conventional; those approaches are introduced in Chapter 13.

Chapter 15 addresses what often is called the "so what" factor of research: What do your findings have to do with the questions you asked in the first place and with the body of knowledge of music education in general? The chapter directs you in interpreting and writing up research findings for the summary chapter of theses and dissertations and explains how to use that information to prepare poster and paper presentations, articles suitable for peer-reviewed journals, or grant proposals. A Recapitulation reiterates what we consider the most important and recurring themes throughout the entire book and concludes with what we hope marks an exciting beginning in your own career as musician-educator-researcher/scholar.

At the time Rainbow and Froehlich published their 1987 edition, the catalogues available were dissertations and journals on compact disc. A few libraries offered catalogue access via direct dial-in Internet for users who owned the requisite technology. Since the advent of the Internet, the amount of searchable information has increased profoundly. Researchers now access online journals, self-published works, massive databases of full articles and a host of tools for investigation and statistical analysis. Note, however, that where there is plenty, there is also much waste. As valuable as the Internet is, inaccurate information, questionable sources, and plagiarism require you to be a skeptic first and trusting reader second. This book therefore seeks to offer guidance for responsible travel not only on the information highway but in the entirety of the research process.

CHAPTER SUMMARY

1) Key elements in good scholarship are tangible and concrete. They range from inquisitiveness and intellectual curiosity to such specific skills as thinking, reading, observing, and publicly sharing the results of such activities. Basic curiosity turns into detailed questions that are addressed by appropriate methods communicated in ways that other researchers accept as good scholarship.
2) Metaphors of the webcam and markers on a lifelong journey can be useful in describing fundamental aspects of research in a field that is diverse and broad-based.
3) Who a researcher is or wishes to become enters prominently into the scholarly process itself. The approaches vary due to the professional allegiances a researcher wishes to hone. This means that decisions vary from person to person as to when and how to (a) zoom in on certain aspects concerning the learning and teaching of music, and (b) omit others.
4) Personal and professional aspirations go hand in hand. Both dimensions therefore need to be considered when developing research skills as an added dimension to the professional person one aspires to be.

TOPICS FOR FURTHER EXPLORATION

1) Reflecting back on your Times Square observations and those of your classmates:
   a. How similar were the times and dates that each of you observed?
   b. How closely did you agree with each other on what you saw? Did observations done at the same time show greater agreement?
   c. What could be seen with the lens zoomed in that you could not detect with the lens zoomed out? Is the opposite also the case; that is, are there details you can pick up with the lens zoomed out that you missed when it was zoomed in?
   d. How alike were your observations to those of your classmates? Would you say that you agreed 100% of the time, 75%, 50%, or less? Where were the greatest differences or similarities? What reasons might you suggest as causing either?
   e. What is your impression of Times Square based on your observations and those of your peers? How accurate or representative of Times Square as you know it are your collected observations? In other words, can you trust your findings? If so, why? If not, why not?
      i. How might the observations be different if you did them at 9:00 am? 2:00 pm? On December 31?
      ii. If you were to select a few of the observed pedestrians for a casual interview, what kind of questions could or would you ask them about their sense of commercialism in Times Square?

2) Consider the following situation and discuss:

For a reading assignment in RC 533, *Prof. E.* had planned to lead the students in a discussion of what they had learned from reading a particular study on the effectiveness of two methods of teaching sight singing skills to 8th graders. The first response came from *Greg* who, seemingly angry and somewhat aggressive, stated: "I don't buy that!" Prof. E., believing in the importance of letting students speak their minds, responded with "what do you mean, you don't buy that? I mean, somebody did this study, and this article explains what they found. How can you . . . I mean, you can. . . ." Greg replied by reiterating what he had said before: "I don't believe in those methods. I use a different approach and know that it works. This study was a waste of time."

Taking Prof. E.'s role, how would you continue the conversation with Greg and the rest of the students? What is your personal position on the subject of the value of research versus personal teaching experience in music education?

---

3) Two Games—Choose one!
   a.   An Association Game

In class, or perhaps afterward, ask a few musician-educator colleagues for five words that describe an inquisitive mind and five words that describe a research mind. Collect the responses and write them down in two columns. Analyze your findings and consider the meaning of your collective responses concerning both terms.

   b.   Bombardment, or "Throw-the-Question-and-See-if-it-Sticks"

As a group decide on a particular concern and bombard it with questions. Take, for instance, sight reading: Divide the entire group into two teams and see who can come up with the most questions in a specified and agreed-upon time frame. We give you a few as start-up:

* What is sight reading? What is it not? What is its purpose?
* Who benefits from it the most?
* Why is it important?
* Who has written about it? Researched it?

Note: Questions asked by both groups do not count in the final tally.

4) Sharpening Your Questioning Skills.

Select a few questions from those you have identified as "real" ones and contrast them to pseudo-questions that

* expect no answer,
* cannot be answered, or
* have an answer already known to the questioner.

REFERENCES

Rainbow, E., & Froehlich, H. (1987). *Research in music education: An introduction to systematic inquiry.* Schirmer Books.

Small, C. (1996). *Music, society, education.* Wesleyan University Press. (Original work published 1977 as *Music-society-education: A radical examination of the prophetic function of music in Western, Eastern and African cultures with its impact on society and its use in education*)

Small, C. (1998a). *Music of the common tongue: Survival and celebration in African American music.* Wesleyan University Press. (Original work published 1987)

Small, C. (1998b). *Musicking: The meanings of performing and listening.* University Press of New England.

PART I

Entering the World of Questioning

Chapters 1 through 3

The first three chapters of this textbook are directed at the reader who is about to become a researcher. The chapters describe the process on which "re"-search depends—the "looking again" that is so essential to the spiral of inquiry mentioned in the Introduction. Chapter 1 asks you to apply "who, what, where, when, why, or how" questions to issues that concern you as a music teacher, a student, or both. Chapter 2 describes early steps in finding, analyzing, and selecting pertinent scholarly literature relevant to such concerns. Chapter 3 pushes you to formulate an initial research purpose and rationale along with purpose specifications to guide your subsequent research decisions.

DOI: 10.4324/9781003057703-2

CHAPTER **1**

The Spiral and Modes of Inquiry

Options, Choices, and Initial Decisions

This chapter describes how your research journey might begin:

- Generating possible research frames
- Considering modes of inquiry
- Focusing your concerns with the Teacher–Learner–Music model
- Getting started with reflective reading.

In this chapter you begin to put concerns that likely originated in personal experience and casual observation into scholarly contexts. By considering a variety of perspectives, modes of inquiry and foci, you generate and imagine different frames for your research ideas. Employing both cursory and reflective reading skills, you learn to look for specific characteristics in a variety of publications.

INTRODUCTION

The research journey begins with accepting that "who, what, where, when, why, and how" questions relative to areas of concern are not always easily answered by simply looking them up on the Internet or by asking experts in the field. Secondly, hardly any answer remains the same once and for all. This is why the "think-read-observe-share" cycle is ongoing: Thinking leads to observing or reading, which may lead to the possible modification of once accepted answers; or reading leads to observations that may make you question previous assumptions or thoughts. Finally, sharing your insights with peers, colleagues and—possibly—the public at large may trigger responses that cause yet more thinking, reading, and observing on your part.

The quest is characterized by exploring and articulating ("framing") researchable questions from which you select one for further examination. The activities become the filters by which you work toward the goal of selecting a topic upon which a complete study can be built. You may visualize it as shown in Figure 1.1.

Notice that the image contains two cones—one inverted, the other upright—that relate to each other. Its purpose is to illustrate that when you engage in thinking, reading, observing, and sharing with increasing specificity, your knowledge base about the field broadens; one cannot happen without the other. Early in the filtering process, you may be inclined to spend much time on thinking/reading, and less on observing/sharing your thoughts and findings (preferably in writing) with your peers. Ideally, however, you should move back and forth between all four activities long before you have fully finalized your plans for executing an actual research project.

DOI: 10.4324/9781003057703-3

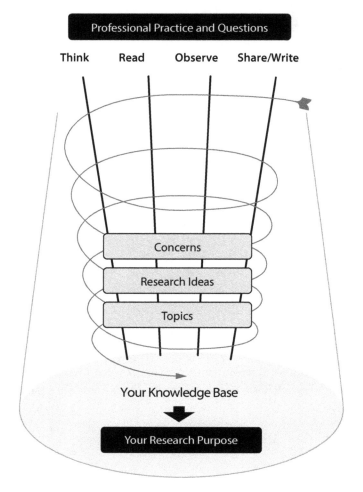

FIGURE 1.1 The Search Process Visualized

Do not be surprised if the spiraling process does not unfold as neatly as visualized in our "textbook description." In fact, at times, you may feel as if the reading and thinking goes in circles, that is, nowhere. This is the proverbial brick wall all scholars run into occasionally, an experience you also know from practicing your instrument. Be assured that moments like that actually may be signs of progress. Uncertainties are an inevitable part of the process of exploring concerns, filtering ideas, and framing topics, because it can be uncomfortable to let one idea go in favor of pursuing another one.

Thinking, reading, observing, and sharing/writing may overlap or take place side by side, albeit at different levels of specificity and precision. Therefore, discuss your concerns, ideas, and topics with friends and colleagues so that you learn to express your thoughts more clearly. At the same time, begin to seek published evidence that addresses your concerns.

Many terms could be used to label the levels of specificity that guide the filtering process. Our labels, chosen deliberately without being necessarily binding, are research *concerns*, *ideas*, *topics*, and *purpose*. Other choices are equally suitable as long as it is understood that the research process evolves through stages of increasing specificity by which a purpose for your project becomes clear to you.

To describe the aim of a research project, some replace "research purpose" with "research question;" still others refer to it as the "research problem." Consider using the term "research problem" cautiously because it tends to imply that a resolution is expected as the outcome. In fact, some research, especially in the philosophical realm, may generate questions rather than solve any one problem in particular. In that case, you might prefer to call the focus of your study the "critical issue" or the "problematic."

TOWARD FRAMING A RESEARCHABLE TOPIC

As you hone your research thoughts from a broad area of concern to a researchable topic, it will be helpful to put an intellectual frame in place. We suggest beginning with a four-sided frame that includes perspective, focus, mode of inquiry, and engagement with the literature. We discussed perspective in the introductory chapter when we visited Times Square via webcam. Two additional frames, mode of inquiry and focus, are described below. The fourth side of the frame, engaging with scholarly and professional literature, is described in detail in Chapter 2.

Generating Possible Research Frames

Music education scholars who study the learning and teaching of music tend to focus on the learner (L), the subject matter of music (M), and the teacher (T), either by themselves or in interaction with each other. To capture the interconnectedness between these component parts, which we call the Teacher-Learner-Music Model, Figure 1.2 likens them to interacting "cogs" (similar to bicycle gears) that cause each other to move, thus resulting in particular processes of learning and teaching.

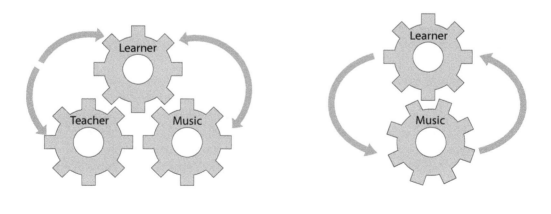

FIGURE 1.2 The Interconnectedness between Formal and Informal Music Learning Situations

In the instructional formality of school music where the teacher guides most musical interactions, these three components shape the interplay of actions in the classroom or rehearsal. When we refer to learning situations as schooling, formal, or instructor-guided, we suggest that they take place with teachers, assigned mentors, or otherwise appointed or declared superiors overseeing the instructional process. Outside of school—away from teachers, mentors, or mediating guides—the learner interacts directly with the music, which changes the ongoing dynamic between learner and subject matter. Calling such situations informal learning does not imply a learning situation that is less important or effective than what goes on in the formality of institutional settings. The opposite may be the case. Presently, both terms—formal and informal learning—are stipulated definitions, still awaiting systematic examination and verification by further evidence (see Chapter 5). Their presence here simply acknowledges that the way in which music learning takes place impacts its results.

Some Thoughts by the Students in RC 533

Most of the students in RC 533 were more interested in issues related to formal music instructional processes than in informal ones. They thought of themselves as teachers who, with varying degrees of experience, had practical "who, what, where, when, why and how" questions about their own involvement in everyday instructional practices. To illustrate:

Christy's efforts to articulate several research ideas stemmed from her question about being an effective teacher in the voice studio. "HOW do I teach differently from others?" she asked. "WHAT and HOW do others teach?" "HOW (and WHY) do I know that I am an effective teacher?" When focusing on music (the music cog in Figure 1.2), Christy began to think about other pedagogues. As a result, she moved away from exclusively focusing on herself. Instead, historical questions began to come to the forefront: WHO have been the most influential vocal pedagogues throughout history? WHAT are they known for and WHAT approaches did they use? HOW did they change what was known or believed about vocal pedagogy? WHY were their ideas influential?

Christy's story illustrates how an original concern (her own effectiveness as a studio teacher) can develop into ideas (previous pedagogy models) of historical significance (what can knowledge about the past teach us about the present?). Clearly, considering whether your own areas of concern deal with questions about teaching or specific actions by your pupils, with events of the past or the present, adds a new dimension to your inquiries. But Christy could also have broadened her initial concern by probing relationships between herself and her students, possibly even adding issues of repertoire choice, teaching strategies, or her students' home backgrounds to the list of ideas she began to gather.

Exploration: Pause for a Moment and Think

Consider the concerns that have come to your mind thus far: Are your interests situated in institutional learning and teaching or in how learning might take place outside of school? Are you looking into the past like Christy had begun to do, or are you more intrigued by what happens in the present? Are you primarily interested in your own or other teachers' behaviors and resultant actions or does the world of ideas about music pique your curiosity? If the latter, how does the world of ideas in music relate to thoughts about education and formal instruction? What questions fascinate you and how could you best articulate them?

Answers to any of the questions posed in the above exploration refer to what we call modes of inquiry. Understanding what they are and knowing differences among them may benefit how you might best articulate specific concerns about various learning and teaching settings. The better and more succinctly you frame such concerns, the stronger all subsequent steps in your research are likely to be.

Modes of Inquiry

All research begins with asking questions about that which is to be examined. Now that you have begun that process yourself, scrutinize the nature of those questions. What specifically are you asking about? Are you interested in the past or in the present; in actions, behaviors, and experiences; or in the study of ideas?

A concern about past events, behaviors, and/or documented experiences would likely lead to a historical study; examining past and present ideas would fall under philosophical inquiries, and examining present events, behaviors, actions, and/or experiences would be empirical in nature—regardless of which methods were used. Interestingly, the etymological origin of all three terms goes back to "learnedness, wisdom, and experience."

"Empirical" derives from the Latin empiricus (or from the Greek empeirikos, empeira, and/or empeiros), *making reference to* experiences that come from "living in the world" as opposed to knowledge that results from studying written documents. A characteristic derived from "learnedness through experience" brings us to the "learned" or "wisdom loving" person. In Greek, philosophos means the same: The person who loves wisdom. The Latin histor means "learned person," suggesting a close connection between "lover of wisdom" and "learned person." A histor, philosophor, and empiricus therefore pursue the answer to a question for the same reason: A need to know. They adhere to principles of both reason and intuition, rely on evidence obtained through the senses as well as through introspection, and engage in the ongoing examination of such principles. In today's understanding of the three modalities, their differences lie mainly in what a question is about: (1) ideas or actions/behaviors/experiences, and (2) those of the past or the present.

Today, each mode has specific conventions and expectations about the nature of the questions asked and the way they are addressed. However, modes of inquiry should never be viewed as being mutually exclusive; one informs the other. There is no reason, for example, why philosophical inquiry could not draw upon empirical resources and use quantitative or qualitative and related research methods to examine (see Chapters 6–13) unresolved issues concerning beliefs and actions. Any of the choices depend on the perspective you bring to what constitutes a "researchable" question.

If you ask, "Why or how did someone do or say something in the past?" you can reconstruct that past either by talking to individuals who witnessed the event or by studying documents that represent or describe those events. The same is true if you want to know what took place at a particular moment in time and why. A philosophical examination might ask why a given statement/idea/belief is important in itself or for practices in music education: How does a particular belief or theory compare to other ideas or beliefs prevalent in our field? How consistently has it been applied to practice over time? To what extent has it guided decision-making processes, and by which educators and/or musicians? Do such choices warrant continuous examination today and, if so, why? Are there seemingly irresolvable differences among current ideas that govern our field today?

Finally, if a question addresses current events, ongoing actions as well as experiences, the investigation would most likely fall into the empirical mode of inquiry. It means that the question addresses phenomena that can be described through sense perceptions of seeing, touching, sensing, hearing, smelling—in short, that which one perceives to exist. Many of the "who, what, where, when, why, and how" questions raised earlier apply here when worded like: Who are the students I am teaching? What is their background? How do they relate to each other and to me? What is their musical taste? How do they spend their spare time? How do any of these questions impact or at least relate to each other and possibly also help me teach better? And, finally, what is "good" teaching? How do others define it? How was the term used in the past? How can I observe it?

To repeat: The lines between research modes are anything but hard and fast. This is why an understanding of basic methods, techniques and requirements in all three modes should be considered an important attribute of any music education scholar. Making choices requires being informed. Honing in on any one mode of inquiry without thinking of all available options limits your scholarship in the same way as does performing only in one style of music or teaching the same lesson for many years.

Some researchers hold the view that only numerically measurable (quantitative) knowledge should be considered factual. "If you can't see it, label, and measure it," they might say, "how can it provide irrefutable evidence on which to base future actions?" Other researchers counter that because there are so many perspectives by which to look at any given question, there also are many approaches to finding answers; no one mode is to be valued over another. Still others suggest that as long as the research is beneficial to society and follows scholarly conventions, any mode and, with it, any procedure is appropriate as long as it is ethical and meets the methodological demands implied by the question itself.

Focusing Your Concerns with the Teacher- Learner-Music Model

Having considered how changes in the mode of inquiry can change the way you think about your area of concern, we now encourage you to think about your focus. Do your queries have more to do with the teacher, the learner, the music, or some combination? Are your concerns driven primarily by questions about the music itself or by matters of teaching and learning that are specific to music, or perhaps even applicable to other subjects? Do you have concerns about purposes of education and schooling in general or do you focus most on gaining better insights about instructional strategies in the classroom or rehearsal space? Do those concerns originate from how you think of yourself either as a musician-teacher or musician-performer? Both equally? Finally, what might any one of those viewpoints mean for the way you articulate your concerns as being relevant for past or current music education practices?

Carlos had been seeking, in his words, a "foolproof" way to assess his concert band students in the ensemble setting. When *Prof. E.* asked him to identify his focus, however, he realized that he had only been thinking of his own convenience. Using the teacher-learner-music model led him to wonder about assessment from his students' point of view. What did *they* think about assessment? How could assessment help his students learn? Coming from the vantage point of the music itself, Carlos wondered whether different styles of music might tell him more about what students were learning—perhaps idiomatic etudes, chamber music, solo repertoire, or even popular music. These questions evolved into thinking about the purpose of assessment, at first perhaps a less tangible concern for him, but one that grew in importance the longer he thought and read about the ways music teachers and scholars thought about assessment in the ensemble setting.

Figure 1.3 illustrates Carlos' efforts. We suggest that you also follow this process, as it will help you consider alternate ways to focus the questions from your areas of concern.

Carlos was not certain at this point, of course, which questions would ultimately guide his research. But by considering alternative ways to focus his area of concern, he had broadened his thinking into a wide variety of possible ideas, each of which interested him in some way.

T		**Teacher-focused:** HOW can I assess band students in the ensemble setting without using up precious rehearsal time?
L		**Learner-focused:** WHAT do band students learn from the assessment process? HOW might students prefer to be assessed?
M		**Music-focused:** WHAT type of music is best suited to assess student learning in the ensemble setting?
T&L		**Teacher & Learner focused:** WHAT can assessments tell me about students' interests and learning needs?
T&M		**Teacher & Music focused:** HOW can I build assessments from the music we work on for each concert unit?
T&M		**Learner & Music focused:** WHAT kinds of music will motivate students to want to do well on end-of-term assessments?
T&L&M		**Teacher & Learner & Music focused:** HOW can I generate a learning environment that is self-guided and allows students to explore new approaches to mastering musicianship skills?

FIGURE 1.3 Focusing your Area of Concern with the Learner-Teacher-Music Model

When you similarly filter your own concerns, notice how the words you use can suggest different perspectives, foci, or modes of inquiry. Because different wordings have consequences for how you might go about addressing a research question, be sure that when you write down your questions you also make a few notes about them. Your notes become important building blocks for working toward a research topic and purpose as you move on in the spiral of inquiry that you now have begun.

A Moment for Reflection and Discussion

Should or can all professional concerns be reduced to "who, what, where, when, why, or how" questions that can be answered with certainty? "Not exactly" would be the reply by many experienced scholars inside and outside of music education (e.g., Barrett & Stauffer, 2009; Blikstad-Balas, 2013; Bowman, 1998, 2002; Deemter, 2010; Elliott, 2002; Keefe, 2000; Sorensen, 2001) who philosophically would favor grey shades over black and white; ambiguity over certainty. Nonetheless, at this point in the process you should err in favor of exercising precision. Later in the process the rules might relax, akin perhaps to how many music students learn to do counterpoint: First follow the rules faithfully; once you have something to say musically, step outside certain rules for the desired compositional effect.

When the students in RC 533 considered each other's question in class discussion, informal conversations arose about career goals and how performing, teaching, and research might contribute to those goals. Some of the questions evoked responses by students who had read materials that seemed applicable to the question at hand, and others seemed to spearhead new inquiries beyond the classroom.

Isaac's questions inspired him to ask his conducting teacher what she considered to be signs of "good conducting." She talked at length about score study and people skills, but also referred him to writings and recordings by other conductors. She further suggested that he look at trade magazines that regularly publish interviews with successful conductors and instrumentalists about their work.

Having already completed a master's thesis, *Dale's* questions were specific enough that he decided to have an informal conversation with some teacher-colleagues in his former school district about how the recent focus on teacher assessment had impacted their work conditions. His question "WHY do I want to know this?" prompted him to formulate reasons why knowing about the impact of teacher assessments on the work conditions of experienced music teachers might be important. As he thought about those reasons, he realized that they triggered further questions and he became excited about what lay ahead.

Not everyone in RC 533 was as excited about what lay ahead as Dale. *Christy, Isaac, Liam,* and *Muna* wondered why they should get involved in doing research when their career goals were more aimed at music performance and/or community music. How could they possibly benefit from spending precious time on more academic courses when they barely found enough time for practicing or working on assignments in music history, literature, and conducting?

Christy felt those pressures more pointedly than some of the other students and did not hesitate to let *Prof. E.* know her feelings. To her, questioning accepted ways of doing things or searching for new approaches seemed to impede on "getting things done." Would it not be sufficient, she asked, to be taught by master teachers who themselves learned through successful coaching and personal experience what to pass on to the next generation of musician-teachers? Had it not already been shown by example that this master-apprentice model worked especially well in the arts?

Exploration: Consider the Conversation in RC 533

After reading the issues raised by the students in RC 533, share with your class-mates your thoughts about the points below, Positive, Negative, Undecided:

1) The impact of scientific research on your everyday lives.
2) The place of scientific thought and research in the arts, and specifically in music.
3) The benefits and drawbacks of the master-apprentice approach in music as compared to other fields.
4) Whether language can get at the essence of the artistic process and/or experi-ence. If so, what does it accomplish? If not, what are the benefits of scholarly discourse about the arts?
5) Commonalities between the processes of performing and doing research.

GETTING STARTED WITH REFLECTIVE READING

Reading is most pleasurable when it is "just for fun." It might resemble noodling on an instru-ment—it feels successful and you already know how to do it. But if noodling was the extent of your musical aspirations, you would never master your instrument. When reading scholarly litera-ture, you should make a similar distinction between "just for fun" and "making a deep dive." Both are likely to be the case when you begin reading with the intention of finding a topic suitable for scholarly research. As a scholar, the library—whether virtual or physical—is your practice room and, like practicing your instrument, it can launch an enjoyable and exciting journey of discovery!

Research in this context is quite different from the "library research" you did as an under-graduate student. Then, you wrote a report that summarized information about a topic, possibly in your own words. Now, you read and write not to summarize, but to deeply process essential information, scrutinizing and analyzing *how* various scholars have addressed particular issues, and comparing their thoughts to each other's as well as to your own. In the following section, we describe the types of sources you are likely to encounter, query the functions of research, and liken scholarly reading to having an in-depth conversation with the authors whose works you read.

Exploring Published Sources

One of the first steps in scholarly reading is becoming acquainted with the nature of publications that make up the overall body of music education literature. When dealing with information gleaned from scholarly as well as general interest sources (i.e., academic journals, trade journals, books, magazines, even blogs and websites), be mindful that publications are designed to reach different audiences and fulfill distinctive functions. The same is true for research—a thought you should keep in mind at this early stage of getting acquainted with the literature.

There is a great deal of variety across types and purposes of publications. Books, for instance, tend to be published once under a single title, and updated infrequently, if at all. They may be intended for students (as is this textbook), for professional development (for instance, Battisti & Garofalo's *Guide to Score Study*), or to disseminate scholarly research and theory (such as *The Routledge Handbook of Sociology and Music Education*). Books may be written by one author (sometimes called a monograph) or multiple (contributing) authors, the latter typically compiled and organized by one or more editors. Chapters in edited volumes may have begun as conference papers or they may have been invited because they represent certain points of view.

Publications released in a serial fashion, whether by day, week, month, quarter, or even year, are known as periodicals. Like books, periodical publications differ according to whether they are intended for professional reading, sometimes called trade publications (i.e., *Music Educators Journal, Instrumentalist, Teaching Music*), or for the dissemination of research and other academic/scholarly pursuits (i.e., *Journal of Research in Music Education, Arts Education Policy Review*). Online publications such as blogs may also be considered periodicals.

General interest essays that inform you about concerns within the profession and allow you to ascertain where you stand on a particular issue are most likely found in periodicals such as trade journals and professional magazines. Those may reach a readership with either very specific interests (e.g., *Flute*, the quarterly journal of the British Flute Society) or a comparatively broad readership (e.g., *The Instrumentalist*). Specific to music education, similar differentiations could be made, for example, between *UPDATE* and the *Music Educators Journal*, both published by the National Association for Music Education (NAfME). Both journals contain articles of interest and are purposefully kept non-technical, but one is intended for a broader readership than the other.

One important distinction is that of peer review. Both trade and scholarly publications that have been peer-reviewed have been examined, critiqued, and identified as worthy of consideration by a committee of peers prior to its publication. We suggest that you focus on finding peer-reviewed sources.

Remember the old adage "don't judge a book by its cover?" We recommend that you don't judge, but that you do notice. The appearance and layout of a publication can tell you a lot about its intended audience. Some publications, for instance, feature photos and graphics while others use only words. Words and graphics may be complex or simple, based on what speaks to their intended audience. Similarly, a good number of popular trade journals and professional magazines prohibit footnotes because the latter take space away from possible advertisements or other, more pressing printed matter. Technical information, on the other hand, is provided in scholarly journals specifically to allow readers to follow and critique an author's line of reasoning and investigative choices.

Exploration: Examining types of sources

We suggest examining several different types of sources even before you begin looking in earnest for literature to support your research ideas:

1) Work with colleagues who have similar interests to find many different kinds of published sources related to those interests. Note similarities and differences in the way the topic is covered, and also in the look and contents of each source. Are the sources you find parts of larger publications (journals, websites, or even recordings) or do they stand on their own (books, for instance)?
2) Alternatively, work with a librarian to gain access to a diverse array of types of music education sources. These may be hard-copy or electronic, or a combination. Compare the way the content in those sources is featured and organized.

As you peruse different journals and books, you will come to appreciate the enormous volume of research relevant to music education. You are likely to find that some publications seem more "esoteric" than others—lacking application to classroom or performance—while other studies speak to those activities directly. That observation will make it easy to understand that research can serve many different functions.

Distinctive Functions of Research

The primary function of all research should be to continually ask questions about that which is uncertain or unknown and to assure that no one source of evidence dominates over any other without justification. In addition to these fundamental functions, researchers in many disciplines distinguish between basic and applied functions of research. Basic (sometimes also called "pure") research discovers, describes, and/or develops theories for the sake of advancing explanations or confirmations of how things work. Research designed to solve a practical problem tends to be called applied (Booth, Colomb, Williams, Bizup, & Fitzgerald, 2016, p. 20). Both kinds of research—basic and applied—are needed for a field of inquiry to move forward.

Disciplines in which research and development are fully integrated components tend to recognize three categories of applied research (Gates, 1999, p. 10). Following Gates, we suggest the following designations for applied research in music education: (1) pedagogical "engineering," (2) field studies, and (3) context studies.

Pedagogical "engineering" would include such areas as testing the advantages of one teaching approach over another, and investigating the usability and appropriateness of tests and other measurement tools. Field studies would comprise observations in natural settings, curriculum development, practitioner inquiry/action research, and the advancement of instructional technologies. Context studies would be those that include surveys of specific practices or opinions on practices, policy studies, and the articulation of rationales for music education, as well as biographies and historical accounts of important events. This four-level structure (basic, pedagogical-engineering, field, and context studies) might explain why one study speaks to you immediately while another seems further removed from your interests. However, as in other disciplines, each function is needed and contributes to the field so long as the research is done well and its findings interpreted with care.

In music education, studies geared toward advancing our knowledge about music and learning through theoretical constructs function as basic research. Many such investigations exist on the nature of specific responses to a variety of musical stimuli, often describing, comparing, and experimenting with them. Basic research also examines the validity of psychological, physiological, and sociological constructs for describing or explaining music teaching and learning, and questions traditions and practices in light of philosophical worldviews. The primary purpose of such investigations is not so much to solve the practical problems each of us encounters in daily teaching as to direct our attention to principles of thought that might help us understand why we encounter the realities we do. Through such deeper understanding, even basic research has the potential to impact practical matters in the classroom.

While basic research may sometimes be applied to practice, it may also happen that the desire for easy applications to everyday life problems results in the misinterpretation and misuse of basic research findings. As an example, we offer the story of the popular response to the "Mozart Effect" studies:

In the early 1990's, three neuroscientists—Frances Rauscher, Gordon Shaw, and Katherine Ky—designed an experiment to test a possible connection between music cognition and mathematical reasoning. They subjected thirty-six college students to three listening conditions (Mozart's "Sonata for Two Pianos in D Major," K. 448, a relaxation tape, or silence), and immediately followed each listening experience with a published test of spatial reasoning. The researchers found that the students' performance on the test improved more after listening to the Mozart sonata than after the other conditions (Rauscher, Shaw, & Ky, 1993). Published in the journal *Nature*, the results were embraced by music educators and the music industry as evidence for the practical importance of music education. Subsequent attempts to replicate the research, however, were not successful. Dr. Rauscher later indicated that this was because the results of the original study had been misinterpreted. The evidence from the original study supported only the three spatial-temporal tasks that had been reported in the original report, as measured by a specific test, and were not intended to represent an improvement in general IQ or other aspects of intelligence. In other words, practical applications of this research misinterpreted both its purpose and its results (Steele et al., 1999).

Reading as Conversation

When you read, whether a journal or magazine article, book, pamphlet, or website, guard against initial reactions such as "I like this, therefore it is good" or "I do not agree with the author and therefore find this publication useless." Instead of relying on such a gut feeling, take the next step and become *an active partner in conversation with the author.*

As you react to what you read, examine your reasoning: Are you responding to a poor quality of writing and research or are your ideas being challenged by evidence that does not match your experience or your beliefs? Do the author's ideas express personal opinions or are they backed up with reliable and valid evidence? Does the author acknowledge contradictory evidence and, if so, how is such evidence presented?

When you ask these questions and look for answers to them in the text you are reading, you begin the process that scholars call critical reading. Do not confuse the word *critical* with *negative*. It is understandable if at first you feel uncomfortable questioning the work of published authors.

After all, you have possibly learned to consider printed word as coming from experts who presumably know more than you do. While that may be true, it should not stop you from analytically examining what you read. Learning to think and read critically requires that that your thinking 1) is novel and not based simply on previous situations, 2) is self-directed rather than other-directed, and 3) follows conventions of critical thinking, including that you, "consider both sides of an issue," "offer evidence for claims made," and "don't let emotion interfere with reason" (Willingham, 2019, p. 3). Critical reading, then, is the trademark of a good scholar, regardless of the mode of inquiry or topic.

We suggest you begin with the tangible step of determining the relevance and trustworthiness of a published piece. Regarding relevance: First, is it applicable to your interests? If so, how does it contribute to or challenge your own thinking? If not, why not? In subsequent chapters, we recommend more specific questions. Regarding trustworthiness, consider (1) how the authors used the evidence they referenced, (2) whether and why those sources and their content can be trusted, and (3) how the authors adhered to accepted principles of scholarly inquiry. This chapter outlines preliminary steps in that process; later chapters provide more detail.

Identifying Trustworthy Sources of Evidence

"*Consider the source!*" means having background information about a source itself. When a trusted friend tells you a first-hand experience, you are likely to accept that information as true. If, however, you believe your friend's perception to be biased, you will seek verification from another person that the friend's description of the experience was trustworthy. Of course, it is possible that the second person's testimony stems only from hear-say; it may not be a good source of information at all. Similar situations exist in published sources.

Good scholars always give credit where credit is due. In the context of writing, this means that all thoughts not the author's own are acknowledged with reference citations—either parenthetical (cited in parentheses within the narrative), footnotes or endnotes, or in a reference list at the end of the publication. There should be consistency between page numbers at both places; sloppy reporting at this level suggests poor quality work. This is one of the first things you should check as you decide whether the sources you examine meet the criteria for scholarship.

Reference citations should accurately reflect the words and meanings of the source to which they refer. To check this, you might locate and examine a small number of cited references. If the information in both places coincides, trustworthiness in the author's work is at a higher level than if you find several mistakes. Carelessness may not weaken an author's overall message but, as in a musical performance, technical mistakes tend to lessen the overall appeal and—possibly—trustworthiness.

Another indicator of good scholarship is the use of sources that are as close to the original as possible. You know this principle of research from being a performing musician: When you want to understand a composer's rather than an editor's intent, you try to find an edition that is as close as possible to the manuscript itself (called the *urtext*, the first published source of a composition).

Common sense suggests that the original, first source, called in research terms a *primary* source, is the most trustworthy. A source that uses information from the primary source as a reference in its own context is known as a *secondary* source. *Tertiary* sources, accordingly, are references that utilize secondary information about a primary source. Research ethics as well as good scholarly sense suggest that an author utilize primary rather than secondary or tertiary sources as much as possible.

Secondary or tertiary sources can be helpful in finding primary source material. However, finding that a publication is full of secondary and tertiary source citations at the expense of primary ones should lower your confidence in that writer's scholarship. For right now simply keep in mind that a primary source is always the one closest to an actual event or observation. That knowledge can serve as a good gauge by which to judge the nature of referenced information in any mode of inquiry.

Exploration: Consider the Source

To practice source verification, we invite you to locate, read, and compare Vaughn and Winner (2000), Deasy (2002), and Ruppert (2006). All of these sources speak to the issue of arts advocacy, but the latter two rely on the first as one of their sources. Below is a summary of Vaughn and Winner's article.

One of many music educators' ongoing concerns is to establish evidence that academic achievement in school is positively tied to participation in the arts, including music. Vaughn and Winner's study involved multiple statistical analyses of 10 years of data gathered by the United States College Board from students taking the nationally standardized Scholastic Aptitude Test (SAT). Results indicated that students who were involved in arts courses had higher test scores than students who were not involved in arts courses, and that students with more high school arts experiences (according to the number of years they had taken arts courses) tended to score higher than lower scoring students. Because these results were derived from survey data, however, the authors suggested merely a correlation, not a causal relationship. In addition, the authors suggested that their study results should be viewed with caution because "an even stronger link exists between SAT scores and study of academic subjects" (p. 87).

In light of Vaughn and Winner's caution, ascertain how Deasy (2002) and Ruppert (2006) presented the findings of the original study in their respective works.

To begin the next phase of your research journey we suggest consulting secondary sources such as handbook chapters, reviews, summaries and even textbooks. Described further in Chapter 2, such publications provide broad overviews of a variety of topics. Learning how scholars and other professionals address your interests will provide you with direction and help you move toward a research topic. We wish you luck in this endeavor!

CHAPTER SUMMARY

1) The cyclical nature of research as "think-read-observe-share" demands that no one action stands on its own. One calibrates the others, thereby moving the process forward.

2) Recognizing the perspective, mode of inquiry, and focus of your professional concerns allows you to see connections between your ideas and the larger context of the learning and teaching of music.

3) Many different kinds of books, articles, and trade magazines make up the body of literature music educators have at their disposal. To sort through them and organize them for use in your own professional quests is an important step in becoming a music education scholar.

4) Critical reading does not mean to find fault; instead, it means seeking the building blocks that make a publication fit the bill of scholarly work. With critical reading, you determine how accurate, complete, and dependable (trustworthy) newly found information is.

5) Many commonalities exist between the processes of teaching, performing, and doing research. They should be stressed over seeming differences because one set of skills informs the other and can provide guidance in how to become the best music educator possible.

Topics for Further Exploration

1) Processes for framing research ideas.
2) Similarities and differences in the contents in the *Music Educators Journal*, *The Instrumentalist*, *Update: Applications of Research in Music Education*, and the *Bulletin of the Council for Research in Music Education*, or a similar combination of scholarly and trade periodicals.
3) Functions of scholarly research.
4) Characteristics of critical reading.

Suggested Assignments

1) Create your own music education questions based on Figure 1.3.
2) Reflect on how your musician, teacher, and researcher selves worked together to filter your areas of concern through the process of thinking-reading-observing-sharing.
3) Find an example of basic research in a music education or general education research journal. Summarize it and report to your colleagues.
4) Find an example of each type of applied research in a music education research journal. Summarize them and report to your colleagues.
5) Find a tertiary source of information related to your area of concern. Follow the references to find the secondary and/or primary sources the author references. As you begin to look through printed source material, keep your eyes open for primary, secondary, and tertiary materials about same information.

REFERENCES

Barrett, M. S., & Stauffer, S. L. (2009). *Narrative inquiry in music education: Troubling certainty*. Springer Science + Business Media.

Blikstad-Balas, M. (2013). Vague concepts in the educational sciences: Implications for researchers. *Scandinavian Journal of Educational Research*, *58*(5), 528–539. https://doi.org/10.1080/00313831.2013.773558

Booth, W. C., Colomb, G. C., Williams, J. M, Bizup, J., & Fitzgerald, W. T. (2016). *The craft of research* (4th ed.). University of Chicago Press.

Bowman, W. D. (1998). *Philosophical perspectives on music*. Oxford University Press.

Bowman, W. D. (2002). Educating musically. In R. Colwell & C. Richardson (Eds.), *The new handbook of research on music teaching and learning* (pp. 63–84). Oxford University Press.

Deasy, R. J. (Ed.) (2002). *Critical links: Learning in the arts and student academic and social development.* Arts Education Partnership. www.aep-arts.org/wp-content/uploads/Critical-Links_-Learning-in-the-Arts-and-Student-Academic-and-Social-Development.pdf

Deemter, van, K. (2010). *Not exactly. In praise of vagueness.* Oxford University Press.

Elliott, D. J. (2002). Philosophical perspectives on research. In R. Colwell & C. Richardson (Eds.), *The new handbook of research on music teaching and learning* (pp. 85–102). A project of the Music Educators National Conference New York: Oxford University Press.

Gates, J. T. (1999, February 15–18). *Music education research at the dawn of the third mediamophosis* [Conference presentation]. Desert Skies Symposium, University of Arizona, Tucson.

Keefe, R. (2000). *Theories of vagueness.* Cambridge University Press.

Rauscher, F. H., Shaw, G. L., & Ky, C. N. (1993). Music and spatial task performance. *Nature, 365*(6447), 611. https://doi.org/10.1038/365611a0

Ruppert, S. S. (2006). *Critical evidence: How the arts benefit student achievement.* National Assembly of State Arts Agencies. www.americansforthearts.org/sites/default/files/critical-evidence_0.pdf

Sorensen, R. (2001). *Vagueness and contradiction.* Clarendon Press.

Steele, K. M., Dalla Bella, S., Peretz, I., Dunlop, T., Dawe, L. A., Humphrey, G. K., Shannon, R. A., Kirby Jr., J. L., & Olmstead, C. G. (1999). Prelude or requiem for the "Mozart effect"? *Nature, 400,* 827. https://doi.org/10.1038/23611

Vaughn, K., & Winner, E. (2000). SAT scores of students who study the arts: What we can and cannot conclude about the association. *Journal of Aesthetic Education, 34*(3–4), 77–89. https://doi.org/10.2307/3333638

Willingham, D. T. (2019). *Occasional paper series: How to teach critical thinking.* New South Wales Department of Education. www.danielwillingham.com/uploads/5/0/0/7/5007325/willingham_2019_nsw_critical_thinking2.pdf

CHAPTER 2

Finding and Mapping Sources of Information

This chapter suggests steps to make the reading tasks involved in conducting research as efficient as possible. The steps include:

- Exploring preliminary sources,
- Framing a research idea,
- Collecting scholarly evidence related to your research idea, and
- Constructing a literature map.

The chapter portrays the search for scholarly literature as a process of identifying, describing, and evaluating relevant literature, forming a collection to guide your research study. In the process, you progress from having voiced a concern to specifying a narrowed research idea situated in an organized body of literature. Constructing a literature map then helps you imagine ways to address your research idea.

INTRODUCTION

Most musicians and educators acquired professional expertise with a combination of formal and informal knowledge, obtained from former teachers, explored in publications, and solidified with personal experience. Professional expertise is distinguished from formal knowledge that is collectively shared by the profession as a whole because the latter is expected to be based on fact and tested evidence. What constitutes fact and what qualifies to be called evidence continues to be under debate by scholars. There seems to be considerable agreement, however, as to what constitutes scholarly communication; that is, scholarly writing. This chapter is about recognizing those characteristics in what is known as the body of literature relevant to a given field.

Coming to understand that body in reference to your chosen research idea is a first step in any scholarly endeavor. The process of finding and using literature for a research project generally occurs in three phases as illustrated in Figure 2.1: (1) exploring preliminary sources, (2) framing a research idea with the vocabulary from those sources, and (3) collecting literature relevant to that idea. Later, you will assess each collected source, describing its contents and evaluating how well it adheres to scholarly conventions and addresses your research idea. Most often this results in a review of the literature—an analysis, evaluation, and synthesis of how other scholars have studied your research interest. Such a review can stand on its own as a term paper or article, or provide background for a research proposal, whether for a class project, thesis, dissertation, or grant proposal.

DOI: 10.4324/9781003057703-4

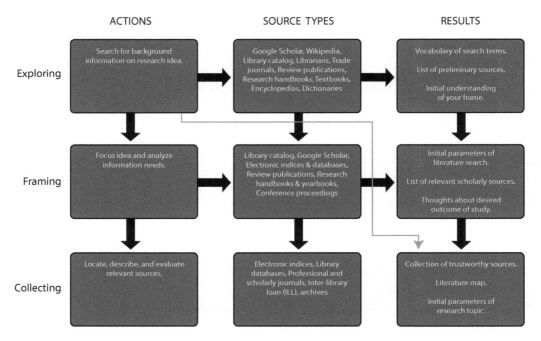

FIGURE 2.1 Steps in Exploratory Reading

EXPLORING YOUR AREA OF CONCERN

Like most new researchers, you began the information search at the level we call *area of concern*. As suggested in Chapter 1, such concerns are often derived from "burning questions" about your work as a music educator. At this level, most new researchers name their research concerns in general terms—"music technology in the high school music program," "the history of scat singing," or "culturally relevant string ensemble pedagogy." Working through Chapter 1, you experienced the next step: narrowing your concern into a research idea by considering possible perspectives, modes of inquiry, and foci. Next, you need to discover (1) the terms scholars use to discuss issues related to your research idea, (2) the extent of previous related research, and (3) the best places to seek information. The exploration stage of the literature search therefore involves preliminary searching: locating preliminary and overview sources, browsing to see what is available, skimming to see what may be relevant, making note of specific vocabulary and terminology, and deciding on a record-keeping strategy that works for you.

Locating Sources in an Academic Library

Whether virtual or "brick and mortar," the library is a place to search for information about any subject, including music and education. Efficiently using a university library requires knowing how to navigate the online catalog, use available search databases, and distinguish reliable and relevant sources from unreliable or irrelevant ones. If you will use an on-campus library, you must learn its location(s), the organization of its holdings, the types of holdings that will best serve your needs, and the procedures for finding materials. Either way, as described later in this section, you must develop an efficient way to keep track of your findings. This skill will serve you for a lifetime.

Navigating Your Library—Virtual or Physical

Your library's catalog may direct you to electronic or print holdings depending both on copyright and the resources available to the specific library. Electronic holdings range from computerized databases to online journals to e-books to electronic media (such as video and audio recordings). (These are further described later in this chapter and referenced in supplemental online materials, see inquiryinmusiceducation.com.) The catalog traditionally refers to hard copy holdings such as books and periodicals housed in the library building as print holdings.

Libraries employ trained personnel who are good at helping researchers make sense of the available search options for electronic and print sources. Make sure to seek their help. While it may seem like an extra step, it can actually save a lot of time. Although most libraries offer help through email and instant messaging (so patrons do not have to actually visit the library), we suggest making personal contacts with library personnel early on.

On-campus library buildings have specific areas for different types of resources: reference materials, books (fiction and non-fiction), periodicals, media, special collections, archives, and often rooms for reading or working on computers. Print versions of standard dictionaries, encyclopedias, professional yearbooks, and conference proceedings are generally located in the reference section, usually in a central place in the library. Print books are housed in "the stacks," classified either according to the Library of Congress system (academic libraries in the United States; note that other countries have similar systems) or the Dewey Decimal System (school and public libraries). It may be helpful to become familiar with the music classifications in one of these systems. Periodicals, including scholarly research publications, trade journals, magazines, and newspapers, are often found in a special reading room, although you will find that most can be accessed electronically. Most libraries also provide an interlibrary loan service by which books, articles and other media can be obtained from other institutions. Researchers interested in historical topics should ask about the procedures for viewing microfilm and microfiche versions of older sources that are not available electronically, and later in the search, for accessing the university archives.

Some academic libraries have separate facilities for undergraduate and graduate students; others decentralize library buildings according to disciplines. The education library, for instance, may not be close to the music library; and music scores, sheet music, music books, and anthologies may be in a different location than professional music education journals or books on music teaching. Be prepared, therefore, to spend time in more than one locale.

Finding What You Are Looking for

At the exploration stage, you learn how scholars describe and discuss the ideas that will form the basis of your project. Sources useful during this stage include *Google*, *Wikipedia*, your library's catalog, librarians, trade journals, review publications, research handbooks, textbooks, and even encyclopedias and dictionaries. When you use your library's electronic catalog, make sure you know how to 'limit' your search. For instance, the "search all" category search may provide a large number of irrelevant findings. Limiting your search to books and media, journal titles, or library databases may be a better use of your time.

Although you will focus later on scholarly sources to collect the evidence that will direct you toward a research idea, trade journals and review publications may be useful at this exploratory stage. Whether intended primarily for performers (i.e., *Horn Call*, *Flute*, *Percussive Notes*, etc.) or music educators (i.e., *Music Educators Journal*, *Teaching Music*, *Music Teacher*, *The Instrumentalist*, etc.) trade journals and magazines can contribute to further inquiries or help to clarify your thoughts on a subject. But do not let them form the bulk of your sources. Review publications, often featured in *Update: Applications of Research in Music Education*, or in one of the many music education research handbooks, provide overviews of topics that are important to our field. Even general interest books and newspaper articles can serve to clarify your concern and ideas. Likewise, lexica (encyclopedias and dictionaries—subject specific as well as general) should never be far from your fingertips or desktop.

Exploratory Searching

At the exploring stage, you are seeking preliminary sources that will guide you to more in-depth materials that are appropriate for your research idea. You therefore begin with browsing, a surface-level exploration for the purpose of getting an overview of "what is out there." Browsing those items that look most interesting helps you learn how scholars describe and discuss your area of concern.

Discovering Search Vocabulary

Begin your literature search by entering words or phrases related to your research idea into a familiar source such as *Google* or *Wikipedia*. (Note: Because it is not peer-reviewed, *Wikipedia* is not a dependable source for scholarly research, and should not be used beyond this exploratory stage.) However, typing your research concern in your own words may not necessarily result in any "hits," or useful sources. Dividing your initially worded concern into its component parts, that is, nouns and/or verbs, is the first step in finding the most useful search terms (sometimes called keywords). Whether you are using an electronic search engine such as *Google*, a library catalog, or a subject-specific index, the correct vocabulary can make or break your search. In fact, discovering appropriate search vocabulary is an important aspect of moving into the framing stage of your literature search.

Also be reminded to cast your net of key terms wider than you first believe necessary. For instance, a search for "improve conducting skills" may produce fewer results than "research, conducting, band music." The opposite can occur as well: Your initial search terms yield thousands of seeming hits but none of them actually relate to your actual interest. You will then need to devise more limits and narrow your search by adding more keywords.

It may also happen that sources are scarce because you have come up with a relatively new territory of exploration. In such a case you may have to seek literature beyond music education sources. If that search also yields only a few results, document that lack of evidence and work with your course instructor or project advisor to develop a plan of action. It may be that your literature search will set the stage for a new area of music education research.

Interested in comparing the experiences of Black music students in what are known as *historically black colleges and universities* (HCBUs) and *predominantly White institutions* (PWIs), *Jeannette* began a *Google* search with the words "Black music student experience. . . ." Immediately, *Google's* algorithm finished her sentence and provided numerous "hits" ranging from journal articles to newspaper articles to *YouTube* videos. Although none of these directly addressed music students, she had clearly hit on a timely research idea.

Isaac's search was not quite as fruitful—at least not at first. Googling "improve conducting skills," provided a hodgepodge of entries that were of little use, either because they were too basic or based on a different definition of the word *conducting*. However, when he moved to *Google Scholar* and divided his idea into "research, conducting, band music," he found links to several scholarly journal articles including reviews by Dickey (1992), Vallo (1990), and Kelly (1999). Those review articles would inform Isaac about how scholars discussed those ideas.

Dale, an experienced reader already, developed terms that would help him find literature related to work conditions in general. Thus, he broke his initial concern about how the new teacher assessments impacted the job satisfaction of experienced music teachers into the following search terms:

- Music teachers;
- Teacher assessment; and
- Occupational/job satisfaction.

These combined terms yielded enough "hits" that Dale felt he could move forward in his search for relevant literature.

Keeping Records of Your Search

Early in the search process it is necessary to devise a way to keep track of what you have found and how you found it. Note-taking becomes much more important at the next stages of the literature search, but at this point we recommend a two-part record-keeping strategy: a database of keywords and search findings, and a process for note-taking.

A template for keeping track of your keywords is shown in Figure 2.2. Enter the search term(s) and date under the name of each database you used. If you used a database outside your university library, make sure to include its URL in your records.

Note-taking begins with keeping track of the bibliographic information for each pertinent source you find so you do not have to find it again later. This means (1) the full names of all authors or editors, in the order they are written in the source, (2) the full title of the source and, if applicable, the work in which the source appears (such as a chapter in an edited book or the volume, issue and year of an article in a periodical), (3) the publisher and place of publication for a book or dissertation, (4) the genre of the source (book, periodical, doctoral dissertation, website, etc.), (5) the pages or paragraph numbers that interest you, and (6) retrieval information—URL's or DOI's for electronic sources. Fortunately, most universities subscribe to a reference management system that will do much of this work for you. The most popular as of the writing of this edition are *Zotero*, *Mendeley*, *EndNote*, and *RefWorks*. We base our discussion here on Zotero, but the process is similar for each system. (Note that both *Zotero* and *Mendeley* are available for free.)

	Database 1	Database 2	Database 3	Database 4
Term(s) 1				
Term(s) 2				
Term(s) 3				
Term(s) 4				

FIGURE 2.2 Keeping Records of Your Search(es)

You will typically be required by your university to use one of several specific formats to complete writing assignments, usually based either on the style requirements of the American Psychological Association (APA), the *Chicago Manual of Style*, or the Modern Language Association (MLA). Each organization publishes a style manual, and you should add the one required by your university to your personal collection. In addition, several online sources provide free access to style guidelines; Purdue University's user-friendly *Online Writing Lab* is used by many graduate students for that purpose (https://owl.purdue.edu/owl/purdue_owl.html). Speaking from experience, we suggest that you learn the rules early. Even at the preliminary stage, set your software so that it will make bibliographic notes in the appropriate format, and make sure to double-check the entries that are housed there, as none of the software programs is perfect every time.

Exploration: A Library "Scavenger Hunt"

- **Start by visiting your university library homepage**
  - Enter the library URL_____
- **Locate and describe the following pages, tools, and/or service. (Please adapt to fit your local library):**
  - Interlibrary Loan & Article Service
  - Citation Guide
  - Reference Management Software
  - Subject Guide for Music
  - Equipment Borrowing
  - Live assistance
  - Other page of interest (URL, name and description)
- **Using search terms related to your research idea (see** Figure 2.2**), conduct a search of the library's electronic catalog AND at least three databases to which your library subscribes.**
  - Possible databases might include ProQuest Dissertation Abstracts, Academic Search Complete, and Sage Premier e-Journals.
  - Create a table like the one in Figure 2.2 to hold your search records.
  - Using vocabulary from Figure 2.1, list the types of sources you found (i.e., textbooks, scholarly journals, trade journals, newspapers, etc.).
- **Create an account in Zotero or another database of your choice.**
  - Make a folder to hold any promising findings.

- Generate a reference list in your university's required style and turn it in for homework.
- **If using a brick-and-mortar (physical) library:**
  - Find all libraries on your campus. How many are there?
  - Find a librarian, introduce yourself, describe your research interests, and ask about their area(s) of expertise.
  - Locate the following and give an example of each:
    - *Music holdings (Call numbers starting with M, ML, MT)*
    - *Education holdings (Call numbers starting with L)*
    - *Periodicals (professional or trade journals and scholarly journals)*
    - *Reference section*
    - *Reserve section*

After you have found and consulted a variety of general sources and discovered useful search terms, you now have a better idea of how scholars and other experts describe and discuss topics related to your area of concern. But before moving to the next level in the spiral of inquiry, take a moment and reflect: How have your research ideas changed after this initial search?

FRAMING A RESEARCH IDEA

At the framing stage of your search, you use what you learned in the previous state to refine and focus your ideas and analyze your information needs. At this state it is critical that you find reputable sources. Tools for searching might include *Google Scholar* as well as general and subject-specific academic databases from your library, described briefly below. When accessed through your library, they provide sources free-of-charge. Additional information may be found in online supplemental materials (see inquiryinmusiceducation.com).

Using Publication Databases

Publication databases (also called indices) provide trustworthy information about scholarly sources in particular fields of study. After becoming acquainted with them from the "scavenger hunt," you should continue to use them. Libraries subscribe to such databases, enabling patrons to use them for free.

Publication databases vary by purpose and content. You might use *WorldCat* (www.worldcat.org, "the world's largest network of library content and services") to find books and other materials in your area of interest and learn where they are housed. *Academic Search Complete* indexes and abstracts over 8,000 journals in the social sciences and education. The *RILM Abstracts* (short for the French term *Répertoire International de Littérature Musicale*) is a music bibliography index, holding records for a variety of musical sub-disciplines. These and other databases are listed for your information in supplemental online materials (see inquiryinmusiceducation.com). Note that two large companies, Ebsco and ProQuest, are the vendors most frequently used by academic libraries in the United States, and both have similar functionality.

Using electronic databases well may require learning additional "subject term" vocabulary. For instance, *Academic Search Complete* uses the phrase "music—instruction and study" to designate "music education." In most cases the website that hosts such an index will have a web-based "button" or other symbol where you can search for the terms used by that source. Figure 2.3 displays the interface for that index. You may also want to look ahead to Figure 4.1 (Chapter 4), which lists many such key terms, fields of study, and subject headings.

Web-based databases may be organized by content area (such as arts and education) or according to whether they are free or require a subscription. If you have university access, for instance, the *RILM Abstracts of Music Literature* (for music) or *Academic Search Complete* (for education) are efficient preliminary sources. If you lack such access, you may wish to try the *Music Research Nexus*

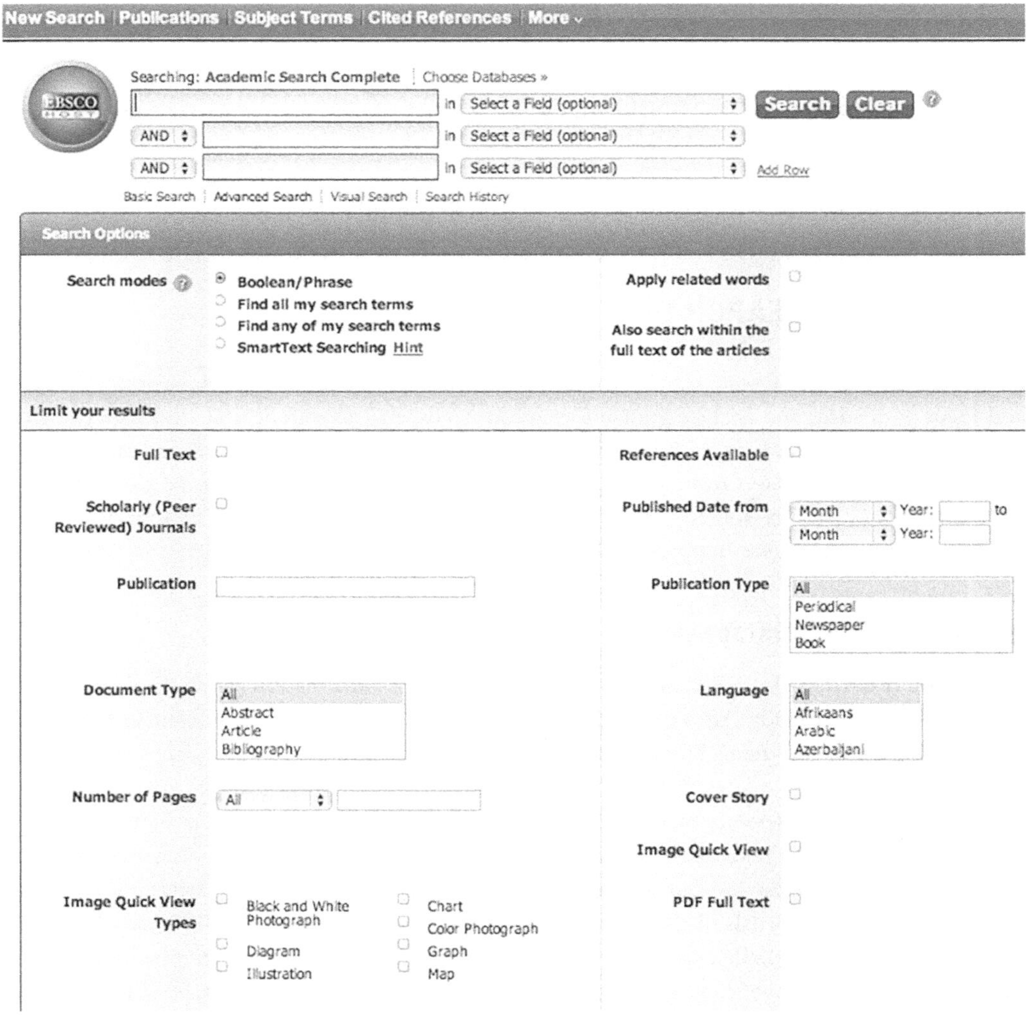

FIGURE 2.3 Sample Search Page from Academic Search Complete. This illustration is used by permission of EBSCO Information Services.

(http://musicresearchnexus.com/) or the Education Resources Information Center *(ERIC)*. *Google Scholar* tends to straddle this distinction; you may use it for free to find citations, but accessing those sources often requires a fee. In such a case, check with a university or public library about interlibrary loan (ILL) services.

A well-planned search of publication databases should yield a long list of publications of potential interest to you. Continuing to keep track of the databases you search and the terms you use will make your search more efficient in the long run. Continue your use of a form similar to that shown above in Figure 2.2 as your search moves forward.

At this stage, we recommend research handbooks, research periodicals, conference proceedings, and occasionally anthologies that are peer-reviewed (meaning a manuscript was reviewed and accepted for publication by a committee of professionally established experts in the field). Peer-reviewed sources are expected to contain a clear and well-defined line of reasoning, use appropriate methods for data gathering and analysis, and have findings and conclusions that speak to their stated purpose.

Databases help you locate sources and tell you where to find them, but not all of them provide access. Some give minimal information—article title, author and source—leaving you to find the journal through another search. Many records link to an abstract (synopsis) of the article, helping you decide whether the source might be helpful for your investigation. More and more, records link directly to the full text of an article, either an electronic (html) publication or an electronic version of a print article (usually in pdf format). (As noted above, those accessed via your library should not have a fee attached.) An important note, however: It is neither acceptable nor wise to limit your search to articles that can be found in full text online.

Most full-text databases allow users to save the pdf version of an article for their personal files, and *Zotero* (as well as some other reference management systems) allows you to keep pdf versions within your records. You may also be able to locate the table of contents for a book on the Internet. If neither of these is possible, consider copying or scanning the table of contents and the introduction and conclusion of key works. You may also wish to copy or scan important pages or lengthy paragraphs that are particularly interesting. Make absolutely sure to note page numbers of any direct quotations in your notes, no matter how small or insignificant. There is nothing worse than having to return to a source at the end of a project to find the page number for a key quotation, or even having to delete a source from your reference list for lack of an appropriate citation.

Skimming Overview Sources

The most important publications for the framing stage of your search are likely to be "overview" sources, usually from within the scholarly music education literature. These often have the word "review" in the article or chapter title, or "handbook" in the book title. Both Routledge and Oxford have, since 1992, published a number of music education research handbooks; the American Educational Research Association and other publishers have done the same for general education and related fields. These and other text-based overview sources can be found through your library's online catalog. The supplemental online materials (see inquiryinmusiceducation. com) include lists of additional sources that you should become familiar with during this stage of exploration, including journals that specifically publish literature review articles, major lexica (encyclopedias and dictionaries) in music and education, and scholarly research periodicals you may consult later in your search.

Carlos' experience was fairly typical. Seeking to find and test a "foolproof" way to grade students in his high school concert band, he initially did a simple *Google* search with the terms *Grading* and *Concert Band*. He found plenty of "hits," but was not quite sure what to do with them. *Prof. E.* suggested that using more specific search terms with *Google Scholar* or one of the library's search databases might be more successful. When he used the terms *"research," "grading," and "music ensemble,"* Carlos found two overview sources: Denis' (2018) literature review in *Update: Applications of Research in Music Education* and Vaughan's (2019) review of "Assessment Practices of American Band Directors" in Brophy's (2019) two-volume *Oxford Handbook of Assessment Policy and Practice in Music Education*. Although the readings did not provide the "quick fix" Carlos had hoped for, he learned about the terminology used by scholars and researchers to discuss assessment in the ensemble setting. In fact, Carlos observed that he had been using the word *grade* (implying judgment) when he really wanted to know more about *assessment* (implying learning). This insight helped him specify his research interest more clearly.

Like Carlos, you may find that overview sources help you place your research interests into a larger and/or more clearly defined context within the field of music education.

Once you have located a good number of overview sources related to your concerns (between 5 and 10), you should skim-read, quickly looking through them to determine their relevance. If you are new to scholarly reading, this can appear to be a daunting task: "I have to read 10 sources in a week?!" You can manage such a number if you focus on whether a publication is relevant to your research idea. You do this by reading selectively. Beginning with the initial paragraphs that may be labeled "introduction," look at the first sentence or two in each paragraph. Go through the entire paragraph only if something interesting is stated in the opening sentence. Finally, read the last paragraphs, which are often but not always labeled "conclusion." If your reading of the conclusion indicates that you missed something important, go back and find it. Otherwise, make note of what you found—broad ideas, terms, subject areas, and one or two sentences that explain your thoughts about the source—and move on to skim another source. At this stage your purpose is to identify the literature that applies to your research idea. Later in the process you will read in a much more detailed and analytical way, but at this stage, skim-reading is both necessary and efficient.

Sometimes a research idea changes as a result of such reading because the topic becomes substantially broader than the initial question, or branches off in another direction entirely. This is appropriate at this stage but be careful that you do not lose sight of your research idea. If that happens, you may find yourself going down the proverbial "rabbit hole" with no end in sight. For this reason it is important to keep track of the steps you followed, because you may need to return to the very earliest sources you found.

It is important at this stage to bombard your research idea with "real" questions (see Introductory Chapter) in light of (1) what you have found in your exploratory literature search, and (2) what you find in further, more detailed reading. Similar to the first level, this involves examining, re-wording, thinking ahead, and specifying further the nature of your research interest. Because scholarly reading is less about seeking a single solution than examining suggested solutions for their validity, trustworthiness, or usefulness, asking the right questions is more important than finding "one right answer." At this stage, your questions should be about specifics ("where-why-when-how-what") and also include practical, mediating factors that may impact your project and the breadth (parameters) of your search.

Examining Your Research Idea in Light of the Overview Literature

In your initial browsing and skimming of the literature, you most likely encountered differences in the ways authors addressed your concern. You may even have found discrepancies between their thoughts and your own. At this point, your purpose is not so much to resolve those differences or to mediate between them as to analyze them and determine whether they are worthy of further study.

Revisiting Your Frame(s)

Most initial areas of concern are broad and touch on many possible research questions within the field of music education. To address those questions, you must break them into more specific sub-questions. Those sub-questions are more likely to correspond to a body of literature, and a critical assessment of that literature will help you to define and narrow your questions still further. This process continues until your question has become so focused that its potential answer may be considered a contribution to knowledge in music education.

Mode of Inquiry

Once you have a coherent research idea, imagine how it might change if it were asked from each mode of inquiry.

Despite her ongoing interest in understanding the university experiences of music students of color, *Jeannette* also contemplated writing a history of the National Association for the Study and Preservation of African-American Music (NASPAAM) and discussed this option with her peers. She clearly felt pulled to address what might be called culturally appropriate, culturally responsive, and/or culturally equitable music education for students from traditionally under-represented communities. She also considered whether she could use a qualitative or quantitative approach to examine music education in such places. In fact, she contemplated replicating a qualitative study such as Ladson-Billings' *The Dreamkeepers* (2009) with a focus on collegiate music study. When she came upon McCall's 2015 study, she was inspired to return to the idea of exploring the experiences of collegiate music students of color and wondered how she might build on McCall's findings.

Thinking Ahead

As you sort through the literature, ask yourself some pertinent questions about the search process itself: What do you hope to get out of this project? What are realistic limitations of your time, financial resources, expertise, and professional aspirations? Are you working toward a doctorate or are you about to finish your master's degree?

Michelle's exploration of the literature helped her realize how broad her research idea actually was; her search needed to be focused substantially if she eventually wanted to conduct a study herself. Because Michelle found that she enjoyed the reading process, she got permission from *Prof. E.* to continue reading and produce as her semester project a comprehensive literature review, always remaining open for eventually focusing in on a more limited research topic.

Greg did not feel nearly as good about this stage of his literature search. Still uncertain about pursuing the degree, he found it difficult to commit to the research process. Somewhat aimlessly, therefore, he collected the titles and bibliographic details of method books and articles concerning string education in public schools and took notes on many of them. But he still was unsure of the purpose of that activity because he found it difficult to ask further questions about what seemed to him to be obvious and known information.

Undoubtedly, you have your own questions at this point and it might be necessary to discuss them with your class instructor or mentor. You may also find it helpful to engage in conversations with your friends and peers.

Quite set on finding efficient ways to assess his high school band students, *Carlos* was not sure why he needed to ask further questions. How much more specific could he get? A bit frustrated with the slow process of finding good sources and more "doable" questions to ask, he turned to *Dale* for additional advice. Going beyond Dale's questionnaire, he began to read the entire thesis. Doing so gave him confidence that he could move forward because he saw possibilities that made sense to him.

Because *Chi-Hui* was to return to her home country after completing her master's degree, she made the practical decision, together with *Prof. E.*, to focus on literature in the field of Comparative (or International) Music Education. Not only did that decision shorten the initial broad-scaled search process, but it also provided Chi-Hui with a subject—music education in the United States—that she could report to her colleagues in her home country.

Whether you are doing a literature review that is limited to a few weeks, expands over several weeks or a semester, or—as with a doctoral dissertation—might take a year or so, avoid rushing this phase of your project. The better informed you are about the literature, the easier it will be to articulate what interests you professionally. And, as it is with the musician in you: The more passionately you care about something, the better you are as a professional. Try to frame an idea that truly intrigues you, contributes to your professional growth, and has broad applicability to future work.

At the master's level, your task will be easier if your research idea is related to your present job or future jobs. Consider also whether your topic involves sources that are relatively easy to find and does not involve subscriptions and other materials beyond those available at your library. At the doctoral level, however, you are at the beginning of a research agenda that will drive your future career as a college professor, at least in the first few years. In this latter case, practical concerns may be less important than topics that address issues that are important for the future of the field.

Specifying the Boundaries of Your Search

Based on the considerations above, decide on the boundaries of your literature search. What approaches seem to hold promise for explaining your articulated concern? What aspects addressed by others are of less interest to you personally? If the purpose of your literature review is to lead you toward proposing and conducting your own study, pay close attention to the methods and procedures used by researchers whose work you are reading. Which ones seem manageable to you and which ones might require a larger commitment of time or money than you can manage?

Dale decided on the following boundaries:

- He was interested in exploring the job satisfaction of mid-career music teachers.
- Recent school reform initiatives required teacher assessments that had not been examined in the music education literature.
- He wanted to make a connection between Paolo Friere's ideas, which he had explored in one of his courses.

As *Michelle* began building a bibliography of research studies related to online music applications for her school district, she discovered several music education research handbooks. *The Oxford Handbook of Music Education, Volumes 1 & 2* (McPherson & Welch, 2012) covered many aspects of music education. *The Oxford Handbook of Social Media and Music Learning* (Waldron, Horsley, & Veblen, 2020) was specific to social media and music learning, and *The Oxford Handbook of Technology and Music Education* (Ruthmann & Mantie, 2017) addressed technology and music education. She also discovered a periodical, the *Journal of Music, Technology and Education*, which had many articles of interest to her. Michelle was amazed at the amount of information collected in those sources and at the many possibilities they suggested for her research idea.

COLLECTING EVIDENCE FROM THE RESEARCH LITERATURE

By now you have learned to use publication databases and distinguish various source types and genres from each other by paying attention to layout and format differences as well as content. You know how to separate trade sources from scholarly ones and overview sources from research articles. Having drawn some boundaries around a research idea and decided on a first set of project parameters, you have reached the collecting stage of the literature search. It now is time to collect scholarly sources that are pertinent to your research idea, describe them in detail, and evaluate their content in terms of how they relate to your research idea. This involves what we referred to in Chapter 1 as critical or reflective reading. The collecting stage requires taking detailed notes as described below.

Describing Source Content

Notes at this stage of the literature search are known as annotations, and are more comprehensive than the basic bibliographic information you began collecting earlier. It is important, therefore, that you develop a note-taking process that will serve you over the long haul. Our students have had success with one of these processes:

1) Add notes to the bibliographic information in your chosen reference management system (i.e., *Zotero*, *Mandelay*, etc.). Some systems allow note-taking, tagging and cross-referencing.
2) Use a note-taking app such as *OneNote* or *Evernote*.
3) Use qualitative data analysis software, discussed in more detail in Chapter 8.
4) Create documents with word-processing software such as *Word* or *Google Docs*.

Annotations for the purpose of reviewing literature should both describe and evaluate each source. When *describing* a source, you need to:

- Note basic question(s) the source purports to examine. Sometimes this is an explicit "purpose statement"; other times you must deduce it from the author's words or the title of a publication.
- Establish the *mode of inquiry* addressed by the source; that is, whether the source deals with ideas, or describes present or past actions, events, and experiences. If you cannot clearly identify the primary mode in which a study is conducted, make note of that fact.
- Find the author's logical explanation about the importance of their purpose.
- Identify the author's description of the approach used to answer their research question.
  - For sources based on quantitative research, note the reported *reliability* and *validity* (or absence thereof) of any data-gathering tools (i.e., tests, observational systems, attitudinal and rating scales, questionnaires, formal or informal interviews).
  - For sources based on qualitative research, note the author's description of reflexivity, ethics, and quality controls.
  - For instructional research this may involve both a teaching and a research approach.
- Paraphrase or quote the study's findings (often called results in quantitative studies).

It is advisable to describe each source in enough detail to keep from having to return to the original later for more information. Realistically, however, since your reading purpose changes over time and according to the project you are working on, you should leave enough space in your notes to add further details as the need arises.

Evaluating Source Content

Evaluating a source involves two parts. First, notice whether the author(s)' work adheres to conventions of good scholarship:

- Are the arguments logical?
- Does the author reference trustworthy sources?
- Do the methods and procedures make sense, given the author's stated purpose or intent?
- Do the study's findings address its stated purpose?

If you find that an author uses trustworthy evidence and logical arguments, you may conclude that the source is suitable for use in your own quest.

The second part of source evaluation is where you respond to how each source applies to your research idea. A given source may support your ideas, or it might form the basis for a new way of thinking about an issue. A source that appears to be of poor quality may give you a reason to argue that more research on the topic is needed. Recognizing gaps or contradictions in the existing evidence is the start of identifying possible topics for research.

It is important that you approach the sources you find as a reasoner and skeptic rather than a receptive acceptor. Keep track of questions raised by what you read and pursue answers to those questions through continued searching. These questions represent the starting points for your eventual research topic and purpose. It is also important that your notes differentiate your own ideas from those of the authors whose work you are reviewing, and also that you use your notes to make connections to other sources you are reading. Depending on the purpose for which you are reading, of course, your evaluation of the content of a publication may differ in depth and focus.

Once you have found a number of studies that clearly connect to your research idea, your collection of individual sources becomes a body of knowledge. When you establish categories and sub-categories within that body, you are on your way to finding possible researchable topics within your research idea. Carlos' experience may serve as an example.

Carlos initially cast a wide net to find sources, which resulted in a large collection. He initially organized them by type, putting trade sources in one group and research sources in another, but realized that would not help him address his research question. Skimming further, several sources caught his eye. He appreciated the concern described by Almqvist, Vinge, Väkevä, and Zandén (2017) with "'Criteria compliance' replacing 'learning'" in music education. Denis (2018), an overview source, helped him articulate pertinent assessment concepts in music education. He loved Dunbar's (2012) idea of "Performance assessment in 30 seconds or less," but wondered how and whether that might work in the concert band setting. Could these sources form the basis of a project? When he described his findings during the next class meeting, *Prof. E.* suggested that a literature map might offer further direction for his work.

CONSTRUCTING A LITERATURE MAP

A literature map can help you narrow your thinking from a research idea to a workable research topic. Creating a graphic representation of the categories and relevant publications in a literature collection (see Hart, 2018; Creswell & Creswell, 2017) will (1) show you visually which studies are most pertinent to your evolving research topic, (2) help you to recognize important sub-topics within your literature collection, and (3) bring to light some possible connections between sources that may not be obvious when you consider them individually.

> *Carlos* first gave his map a tentative title ("Building Practical and Meaningful Assessments for Concert Band") and then named two main categories within his literature collection: "Perspectives on Assessment" and "Approaches to Assessment." He then examined the sources in each category more closely, which helped him define sub-categories within the main categories.
>
> Within the "Perspectives" category, he noticed a difference in the sources that reviewed research and the ones that actually did research. Within the latter, authors tended to do large-scale studies that explored how ensemble director-teachers were doing assessment, or smaller-scale surveys that investigated the assessment preferences of parents, students, or administrators (called "stakeholders."). Within the "Approaches" category he created two sub-categories, one with specific ideas for how to assess and another that suggested strategies for incorporating assessment over the long term. Carlos created a third category for the sources that most spoke to his own priorities, and added NAfME's *Model Cornerstone Assessments* to this category. The map helped him to clarify his ideas and move toward a researchable topic.

Carlos' complete literature map can be seen in Figure 2.4.

Organizing the sources you have collected into a literature map can point out strengths and weaknesses in your literature collection, including:

1) which studies are most pertinent to your evolving topic,
2) what sub-topics are dealt with by particular researchers,
3) whether there are any "holes" in the literature that still need answers, and
4) how other researchers designed studies for topics similar to yours.

Such clarification requires, however, that only well-conducted studies be included in the map. These are studies for which you know the purpose, applicable terms and their definitions, mode of inquiry, research methods, data gathering and analysis tools, and results and conclusions as stated by the author. It should be clear that the results of each study address the author's stated purpose; the conclusions are truly based on the results; and any limitations in design are properly acknowledged.

A literature map can also help you to tie together or synthesize the findings from your literature search, or even re-calibrate the parameters of your research idea. Chi-Hui, for instance, might have used the literature map to reorganize her literature collection by categories.

When you construct your literature map, use only those sources that most closely relate to your evolving research idea. This means revisiting your notes to be sure each publication pertains specifically to your research idea. You may find that information you once considered relevant is no longer applicable. For Carlos, for example, this meant discarding references that had been important in the earlier phases of his search, but were no longer needed. If your literature map does not end up looking as neat as the one Carlos created, keep in mind that its purpose is to help

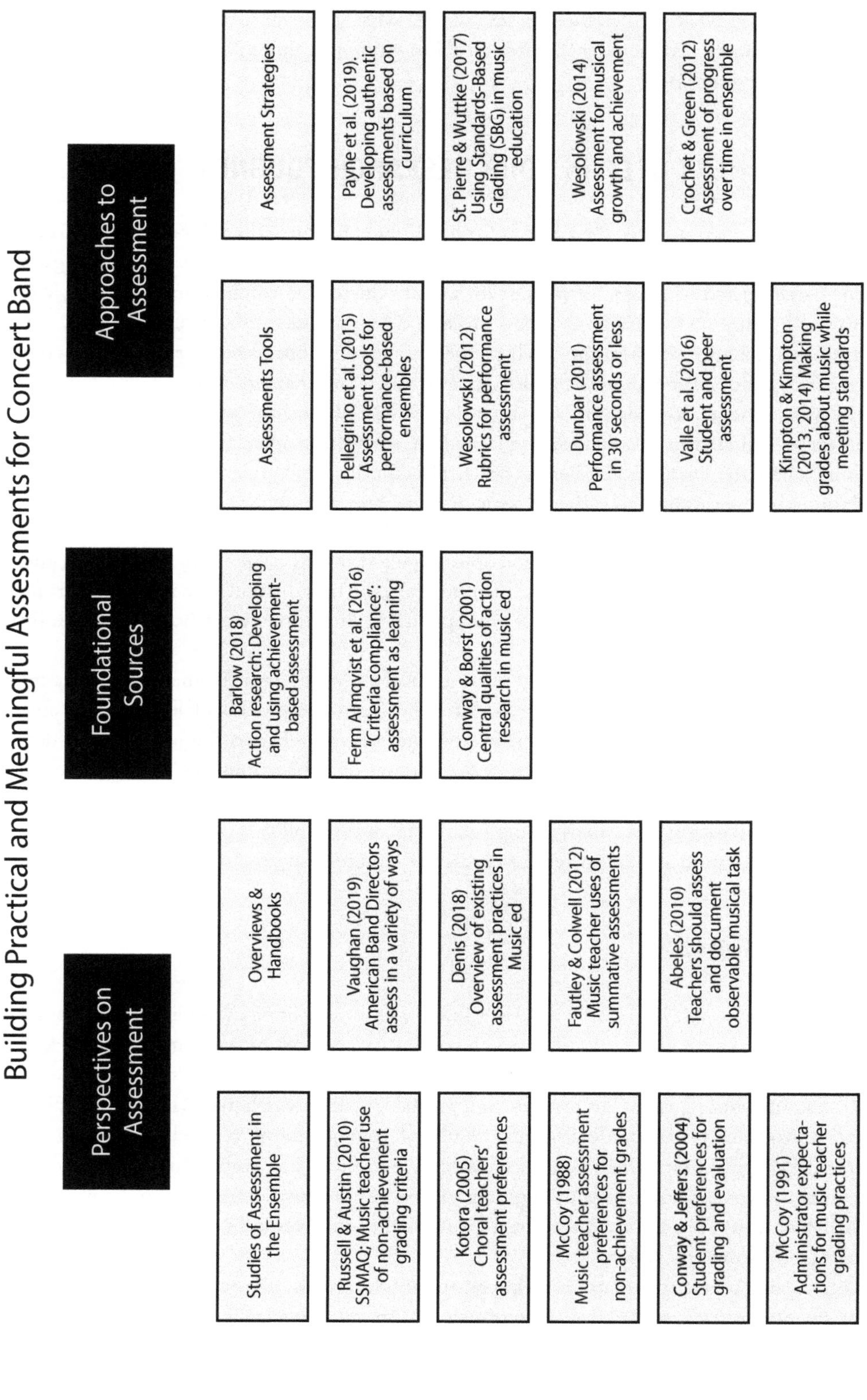

Building Practical and Meaningful Assessments for Concert Band

Perspectives on Assessment

Studies of Assessment in the Ensemble
- Russell & Austin (2010) SSMAQ; Music teacher use of non-achievement grading criteria
- Kotora (2005) Choral teachers' assessment preferences
- McCoy (1988) Music teacher assessment preferences for non-achievement grades
- Conway & Jeffers (2004) Student preferences for grading and evaluation
- McCoy (1991) Administrator expectations for music teacher grading practices

Overviews & Handbooks
- Vaughan (2019) American Band Directors assess in a variety of ways
- Denis (2018) Overview of existing assessment practices in Music ed
- Fautley & Colwell (2012) Music teacher uses of summative assessments
- Abeles (2010) Teachers should assess and document observable musical task

Foundational Sources

- Barlow (2018) Action research: Developing and using achievement-based assessment
- Ferm Almqvist et al. (2016) "Criteria compliance": assessment as learning
- Conway & Borst (2001) Central qualities of action research in music ed

Approaches to Assessment

Assessments Tools
- Pellegrino et al. (2015) Assessment tools for performance-based ensembles
- Wesolowski (2012) Rubrics for performance assessment
- Dunbar (2011) Performance assessment in 30 seconds or less
- Valle et al. (2016) Student and peer assessment
- Kimpton & Kimpton (2013, 2014) Making grades about music while meeting standards

Assessment Strategies
- Payne et al. (2019). Developing authentic assessments based on curriculum
- St. Pierre & Wuttke (2017) Using Standards-Based Grading (SBG) in music education
- Wesolowski (2014) Assessment for musical growth and achievement
- Crochet & Green (2012) Assessment of progress over time in ensemble

FIGURE 2.4 Carlos' Literature Map

you think about (1) what you are looking for, and (2) what you expect to do with the information once you found it. Remember that it is a tool to guide you through the process rather than a product of your research.

TAKING THE NEXT STEP IN YOUR RESEARCH JOURNEY

The way you will communicate the findings from your literature analysis differs according to why the review was undertaken in the first place. If your purpose is simply to gather and organize extant research related to a topic of interest for an introductory research course, you may write a scholarly literature review paper as a class project. If you are designing a research study, your analysis of the literature will become the basis for your research purpose and rationale (discussed in Chapter 3), and suggested research design (elaborated in Chapters 5–13). For publication, scholarly articles frequently combine the discussion of related literature with the rationale, while master's theses and doctoral dissertations typically have an entire chapter, frequently titled "related literature," where the writer establishes his or her place in the topic under consideration.

If your purpose is simply to gather and organize the literature about a topic of interest, it may be acceptable to create an annotated bibliography. You do this by collecting the notes about your sources, following the guidelines for annotation suggested in this chapter, and organizing them in a way that is useful to you: alphabetically, historically, or by sub-topic, for instance. For most scholars an annotated bibliography is the starting point of a literature review, however, rather than the end product.

Do not be intimidated by what may seem an overwhelming task. Remember that it took years to become an accomplished musician, but you began the process of learning and never looked back. We think the same will happen now that you have begun the journey into doing research. After having evaluated and abstracted a number of publications, we are confident that you will begin to develop a sense for what separates strong and trustworthy publications from weak and less convincing ones. Developing such a discerning ability is one of the most crucial skills in your preparation as a competent researcher. It requires expertise that grows over time.

CHAPTER SUMMARY

1)   Exploring a research idea involves: (a) getting to know your library's holdings and resources; (b) preliminary searching to discover search vocabulary and preliminary sources; and (c) keeping track of search terms and results.
2)   Re-framing your research idea prior to your formal literature search makes for a more efficient search. You do this by considering the results of your preliminary search, imagining multiple perspectives from which your idea might be examined, and considering which mode of inquiry is most applicable to your questions. These steps help you engage with the literature.
3)   Analyzing your collection of literature-based evidence involves both describing and evaluating the literature you collect.
4)   Constructing a literature map can help you specify the details of your research topic. You do this by looking for a) studies that are pertinent to your research ideas, b) sub-topics within your literature collection, and c) connections between sources that might not otherwise be obvious.

Topics for Further Exploration

1) Preliminary sources versus research sources.
2) Formatting requirements of your institution or publisher.
3) Differences between taking notes and critical engagement with the literature.

Suggested Assignments

1) Research "speed dating." Team up with a colleague for a 10-minute session in which each of you interviews the other for 5 minutes about experiences exploring the literature. Be as specific in your interview as possible, covering as much of the process as possible. After about 10 minutes rotate to other colleagues for the same process. Continue until each member of the class has been interviewer and interviewee at least once. Compare the answers and identify commonalities and differences among your experiences. Assess how the questions were asked and which questions yielded the most detailed responses.
2) Locate in the library the major databases relevant to research in music education.
3) Find one or more music education or general education handbooks related to your topic. Skim the table(s) of contents and describe to your classmates. A list of recent handbooks can be found in supplemental online materials (see inquiryinmusiceducation.com).
4) Initiate a computer search for references.
5) Locate some of the research periodicals listed in the supplemental online materials and develop a list of sources that may be useful for your research interest.
6) Read three articles from research journals and evaluate them according to the criteria described in this chapter.
7) Examine Library of Congress classifications (or another classification scheme) using a minimum of three books from a particular Library of Congress number (i.e., MT1). Categorize according to purpose and targeted readership(s).
8) Construct a literature map for your literature collection. Explain it to your colleagues.
9) Compare the purpose statements for three sources from your preliminary search. Skim each source and determine the steps the author(s) took to fulfill their stated purpose(s). Share your findings with your colleagues.

Recommended Reading

On Literature Mapping

Creswell, J. W., & Creswell, J. D. (2017). *Research design: Qualitative, quantitative, and mixed methods approaches* (5th ed.). Sage.
Hart, C. (2018). *Doing a literature review: Releasing the research imagination* (2nd ed.). Sage.

On Literature Reviews

Cooper, H. M. (1985). *A taxonomy of literature reviews.* Paper presented at the annual meeting of the American Educational Research Association, Chicago. ERIC Document Reproduction Services No. ED254541. www.eric.ed.gov/
Hart, C. (2018). *Doing a literature review: Releasing the research imagination* (2nd ed.). Sage.

On Print and Electronic Music Sources

Gottlieb, J. (2016). *Music library and research skills* (2nd ed.). Oxford.

On Publication Manuals

American Psychological Association. (2020). *Publication manual of the American Psychological Association* (7th ed.). https://doi.org/10.1037/0000165-000

Modern Language Association. (2021). *MLA handbook for writers of research papers* (9th ed.). Author.

Purdue OWL. (2020). *Purdue online writing lab*. Purdue University. https://owl.purdue.edu/owl/purdue_owl.html

The University of Chicago Press. (2017). *The Chicago manual of style* (17th ed.). Author.

REFERENCES

Abeles, H. F. (2010). Assessing music learning. In H. F. Abeles & L. A. Custodero (Eds.), *Critical issues in music education* (pp. 167–93). Oxford University Press.

Almqvist, F. C., Vinge, J., Väkevä, L., & Zandén, O. (2017). Assessment as learning in music education: The risk of "criteria compliance" replacing "learning" in the Scandinavian countries. *Research Studies in Music Education, 39*(1), 3–18. https://doi.org/10.1177/1321103X16676649

Barlow, S. (2018). Assessment and engagement in music classes: Are they mutually exclusive? *Australian Journal of Music Education, 52*(1), 19–27.

Conway, C. M., & Borst, J. (2001). Action research in music education. *Update: Applications of Research in Music Education, 19*(2), 3–8. https://doi.org/10.1177/87551233010190020102

Conway, C. M., & Jeffers, T. (2004). Parent, student, and teacher perceptions of assessment procedures in beginning instrumental music. *Bulletin of the Council for Research in Music Education,* 16–25. www.jstor.org/stable/40319215

Creswell, J. W., & Creswell, J. D. (2017). *Research design: Qualitative, quantitative, and mixed methods approaches* (5th ed.). Sage.

Crochet, L. S., & Green, S. K. (2012). Examining progress across time with practical assessments in ensemble settings. *Music Educators Journal, 98*(3), 49–54. https://doi.org/10.1177/0027432111435276

Denis, J. M. (2018). Assessment in music: A practitioner Introduction to assessing students. *Update: Applications of Research in Music Education, 36*(3), 20–28. https://doi.org/10.1177/8755123317741489

Dickey, M. R. (1992). A review of research on modeling in music teaching and learning. *Bulletin of the Council for Research in Music Education, 113,* 27–40. www.jstor.org/stable/40318509

Dunbar, L. (2012). Performance assessment of the masses in 30 seconds or less. *General Music Today, 25*(2), 31–35. https://doi.org/10.1177/1048371311406266

Fautley, M., & Colwell, R. (2012). Assessment in the secondary music classroom. In G. E. McPherson & G. F. Welch (Eds.), *The Oxford handbook of music education* (Vol. 1). Oxford University Press. https://doi.org/10.1093/oxfordhb/9780199730810.013.0029

Ferm Almqvist, C., Vinge, J., Väkevä, L., & Zandén, O. (2017). Assessment as learning in music education: The risk of "criteria compliance" replacing "learning" in the Scandinavian countries. *Research Studies in Music Education, 39*(1), 3–18. https://doi.org/10.1177/1321103X16676649

Hart, C. (2018). *Doing a literature review: Releasing the research imagination* (2nd ed.). Sage.

Kelly, S. N. (1999). Using conducting gestures to teach music concepts: A review of research. *Update: Applications of Research in Music Education, 18*(1), 3–6.

Kimpton, P., & Kimpton, A. K. (2013). *Grading for musical excellence: Making music an essential part of your grades*. GIA Publications.

Kimpton, P., & Kimpton, A. K. (2014). *Common core: Re-imagining the music rehearsal and classroom: Standards, curriculum, assessment, instruction*. GIA Publications.

Kotora, E. (2005). Assessment practices in the choral music classroom: A survey of Ohio high school choral music teachers and college choral methods professors. *Contributions to Music Education, 32*(2), 65–80. www.jstor.org/stable/24127154

Ladson-Billings, G. (2009). *The dreamkeepers: Successful teachers of African American children* (2nd ed.). Jossey-Bass.

McCall, J. M. (2015). *Degree perseverance among African Americans transitioning from Historically Black Colleges and Universities (HBCUs) to Predominantly White Institution (PWIs)* [Doctoral dissertation]. Arizona State University. ASU Library: Digital Repository. http://hdl.handle.net/2286/R.A.150878

McCoy, C. W. (1988). An exploratory study of grading criteria among selected Ohio ensemble directors. *Contributions to Music Education, 15,* 15–19. www.jstor.org/stable/24127441

McCoy, C. W. (1991). Grading students in performing groups: A comparison of principals' recommendations with directors' practices. *Journal of Research in Music Education, 39*(3), 181–190. https://doi.org/10.2307/3344718

McPherson, G., & Welch, G. F. (2012). *The Oxford handbook of music education* (Vol. 1 & 2). Oxford University Press. https://doi.org/10.1093/oxfordhb/9780199730810.001.0001

Payne, P. D., Burrack, F., Parkes, K. A., & Wesolowski, B. (2019). An emerging process of assessment in music education. *Music Educators Journal, 105*(3), 36–44. https://doi.org/10.1177/0027432118818880

Pellegrino, K., Conway, C. M., & Russell, J. A. (2015). Assessment in performance-based secondary music classes. *Music Educators Journal, 102*(1), 48–55. https://doi.org/10.1177/0027432115590183

Russell, J. A., & Austin, J. R. (2010). Assessment practices of secondary music teachers. *Journal of Research in Music Education, 58*(1), 37–54. https://doi.org/10.1177/0022429409360062

Ruthmann, S. A., & Mantie, R. (Eds.) (2017). *The Oxford handbook of technology and music education.* Oxford University Press. https://doi.org/10.1093/oxfordhb/9780199372133.001.0001

St. Pierre, N. A., & Wuttke, B. C. (2017). Standards-based grading practices among practicing music educators: Prevalence and rationale. *Update: Applications of Research in Music Education, 35*(2), 30–37. https://doi.org/10.1177/8755123315604468

Valle, C., Andrade, H., Palma, M., & Hefferen, J. (2016). Applications of peer assessment and self-assessment in music. *Music Educators Journal, 102*(4), 41–49. https://doi.org/10.1177/0027432116644652

Vallo, V., Jr. (1990). Conducting and music education: A review of selected research. *Update: Applications of Research in Music Education, 9*(1), 13–16. https://doi.org/10.1177/875512339000900104

Vaughan, C. J. (2019). Assessment practices of American band directors. In T. S. Brophy (Ed.), *The Oxford handbook of assessment policy and practice in music education* (Vol. 2, pp. 351–378). Oxford University Press. https://doi.org/10.1093/oxfordhb/9780190248130.001.0001

Waldron, J. L., Horsley, S., & Veblen, K. K. (2020). *The Oxford handbook of social media and music learning.* Oxford University Press. https://doi.org/10.1093/oxfordhb/9780190660772.013.3

Wesolowski, B. C. (2012). Understanding and developing rubrics for music performance assessment. *Music Educators Journal, 98*(3), 36–42. https://doi.org/10.1177/0027432111432524

Wesolowski, B. C. (2014). Documenting student learning in music performance: A framework. *Music Educators Journal, 101*(1), 77–85. https://doi.org/10.1177/0027432114540475

CHAPTER 3

Toward a Rationale and Research Plan

Writing a Contract With Yourself

This chapter suggests steps for developing a plan to complete a literature review or research proposal:

*   naming a research topic,
*   crafting a purpose statement,
*   articulating a rationale, and
*   determining the parameters of a project.

Having collected literature related to a topic and examined the place of your topic in the broader scope of music education knowledge via your literature map, you now craft a purpose statement and articulate a rationale as part of making plans for the next steps in your study.

INTRODUCTION

In the fourth week of RC533, *Carlos* announced to *Prof. E.* that he had made arrangements to distribute a questionnaire about assessment in the ensemble classroom to the music teachers in his home school district. He had based his survey on the one from Dale's thesis. Proudly displaying a draft created with *Qualtrics*, Carlos was surprised (and somewhat frustrated) when Prof. E. did not even look at the questionnaire but simply asked for clarification about his research topic and purpose, expressing concern that his plan seemed vague and also had not been "approved" by certain committees. As he tried to answer Prof. E.'s questions about topic and purpose, Carlos realized that he could not articulate either of them clearly. Reluctantly, he had to admit that he had, "put the cart before the horse" by trying to gather data before his research plan—purpose, rationale, and methods for data collection and analysis—was fully complete.

A research plan—what we call a contract with yourself—divides a project into specific tasks that direct your actions and reminds you (and perhaps others) of what must be accomplished to complete the project. As you develop your research plan, keep in mind the experiences of the

DOI: 10.4324/9781003057703-5

students in RC 533. Like them, some of you will focus more on the "search" aspect of thinking and reading, with a *review of the literature* as your desired outcome. That may be the extent of your work for the time being, while others will use their literature review as the foundation for a *research proposal*. If you are a master's or doctoral student, this proposal may become the basis for the final project of your degree—a *master's thesis* or *doctoral dissertation*.

In a single semester, you may expect to get a good start on your literature collection, purpose, and rationale. If planning to do original research for a thesis or dissertation, you will learn the basics of the research methods with which you plan the design of your research. However, no student in RC533 completed an entire research study in a single term, and the same is likely true for you.

Developing Your Preliminary Plan

Do not rush into submitting an official proposal without laying out a clear plan and asking for feedback. As you go through the semester, you will continually tighten and revise your plan by learning more about the methods and designs that are common in each respective research mode and about different proposal formats (see Chapters 5–13 and 14.) Dealing with each aspect of the plan systematically will help you move forward in the spiral of inquiry. This is so even if, at times, the multiple demands of critical reading, working on class assignments, and continuing with life outside of class may look insurmountable. Remember that you became an accomplished musician step-by-step; the same is true for becoming a researcher. Engaging with research is a process . . . one that requires, like musical performance, continuous refining.

A good first step is to formulate in writing:

- a clearly articulated research topic,
- rationale, and
- purpose statement.

The next section serves as a bridge between the topic examination you did with the literature map and the development of a research purpose and a rationale. Whether the outcome of your research is a stand-alone literature review, a research proposal for a class project, or a proposal for a thesis, dissertation, or grant, these steps are necessary to determine the scope and the direction of your project.

ARTICULATING YOUR RESEARCH TOPIC

Liam came to class one evening rather upset. His mapping of the research related to the scat singing techniques of Louis Armstrong had led him to question the basic premise he voiced at the beginning of the semester. Rather than viewing the music of Louis Armstrong as a technical singing accomplishment, his non-musical sources (i.e., historical, social science) suggested that the practice of scat singing was the result of a long line of African-American musical and social factors. The sources seemed to suggest that Louis Armstrong used scat singing to build up his own stage persona, but that he did not originate the practice. After sharing this new perspective with his colleagues in RC533, Liam realized that bringing together these seemingly disparate ideas would make his research stronger. "So now, what I want to know is: What are the differences between the reality of the origins of scat singing and the myths surrounding it?"

Contradictions like the one Liam encountered can be the basis of well-defined research topics and purposes. A similar contradiction was the basis of a research question pursued by Montemayor and Moss (2009). Several professional sources (among them, Battisti & Garofalo, 1990; Lisk, 1991) suggest that musical score study without a recorded model is preferable to study with a recording. Montemayor and Moss (2009), however, found an inconsistency with that belief in the research literature. Some studies suggested pitch and rhythm error detection by student conductors was superior when recordings were used, whereas other studies did not report such findings. Their topic thus became error detection skills with and without the use of recordings. Already quite well defined, articulating the actual purpose statement would be a matter of clarifying the context of the research, its specific questions, design, and methods. It eventually reads, to investigate "effects of aural-supported rehearsal preparation on selected behavioral and evaluative elements of novice teachers' rehearsals" (p. 236).

Crafting a well-defined purpose will ultimately help you create a title that clearly communicates your intent. The published title of the study above, for example, reads "Effects of Recorded Models on Novice Teachers' Rehearsal Verbalizations, Evaluations, and Conducting" (p. 236). You may think that deciding on a title may seem a "final" activity, but we suggest even at this preliminary stage of the process to come up with a "working title" that you will sharpen as your project takes shape.

Not all projects move smoothly from topic to purpose to title. However, the more clearly you pinpoint your research topic, the more likely it is that a well-articulated purpose and rationale will follow. Narrowing your research ideas to a single topic, therefore, means becoming ever more exact about what and how you wish to observe, describe, or examine. You may consider several options before committing to a single topic. Carlos' earlier struggles illustrate this process: From what perspective would he consider this issue? Did he wish to know how other teachers implemented, processed, and analyzed student assessment? Or was he more interested in investigating how students perceived assessment, so he could better meet their instructional needs? Was he interested in documenting changes in musical achievement? Or did he just want to know what the options were?

Because the research journey differs from person to person, there is no single way to narrow your thoughts from general to specific. We therefore return to three of the RC 533 students to illustrate what it means to commit to a research topic. As you will see, this was easier for some students than for others:

Chi-Hui hoped to limit her search to studies in International (also called Comparative) Music Education. From cursory reading on that subject, she learned that investigating similarities and differences in the development of formal music education in different countries was a legitimate research project.

Christy had begun the semester wanting to study vocal pedagogy. Interested in the history of that area, she had narrowed her research idea to a study of how evolving thoughts about educational pedagogy had influenced vocal pedagogues from 1800–1900. But there was little explicit mention of pedagogical thinking in the literature she found. Should she expand her search in some way, or narrow it to focus more on individual pedagogues? Her interest was piqued and she began to look more carefully at the pedagogues that had originated the methods. As she did so, she took note more about the historical context of those methods than about their contents and pedagogical strategies.

Thinking and reading about connections between the component parts of her topic led *Michelle* to visualize her research idea as a puzzle. She felt like the music teachers in her district were fairly comfortable with music technology in the classroom, but that what they were doing in the classroom did not seem to connect to the students' participatory music-making at home. This, of course, had been compounded by the experience of teaching and learning music during the recent pandemic. She therefore saw her research task as finding a way (maybe more than one way) to fill in the missing pieces. This image gave her the idea to look for ways to bring together students' music-making at home and at school.

Imagination caused the three students to think broadly, yet in ever more specific terms. Becker (1998) calls that process "visualizing" your research, literally imagining what a study might look like when the topic is worded this or that way. Think creatively about new ways of seeing what seemed fully examined before. Make concrete connections between what you read and think about as well as what you begin to observe, describe, and examine. Live with the ideas for a while so that they take on a life of their own.

Initial interests in practical matters such as musical actions in the classroom can be addressed philosophically when you turn them into quests about ideas and constructs of thought. Marguerite might transform her excitement about Christopher Small's ideas into a research study by exploring how relationships are affirmed and celebrated "every time we take part in a musical performance" (Small, 1997, p. 4). She especially liked the question: "What does it mean when this performance takes place at this time, in this place, with these participants?" (p. 3). She wondered, though, whether she wanted to explore this idea philosophically or empirically. Might she be able to imagine a context where it could be explored? Although the idea might still sound abstract to an uninvolved bystander, for Marguerite it was a natural outcome of her earlier voiced concerns.

CRAFTING THE RESEARCH PURPOSE

The purpose statement communicates the intent of a particular project. As such, its wording should be succinct and unambiguous. It should clearly state the scope and boundaries of your research project—nothing more and nothing less. Returning to Gates' (1999) functions of research, described in Chapter 1: Are you more interested in examining theories and principles applicable to music learning and teaching in general or do you favor inventing technological and other learning tools? Is your perspective that of an "engineer-type" educator or a philosopher-educator? Do you want practical answers to "how to" questions or are you primarily interested in generating more questions?

How you respond to any of these queries guides the wording of your purpose statement. If you are not sure, examine purpose statements used by authors whose work resonates with your own thinking. Initially, you may begin simply: "The purpose of this study is to investigate/ examine/explore . . ." Fill in the component parts of your topic as they speak to your expectations of what the study should accomplish. Provide a sense of (1) the mode of inquiry (i.e., historical, empirical, or philosophical) employed in the study; (2) the focus—learner, teacher, music, or a combination; and (3) whether the study is based on descriptive (qualitative or quantitative), relational, experimental or mixed methods. (For more information about methods, see Chapters 5–13.) However, you should avoid specific reference to any particular data gathering device unless your purpose is developing a tool. As your purpose takes shape, share it with colleagues in and out of class, as their perspective will help you to make sure your purpose is as clear as possible.

Exploration: Formulating Purpose statements

Below you find first attempts by many of the students in RC 533 to formulate purpose statements. What feedback would you give them?

Carlos . . . to examine ways to build practical and meaningful assessments for high school Concert Band.

Chi -Hui . . . to explore research related to the formal teaching of Western art music in Taiwan and North America.

Christy . . . to examine the historical contexts of influential vocal pedagogues between 1800 and 1900.

Dale . . . to investigate how mid-career music teachers in his home state perceive recently implemented teacher assessments.

Jeannette . . . to explore the experiences of collegiate music students from Black and other traditionally underserved populations.

Keisha . . . to study the effects of speech-based rhythm patterns on the rhythmic achievement of young children.

Liam . . . to explore stories about the cultural and musical origins of the practice of jazz scat singing.

Michelle . . . to look for ways classroom music teachers could bridge school music and students' participatory music-making at home.

Note from these examples how a purpose statement triggers expectations about what a proposed study might look like. Make suggestions for clarifying and sharpening the focus where necessary and ask about the implications of the words each student used. Consider your own developing purpose statement in light of the advice you give to the students in RC533.

Purpose Specifications

It is common for researchers in all modes of inquiry to specify the parts of their purpose with research questions, sub-purposes, or hypotheses. Many students who are preparing a research plan for the first time find this activity helpful for delineating the scope of their research project. Writing down your purpose specifications can clarify whether you have (a) addressed all necessary variables or questions, (b) chosen the appropriate mode of inquiry and research methods for collecting and analyzing data, (c) learned the requisite skills or techniques for completing the research successfully, and (d) gained access to the resources necessary to complete the study in a timely fashion.

How you choose to format your research specifications is a matter of personal choice, but it also depends on the traditions within the mode of inquiry and methods with which you work. *Research questions* are typically used by philosophical, historical, and qualitative researchers. Quantitative researchers may also use that term or may call the delineations of their purpose *sub-purposes* or *hypotheses*. The latter term—hypotheses—has a specific mathematical connotation and is used most frequently in ex post facto and experimental research (see Chapters 9 and 12). And a word of caution is in order for the word "effect." It suggests causality between what is being observed and leads to particular considerations about research method and design—whether quantitatively or qualitatively, historically or philosophically. If your research plan includes original research, your clearly written purpose statement, purpose specifications, and evidence from your literature review should make a case for your plan. Every aspect of your stated purpose must be reflected in your plan.

Failing to clearly address all purpose specifications can lead you into a research "rabbit hole," in other words, into ideas and activities that are not pertinent to your research purpose. That danger is particularly strong with purpose statements that are rather general in nature. When researching the essence of ideas and philosophical concepts (as opposed to actions), purpose specifications must provide parameters that determine, beyond the purpose statement, the major line of argumentation. A preconceived line of argumentation is essential if you wish to avoid a thinking-while-you-work approach.

Regardless of the form in which purpose specifications are presented, they should express what aspects of the topic the investigator intends to study. They should not reflect, however, how these aspects are to be investigated. Issues such as the development of a measurement tool, test, questionnaire, or observational system belong to the method section of an investigation because they refer to the procedures by which a purpose or quest is addressed. You may face difficulties in developing a measurement tool or test, but facing those difficulties is generally not the purpose of your study. Of course, there are exceptions to nearly all rules. For instance, you might think of yourself as an engineer who tries to work out technological difficulties in some music hardware or software. As a result, you eventually might find new ways of doing things, truly a sign of leadership in music education scholarship.

CONSTRUCTING A RATIONALE FOR YOUR RESEARCH PURPOSE

A rationale is a reasoned explanation of why something exists. In a literature review, research proposal, or research report it is usually a logical argumentation (see Chapter 4) constructed to underscore the importance of the research purpose in light of the literature. The rationale has a dual function: (a) For you as researcher it represents the logical framework for the stated purpose of the investigation, and (b) it explains to readers why your research purpose is important, and establishes the theoretical framework by which its results can be interpreted.

A good way to learn to construct a rationale is to analyze rationales written by other researchers. Before investigating published rationales, however, we briefly introduce elements of written logic that are common in research rationales.

Logical Reasoning in Research Rationales

Applying rules of logic ("the study of the principles of reasoning," *American Heritage Dictionary of the English Language*, 2020) to your own and other people's thinking and writing is important not only in scholarship but in everyday living (e.g., Allen, 2004; Cannavo, 1998; Hult, 1996). As Tragesser (1977) and Leonard (1957) have pointed out, there are, in fact, several logics. Informal-propositional logic, also referred to as Aristotelian logic, is implied most often when people refer to "logic" as "clear thinking." However, not all scholarly writings follow that approach. In this chapter, we therefore contrast Aristotelian logic with *dialectic* reasoning; in Chapter 4 we introduce a few other logical options for your information, and in Chapter 5 we introduce the concept of fallacy. Your increasingly critical eye will likely discern these and similar forms of reasoning in current music education literature. Take note of how each speaks to you.

Aristotelian Logic

Very common in Western thinking, Aristotelian logic underlies the way most students are taught to think and write, particularly in the West. Written conversations based on this logic are known as *argumentations* or simply arguments. Such arguments do not, however, assume antagonism on the part of the writer or reader. Instead, they presume the back-and-forth of lively conversation.

The simplest argument consists of two claims, or declamatory statements. "Because it rained last night, therefore the street is wet" is an argument that contains evidence and a conclusion. In the English language, sentences that contain "because," "since," or "although" suggest linear inferences from one point to another. Grammatically, inferences make use of compound prepositions of "therefore," "hence," or "consequently" to assert a claim.

To be convincing, a claim should be followed or preceded by a reason that contains sufficient evidence to qualify as such. If the evidence is weak, the reason is also weak, which then threatens the veracity of the claim and, therefore, the argument. The building blocks in the argument may go in any order as long as all of them are present. To build a valid line of argumentation, then, weave several arguments together in such a way that the final conclusion seems inevitable. It makes the argumentation linear because only that evidence is being used that contributes to the conclusion.

As an example think of what lawyers do in their roles as prosecutor and defense attorney, respectively: Each start from the same Point A, the defendant being accused of being guilty. Then both lawyers argue in a straight line toward two very different end points in their respective argumentations: The prosecutor ends with "therefore, the defendant is guilty" and the defense attorney with "therefore, the defendant is not guilty." Both lawyers build their reasoning on different evidence (in both cases presumably air-tight) spiced with emotional rhetoric (often quite graphic), by which to make the jurors believe that each Point B is inevitable (and, thus, a "logical") conclusion.

Dialectic Logic (Dialectics)

The *American Heritage Dictionary of the English Language* (2020) defines dialectics as: "The contradiction between two conflicting forces viewed as the determining factor in their continuing interaction." Dialectic reasoning moves from a claim (the *thesis*) to a counterclaim (the *antithesis*) to a synthesized claim (the *synthesis*). Still inferential, the reasoning takes both argument and counterargument into consideration when making a case.

"Being—not-being—becoming" is such a dialectic (Mautner, 2005, p. 159), but the synthesis ("becoming") is not so much a conclusion as it is the new thesis which immediately creates its own opposition, "not-becoming." Again, in the tension between becoming and not becoming lies the next synthesis.

Some music education authors describe as dialectic the tensions that lie in such binaries as product-process, informal-formal learning, or teacher-guided and student-initiated learning. While possibly descriptive, such polarities do not in themselves represent dialectic reasoning as long as there is an assumption that the tensions created by the polarities can be resolved. Rather, dialectic reasoning tends to question the possibility of any permanent resolution. Think, for example, of music as both an aesthetic and also a social object; as an artistic product as well as a subjective, entertaining act; a social-political, yet highly personal, emotional force; a self-serving but also an educational instrument.

Figure 3.1 portrays both propositional and dialectic logic as described above. As straightforward as the images appear here, their equivalents in scholarly literature are not always easily identified. Rhetoric and stylistic "fillers," while at times important writing tools, can cloud the clarity of authors' reasoning. Still, as you read and think about the rationale for your own project, identify claims, reasons, and data as well as original claims, counterclaims, and synthesized claims.

In the Recommended Reading at the end of this chapter we list research articles that vary according to philosophical, historical, and empirical modes of inquiry, and represent qualitative, relational, and experimental methods. Despite their seemingly different formats, each contains the elements of rationale and purpose in some explicit form. For the sake of brevity, each is from a published research article. We suggest, in addition to these, skimming multiple dissertations and research articles related to your own research purpose so you can see (1) how authors present similar

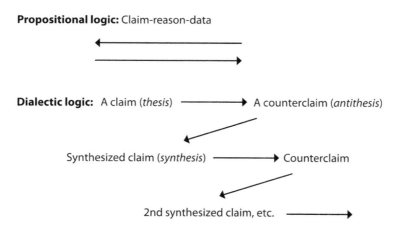

FIGURE 3.1 Diagrams of Propositional and Dialectic Argumentation

information (rationale, purpose) in different ways, and (2) the difference between the breadth, depth, and level of detail in a thesis or dissertation rationale as opposed to those printed in published studies.

Once you have examined several rationales written by other researchers it is time to begin to construct your own. As you get involved in crafting your argumentation, you will come to understand more clearly how your research should be designed. What follows are two examples, one by Rawlings (2016) and the other by Cronenberg (2017).

After introducing the study and reviewing related literature, Rawlings (2016) concludes his introduction with this rationale:

> Students who are different from the established school ensemble culture, but who still volunteer to join the musical group, may be targets for antisocial-aggressive behaviors from their peers. This type of behavior has been documented in only a few studies involving school ensembles; however, additional evidence of hazing and harassment behaviors in collegiate music ensembles exists with late adolescent populations (Alvarez & Brown, 2011; Brinkley, 2014; Carter, 2013; Silveira & Hudson, 2015). With the prevalence of bullying in schools as publicized in modern mainstream media and research studies in music education as well as a growing wealth of empirical research in general education about aggression and bullying (Espelage, Green, & Polanin, 2012; Espelage & Swearer, 2004, 2010; Mishna, 2012), further studies are needed to understand bullying from inside the music classroom (Allsup & Shieh, 2012; Hubbs, 2010).
>
> (p. 10)

Rawlings' linear rationale suggests this study as a response to the need for further evidence about bullying in school music classrooms.

Cronenberg's (2017) rationale follows an introduction in which she acquaints readers with the music teachers who are the focus of her narrative research study, and provides a brief background that explains how her own experience led to this particular study:

> I use Jorgensen's dialectic of making and receiving as a framework to address a question Jorgensen (2001) herself asks: "What are the principles by which teachers and their students adjudicate the dialectics they face?" (p. 18). Both Rachel and Beth make choices for their music classrooms guided by specific principles developed throughout their lifetime of musical experiences and by their preparation for and work as music educators. In sharing their practices and experiences, I present two teachers who adjudicate the making and receiving dialectic in ways relatable to many music educators. I place them together in this study not to present two ends of a dichotomy, but rather to place their perspectives in dialogue with each other as well as with the perspectives of those reading. The intention of Jorgensen's dialectic is to raise issues and generate dialogue, as is my purpose here.
>
> (p. 85)

Cronenberg's rationale illustrates the way dialectic reasoning can "raise issues and generate dialogue" rather than suggesting a resolution to a problem.

Other rationales may be derived from such reasoned needs as:

1) the exploration of seeming contradictions in empirical, philosophical, or historical studies,
2) the synthesis of ideas from disparate sources, resulting in a new way of thinking about a familiar issue,

3) the creation of a narrative about a particular aspect of music teaching and learning in the past, or,

4) the systematic exploration of constructs of thought related to the learning and teaching of music.

Differences in the written forms of a rationale depend on the kind of document you are working on, but the basic structure and intention of the rationale should remain the same. To summarize: Consider whether your research is guided by one of the reasons listed above. Ask your peers to review the plan and check your reasoning. Sharing your research purpose and rationale with your colleagues can ensure that your thoughts are logical and you are not missing any factors of importance. Discussing your plans with others may also help you in considering practical matters, which we discuss in the next section.

MOVING FORWARD WITH THE CONTRACT

As was true with Carlos at the beginning of this chapter, it is premature to begin a research project until you have fully developed your research plan and presented it in writing. When completed, your plan is called a research proposal, an official document that likely requires approval from at least one committee in your academic department as well as from an Institutional Review Board (IRB, described below) and sometimes the university as a whole. Here, we describe preliminary steps for completing a proposal. As you continue to review literature and determine which of the methods described in subsequent chapters best addresses your research purpose, you will add details to your proposal. Once formalized in writing and accepted by your department or institution, it is a *bona fide* contractual agreement: You have indicated what you will do to meet the institution's research requirements and the institution has approved your proposed actions.

Determining the Parameters of Your Project

We use the word parameters to mean the boundaries of your project: type, scope, and method. Like much of the research process, there is a cyclical relationship between the parameters of a research project and its stated purpose and rationale, and a project cannot be commenced until all of these have been agreed upon with your instructor or graduate committee.

As described in previous chapters, most readers of this textbook will complete a stand-alone literature review or a literature review for the purpose of proposing a research project, the latter either as a course requirement or a first step in fulfilling the research requirement for a graduate degree (commonly called the thesis or dissertation).

The Literature Review as a Stand-Alone Project

The aim of a stand-alone literature review is to demonstrate an understanding and critical analysis of previous research (and sometimes professional writing) on a topic. While a formal proposal to your institution is likely not needed for such a project, many course instructors require that students complete a project proposal to guide their work. The scope of such a project may be exhaustive, selective, or representative, depending both on the specifics of your interests and on what is available (see Cooper, 1985). Writers of stand-alone literature reviews will find Chapters

4–13 to be useful for understanding the details as well as the strengths and weaknesses of the types of research and other writing that you analyze for your literature review.

Typically, stand-alone literature reviews are organized according to the author's purpose specifications, although your course instructor may suggest other organizational schemes. It is not a "review" in the sense of a book or performance review; nor is it simply a collection of summaries. Instead, it is an analysis and synthesis of what has been written, how and why that writing came about, and what remains to be done or at least considered. Your written conclusion should reflect deep processing of the information you have found, and include the principle ideas in the body of knowledge as well as their strengths and weaknesses. As you near the end of the project, you will find Chapter 15 useful for imagining and communicating what we call the "so what"; that is, the importance of what you have found in your analysis. Successfully completing a literature review is part of becoming an expert in a scholarly topic.

The Literature Review as Part of a Course-Required Research Proposal or a First Step in Proposing a Scholarly Research Project

A writer who intends to propose original research, whether as part of a course requirement or to commence a scholarly research project, uses the literature to make the case that there is a need for their proposed study, and that their research design (i.e., methods and procedures, described further in Chapters 5–13) offers a logical, ethical, and practical means for filling that need. The initial process (what we've described as *explore, frame, collect*) is similar to that of the person writing a stand-alone literature review. However, if you are reviewing literature for the purpose of proposing original research, it is critical that you consider the strengths and weaknesses of each author's approach, not only from their perspective, but also in regards to your proposed research project.

The specifics of the proposal depend upon policies of the institution under which you conduct your research as well as on your objectives as a researcher. Typically, a proposal for original research requires a literature review as well as an explanation of your plan for collecting, analyzing, and evaluating data. Note that you will find additional details pertinent to specific methods and procedures for philosophical, historical, and empirical research (both qualitative and quantitative) at the end of each methods chapter (see the Table of Contents for specific chapters). Information about completing the final report and options for publication is included in Chapter 14 and supplemental online materials (see inquiryinmusiceducation.com).

Institutional Review Boards (IRBs)

All research that includes interaction with people (called "human subjects" in research terms) and that is done under the auspices of an institution that receives United States government funds is subject to the Code of Federal Regulations for the Protection of Human Subjects (45CFR46). This code, also known as the "Common Rule," is administered by the Office for Human Research Protections (OHRP), part of the U.S. Department of Health and Human Services. The most recent revision of the Common Rule was in 2018.

Because of this law, all educational institutions that support research have policies for compliance. Whether you are a professor at a research university, an itinerant music teacher working in a school, or someone working with a community arts organization that receives government funds, research that involves interaction with people other than yourself is subject to these rules (as is research done by your students, if you teach research in some capacity). Other governments around the world have similar laws; if your research is being done outside the United States you should become familiar with the laws of the country in which you are working (and that which is funding your research, if different).

An appointed committee within each institution, known in the United States as an Institutional Review Board (or IRB) is tasked with assuring that all institutional research complies with the requirements for ethical conduct as outlined by the Federal government. Other governments have similar requirements. This board reviews proposed research to make sure each research plan adheres to the government's requirements for ethical research: respect for persons, beneficence, and justice. One key element of these requirements is the idea of *informed consent*; that is, that research participants have been informed of the procedures and risks involved in a given study and have consented to participating. In addition to the IRB, research done in a school district is typically subject to approval by the board of education. Smaller community arts organizations may not have research policies, but this does not release researchers from the obligation to make sure their research is safe and ethical. Fortunately, many of the contexts music educators typically study are exempt from a full IRB review. Note, however, that it is your institution's IRB that makes the determination of exemption, usually through an expedited review process. As a researcher it is your responsibility to know the law and abide by it. More information can be found in the sources under "Recommended Readings" at the end of this chapter.

Practical Considerations for Planning Research

You may also want to think about issues beyond those discussed in the literature:

Dale, quite clear about his career path, had the following practical and personal concerns:

- My desired outcome is to be a music education professor. Focusing on popular music as a way to diversify the band curriculum might mean being labeled as a "popular music" scholar. Is that what I want?
- I want to finish the doctorate as quickly as possible.
- I want to use the expertise gained from my master's thesis.
- I have young children at home. It is important to me to choose a topic that does not take me far from home for long periods of time. What kind of study would allow me to work mostly from home?

Most master's level research projects address a practical question posed by the researcher, or focus empirical or historical attention on a local entity such as a music school, influential pedagogue, or community ensemble. While action research projects (discussed in Chapter 13) exemplify this idea, master's level research may use any of the methods suggested in this textbook. Doctoral level research is expected to be unique, valuable, and ideally of enough interest to the music education profession that it will be accepted as a journal article, book chapter, or even a full-fledged book.

As you consider the details of your preliminary proposal, we suggest that you consider what you stand to gain from the research, and also that you think about personal factors that will impact your abilities to complete the project. We offer these questions for your consideration; you, as well as your colleagues and your instructor may add others:

- How much time do you have to complete the study? Is there a best or worse time of year for you? For your participants? What pending work-related or personal duties or activities might limit your time?
- Will your topic involve travel or other expenses? How will you pay for these?
- What group(s) of people do you have access to or want to gain access to? How might you do that?

Because it is always advisable to consider practical issues from the beginning, such questions as the number of individuals in your study, the perspective from which you observe, the type of data you collect, and the time frame within which to observe, measure, or otherwise collect and analyze data are important.

CHAPTER SUMMARY

1) Deciding *how* you will do your research—that is, the method by which you want to carry out a study—is premature until you have determined the parameters of your research plan.
2) Clearly articulating your research topic means being ever more exact about what and how you wish to observe, describe, and/or examine. This takes imagination, thinking broadly yet in ever more specific terms.
3) Paying attention to the wording of the purpose statement is essential for communicating the intent of your study in an exacting and clear way.
4) A research rationale serves two purposes: representing the logical framework for the stated purpose of the investigation, and explaining the purpose of the study and the theoretical framework by which its results can be interpreted.
5) Original research done under the auspices of any institution (i.e., educational or cultural establishment or non-profit grantor) typically requires an approved research proposal.
6) If you plan on working with human subjects, your research must be reviewed by your institution's Institutional Review Board.
7) The design of your research should not be determined until the other aspects of your study are in place. It is useful, however, to consider practical and theoretical elements of the design prior to making final decisions.

Topics for Further Exploration

1) The characteristics of a clear purpose statement.
2) The varying ways scholars construct rationales.
3) The relationship between research purpose, rationale, and methods.

Suggested Assignments

1) Apply steps similar to those followed by Liam, Christy, Michelle, and other students to narrow your research topic as much as possible.

2) Articulate in writing at least three possible *research purposes* that might originate in your chosen *research topic.*

3) Write a preliminary purpose statement and rationale for your research project. Explain your choice of wording to your colleagues.

4) From a scholarly source in your literature collection, trace an author's stated purpose, rationale, research design, results or findings, and conclusions.

Recommended Reading

About Research Proposals

Creswell, J. W., & Creswell, J. D. (2017). *Research design: Qualitative, quantitative, and mixed methods approaches* (5th ed.). Sage.

Locke, L. F., Lawrence, R., Spirduso, W. W., & Silverman, S. J. (2013). *Proposals that work: A guide for planning dissertation and grant proposals* (6th ed.). Sage.

On U.S. Government Research Regulations

National Commission for the Protection of Human Subjects of Biomedical and Behavioral Research. (1979). *The Belmont report: Ethical principles and guidelines for the protection of human subjects of research.* U.S. Department of Health and Human Services. www.hhs.gov/ohrp/humansubjects/guidance/belmont. html

National Science Foundation. (n.d.). *Frequently asked questions and vignettes: Interpreting the common rule for the protection of human subjects for behavioral and social science research.* Washington, DC: Author. Retrieved November 10, 2020, from www.nsf.gov/bfa/dias/policy/hsfaqs.jsp#exempt

About Dialectic Reasoning

Jorgensen, E. R. (2001). *Transforming music education.* Indiana University Press.

Sample Research Rationales

Allsup, R. E. (2003). Mutual learning and democratic action in instrumental music education. *Journal of Research in Music Education, 51*(1), 24–37. https://doi.org/10.2307/3345646.

Baughman, M. (2017). An Examination of methods used to teach practice strategies in the college voice studio. *Update: Applications of Research in Music Education, 35*(2), 15–22. https://doi.org/10.1177/8755123315593325

Cayari, C. (2018). Connecting music education and virtual performance practices from YouTube. *Music Education Research, 20*(3), 360–376. https://doi.org/10.1080/14613808.2017.1383374

Fitzpatrick, K. R. (2006). The effect of instrumental music participation and socioeconomic status on Ohio fourth-, sixth-, and ninth-grade proficiency test performance. *Journal of Research in Music Education, 54*(1), 73–84. https://doi.org/10.1177/002242940605400106

Froehlich, H. C., & Cattley, G. (1993). Language, metaphor, and analogy in the music education research process. In E. R. Jorgensen (Ed.), *Philosopher, teacher, musician: Perspectives on music education* (pp. 243–258). University of Illinois Press.

Meissner, H., & Timmers, R. (2019). Teaching young musicians expressive performance: An experimental study. *Music Education Research, 21*(1), 20–39. https://doi.org/10.1080/14613808.2018.1465031

Montemayor, M., & Moss, E. A. (2009). Effects of recorded models on novice teachers' rehearsal verbalizations, evaluations, and conducting. *Journal of Research in Music Education, 57*(3), 236–251. https://doi.org/10.1177/0022429409343183

Palkki, J. (2020). "My voice speaks for itself": The experiences of three transgender students in American secondary school choral programs. *International Journal of Music Education, 38*(1), 126–146. https://doi.org/10.1177/0255761419890946

Richerme, L. K. (2016). Measuring music education: A philosophical investigation of the Model Cornerstone Assessments. *Journal of Research in Music Education, 64*(3), 274–293. https://doi.org/10.1177/0022429416659250

White-Hope, S. (2019). Elma Lewis, her school of fine arts, and her vision of arts education as cultural emancipation. *Bulletin of the Council for Research in Music Education, 219*, 47–60. https://doi.org/10.5406/bulcouresmusedu.219.0047

REFERENCES

Allen, M. (2004). *Smart thinking: Skills for critical understanding and writing* (2nd ed.). Oxford University Press.

American Heritage Dictionary of the English Language. (2020). Dialectics. In *The Online American Heritage dictionary of the English language* (5th ed.). Retrieved April 22, 2021, from www.ahdictionary.com/word/search.html?q=dialectics

American Heritage Dictionary of the English Language. (2020). Logic. In *The Online American Heritage dictionary of the English language* (5th ed.). Retrieved April 22, 2021, from www.ahdictionary.com/word/search.html?q=logic

Battisti, F., & Garofalo, R. (1990). *Guide to score study for the wind band conductor.* Meredith Music Publications.

Becker, H. S. (1998). *Tricks of the trade.* University of Chicago Press.

Cannavo, S. (1998). *Think to win: The power of logic in everyday life.* Prometheus Books.

Cooper, H. M. (1985). *A taxonomy of literature reviews.* (ED254541). ERIC. https://files.eric.ed.gov/fulltext/ED254541.pdf

Cronenberg, S. (2017). Making and receiving: Possibilities for middle school general music. *Bulletin of the Council for Research in Music Education, 210–211*, 81–99. https://doi.org/10.5406/bulcouresmusedu.210-211.0081

Gates, J. T. (1999). *Music education research at the dawn of the third mediamophosis* [Conference presentation]. Desert Skies Symposium, February 15–18, 1999, University of Arizona, Tucson.

Hult, C. A. (1996). *Researching and writing in the humanities and arts.* Allyn and Bacon.

Leonard, H. S. (1957). *Principles of right reason.* Henry Holt.

Lisk, E. S. (1991). *The creative director: Alternative rehearsal techniques* (3rd ed.). Meredith Music.

Mautner, T. (2005). *The Penguin dictionary of philosophy* (2nd ed.). Penguin Books.

Montemayor, M., & Moss, E. A. (2009). Effects of recorded models on novice teachers' rehearsal verbalizations, evaluations, and conducting. *Journal of Research in Music Education, 57*(3), 236–251. https://doi.org/10.1177/0022429409343183

Rawlings, J. R. (2016). Middle school students' perceptions of bullying. *Bulletin of the Council for Research in Music Education, 209*, 7–26. https://doi.org/10.5406/bulcouresmusedu.209.0007

Small, C. (1997). Musicking: A ritual in social space. In R. Rideout (Ed.), *On the sociology of music education* (pp. 1–12). Proceedings of the Oklahoma Symposium for Music Education in April, 1995, Oklahoma University School of Music, Norman, Oklahoma. http://jlarrystockton.com/Stocktoj/small.pdf

Tragesser, R. S. (1977). *Phenomenology and logic.* Cornell University Press.

PART II

Methods in Modes of Inquiry
Chapters 4 through 15

Part II is about specific methodological considerations embedded in different modes of inquiry. Whether your questions are about the past or the present, events, actions, behaviors, experiences, or ideas; you now learn about ways by which to address them. Your task lies in finding the best possible approach among several options by which to collect and examine the evidence you need to fulfill your stated study purpose. Such decision requires careful thought and analysis.

We begin this section with philosophy because choices about research paradigms, theories, and beliefs—the purview of philosophical reasoning—impact all modes of inquiry. You best understand the relationship between modes and their respective methods once you grasp philosophical differences about what constitutes knowledge and evidence in any form of research. Furthermore, all modes of inquiry demand the ability to convey your thoughts well-reasoned and convincingly. As already suggested in Chapter 3, logic becomes an essential research tool in whatever you choose to investigate. Chapter 4 provides a background in the kind of thinking that underlies all scholarship, while Chapter 5 describes processes for undertaking a philosophical study.

Following the philosophical mode of inquiry, Chapter 6 is a comprehensive description of historical research in music education. The chapter provides a glimpse into the rich world of examining past events, actions, behaviors, and documented experiences in music and music education. The chapter also sets the tone for the broad scope of qualitative research methods described in Chapters 7 and 8. Conceptually, research purposes that suggest the use of qualitative research methods require knowledge of specific traditions and philosophical underpinnings that have guided and continue to guide researchers. The methods continue to evolve as new thought processes bring about new questions and ideas for study. Chapter 8 must therefore be understood as a snapshot of currently favored qualitative research designs.

Chapters 9–13 introduce you to basic research designs common in quantitative-empirical investigations. Purposefully brief, chapter 9 addresses measurement theory to aid you in understanding the meaning of numbers in statistical analyses. More advanced philosophical and mathematical theory are kept to a minimum. Chapters 10–12, too, are limited to basic information about descriptive statistics, simple correlations, *ex post facto*, and experimental designs. Advanced knowledge about more sophisticated design options and measurement procedures should be gained from sources outside the purview of the type of class for which this book was written. Chapter 13 features three traditions that utilize qualitative and quantitative procedures: Mixed methods, practitioner inquiry/action research, and arts-based and arts practice research.

Chapter 14 features basic information about the content and construction of gathering tools used across the research approaches described in the previous chapters. This chapter emphasizes

DOI: 10.4324/9781003057703-6

that all modes of inquiry can benefit from carefully developed observation forms, interview schedules, and tests.

Chapter 15 addresses the "so what" factor of a completed study. It is the question most everyone asks after the data are gathered and analyzed. The chapter, however, is not only about interpreting your findings and completing your degree requirements, but also about making your original research accessible to different audiences. Such sharing can be in the form of specialized research or general interest articles, scholarly papers or workshops, grant applications or designing new or ongoing research. The book ends with what we call "Recapitulation," a review of those components in scholarship that should be considered essential in all modes of inquiry.

Ways of Thinking and Their Consequences

This chapter introduces contexts and ways of thinking that delineate scholarship within the field of music education and beyond:

- Historical and conceptual contexts as landmarks of scholarly thought,
- Perspective as awareness of point of view and researcher position,
- Logic as a tool for critical thinking,
- Identifiable laws, theories, paradigms, or belief systems, and
- Skills of reasoning as research tools.

The perspectives and concepts described in this chapter introduce you to thinking as a research activity.

INTRODUCTION

Thinking as a research activity cannot be done in a vacuum. Rather, making critical judgments about extant studies, as well as your own research purpose and rationale, requires contextual knowledge. The distinct research traditions and scholarly predilections that describe music education as a field of study have developed over time. Having a sense of the process of that development and the conceptual thinking behind it will help you place your own ideas and those you read about into the body of scholarly music education knowledge. Therefore, we encourage you, when you read this chapter, to place your own articulated and mapped research interests (see Chapter 2) into the larger historical and conceptual frame of the field. You will soon discover that historical and conceptual precedents already shape the way you think.

A BRIEF CHRONOLOGICAL AND CONCEPTUAL OVERVIEW OF MUSIC EDUCATION SCHOLARSHIP IN THE UNITED STATES

Both chronological and conceptual contexts have shaped our professional field and literature. This brief overview is intended to illustrate that what has transpired over time impacts the how, why, and what of today's research.

DOI: 10.4324/9781003057703-7

The Chronological Context

The first peer-reviewed research publication in the field of music education in the United States appeared in the Spring of 1953 with the *Journal of Research in Music Education*. In 1963, the *Bulletin of the Council for Research in Music Education* debuted under the supervision of the College of Education and School of Music of the University of Illinois and the Office of the Superintendent of Public Instruction, Urbana, Illinois. Both journals gave music educators a forum for disseminating information pertinent to the research community. Prior to the establishment of those two publications, observations about musical actions and ideas, present and past, were gathered by researchers of many different disciplines and published in journals specific to education, psychology, musicology, and music theory.

A third landmark publication was *Basic Concepts in Music Education* (Henry, 1958). The chapters in this edited book describe the scope of interdisciplinary concerns paramount to and typical of music education as a field of study in the mid-20th century. Specifically, the book acknowledged the relationship of music education to such disciplines as philosophy, psychology, and sociology. Richard Colwell (1991), editor of the second edition, asserted that there had been few changes in the basic concepts across the field of music education between 1958 and 1991. However, Colwell also observed the rapid growth of the field since 1991, an observation substantiated by the following:

- The number of research journals has steadily increased (see list in supplemental online appendices, inquiryinmusiceducation.com). This may be partly due to cooperative efforts by music education researchers and MENC (now known as NAfME) in the late 1970s and early 1980s to constitute Special Research Interest Groups (SRIGs).
- The Internet has enabled music educators to share publications from around the world, resulting in an international community of readers and authors.

Between 1953 and the 1990s, research on the pedagogy of jazz, singing, and various instrumental specializations increased as well, as evidenced by the emergence of peer reviewed journals in which performance specialists examine pedagogical techniques and repertoire according to scholarly principles (e.g., *Journal of Band Research, Journal of Research in Singing*, and many others). Perhaps as a result of that expansion, Richard Colwell (1992) spearheaded a comprehensive research handbook on the learning and teaching of music, with a second one, co-edited by Carol Richardson, being published in 2002 (Colwell & Richardson, 2002). A third two-volume handbook, the *MENC Handbook of Research on Music Learning* (Colwell & Webster, 2011) further changed the landscape of published music education research in English-speaking countries. Referencing a much larger number of peer-reviewed research studies than were available in the mid-20th century, the topics range from research methodology to the status of knowledge in particular subject areas. Since that time (see list in supplemental online appendices, inquiryinmusiceducation.com), the publication of research handbooks in our field has grown exponentially. Yet despite this growth, research and scholarship in our field remains connected to the ideas first mentioned in *Basic Concepts* in 1958.

Professional symposia and conferences have also multiplied beyond those that were common in earlier years, adding to the published body of knowledge accessible to scholars and practitioners alike. The ease of text and video communication via the Internet and international air travel have made this expansion virtually exponential, as music educators frequently communicate and even co-author with peers from around the world. This plethora of information brings forth another question: How does a researcher prevent information overload? Over time, scholars have developed conceptualizations for obtaining a "bird's eye view" (also called a macro view) of what otherwise might appear to be an enormous and unwieldy amount of isolated information.

A Conceptual Perspective

Central to our definition of music education research as the study of the learning and teaching of music are the terms *learning*, *teaching*, and *music*. This is why the visual model presented in Chapter 1 refers to interactions between the learner, the teacher and the subject matter of music. Figure 4.1 is an expanded perspective of the same three "cogwheels," now surrounded by words representing the fields and areas of study that comprise the body of professional literature related to the learning and teaching of music in its many different contexts. In the case of school music, all three cogs may be visualized in constant motion. In situations where the learner interacts with the music without an intervening expert (such as the teacher), interesting questions arise as to what might be represented by the third cog.

Figure 4.1 lists numerous themes and subject areas in which questions about the teaching-learning processes have been examined. These themes and subject areas may be considered key terms, fields of study, and subject headings under which specific investigations may fall. As you can see, the mosaic that represents research in music education ranges from issues specific to the learner, the music, and the individual teacher to queries that focus on the dyadic or triadic relationship between these three interacting agents. The figure is therefore offered to aid your search

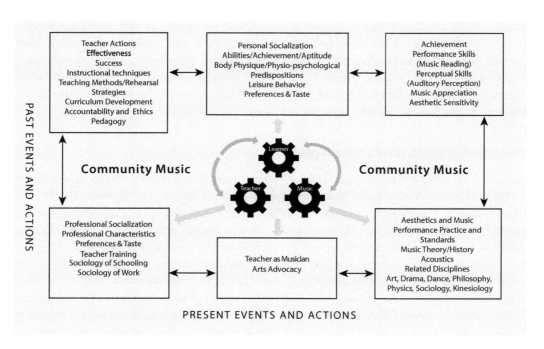

FIGURE 4.1 Suggested Fields, Areas of Study, and Selected Key Terms Relevant to the Study of the Learning and Teaching of Music

for relevant literature and guide you in placing each study you read into the mosaic of extant research.

Because music education circumstances are not always under the control of any of the three "agents," researchers also consider contextual factors as interacting with what goes on in learning-teaching processes. You might, in fact, elect to focus on the contextual factors as your main concern. The options are indeed limitless when you consider the amount of research that has already been conducted on each of the component's parts in the interactive web (and how much still needs to be done).

Music as an Interactive Agent

Research in and about music is often seen as the purview of musicologists, theorists and ethno-musicologists. Music educators rely on such work because musical knowledge is a core of our profession. Our own musical knowledge and skills shape our instructional choices and thereby influence our students' musical knowledge and skills.

The origins of music have been discussed and speculated on by many scholars and in many cultures for thousands of years. Hardly anyone fails to acknowledge the works of Pythagoras (ca. 500 B.C.E.) and Plato (427–347 B.C.E.) as the beginning of modern concepts of studying the physical and aesthetic properties of music in relationship to their cognitive, emotional, and physiological dimensions. Both thinkers sought to describe physical aspects of sound in terms of arithmetic relationships but it was Plato who, additionally, speculated on the manifestation of the beautiful and its relationship to the moral development of the human character.

Today, thanks to the work of many musicologists, ethno-musicologists and anthropologists, we have knowledge of musical traditions that have shaped cultures in Africa, Asia, India, the Mediterranean and Middle Eastern countries. A most interesting account of music in pre-historic times may be Steven Mithen's (2006) evolutionary hypothesis about a "music-like communication system" among the Neanderthals "that was more complex and more sophisticated than that found in any of the previous species of Homo" (p. 234). For later times, Cho (2003) refers to early writings on the music of China dating back to about 122 B.C., in which the pentatonic pattern and the twelve semitones within the octave are described.

The Learner as an Interactive Agent

Studies on interactions between music and the learner have facilitated information about how learners perceive and respond to music at different ages and levels of training and exposure. Out of such research have sprung questions as to whether different kinds of music might cause different kinds of responses among listeners of varying characteristics. Matters of technology in the classroom, whether virtual or face-to-face, and in application to music itself are more important than ever.

Issues of power and control among groups of unequal standing deserve attention as they impact learners' socio-economic conditions, socialization, and enculturation. In light of those issues, informal learning gains have been contrasted to formal gains and self-guided learning strategies to teacher-designed instructional strategies. Philosophically, questions prevail about what it means to "educate musically" (Bowman, 2002) both inside and outside of school and about the multifaceted nature of curriculum that guides formal instruction.

Scholars in various disciplines have addressed aesthetics and aesthetic education as evidenced in matters of musical identities. Preferences and taste in and out of school settings have been investigated by music psychologists, educators, sociologists, and philosophers. Theories that explain how the brain processes musical stimuli have been developed in child and adult psychology, education, medicine, and neurology.

Studies exist on the appropriate sequence of learning tasks for children of different age groups as well as on the measurement of musical ability and achievement. Quantifiable measures for assessing music performance have been studied separate from and together with qualitative methods that use personal, verbal-comparative judgments in assessing achievement and aptitude. Consistency in both measurements and judgments has been central to relating performance outputs of learners and teachers to each other. In the name of arts advocacy, researchers have collected data to document the benefits of music instruction on general learning skills, notably literacy and mathematical comprehension. Such investigations have often led to public debates about the purpose of the arts and music in the curriculum as well as in society.

The Teacher as an Interactive Agent

In efforts to increase instructional effectiveness, researchers have measured the time teachers typically devote to activities that routinely shape lessons or rehearsals. Proportions of time spent on specific lesson components are related to the use of verbal and nonverbal instruction and on the relationship between forms of instruction and classroom management. Research conducted by school music supervisors has compared teachers to each other or has related their teaching skills to student performance.

As representatives of music and education, music teachers are often considered the best advocates for music and the arts in the curriculum. To make and present that case skillfully and convincingly, data are needed to support that claim, and careful thought must be given to what is in the best interest of a student educationally. Resultant conflicts have only begun to be debated in the music educational research literature and among cultural theorists.

An area of recent interest among researchers is the study of how music teachers become who they are. Using terms such as identity construction, social psychology, and sociological studies, researchers examine connections between personal and professional identity, instructional values, and what goes on in classrooms and rehearsal halls across the country. Such knowledge is considered relevant for decisions about curricular reforms in music teacher training programs.

Contextual Factors as Interacting Agents

Spearheaded by researchers interested in the application of social-psychological and sociological theory to music education, the contexts underlying music learning and teaching of varying kinds have become major investigative topics. Requiring interdisciplinary approaches, such questions query educational goals and purposes within different institutional and political settings; the social acquisition of musical values; and the ways upbringing, social status, and cultural/artistic opportunities impact learning styles, patterns, and motivations. Decisions about educational goals, music repertoire selections, disciplinary measures in the classroom, and what constitutes appropriate instructional sequences at various levels of schooling are dependent on those forces.

As in the case of research on other "agents" listed in Figure 4.1, engaging with the music education research literature over several decades makes you aware that certain questions come up repeatedly but are viewed differently by researchers from different generations and philosophical perspectives. You may also notice that certain facts in the field have changed whereas others have remained constant. To conclude, no single answer is ever satisfactory for very long because perspectives change. To respond to such changes and remain useful, research must be ongoing. Therefore, do not reject a study because it is old; similarly, do not put trust into findings just because they are recent.

Having determined that he wanted to explore the job satisfaction of mid-career music teachers, *Dale* next considered his researcher-perspective. He had liked the detached nature of the survey methodology used for his master's thesis. But his evolving interest in Freire's *Pedagogy of the Oppressed* (which he had encountered reading Bernard's 2015 dissertation) suggested an expanded view of pedagogy, one that might benefit from a more personal approach with a small number of participants. The change in his point of view would necessitate a change in the methods he would use.

WAYS OF THINKING: PERSPECTIVES AND THEIR CONSEQUENCES

In our introductory chapter, you conducted observations by zooming in or out of New York City's Times Square via webcam images. Depending on the position of the lens, you either obtained a "bird's eye view" of the entire scene or were able to pay attention to minute details about a few people in the picture. Looking at the large picture is sometimes called a macro-view; correspondingly, zeroing in on details becomes a micro-view. The choice in between—the meso view—articulates how the minute details fit into the larger picture.

Describing views "from a higher plane" (Popper, 1945, p. 3) can be as necessary and beneficial as detailing one part of the larger picture from the ground up. Each approach is important because one is needed to inform the other. But each view also has drawbacks because in either case important information can get lost. After all, you might fail to see the proverbial "trees in the forest."

Figure 4.2 illustrates two observational positions similar to those just described. However, rather than dealing with micro and macro perspectives, the images speak to the role the observer takes in different research settings. Image A portrays a curious but personally uninvolved bystander—a *nonparticipant* observer—in a research setting. By viewing the setting from the outside, the researcher is expected to remain "objective," personally detached from that which is being observed. In Image B, the researcher is accepted as integral to that which is being examined; they acknowledge their own subjectivity as well as that of those whose "lived" experiences they seek to interpret.

Image A stands for the classic scientific model of research which, in most instances, guides quantitative approaches to inquiry. It is representative of what philosophers call a modernist point of view, a firm belief in the power of "objectively" reasoned and observed evidence (the data) in support of what is factual and therefore true. If the observed evidence is measurable (i.e., quantifiable) in the form of *variables* and can be replicated, what was a theoretical belief becomes accepted fact. Philosophically known as "empirical" or "logical positivism" (now more often post-positivism) this trust in tested evidence as truth favors physical observations and mathematical logic over intuitive insights or spiritual and otherwise intangible beliefs.

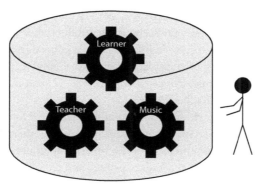

The Researcher as Bystander:
Non-Participant Observer, Involuntary
Contributor to All Observed Interactions
IMAGE A

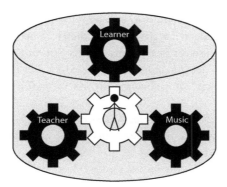

The Researcher as involved Agent:
Conscious Contributor to All Recorded Interactions
IMAGE B

FIGURE 4.2 The Researcher's Role as Participant and Non-Participant

Image B stands for those theoretical perspectives that favor qualitative approaches to data gathering and analyses. Believing objectivity to be impossible, researchers with this worldview recognize and acknowledge the contextuality of what they themselves experience as they seek to observe what goes on around them. Philosophically, image B illustrates what are known as interpretive beliefs. More recently, new labels for such viewpoints have sprung up in response or reaction to the variety of different philosophical positions about what constitutes research, knowledge, fact, and truth (for more, see Chapter 5).

Our approach to defining research modes (see Chapter 1) emphasizes that empirical approaches may be quantitative or qualitative in nature so long as they look at present day events, actions, and experiences. Just as in the case of macro or micro views, neither the quantitative nor the qualitative way of thinking is "right" or "wrong;" instead, each has consequences for how research findings become part of what we know as the body of knowledge of music education.

Researchers might also decide to combine quantitative and qualitative practices. The approach is known as mixed methods research when findings from both quantitative and qualitative approaches are integral to the results (Fitzpatrick, 2014, p. 172). However, it is also possible that an investigator who identifies as a post-positivist might conduct informal conversations with a few likely research participants prior to developing a large-scale measurement tool, or use intuitive language to explain the meaning of their data. (Qualitative approaches are discussed further in Chapters 7 and 8; quantitative approaches in Chapters 9 to 12; and mixed methods, practitioner inquiry, and arts-based research in Chapter 13.)

Historians, viewing music teaching and learning through the lens of the past, are expected to maintain detachment and avoid bias on the one hand and, on the other, show intuition and empathy for the social and political circumstances of the time frame under investigation. When interpreting people's words and actions on the basis of printed and pictorial evidence, for example, such intuitive knowledge would stem from being well-grounded in knowledge about how people lived and thought during the time period in question. (For more on historical research, see Chapter 6.)

Philosophers, too, understand that both quantitative and qualitative research approaches are necessary to explore the world of ideas fully—be they of the past or in the present. Philosophically, in fact, their connection is crucial to appreciating the relationship between the angles chosen to pose a question, the methods used to address it, and how the findings are interpreted. Both the philosophical lens and the role a researcher chooses have therefore become important philosophical topics of debate in and of themselves (see Chapter 5). As you read critically, you should try to become more familiar with those debates, at least to some extent. For instance, as you think about the angle from which an author has approached a study, ask yourself these questions:

- What are the acknowledged lenses and roles you recognize?
- How have those contributed to the question(s) asked and answered in each reported investigation?
- How do you yourself think about the idea(s) under consideration?

Any serious efforts to address such questions turn your reading into thinking as a research activity.

Thinking as a Research Activity

The art and science of thinking has been subject to systematic study in many countries, by many individuals of different scholarly disciplines, and for many centuries. You might say the body of scholarly knowledge—across disciplines, around the world, and over time—is the repository of those efforts. You join in on the scholarly conversation by learning to discern how researchers:

- draw valid inferences from observations, statements, or sources,
- think about things in a deliberate way,
- know whether or when they present "certain" knowledge as compared to belief or perceived reality,
- reflect their own worldviews in comparison to those held by others, and
- approach and describe ethical decisions in the course of their reported work.

Philosophically, the bulleted points have to do with the way researchers see and describe the world. Each study you read reflects the author's perspective even if it is not stated explicitly. Quantitative empiricists and scientifically trained philosophers, for example, may look for indisputable and replicable facts as their data whereas qualitative constructivists, interpretivists, phenomenologists and others with postmodern views may accept that shared knowledge and beliefs represent certain truths only for the time being, if at all.

As a reader, you will learn to discern whether or not (1) a report is clearly written and logically convincing; (2) methodological decisions seem to be ethical; and (3) beliefs about teaching and learning are theoretically grounded as well as evidence-driven. A major tool in obtaining answers to these questions lies in your knowledge and use of logic, an important domain (or branch) of the field of philosophy. Logic also is an indispensable tool in many other aspects of doing research and should therefore be seen as the foundation of all scholarship—whether in the so-called hard or soft sciences, music education included.

Logic as a Major Research Tool

Knowing how to apply rules of logic is helpful not only for writing, but also for everyday life. To describe both skill sets, this chapter relies in large part on Copi, Cohen, and McMahon (2019), Hart (2018), van den Brink-Budgen (2010), Weston (2009), and Wheelwright (1962). Details about how to construct lines of argumentation are provided about informal-propositional (called, in short, informal) and dialectic logic. Other forms of reasoning are addressed further below and in Chapters 7 and 8.

Using Informal Logic

Even before you read this book, you likely used components of informal logic in composing term papers and other written assignments for various classes. You made claims (philosophers call them premises or propositions) that you strung together to make a final point, often called the conclusion. Philosophers call any writing that contains at least one premise and a conclusion a *syllogism* (e.g., "if **p**, then **q**"). It is the building block for entire lines of propositional argumentation in which **q** (as conclusion) becomes the proposition (**p)** in the next argument. There are many concrete guidelines about the "do's and don'ts" of informal-propositional logic because centuries of scholarship have helped systematize this form of reasoning. Figure 4.3, adapted from Weston (2009, pp. 1–57) provides a summarized guide to developing valid lines of argumentation in informal logic. Any entries that have an asterisk before or directly behind them are our additions.

The cells in the figure advise you how to think and subsequently write: Start with reliable premises, outline your line of argumentation, use representative examples, be cautious about claims of fact, consider objections and alternatives, and be mindful of the fact that definitions do not substitute for arguments. When you extend an argument by exploring a sideline issue, make sure you inform the reader of such a "side trip." If your initial efforts at this sort of writing feel a bit stifled or stiff, be reminded, once again, that writing is like performing: You are likely to get better as you practice. To examine your own skills in propositional writing, we suggest you examine the extent to which you follow the rules of informal propositional logic faithfully and completely in your own written work.

Dialectics

Already briefly explained in Chapter 3, dialectics use opposites, conflicts, or contradictions that are stated as thesis and antithesis and serve as evidence in a temporary resolution called synthesis. A simple example might be the thesis that "music can do no harm." Contrast that statement with

	RULE 1	RULE 2	RULE 3	RULE 4	RULE 5
Short Arguments	Identify premises and conclusions	Develop your ideas in a natural order	Start from reliable premises	Be concrete, concise, and consistent	Avoid rhetoric when it gets in the way of an argument*
Generalizations	Use more than one example UNLESS: ⇩	Use representative examples	Be cautious about claims of fact (including numbers and statistics)*	Think of ratio between examples that fit **and** those that don't fit your point	
Arguments by Analogy	One example suffices if it is used as an analogy	Make sure the analogy holds	Use analogies sparingly*		
Arguments About Causes	Causal arguments start with correlations	Correlations may have alternative explanations	Work toward the most likely explanation	Expect complexity	
Deductive/ *Inductive Arguments	Syllogisms [If **p**, then **q**] or: **p**. Therefore, **q**.	[If **p**, then **q**] Not-**q**. Therefore, not-**p**.	Hypothetical syllogism: If **p** then **q**. If **q** then **r**. Therefore, if **p** then **r**.	Dilemma: **p** or **q**. If **p** then **r**. If **q** then **s**. Therefore, **r** or **s**.	Reduction to absurdity ("Reductio ad absurdum") To prove: **p**; Assume the opposite: **not-p**. Argue **q** as the conclusion Show that **q** is false (not true) Conclude **p** as being true.
Extended Arguments	Explore the issue	Spell out basic ideas as arguments	Defend basic premises with arguments of their own	Consider objections & alternatives	Definitions don't replace arguments

FIGURE 4.3 Basic Rules of Propositional Argumentation

"music can be harmful to the ears." Both statements together form the basis for a synthesis such as "music can have differential effects on the listener's or performer's ears." However, the analysis does not conclude at this point, because the synthesis—as the next thesis—calls for a further antithesis, again qualifying the synthesis. Your next point might be to say that below a certain decibel level, the differential effects are negligible. And so you continue the process by inductively examining the complexities of music performance as an art, craft, practice, medical issue, and business.

The example may seem simple, but the technique is not. It goes back to a lineage of dialectic philosophers of the late 19th and 20th centuries, notably G.W.F. Hegel, K. Marx, F. Engels and later, critical theorists, such as J. Habermas, P. Bourdieu, P. Freire, I. Illich, and others. As a method, dialectic reasoning is well suited to taking a macro view of the many antithetical forces in society that seem to stand in the way of providing equal access to all resources a society has available. Critical theorists examine such given polarities in their meaning for taking action: Calling for social justice in unequal societal class structures; pointing to how knowledge as social capital is selected by and for the economically ruling class(es); and attributing unequal economic and sociocultural conditions within a country and across the globe to unequal access to knowledge as social capital. Critical pedagogues carry such analysis into calls to transform formal education in society rather than merely revise or reform.

Because of the inferential nature inherent in dialectic reasoning, proponents of the method— particularly those following in Hegel's footsteps—view it as the most stringent scientific form of philosophical inquiry. No other approach, they argue, is as inductive in nature as dialectic reasoning. Needless to say, there are philosophers who dispute that claim. In summary, along with thinking and writing and working with words, dialectic reasoning demands:

- detailed knowledge of the literature in support of and contradiction to particular theories, practices, thoughts and beliefs, and

- remaining open to the irresolvable tension of wanting to draw finite conclusions even if the inquiry promises to be ongoing.

As Tragesser (1977), Leonard (1957), and a number of other logicians have pointed out, there are several logics. Aristotelian/informal and dialectic may be the most familiar, but it is worth knowing about some of the others. Thus, before leaving the topic of logic, we introduce phenomenological reasoning and interpretive thinking.

Phenomenological Reasoning

Phenomenological reasoning (or phenomenology) has been "practiced in various guises for centuries" (Smith, 2018, para. 2). It is an intentional "first-person view" (Smith, 2018, para. 1) by which the quality of an experience is described. Such description allows for speculation, emotion, and reason to be used as equally important means to convey meaning. Such "free form" investigation combines observation with personal insights to fully understand the phenomenon as it presents itself to the researcher.

The term "understand" in this context is often referred to by phenomenologists as *verstehen* (fer-shtee-hen), the German word for understanding. Although not much different in its meaning from the English term, the word as used by German philosopher Martin Heidegger implies bringing to life the relationship between what you observe and your role in it. Such descriptions of "lived experiences" become both claim and evidence (data) because what a writer claims to be true should be accepted as long as the descriptions are honestly delivered. You learn more about phenomenology in Chapters 7 and 8.

Interpretivism

Similar to phenomenology but not necessarily written in a first-person view, interpretivism is at the heart of those qualitative studies in which researchers do not separate themselves from that which they study (Image B in Figure 4.2). In its strictest sense, the technique derives from *hermeneutics*, a term that means text analysis or interpretation. Originally coming from the field of theology, hermeneutics keeps close to the text, which means that it only seeks to explain what is there rather than question or speculate beyond it.

Interpretivism is applied to qualitative data in music education that require honest and reflective interpretation in response to the research questions posed. Unlike phenomenologists, interpretivists tend to avoid broader speculations even when perhaps feasible and interesting. In fact, some qualitative researchers who base their work on the tenets of interpretivism insist that no method of reasoning should ever override the need to deal with a particular phenomenon in its own way and language (for more information, see Chapters 7 and 8).

Fact and Belief in the Study of Music Learning and Teaching

Scientists use specific vocabulary to describe what is known about the physical world. Facts that have remained constant over time are couched in statements known as "laws." Many such laws have been with us over time as, for instance, the law of gravity or Newton's law of motion (in short: to any action there is an equal reaction). A physical law with implications for music might state that sounds are compressional waveforms perceived by human ears. The law might further assert that sound waves are perceived differently by younger and older adults due to age-related, physical changes in the ears. Either of the two laws can be confirmed by means of repeated observations. However, laws can be disproven if new evidence makes such a move inevitable.

Laws that have changed over time may be called *paradigms* (Kuhn, 1970). A field is paradigmatic when it accepts and acts upon extant laws uniformly and consistently. Because disciplines in the humanities allow many viewpoints to live side by side, Kuhn called humanities research *non-paradigmatic*. Whether or not that assessment is entirely true may be subject to debate among scholars. But it certainly seems to be true that music education scholarship is characterized by the co-existence of many theories, models, and beliefs about the learning and teaching of music. As a reader of research you should know how a particular work contributes to what the profession declares to be its accepted body of knowledge. As a research practitioner, you should be clear in your own mind as to whether a question contributes to affirming a law or examining a belief. You should also be aware of how evidence functions in either case.

About Scientific Laws, Paradigms, Theories, Models, and Beliefs

Physical laws are paradigms—accepted principles of operation; so are many agreed upon principles in the medical field. For example, the medical community holds to a common paradigm about the distinction between a cold and the flu. One should not be treated like the other. But it can also happen that scientific paradigms change over time. Bloodletting by way of leeches, once a medicinal paradigm, has long been abandoned for newer treatment conventions.

Following Kuhn, we define a paradigm as a theory with tested laws that are widely believed to override others in a scientific field or discipline. As such, a paradigm should be time-proven. However, you probably know that what is or is not factual is subject to debate among philosophers and physical scientists alike. Beliefs and the principles guiding them, then, play an important role in all research—even in the physical sciences.

Like paradigms, principles emerge once similar findings for like questions get confirmed over time, giving reason to trust a researched explanation as long as no contradictory evidence emerges. Beliefs require the largest amount of trust in what is merely at the earliest stage of testing or is still untested personal experience, common sense knowledge, or casual observation.

A paradigm (or principle) of importance to music education researchers might be that humans process sounds cognitively and emotionally in different ways regardless of any physical hearing acuity. What triggers different kinds of processing in the listener or performer then becomes the subject of further research, possibly leading to new theories and/or new questions. The angles that inform how we ask new questions are known as theories.

Educational psychologist Guy Lefrançois (2000) describes a theory as:

> . . . a statement, or more often, a collection of related statements whose main function is to summarize, simplify, organize, and explain observations and to permit prediction about events relating to this set of observations. Some of those statements may be described as laws, others as principles, and many as beliefs.
>
> (pp. 10–11)

Lefrançois' definition separates laws from principles and beliefs. Again, how much each of them contributes to the building of a theory depends on the strength of the evidence behind them. Just as accepted facts are confirmed or refuted because of newly gathered evidence, so too are theories; for instance, when because new insights question or reaffirm old explanations. Explanations should simplify rather than complicate the observations (or known facts). Therefore, a theory should always be "practical," that is, provide insights you did not have before. If a theory is less clear than its underlying observations, you may have reason to question its need.

You can find different, even conflicting, theories in the music education literature about levels of processing music. The theories come from various fields of knowledge, often proposing interdisciplinary ways by which to explain human responses to music. You have, for instance, theories of perception, musical taste, and aesthetics. Some of them originated in psychology, sociology and philosophy; others are from musicology, ethnomusicology, anthropology, and culture studies. Only theories that account for the ongoing and undeniable interaction between organism and environment, between context and action, are believed to truly explain human behavior in all its forms. Such thinking is inter- and multi-disciplinary, reaching across artificially set boundaries of subject matter and knowledge. Educational theorist John Dewey always thought in interdisciplinary terms, connecting education with the arts, politics, psychology and social psychology.

Lesser known theoretical frameworks generally require more detailed documentation than do familiar or commonly known theories. For instance, the theory of behaviorism, widely applied to research in music education over many years, may require less explanation than its underlying framework of *Cartesianism*, a thought process going back to philosopher René Descartes and instrumental for understanding behaviorism.

To word your own thoughts and questions according to the language common to a particular theory, familiarize yourself with the field(s) integral to it. Subsequently, think about how you might describe your own thoughts either verbally, visually, or even artistically.

Considering the Interdisciplinary Nature of the Field

As a composite of at least two fields of knowledge (music and education), questions about the learning and teaching of music tend to be situated between the research traditions and concerns of several disciplines. Since the middle of the 20th century, such disciplines have not only included psychology, but also neuroscience, medicine, and sociology. It is likely, therefore, that some of the studies you read have an interdisciplinary twist.

For example, an investigation of the effect of hearing loss on performance acuity may deal with musical, neurological, and physical constructs of sound perception and its measurement. Research on motivation probably includes relevant sources in psychology, education, and sociology. Researchers interested in past events and actions may draw from the political history of a particular time frame to distill questions that deal with relationships between population statistics and major cultural movements that may have influenced music instruction in the schools. Other researchers may originate relevant questions by examining thoughts in sports psychology, marketing, and other fields that address various forms of skill training, communication, and motivation.

You should expect that researchers who draw from one discipline to investigate questions in another show at least rudimentary familiarity with the technical know-how of the secondary field. Of course, you must similarly have a basic familiarity with the terminology and ways of doing things in other fields. Staying abreast of the broad array of research traditions that connect to the study of the learning and teaching of music is not only necessary but exciting; consider it an added bonus of becoming a music education scholar.

Using Theories to Model Your Thoughts

You may find it helpful to use theories from inside or outside music education to model your thoughts. Such models may be verbal, guiding readers through a carefully crafted process of clearly defined constructs and terms, or they may be presented in a graphic or artistic rendition that illustrates your thinking. A verbal example might be that of Gates (1999), briefly introduced in Chapter 1. Gates suggested that because of ongoing technological changes, music education scholars should borrow ideas from large fields such as "medicine, psychology, social work, management, and manufacturing" (p. 9) and "recognize at least four different levels of research activity":

- basic research (discovery, description, theory development),
- pedagogical "engineering" (test development, hypothesis testing),
- applications/technology (field trials, action research, materials development),
- and profession studies (survey of practices, curriculum research, policy studies, rationales, biography, history) (pp. 9–10).

Our use of interacting cogs as illustrations in this textbook represents the influence on our thinking of a theoretical framework known as *social interactionism*, a belief system derived from *pragmatism* as an interdisciplinary way of looking at how individuals and groups of individuals interact with each other in particular contexts.

Other scholars have built graphic models, sometimes called heuristics, to categorize their analysis of the literature and guide their own research or that of future scholars. See, for instance (Butler, Lind, & McKoy, 2007; Webster, 2002; Shaw, 2021; Stern, 2021). Others create models to represent research findings (see van der Merwe & Habron, 2015). Many other organizing principles exist; we suggest exploring them as you advance your reading and research comprehension skills.

Certain music educator/artists hold that valid research in the arts may be situated in the artistic product itself. Composing, then, is "doing research"; understanding a musical work by performing it means to grasp its underlying theory. Often referred to as "arts-based research" (e.g., Leavy, 2020; Greenwood, 2019; Springgay, Irwin, Leggo, & Gouzouasis, 2007; Barone & Eisner, 2011), theory formation lies in the doing of music, in the doing of art. When it expresses what it is supposed to express, theory and evidence become one. For more information, see Chapter 13.

Exploration: Articulating Your Thoughts

State in writing what you believe as a teacher, a student, and a researcher about the relationship of knowledge to fact, beliefs to truth, and "subjectively" perceived to "objectively" measured experiences. Connect your thoughts to readings from your research class and elsewhere. Give your essay a title that reflects its content.

The Function of Evidence in the Research Process

Some scholars hold that the more observations a researcher has in their data pool, the better their findings corroborate extant theories and beliefs. An opposing viewpoint is that certainty of belief is impossible because uncertainty is a basic principle of human existence. In between those two viewpoints (for which there are many philosophical labels, see Chapter 5) are a considerable number of others that speak about the place of science, knowledge, the arts, and teaching in relationship to each other.

A recurring theme among scholars across many disciplines is the question of how evidence functions as a contributor to theory. Asked more directly: What comes first? A basic "hunch" (or assumption) of what causes certain behaviors and actions to occur, or many observations that lead to conclusions as to why the observed behaviors or actions might have occurred in the first place? Does evidence contribute to knowledge *inductively* or *deductively*? Does the theory drive the observations (deduction) or do the observations drive the development of a theory (induction)?

Inspired by and indebted to Pidwirny and Jones (2010), we visualize the question in Figure 4.4. We then draw on Rothchild (2006) when we use the model to illustrate how the elements of observed reality might lead to our understanding of that reality. Our earlier visualization of the relationship between data and claim in lines of reasoning is similar to how the arrows are used here.

Inductive and Deductive Reasoning

Deduction seeks to confirm theory by collecting evidence after the fact (the theory occurs *a priori*); induction formulates a theory in advance (*a posteriori*). Although you may recognize in this description elements of the proverbial "chicken and egg" question, you may also realize the implications of such a distinction: When you begin with a theory and collect data to test it, you run the risk of only looking for those data that support the theory from the onset. When you

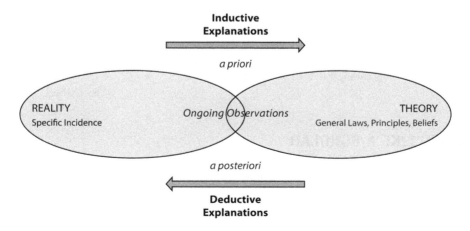

FIGURE 4.4 Scientific Understanding: Inductive and Deductive Reasoning

collect data to eventually formulate a theory, you never can be certain that another set of data will not falsify the theory.

This story, as told by the late Irving Rothchild (2006) professor emeritus of reproductive biology at Case Western University, is a reflection on an essay by Vicky Hearne that contrasted the behavior of highly trained primates. Rothchild's story concludes with questions we want to ask you as well:

A chimpanzee and an orangutan, housed separately, were each given a small hexagonal block of wood and an assortment of differently shaped openings into only one of which the block would fit. They knew they would be rewarded for making the right choice. The chimp examined every detail of the floor, walls, and ceiling; the openings and every side of the hexagonal block; smelled it, tasted it, and, after trying one opening after another, found [an opening] the block would fall into. The orangutan scratched his back with the block, and then sat with a far-away look in his eyes for what seemed to the human observer like forever. He then put the block directly into the hexagonal opening. Was the chimp an inductivist? Did the orangutan consider the problem, form a hypothesis, then test it? Which one was the scientist? (Rothchild, 2006, p. 2).

Popper (1968) argued that no observation can ever be made without a pre-conceived perspective (theory), thereby rendering the distinction between inductive and deductive research a moot point. Rothchild (2006) objected to that point of view and used Hearne's story to argue, instead, that:

Induction and deduction are two, usually different but never contradictory, approaches to problem solving. The problem must be solved by testing the validity of the conclusion or inference, etc., reached from either direction. Induction and deduction are thus valuable, often complementary, tools that facilitate problem solving.

(Rothchild, 2006, p. 3)

At the center of the process in both cases are ongoing observations. To return to the chimp, the orangutan, and Rothchild's questions: "Were both scientists? Yes. Was the orangutan more so than the chimp? No. He was only different" (p. 4).

Scientific inquiry, then, can occur in a variety of ways, but all holding to the same principle of learning through observation and examination. Again, Rothchild:

The only true scientific method is to use whatever tools we can to make observations, ask and answer questions, solve problems, test a theory, etc., and it doesn't matter whether we use induction, deduction, or any other kind of reasoning to do so; it would be a heresy to deny the validity of *any* method that helps us learn to know.

(Rothchild, 2006, p. 4)

THINKING LIKE A SCHOLAR

The ways of thinking described in this chapter undergird the work of all scholars. They are the basis of the think-read-observe-share spiral of inquiry that is the foundation of this textbook. Your research tasks thus far in the process have involved mostly thinking and reading, but soon you will add observation—whether analyzing patterns across your reading or doing original research—and then sharing those observations in writing.

When you apply scholarly thinking to your current reading, you should be able to confirm that (1) the researcher's perspective and position are clear throughout, whether or not they are stated explicitly; (2) all stated questions are true rather than rhetorical, (3) research specifications are addressed exhaustively and in good faith; and (4) conclusions drawn from presented evidence either address the stated questions or lead to new ones.

Applying these same criteria to your own writing, you should:

- Be clear about connections between your perspective, your position, and your research purpose,
- Be consistent in wording your purpose, questions, and/or named intent throughout a study,
- Conceptually frame your questions and place them into the larger body of extant professional literature,
- Use a recognizable form of argumentation that is explicitly laid out so that the reader can easily follow it (see also Chapter 5).

CHAPTER SUMMARY

1) How you perceive the world, know the world, and judge and justify your own actions and those around you as good and desirable should become the starting point for any question you consider important enough to ask. Keep those ideas in mind as you engage with scholarly writing—your own and that of other scholars.
2) Different forms of logic guide the way in which authors articulate their beliefs. Examine those forms and apply them to the way you think and write.
3) Researchers disagree about the veracity of worldviews and beliefs; about what is factual and what is not. Nonetheless, they respect scholarly argumentation when it is forthright and clear.
4) Distinguishing between theories, paradigms, laws, principles and beliefs in music education research might allow you to determine the respective strength and weaknesses of many studies you read.
5) As a critical reader and novice scholar, you should strive to locate evidence that:
   - connects to and supports extant research, and
   - provides further explanations for or confirmations of evidence that strengthens extant theories and their explanatory power.
6) To organize the material you read, you might want to keep in mind the model of learner, teacher and music, and how the three relate as interactive agents to each other.
7) The ways of thinking described in this chapter form the basis of the think-read-observe-share spiral of inquiry.

Topics for Further Exploration

1) Briefly review the main differences in propositional and dialectic argumentation, highlighting their respective strengths in music education scholarship.
2) Obtain copies of one or more published music education handbooks. (See supplemental online appendices: inquiryinmusiceducation.com)
   a. Examine the Tables of Contents for recurring themes that could be placed into the schematic of Figure 4.1.

b. Read comparable chapters from two handbooks that are several years apart and trace the changes in thinking about music education portrayed by the selections. (For example: Compare Swanwick's 2011 chapter "Musical development: Revisiting a generic theory" with Runfola and Swanwick's 2002 chapter "Developmental characteristics of music learners.")

Suggested Assignments

1) Working with a colleague, agree to provide honest critiques of the logic and argumentation each of you used in a recent class assignment. Even if the assignment received a good mark, invite your colleague to make suggestions to improve your work. (Note that this is a common activity among published scholars, likely including your professor!)

2) Find sources comparable to the music education *Handbooks* in education and psychology and look for (a) similarities and differences in these sources as compared to those mentioned above, and (b) themes and topics not addressed in the music education handbooks.

3) Choose an issue of a scholarly music education journal published since 2000. Examine its Table of Contents and place each title into the schematic of Figure 4.1.

Recommended Reading

Mackenzie, N., & Knipe, S. (2006). Research dilemmas: Paradigms, methods and methodology. *Issues in Educational Research, 16*. Retrieved from www.iier.org.au/iier16/mackenzie.html

Pine, R. (2011). *Essential logic: Basic reasoning skills for the twenty-first century (online ed.).* Retrieved from http://www2.hawaii.edu/~pine/EL/book2-am.htm

REFERENCES

Barone, T., & Eisner, E. W. (2011). *Arts based research.* Sage.

Bernard, C. F. (2015). *Ensemble educators, administrators, and evaluation: Support, survival, and navigating change in a high-stakes environment* [Doctoral dissertation]. Teachers College, Columbia University. ProQuest Dissertations and Theses Global (Publication No. 3704455).

Bowman, W. (2002). Educating musically. In R. Colwell & C. Richardson (Eds.), *The new handbook of research on music teaching and learning* (pp. 63–84). Oxford University Press.

Butler, A., Lind, V. L., & McKoy, C. L. (2007). Equity and access in music education: Conceptualizing culture as barriers to and supports for music learning. *Music Education Research, 9*(2), 241–253. https://doi.org/10.1080/14613800701384375

Cho, G. J. (2003). *The discovery of musical equal temperament in China and Europe in the sixteenth century.* The Edwin Mellen Press.

Colwell, R. (Ed.) (1991). *Basic concepts in music education II.* University of Colorado Press.

Colwell, R. (Ed.) (1992). *Handbook of research on music teaching and learning.* Schirmer.

Colwell, R., & Richardson, C. (Eds.) (2002). *The new handbook of research on music teaching and learning.* Oxford University Press.

Colwell, R., & Webster, P. R. (Eds.) (2011). *MENC handbook of research on music learning* (Vol. 1 & 2). Oxford University Press.

Copi, I., Cohen, C., & McMahon, K. (2019). *Introduction to logic* (15th ed.). Routledge.

Fitzpatrick, K. R. (2014). Mixed methods research in music education. In C. M. Conway (Ed.), *The Oxford handbook of qualitative research in American music education* (Vol. 1, pp. 171–187). Oxford University Press.

Gates, J. T. (1999). *Music education research at the dawn of the third mediamophosis* [Conference presentation]. Desert Skies Symposium, February 15–18, 1999, University of Arizona, Tucson.

Greenwood, J. (2019). Arts-based research. *Oxford Research Encyclopedia of Education*. https://doi.org/10.1093/acrefore/9780190264093.013.29

Hart, C. (2018). *Doing a literature review: Releasing the research imagination* (2nd ed.). Sage.

Henry, N. B. (Ed.) (1958). *Basic concepts in music education*. University of Chicago Press.

Kuhn, T. S. (1970). *The structure of scientific revolutions* (2nd ed.). University of Chicago Press. (Original work published 1962)

Leavy, P. (2020). *Methods meets art: Arts-based research practice* (3rd ed.). Guilford.

Lefrançois, G. R. (2000). *Psychology for teaching* (10th ed.). Wadsworth.

Leonard, H. S. (1957). *Principles of right reason*. Henry Holt.

Mithen, S. J. (2006). *The singing Neanderthals: The origins of music, language, mind, and body*. Harvard University Press.

Pidwirny, M., & Jones, S. (2010). *Fundamentals of physical geography: Chapter 3* (2nd ed.). University of British Columbia Okanagan. www.physicalgeography.net/fundamentals/contents.html

Popper, K. R. (1945). *The open society and its enemies*. Routledge.

Popper, K. R. (1968). *Conjectures and refutations: The growth of scientific knowledge*. Harper & Row.

Rothchild, I. (2006). *Induction, deduction, and the scientific method: An eclectic overview of the practice of science*. Society for the Study of Reproduction. http://citeseerx.ist.psu.edu/viewdoc/summary?doi=10.1.1.131.2694

Shaw, R. (2021). Placing the music teacher in an era of reform: Synthesizing research on music teacher networks and isolation. In C. Frierson-Campbell, C. Hall, S. R. Powell, & G. Rosabal-Coto (Eds.), *Sociological thinking in music education: International intersections*. Oxford University Press.

Smith, D. W. (2018). Phenomenology. In E. N. Zalta (Ed.), *The Stanford encyclopedia of philosophy* (Summer 2018). Metaphysics Research Lab, Stanford University. https://plato.stanford.edu/archives/sum2018/entries/phenomenology/

Springgay, S., Irwin, R. L., Leggo, C., & Gouzouasis, P. (Eds.) (2007). *A/R/Tography*. Sense Publishers.

Stern, J. (2021). Marching on an uneven field: A Bourdieusian analysis of competitive high school marching band in the U.S. In C. Frierson-Campbell, C. Hall, S. R. Powell, & G. Rosabal-Coto (Eds.), *Sociological thinking in music education: International intersections*. Oxford University Press.

Tragesser, R. S. (1977). *Phenomenology and logic*. Cornell University Press.

van den Brink-Budgen, R. (2010). *Critical thinking for students. Learn the skills of analyzing, evaluating and producing arguments* (4th ed.). Oxford University Press: How To Books.

van der Merwe, L., & Habron, J. (2015). A conceptual model of spirituality in music education. *Journal of Research in Music Education, 63*(1), 47–69. https://doi.org/10.1177/0022429415575314

Webster, P. (2002). Creative thinking in music: Advancing a model. In T. Sullivan & L. Willingham (Eds.), *Creativity and music education* (pp. 16–34). Canadian Music Educators' Association.

Weston, A. (2009). *A rulebook for arguments* (4th ed.). Hackett Publishing Company, Inc.

Wheelwright, P. E. (1962). *Valid thinking: An introduction to logic*. Odyssey Press.

CHAPTER 5

Approaches in the Philosophical Mode of Inquiry

This chapter focuses on philosophy as a tool for research in music education:

- Understanding what distinguishes philosophical inquiry from other types of research;
- Recognizing valid and clearly defined evidence in philosophical inquiry;
- Articulating your own beliefs in light of new or established belief systems; and
- Initiating a study in the philosophical mode of inquiry.

The "doing" of philosophy is covertly or overtly embedded in all scholarship. But as a mode of inquiry in music education, its main function lies in questioning—interrogating beliefs that underlie extant theories, challenging taken-for-granted habits and practices, and generally pushing the profession to deeply consider the implications of its practices and policies. Common to the many possible approaches should be the presence of traceable lines of argumentation with well-defined and consistently used key terms.

INTRODUCTION

We may note one peculiar feature of philosophy. If someone asks the question what is mathematics, we can give him a dictionary definition, let us say the science of number, for the sake of argument. As far as it goes this is an uncontroversial statement. . . . Definitions may be given in this way of any field where a body of definite knowledge exists. But philosophy cannot be so defined. Any definition is controversial and already embodies a philosophic attitude. The only way to find out what philosophy is, is to do philosophy (Russell, 1959, p. 7).

You may have thought you were "doing philosophy" when you applied for a teaching job and the principal or other school official asked about "your philosophy of music teaching/education." You may have been asked the same question in several of the music teacher preparation classes you took or are taking.

During one of the coffee talks, Liam spoke up about what he hoped to accomplish as a jazz musician. Christy then asked him how those plans fit into his "philosophy of music education." Usually quiet during those conversations, Prof. E. interjected, "Christy, what exactly do you mean?" Christy looked at him incredulously: Surely

---

DOI: 10.4324/9781003057703-8

he knew what a philosophy of music education was! After all, hardly any music educator is not required sooner or later in their career to articulate "a philosophy," that is, a personal statement on the importance of music in the curriculum. Hadn't Prof. E. repeatedly stated how important philosophy was for research? Why, then, this question?

Prof. E. asked this question to bring up the distinctions between simply stating an opinion, engaging in philosophical discourse, and conducting research in the philosophical mode of inquiry. In its most popular usage, philosophy means "love of wisdom" (philo: "loving," sophia: "knowledge, wisdom"). In popular usage, it is demonstrated by any train of thought articulated as a deliberate point of view, sometimes shared with others for the purpose of debate, and at other times carefully articulated as a personal statement about what is important to you in the way you see the world.

What sets such "trains of thought" apart from doing philosophy as a mode of inquiry in the context of research? How is sharing ideas with friends or writing out your own belief system different from using philosophy as a tool for addressing a pressing professional concern? When would such thinking qualify to be called research?

The former is like an informal gathering of friends making music together. Intuition and the immediacy of personal judgments define the moment of performing. An occasional mistake or unwanted chord progression does not diminish anyone's satisfaction with the experience. You and your fellow musicians set the parameters, unencumbered by scrutiny from a body of professional critics.

Such impromptu performances have shaped the creative life of most every music lover, but loving music does not necessarily equate with being a professional musician. That happens once your performances withstand scrutiny and meet standards set by outside experts and audiences. Similarly, expounding a train of thought at the spur of the moment generally "does not a philosopher make." Philosophy must reach beyond an "arbitrarily held opinion" or "personal views rooted in nothing more substantial than sentiment" (Bowman, 1998, p. 5). Rather, you "perform" philosophically by employing skills of reasoning as established by the scholarly collective. Knowing and understanding them is but one of the many requisites for good philosophical scholarship.

Why and When to Engage in Philosophical Inquiry

Having learned through reading that many scholars view Christopher Small's notion of musicking as more philosophical than practical made Marguerite wonder about her own approach. Did she want to examine Small's ideas philosophically or empirically? How would she decide? When she shared her dilemma in the coffee talk, Prof. E. asked: What did she really want to know? Did she want to illuminate and bring forth ideas about informal music practices, or did she want to use Small's (and perhaps other) ideas to examine informal musical practices in present-day settings?

You may consider philosophical study for many reasons: To discover discrepancies between others' ideas and your own, to resolve contradictions between accepted practices and the beliefs they espouse (or your own beliefs), or to seek further clarification about concepts that impact specific practices. Perhaps you want to illuminate or strengthen extant musical and educational theories, constructs and/or paradigms. Any of those can be turned into a research purpose, question, or (as some philosophers call them) a problematic. Even examining the place of rational thought in the arts continues to be a valid topic for examination and scholarship.

So how do you know if your ideas are philosophical? Lauren Kapalka Richerme (2013) suggests that philosophical inquiry in music education aspires to the following:

> Philosophical inquiry interrogates a discipline's underlying values; philosophical inquiry explores questions of a philosophical nature; philosophical inquiry connects multiple disciplines and experiences; philosophical inquiry involves clarifying, integrating, and analyzing preexisting concepts and ideas as well as creating new ones; philosophical inquiry ultimately aims to motivate and mobilize a field's practices and thinking.
>
> (p. 16)

While other modes of inquiry may intend to inform or persuade their audience, systematically conducted philosophical research—despite or across differences in approach—is almost always intended to persuade.

The remainder of this chapter describes working with different forms of logic, defining terms, and articulating the worldview that likely prompted your chosen form of logic. Placing your own beliefs with other systems of reasoning relevant to music, education, and music education concludes the chapter. It emphasizes that philosophizing as a research activity and philosophy as a discipline come together because each informs the other.

SKILLS OF REASONING AS RESEARCH TOOLS

In Chapter 4, you learned to trace lines of argumentation in what you read, to distinguish between scientific laws, paradigms, theories, models, and beliefs, and to consider the function of evidence in the research process. In an assignment at the end of that chapter we asked you to work with a colleague to examine some former papers for logical strength. Below, we go a step further by asking you to consider the strength of the evidence you read and write about. Then we invite you to look for what philosophers call fallacious argumentations. Once you recognize fallacious arguments, you will appreciate valid ones even more.

Examining Strength of Evidence behind a Claim

Through her literature review, *Keisha* realized that many different theoretical frameworks undergird the research relating children's multi-sensory responses to learning rhythmic and pitch patterns. Some authors cited claims supported by theories of perception and cognition, while others cited theories related to learning and teaching. Although a connection was likely and reasonable, the tested tasks underlying those theories did not always seem comparable. How valid was it to group studies from different fields of knowledge as evidence for a single claim?

As Keisha learned, it is not sufficient to rely on the title, type, or abstract of a publication to determine the strength of its evidence. Only the data themselves can prove the validity of a claim. In other words, questioning the content and claims in a cited source is important. So is the way you reference their evidence in your arguments.

In addition, the wording of your arguments may have consequences for the validity of the claims. For instance, it is easy to verify the truth of the following statement:

"In 1987, Rainbow and Froehlich published a research textbook."

The evidence is available in some libraries and bookstores. Similarly, you can validate the statement:

"Rainbow and Froehlich (1987) listed five sources of truth."

The statement is true because you can document the page numbers: pages 7–8. Whether you agree that there are more or fewer sources of truth would be another matter, requiring you to find additional sources in support of your own position.

Next consider:

"There are 5 sources of truth."

(Rainbow & Froehlich, 1987, pp. 7–8)

You now make a claim that—to be convincing—calls for far more evidence than is provided by a single reference. Its content rather than the source becomes the issue.

Fallacies of Argumentation

Philosophers use the term fallacy to describe arguments with weak or faulty evidence. Fallacies tend to be caused by logical and structural weaknesses in arguments such as (1) incomplete, inadequate, irrelevant, ambiguous, or even inaccurate evidence, and/or (2) deficient, weak, or inconsistently used definitions of key terms. Generally unintentional, such deficiencies happen because a writer takes shortcuts in trying to make persuasive arguments. For example, a reference to "big names" or known experts as the sole support for a given statement ultimately renders that argument invalid. Such is not permissible as evidence in any scholarship, regardless of mode. Claiming, "research has found . . ." but citing only one study as reference does not provide enough evidence for building a convincing premise. One of your tasks as a philosopher, then, might be to pinpoint such fallacies and show how they impact the writer's conclusion(s).

Of the named fallacies in many available textbooks on logic, the most commonly mentioned seem to be:

1) An *ad hominem* argument, also called a *straw man* fallacy: An idea is attacked because of what person holds the idea rather than the specifics of the idea itself. This can take two forms: An idea is assumed wrong simply because it came from a *persona non-grata* (undesirable, un-liked, considered inept); or an idea is accepted as good because it is expressed by a person held in high esteem. Neither option is a sufficient reason for accepting or rejecting a stated premise.

2) An *ambiguous* argument: The unclear meaning of a word or phrase in a premise makes it appear valid when it is not. Ambiguous arguments occur when a premise includes one or more words with multiple possible meanings, or when a premise is structured in an ambiguous way. (For more information, see section in this chapter on Defining Terms.)

3) A *circular* argument (see also "*begging the question*"): Something is declared good or bad because the writer says so. This happens quite frequently in the above-mentioned, opinion-rich "philosophies" (justifications) many of us have been asked to articulate in various situations. Because we want to believe that something is true, we declare it to be so—often vehemently. It is what some call wishful thinking.

4) A *slippery slope* argument: Causal relationships are drawn where there are none. "A boy who blows his horn does not blow a safe" refers to the assumed causality between musical training and morally upright behavior. Very little evidence, if any, exists to confirm that causality but statements of similar meaning can often be found in arts advocacy documents (see the Mozart effect studies referred to in Chapter 1).

5) *Begging the question*: The strength of a belief becomes the evidence in support of that belief (see also *circular* and *ad hominem* arguments). Enthusiasm and strength of conviction, both needed in the work music educators do, should not be assumed to replace factual evidence derived from well conducted investigations.

Exploration: Knowing a Fallacy When You See It

1) Document fallacies in argumentations from the popular or professional media that you interact with. What did you find?
2) If you were to take our word that our list of fallacies was sufficient, which fallacy (or fallacies) would you have committed?
3) What other steps could you take to strengthen your own knowledge about fallacies of argumentation in music education research?

Approaches to Defining Terms

A second component of good scholarship, particularly in the philosophical mode, is the consistent use of explicitly defined terms. As Jorgensen (2006) points out, the act of clarifying terms helps to shine a light on intellectual relationships and connections, makes it possible to compare and/or critique ideas, and allows for ideas used in research to be applied in practice (pp. 177–178). Ambiguous or poorly worded definitions, on the other hand, weaken any argumentation (although even the best definition does not replace the evidence needed for a valid argument).

Figure 5.1 shows several approaches to defining terms, labeled *synonymous-stipulated*, *synonymous-lexical*, and *operational* definitions as well as those by *genus* and *difference*. Each carries with it a certain level of credibility, suggesting that not all definitions should be equally trusted, or are equally strong.

Stipulated and/or Operational Definitions

A stipulated definition simply replaces one term with another. Such may be the case when you define "good music" as that which you like. Perhaps not very strong and possibly quite different from what music theorists or philosophers would support or stipulate, the definition may serve its purpose for what you speak or write about.

	Synonymous	*Operational*	*by Genus and Difference*
Stipulated	Author-generated	Author-tested over time	Definition follows scientific format/ structure of class and sub-class
Lexical	Published and literal translation of foreign and/or unusual terms	Professionally agreed-upon definitions	Definition follows scientific format/ structure of class and sub-class

FIGURE 5.1 Types of Definitions

An operational definition requires more than a simple word or phrase replacement. For example, Gordon (1980) coined the term "audiation"; Small (1995/1997, 1998) the gerund "musicking" (with a "k"); and Elliott (1995) "musicing" (without a "k"). Each of these authors explained their reasoning in detail, thus defining the terms operationally. As the profession at large gradually began to include the terms in its vocabulary, the definitions found entry into other authors' writings and, later, into dictionaries as well as peer-reviewed, published glossaries. Thus, operational terms became lexical. An important task of good scholarship is to verify that the lexical use is in keeping with how an author originally stipulated either a new term (as in the case of audiation and musicking) or a new meaning for a known term.

Avoid stipulating circular definitions, defining a word with itself. For instance, stipulating "aesthetics as the study of aesthetic appreciation" makes the definition circular, thus useless. Surprisingly, you find many such examples in lexica, dictionaries, and encyclopedias. Be careful: it is easy to fall into that logical trap.

Operational definitions often describe how a term may be used in a particular context. Such is the case, for example, when "music achievement" is defined by the tasks in a particular music performance or theory test. A collection of tangible behaviors, observable and themselves defined, provide the operational meaning of the word. Because of the context-dependency of operational definitions, it is conceivable that different authors provide dissimilar definitions for the same term. Such differences and contradictions can become the raw material (the raw data) for much needed philosophical studies in our field.

Definitions by "Genus and Difference"

Definitions by "genus and difference" include operationally defined terms when the latter speak to (1) the class or family to which a term belongs (the genus), and (2) the specific attribute(s) that separate(s) the term from the class or family (the difference). A simple example might be to define a violin as a bowed instrument in the string family with a fretless fingerboard, with strings tuned in fifths from lowest to highest as G3, D4, A4, and E5. You first state the genus (string family with fretless fingerboards), followed by the difference (the size and the tuning of the strings; i.e., what sets the violin apart from other instruments in the genus).

Constructing the definition works best if you first list everything that falls under a term (the denotations), and then find the characteristics that are common to all denotations. Those commonalities (the connotations) become the building block for the definition itself. Order the connotations from broadest to most specific so that all qualities are accounted for. Then craft one or several sentences in which the connotations describe the term. Your task is to assure that the term itself is not broader than the definition or that the definition is not broader than the term.

Examining how different researchers have stipulated or operationalized terms in their respective works can result in fruitful philosophical investigations. You might, for instance, address how specific terms have been adopted, adjusted, or changed in various scholarly documents; findings that could serve as springboard for new queries. For example:

In their reading, *Isaac*, *Keisha*, and *Marguerite* found inconsistencies in the way many authors used common words and phrases in both trade and scholarly literature. They identified the following terms as needing additional clarity: aesthetic education; creativity and imagination in the learning and teaching of music; social justice, power, and behavior modification in the classroom; student empowerment and teacher control. They also wondered which of these terms belonged to or were derived from specific theoretical frameworks. Did the studies they read provide enough evidence for the claims made by the authors they engaged with?

EXAMINING PHILOSOPHICAL QUESTIONS

> Philosophical inquiry is a lively and provocative, daunting yet rewarding practice that questions received views, challenges habits and assumptions, and painstakingly investigates how things might be other than they appear to be or better than they are.
>
> (Bowman & Frega, 2012, p. 18)

You might think of philosophers as music education "watch dogs" because of their role in questioning taken-for-granted theories, concepts, and terms that are widely but, at times, somewhat indiscriminately used in music education. Examining and systematically comparing ideas in all modes of inquiry can bring out similarities and differences in meanings and findings across studies and point out weaknesses and strengths in applying certain concepts to practice. Such inquiries can:

> . . . raise issues; question assumptions; open new vistas on what error, or truth, or belief consist of; reassess our realities within newly conceived frameworks; or any of the other ways to stimulate reconstructions of our theories and practices that rigorous examination might reveal as being unproductive or dehumanizing.
>
> (Reimer, 2008, p. 195)

However, philosophy as "*a* systematic, reflective discipline" (p. 3, emphasis in original) can and should not be prescriptive, not so much a guide for action as an examination of "the grounds for belief and action" (Bowman, 1992, p. 3; emphasis ours. See also Bowman, 1998, p. 5). Such grounds are nearly limitless whereas their consequences, the actions themselves, might not be.

Beginning with questions about the nature of music, society, education, music education, and principles of learning and teaching, the options of what to examine philosophically are many. You might, for instance examine the grounds for what is or is not considered important social and musical capital (i.e., valuable musical knowledge and skills) and what various thinkers may mean by schooling and education as societal mandates.

Questions about the Nature of Music and Education

What is the nature of these organized sounds we call music? What makes these sounds "music" rather than just "noise"? What do the variety of human responses to music say about its value in our lives? Are some musics, some responses, and some methods of teaching them "better" than others? Why or why not? Who gets to decide?

Many music educators believe that using the "philosophy of music education" to respond to questions like those above means choosing between aesthetic and paraxial interpretations of music teaching and learning or finding a balance between the two. This is a misconception. Although these two schools of thought have been prominent in music education philosophy, particularly in the United States, since the early 1970s, both stem from sub-branches of philosophy.

Aesthetics stems from axiology, the study of values. For this reason, critical theorists and constructivists tend to reject the notion of examining music educational practices solely from an aesthetic angle. Instead, they address relationships between educational goals and purposes within the axiological context of ethics and politics. Because musical values are socially acquired, they reflect upbringing, social status, and cultural/artistic opportunities. Any decisions about educational goals are as dependent on those forces as they are about decisions about what "good music" might be or what a "well-rounded musical education" might mean.

Similarly, music-making as a practice needs to be more "than an understanding of pieces or works of music." Instead, it must be guided by "actions[s] that [are] embedded in and responsive to a specific context of effort." Such music practice is termed praxis, signifying that "'music' pivots on particular kinds of human doing-and-making that are purposeful, contextual and socially-embedded" (Elliott, www.davidelliottmusic.com/music-matters/what-does-praxial-mean/).

Exploration: An Invitation to Think about Music and Education

Review and compare contrasting philosophical ideas expressed by McPhail (2018); Elliott and Silverman (2012); Reimer (2012); Scruton (1997); Alperson (2011); and Panaiotidi (2002) and the contributing authors in Regelski and Gates (2009) or Bowman and Frega (2012). Focus on whether and how constructs of musicianship should be connected to sociocultural and educational traditions of schooling in general and institutions of learning in particular. Reflect on the influence, positive and negative, of hierarchies of power on your own learning. Determine how interdisciplinary ways of thinking may conflict with subject-specific curricula.

Philosophers have examined such issues as (1) a teacher's role as indoctrinator or facilitator of learning, (2) gender inequalities as manifested in instrument and repertoire choice, (3) addressing the "taken-for-granted" structure of public schooling to better meet the needs of marginalized students, (4) race and gender discrimination in curriculum construction and teaching practices, and (5) differences in urban versus rural versus suburban instructional settings. A few examples are those by Bleiker (2009); Bradley (2007); Gaztambide-Fernández (2010); Gould (2007); Lamb, Dolloff, and Howe (2002); vanWelden (2004); and Williams and Shannon (2004). Use these or similar examples to sharpen your questions on comparable topics; link them to contexts with which you are familiar or that you care about. Consider social-cultural factors with any recommendations you make. Indeed, whatever problematic you choose to investigate, you are well advised to consider opposing data and viewpoints before drawing any conclusions that result in guides for action.

Clarifying Constructs and Theories

The clarification of constructs and theories in our field could contribute greatly to setting a somewhat paradigmatically orientated research agenda for the profession. Efforts to that effect have been spearheaded by music educators of many philosophical persuasions and research preferences. Engaging with a few of those, listed under recommended readings at the end of this chapter, may provide a sense of how systematic reasoning can impact action in the classroom or further empirical and historical research.

To begin, look at how other scholars have proceeded. Start with dissertations and journal articles in which biographical and historical information about the lives and contributions of particular philosophers, musicians, and music educators were connected to their respective beliefs about music, education, culture, and society (e.g., Burrage, 2013; Cee, 2008; Chandler, 2004; Helfer, 2003; White-Hope, 2019; Lee, 1982; Mortyakova, 2011; Orrel, 1995; Reeves-Johnson, 2002; Revkin, 1984; Shiraishi, 2001; Whalen, 2008; Williams, 2017). Or examine studies in which specific instructional actions were described and analyzed from specific theoretical angles (e.g., Countryman & Stewart Rose, 2017; Benton, 2002; Dale, 2012; Garberich, 2008; Kertz-Welzel, 2008; Louth, 2008; Mantie, 2012; Kedem, 2008; Kuehmann, 1987; Tan, 2016). The descriptors came from such areas as cognition and perception; creativity and inspiration; power and ideology in music instructional settings; metaphor and imagery in music; multiculturalism, globalization, and musicianship; age-specific processes of learning; and curriculum theory.

In a third group of studies, researchers combined empirical and philosophical methods to examine particular instructional settings. Often, terms used to describe what was going on in private studios or music classrooms from Kindergarten through college, were derived from the investigator's philosophical worldview or that of known philosophers inside or outside the field of music education. Examples are investigations by Autry (2019), Balija (2015), Cho (2010), Cohen (2007), Dees (2005), Dexter (2014), Eshelman (1995), Field (1997), Jensen-Hole (2005) and Williams (2010). In some instances, the focus was less on philosophical methods than on empirical ones, thereby concentrating a study more on pedagogical actions than on clarifying underlying theoretical constructs.

Recently (and much encouraged by critical theorists in music education) researchers have begun to address apparent dissonances, tensions, or incongruities between specific thought processes, key terms, and practices in extant theories of instruction and music pedagogy. Such efforts require a willingness to step outside the relative comfort zone of accepted ways of instructional practices. And this disposition in turn requires strong skills, because questioning extant practices is more difficult than building on them. Examples include Bates (2019), Bradley (2012), Gaztambide-Fernandez (2010), Hess (2017), and Rosabal-Coto (2016).

Exploration: Crafting a Philosophical Response

Craft a brief philosophical essay in which you affirm, refute, build on, or otherwise respond to the position taken by the author of one of the articles cited above. Apply what you would use in any other mode of inquiry:

- Introduce your essay with an argumentation, a brief story, or a vignette that illustrates the point(s) you plan to make.
- Clearly state the point you are responding to, and articulate your chosen line of reasoning (i.e., premises; see Chapter 4).
- Define key terms and place them into your question(s) and argumentation without replacing either.
- Use those definitions consistently. If your study is actually about defining a term, say so as part of your research rationale.
- Document strength of evidence in specific arguments; point to divergent, contradictory, or even unclear philosophical positions that emanate from different forms of reasoning.

CONNECTING YOUR OWN BELIEFS TO EXTANT WORLDVIEWS

Just as centuries of making and composing music have resulted in a defined body of musical works, describable in styles, genres, and ways of thinking (the discipline of music), so have centuries of thought and argumentation about beliefs contributed to the discipline of philosophy. Systematized as philosophical branches (or domains), the discipline reflects what philosophers have done and continue to do: Examine the relationship between reality, perception of reality, knowledge, fact, and truth from many angles and perspectives. Like the students in RC533, as you engage in philosophical inquiry, you will likely begin to recognize connections between your personal actions and beliefs and the philosophical ideas in this chapter and beyond.

Philosophical Branches

You already learned about the branch of logic as the study of reasoning and you read earlier in this chapter that the branch (or domain) of axiology comprises ethics, aesthetics, and politics. Just as these domains inform all research in music education, so do the remaining branches of:

- epistemology as the study of knowledge,
- metaphysics as the study of the nature of reality, and
- phenomenology as the study of experience.

Each contributes to the questions you ask and the methods you use to address them. Sometimes difficult to separate one from the other, one domain informs the other. Grasping the terminology of each makes you a stronger philosopher and researcher. That is only true, however, if you have a clear understanding of the meaning behind what a particular domain stands for. A word of caution: Use only terms with which you are familiar. Scholarly-sounding multisyllabic words do not make you a better philosopher. Clarity of thought does.

Epistemology and Music Education

As the branch of philosophy that reasons about the nature and origin of knowledge, *epistemology* is central to investigations of what constitutes knowledge in the music classroom and in music teacher training. Different answers about what might be considered accepted canons of musical choices on the one hand and learner preferences on the other shape that discourse in music education.

Recent writings in what has become known as social epistemology focus on "the epistemic effects of social interactions and social systems" (Goldman & O'Connor, 2021, para. 1). Philosophy, sociology, and education intertwine in this discourse, challenging music educators to connect what pupils learn musically outside of school, what they might bring to such learning processes from home, and what school music has to offer them. Thus, social epistemology applied to music learning takes you directly into the why, what, and how of developing music curricula and community programs that are both transmitting knowledge and transforming minds for the betterment of individuals and of society. These, however, are practical questions that also connect to axiological questions of aesthetics, ethics, and political power structures in society.

Metaphysics and Music Education

The branch of *metaphysics* investigates the nature of ultimate reality and is generally divided into *ontology* (the study of being) and *cosmology* (the study of the structure of the universe). Finding a clear-cut definition is not easy because, like aesthetics, the term has undergone major changes of meaning since Aristotle first used it as a label for the treatise that followed *Physics*, a collection of fourteen philosophical lectures (books) on nature itself (van Inwagen & Sullivan, 2020, para. 1).

In more recent times and in everyday language, the term is used most often to refer to what may lie beyond the physical world. In that sense, metaphysical questions have theological or teleological bents, which cannot be explained by scientific means alone. Tangible connections between metaphysics (as it is understood today) and ontology become clear when you think systematically about music and the arts as aesthetic phenomena whose explanation may extend beyond intellectual understanding alone. Emotions, feelings, values, and how these come about take you back to axiology. Ethics and politics enter into educational and artistic decision-making.

Metaphysical examinations of what constitutes aesthetic responses to music often examine the place of the self in the realm of social realities or connected to spiritual experiences. When connected to social realities within the nature and purpose of music schooling, it becomes essential to ask not only what makes a composition great rather than merely good, but also to inquire about whether, when, and where such judgments are "teachable."

Phenomenology and Music Education

In Chapter 4, we described *phenomenology* as a method of reasoning. Philosophically, it is the branch that studies "structures of experience, or consciousness" (Smith, 2018, para. 3). The term itself has undergone changes in meaning across different disciplines and times and therefore requires ongoing clarification. Music education researchers tend to refer to it mainly in the context of qualitative research in which data gathering and interpretation are equally situated in the consciousness of the observer and the observed. Philosophers who subscribe to this approach place themselves into that which they examine. (For more information, see Chapters 7 & 8.)

Phenomenologists accept given perceptions as valid so long as their descriptions are trustworthy. Thus, personal experiences and viewpoints are as valid in phenomenological reasoning as are recallable facts and agreed-upon measurements in quantitative research. Phenomenological scholarship realizes perhaps more clearly than any other philosophical branch that your worldview determines the investigative steps by which to address the questions you may have. Knowledge originates in experience, rather than in observing or being observed. Such an approach invites the first person, or "I" form of writing, a style not always condoned by scholars who favor a formalist, functionalist, or modernist view of the world.

Extant Worldviews or Belief Systems

Your belief system (or worldview) reflects who you believe you are and why you think the way you do. Many such belief systems exist, ranging from long-established religious or theological beliefs to casually formulated secular ideologies. Either form describes what you consider important in life—both personal and professional. Figure 5.2 lists a select few of the many "-isms" you can find in the literature. Those listed, sometimes by themselves and also in combination with each other, have shaped music education discourse in the United States since the mid-20th century.

Many worldviews have labels that describe their key tenet. For instance, *absolutism* professes to an unconditional belief in true, right, and desirable standards of actions and behaviors over false and undesirable judgments and values. *Relativism*, on the other hand, acknowledges that differences in context should allow for differences in judgments about right and wrong, good and bad, or appropriate and inappropriate. *Behaviorism* is a short term for a complex belief system in the power of observable actions ("behaviors") as the basis for what may be considered scientific data.

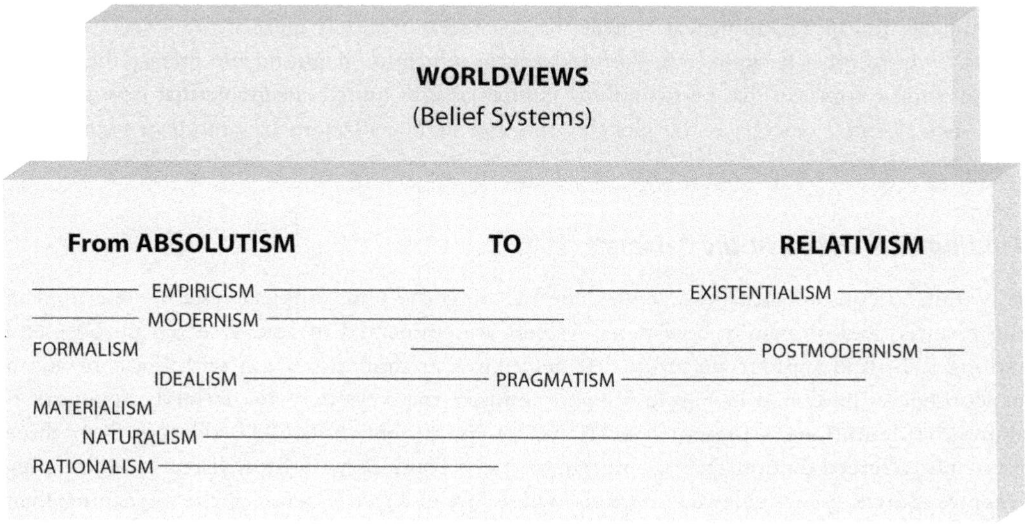

WORLDVIEWS
(Belief Systems)

From ABSOLUTISM   **TO**   **RELATIVISM**

EMPIRICISM ——————   —————— EXISTENTIALISM ——————
—————— MODERNISM ——————————————
FORMALISM   —————————————————— POSTMODERNISM ——
IDEALISM —————————— PRAGMATISM ——————
MATERIALISM
NATURALISM ————————————————————————
RATIONALISM ——————————————

FIGURE 5.2 Selected Worldviews

Terms like absolutism, formalism, functionalism, and relativism may seem more familiar than others because they readily say what they represent. Others are not as easily defined because their everyday meanings differ from their philosophical meanings. An example is *idealism*, often used in everyday language to mean beliefs only a dreamer or unrealistic person might hold. Philosophically, however, the meaning is more complex.

Going as far back as Plato's theory of idea, "idea-ism" suggests that the idea of a thing is more real than the thing itself. The concept—the idea of "tree"—is more concrete in its comprehensiveness than any one tree you see in a forest or parking lot. This is the meaning of the philosophical construct of idealism that can be found in metaphysics, epistemology, and their respective sub-domains. German philosophers of the late 18th and early 19th centuries further added to the meaning of the construct, thereby creating even more definitions (and, possibly, more confusion).

You may encounter a similar discrepancy between the philosophical and everyday usage of the term *pragmatism*. If you examine definitions of the term you may notice that "practical" and "pragmatic" appear to be used interchangeably. Exploring pragmatism in greater depth, however, you find the term's philosophical meaning to be more complex than what some of those definitions suggest.

Not listed in Figure 5.2 is an influential system of thinking known as *feminism*. Summarized by authors in *The Stanford Encyclopedia of Philosophy*, feminist philosophers have:

> introduced new concepts and perspectives that have transformed philosophy itself. They are also rendering philosophical previously un-problematized topics, such as the body, class and work, disability, the family, reproduction, the self, sex work, human trafficking, and sexuality. And they are bringing a particularly feminist lens to issues of science, globalization, human rights, popular culture, and race and racism.
>
> (McAfee, 2018, para. 2)

Feminism has played an important role in questioning whether traditional "-isms," because of their historic representation of the socio-political and cultural perspectives of scholars who were traditionally European and primarily male, have silenced or simply ignored the voices and ideas of people from other backgrounds. Postmodernism, which use linguistic and literary theories to address similar concerns, has been similarly influential. It is quite conceivable that new perspectives, new "-isms" emerge as the globalization and democratization of education systems and cultures continue.

Finding Your Place in the "-isms"

It is time to consider how your own beliefs fit into the philosophical systems described in this chapter, and ultimately how those systems are connected to your research purpose and rationale. To find appropriate terms that describe your thinking, begin with the continuum of worldviews presented in Figure 5.2 and compare the ways they are defined. Appendix B shows the definitions as presented by Rainbow and Froehlich in 1987, selected from three reputable, refereed dictionaries. Comparing these definitions with those listed in online philosophy sources (peer-reviewed and not) will give you a better sense of their meaning than any one source.

Exploration: Working with "-isms"

Compare the definitions in Appendix B with a selection of peer-reviewed sources (e.g., Fieser & Dowden's *The Internet Encyclopedia of Philosophy* (1995) and Zalta's *Stanford Encyclopedia of Philosophy* (2021); and non-peer reviewed sources (e.g., *Wiktionary*, the *Glossary of Philosophical Isms* (2017) and Saint-Andre's "Index of ISMS" (2013, also available via the *Ismbook* blog). Links may be found in References and in supplemental online materials (see inquiryinmusiceducation.com). Examine all definitions carefully, noting similarities and differences among them. Should you recognize the same unreferenced definitions in two or more sources, mark them as possible examples of questionable scholarship. In addition, make note of (1) where you stand on the issues alluded to by the "-isms" listed, and (2) how the issues may be relevant to your work as a musician, teacher, and researcher. For example, where would you place yourself on a continuum between absolutist and relativist? Idealist and empiricist? Pragmatist and formalist?

You may find that juxtaposing one position against another helps you to position your beliefs amongst the "-isms." We suggest you begin by pairing them as shown in Figure 5.3.

If you find any one "-ism" alone to be insufficient to describe your worldview, you are not alone. Many philosophers have also done so. But remember: The level of detail with which you describe your reasoning is more important than the label you give.

When you spend time with the "-isms" and consider how you think, the result may well be a stronger perspective about yourself. A strong perspective, however, is likely to influence the way you ask questions and pursue their answers. As a writer, the philosophical branch within which you place your work and the worldview that guides your thinking signal to your readers the contextual boundaries that define the scope of your argumentation. Be sure you state both succinctly.

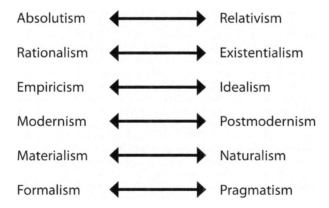

Absolutism	⟷	Relativism
Rationalism	⟷	Existentialism
Empiricism	⟷	Idealism
Modernism	⟷	Postmodernism
Materialism	⟷	Naturalism
Formalism	⟷	Pragmatism

FIGURE 5.3 Selected Paired Worldviews in Juxtaposition to Each Other

Being and Becoming a Philosopher

Do you desire to clarify existing terms, examine taken-for-granted assumptions, and/or connect thinking in music education to ideas from other systems of thought in ways that are characteristically philosophical? If so, your research purpose may display what Estelle Jorgensen (2006, p. 176) calls "symptoms of the philosophical," and you may wish to pursue research in the philosophical mode of inquiry.

We concur with Bertrand Russell (1959), quoted at the start of this chapter: "The only way to find out what philosophy is, is to do philosophy" (p. 7). As a philosopher, your research field is the written and spoken word—digital and analog—and the workspace where your computer is located. Working as a philosopher means taking on many tasks like those explored in this chapter. Perhaps these "explorations" have sparked your curiosity toward further philosophical pursuits. On the other hand, perhaps they have convinced you that doing philosophical research is not for the "faint-hearted." But then, neither is music performance!

Internal restraints may be caused by thinking about things in the quiet of your study rather than talking to others. Feeling the responsibility to articulate your thoughts exactly, you can never be fully certain of success until you submit your writing to peer review. In that process you are likely to discover that trying to clarify, integrate, and analyze "preexisting concepts and ideas as well as creat[e] others" (Richerme, 2013, p. 16) takes time and repeated re-drafting. Therefore, allow ample time for re-writes, self-selected peer reviews, and continuous re-drafting.

Do not be discouraged when answers remain inconclusive, trigger more questions, or set your world apart from that of others. Philosophical inquiry is a form of literary creativity, full of discoveries and opportunities but also relentless in making you more and more aware of the many thoughts that await articulation. You may find that philosophy chooses you rather than the other way around. And, even when you end up conducting research in other modes of inquiry—once a philosopher, always a philosopher!

CRAFTING A PHILOSOPHICAL RESEARCH PROPOSAL

A philosophical research proposal, particularly for a degree requirement, usually has three sections or chapters: (1) Introduction (Thesis Statement or Statement of the Problematic), (2) Narrative, and (3) Conclusions. Its purpose is to connect your specific view of the topic to the published body of knowledge in the field, support your claim that there is a need for your study, and communicate that you have the necessary skills and knowledge to complete the proposed project.

Writing the Introduction

In the introduction you recast the purpose and rationale you wrote in Chapter 3 as a *thesis statement* or a *statement of the problematic*, adding clearly articulated premises that logically present your thesis. Your thesis statement (1) "motivates" your project, explaining its importance to your audience, (2) provides background for understanding the point(s) of view you will present (and briefly acknowledges potential objections to those points of view), and (3) states your thesis and its principal premises in a clear, unequivocal way. As such, your introduction describes and demonstrates the type of argumentation you intend to use (see Chapter 4).

Writing the Narrative

Using the organizational scheme from your introduction, craft a narrative of some length (often stipulated by your university) that describes and demonstrates the type of argumentation you intend to use (see Chapter 4). As premises are the bases of argumentations, your narrative must introduce each premise you intend to examine, supported by the literature. In addition, you must define any technical or ambiguous terms in your thesis statement, anticipate and respond to any likely objections to your arguments, and clearly lay out your plans for completing the project. "Signposting," telling the reader "what you have done, what you are going to do, and about how different parts of your paper relate to each other" (Chudnoff, 2007, p. 49), may be helpful.

Prior to writing the narrative, it may be necessary to expand your literature collection, particularly if your thesis intends to connect "multiple disciplines and experiences" (see Richerme, 2013). Once you are certain that your literature collection supports your thesis, it is time to outline or otherwise re-organize your thinking.

Some music education philosophers have used personal stories to illustrate the points they want to make, and built on those points to make their arguments. See Richerme (2015) and Freer (2019), among others. At other times the argument itself may present a logical organizational scheme. One caution: While it may seem most natural to you as a writer to organize your narrative in the order in which the ideas came to you, a "logical-explanatory order" is most likely to provide a clear path for readers to understand your argument (Chudnoff, 2007, pp. 46–48).

Writing the Conclusion

The conclusion to your proposal explains what your argument might mean for the field of music education. It tells the committee reviewing your proposal whether your expectations are reasonable and do-able, not only for yourself but also for the field at large. While it is true that "researchers engaging in philosophical inquiry ultimately strive to guide, influence, and alter thought and practice" (Richerme, 2013, p. 21), it is also true that "the products of good philosophizing are not new facts but new perspectives on the assumptions, beliefs, meanings, and definitions that inhabit our thoughts and actions" (Elliott, 1995, p. 8). As noted by Wayne Bowman and Ana Lucía Frega (2012), "the most important outcomes of philosophical inquiry . . . are not unequivocal or ultimate answers but the ability to ask better, more useful questions" (p. 4). Your conclusion should reflect this expectation.

CHAPTER SUMMARY

1) Philosophy as a mode of inquiry may be distinguished from the philosophical thinking that underlies all scholarship and also from stated opinions whose claims may be unwarranted or expressed as "wishful thinking."
2) Examining your arguments and those of other scholars for unwarranted and warranted claims, and probing contradictions in extant answers are important tasks of a philosopher-scholar.
3) Identifying strong as well as fallacious argumentations in published works can lead to new questions and "problematics."
4) Defining terms should be part of any form of reasoning as definitions reflect varying degrees of information.

5) A purposefully chosen form of argumentation and explicitly defined terms should also be central to your scholarship.

6) Different worldviews impact forms of argumentation. As they are multidimensional tools in all of research, familiarity with various worldviews is essential for matching your argument (and your method, when applicable) with the most appropriate form of reasoning.

Topics for Further Exploration

1) The role of the philosopher in music education.

2) A comparison of the schools of thought illustrated in Figure 5.2 and their application to education, music, and music education.

3) A discussion of any of the philosophical questions in the section so-named above in light of the continua suggested in Figure 5.3.

4) Arguments for and against Bertrand Russell's assertion that value and dogma should not be the subject of philosophical inquiry because their truth cannot be probed by methods of logical argumentation.

Suggested Assignments

1) Select two of the titles given below that pique your interest (see full citations in *References*). Imagine/envision: (a) what each of them might be about, (b) how you would do titular study in your own mind, and—after skimming the sources—(c) how close your own vision came to the actual work:
   - Bell, A. P. (2015). "Can We Afford These Affordances? GarageBand and the Double-Edged Sword of the Digital Audio Workstation."
   - Bowman, W. D. (2012). "Music's Place in Education."
   - Froehlich, H. & Cattley, G. (1993). "Language, metaphor, and analogy in the music education research process."
   - Gould, E. (2007). "Legible bodies in music education: Becoming-matter."
   - Kronig, F. K. (2021). "Six Fallacies Regarding the Question of Whether we Conceive of Practices as 'Musical.'"
   - Jorgensen, E. R. (2001). "A Dialectical View of Theory and Practice."
   - Parkinson, T. & Smith, G. D. (2015). "Towards an Epistemology of Authenticity in Higher Popular Music Education."
   - Panaiotidi, E. (2002). "What is Philosophy of Music Education and Do we Really Need It?"
   - Richerme, L. K. (2013). *Complicating, considering, connecting: Rhizomatic philosophizing in music education*
   - Scarlato, M. K. M. (2021). *Go Ask Alice: How Is a Raven Like a Band Director?*
   - van der Schyff, D., Schiavio, A., & Elliott, D. J. (2016). "Critical Ontology for an Enactive Music Pedagogy."
   - Whale, M. (2009). *Music as the between: The idea of meeting in existence, music and education.*

2) Using an "In Dialogue" essay from *Philosophy of Music Education Review* as models, craft an "In Dialogue" essay as a written response to one of the philosophical sources in the list above.

3) Randomly select a chapter from one of the scholarly music education *Handbooks* featured in the supplemental online appendices (see inquiryinmusiceducation.com). Then select a paragraph in which an author cites at least three different studies in support of one claim.

Determine whether terms in those studies are used interchangeably despite theoretical/epistemological differences.

4) In a small group, find a seemingly simple object (e.g., a table, chair, or musical instrument) and work out a definition by genus and difference that seems satisfactory to each person in the group. Note issues that seem hard to resolve.

5) Outline major points that describe your own belief system about what should constitute "quality music" in the curriculum. Take a key term from one of those collected points and define it lexically, operationally, and by genus and difference.

6) Select three published articles in the realm of philosophical inquiry and determine a) purpose(s) and/or questions, b) line(s) of argumentation, c) definitions of terms, d) references to pertinent literature (note primary and secondary sources), and e) conclusions drawn. Evaluate the studies according to the criteria described in this chapter.

7) Find or develop examples that fit the fallacies of argumentation provided in this chapter.

8) Examine and try to label the definitions you find in a selected number of published research studies, particular theses and dissertations.

Recommended Reading

On Philosophy in General

Abel, R. (1976). *Man is the measure: A cordial invitation to the central problems of philosophy.* Free Press.

Cathcart, T., & Klein, D. (2008). *Plato and a platypus walk into a bar . . .: Understanding philosophy through jokes.* Penguin Books.

Durant, W. (1961). *The story of philosophy: The lives and opinions of the world's greatest philosophers.* The Pocket Library.

Fost, P. S., & Baggini, J. (2020). *The philosopher's toolkit: A compendium of philosophical concepts and methods* (3rd ed.). Wiley-Blackwell.

Harris, E. E. (2000). *Apocalypse and paradigm: Science and everyday thinking.* Praeger.

Russell, B. (1945). *A history of Western philosophy* (14th ed.). Simon and Schuster.

Whitehead, A. N. (1967). *The aims of education and other essays.* Free Press. (Originally published in 1929 by Macmillan)

Zalta, E. N. (Ed.) (2021). *The Stanford encyclopedia of philosophy.* Stanford Center for the Study of Language and Information, Stanford University. https://plato.stanford.edu.

On Logic

Allen, M. (2013). *Smart thinking: Skills for critical understanding and writing* (2nd ed.). Oxford.

Crosswhite, J. (1996). *The rhetoric of reason: Writing and the attractions of argument.* University of Wisconsin Press.

Hurley, P. J., & Watson, L. (2017). *A concise introduction to logic* (13th ed.). Cengage.

Perelman, C. (Ed.) (1975). *Dialectics.* (International Institute of Philosophy, Entretiens in Varna, 15–22 September 1973). Martinus Nijhoff.

Popper, K. R. (1959). *The logic of scientific discovery.* Basic Books.

Popper, K. R. (1968). *Conjectures and refutations: The growth of scientific knowledge.* Harper and Row.

On Aesthetics (and Music Education)

Duvenage, P. (2003). *Habermas and aesthetics: The limits of communicative reason.* Polity Press.

Macarthur, S. (2002). *Feminist aesthetics in music.* Greenwood Press.

Meyer, L. B. (1956). *Emotion and meaning in music.* Chicago University Press.

Meyer, L. B. (1994). *Music, the arts, and ideas: Patterns and predictions in twentieth-century culture.* Chicago University Press.

Reimer, B. (1962). Leonard Meyer's theory of value and greatness in music. *Journal of Research in Music Education, 10*(2), 87–99. https://doi.org/10.2307/3343992

Reimer, B. (2002). *A philosophy of music education: Advancing the vision.* Prentice Hall.

Reimer, B. (2009). *Seeking the significance of music education: Essays and reflections.* Rowman & Littlefield.

Schwadron, A.A. (1975). Research directions in comparative music aesthetics and music education. *Journal of Aesthetics, 9*(1), 99–109. https://doi.org/10.2307/3331765

On the Aesthetic/Paraxial Conversation

Alperson, P. (2011). Music education. In T. Gracyk & A. Kania (Eds.), *The Routledge companion to philosophy and music* (pp. 614–623). Routledge.

Elliott, D. J., & Silverman, M. (2012). Rethinking philosophy, re-viewing musical-emotional experiences. In *The Oxford handbook of philosophy in music education* (pp. 37–62). Oxford University Press. https://doi.org/10.1093/oxfordhb/9780195394733.013.0003

McPhail, G. (2018). Too much noise in the classroom? Towards a praxis of conceptualization. *Philosophy of Music Education Review, 26*(2), 176–198. https://doi.org/10.2979/philmusieducrevi.26.2.05

Panaiotidi, E. (2002). What is philosophy of music education and do we really need it? *Studies in Philosophy and Education, 21*(3), 229–252. https://doi.org/10.1023/A:1015513807617

Reimer, B. (2012). Uncomfortable with immanence: The nature and value of music and music education as singular or supplemental. In *The Oxford handbook of philosophy in music education* (pp. 111–128). Oxford University Press. https://doi.org/10.1093/oxfordhb/9780195394733.013.0006

Other Recommended Sources

Amedco, G. (2008). Difficulties encountered in the application of the phenomenological method in the social sciences. *Indo-Pacific Journal of Phenomenology, 8.* www.ajol.info/index.php/ipjp/article/viewFile/65428/53118

Barrett, J. R. (Ed.) (2009). *Music education at a crossroads: Realizing the goal of music for all.* R&L Education.

Bowman, W. D. & Frega, A. L. (Eds.) (2012). *The Oxford handbook of philosophy in music education.* Oxford University Press. https://doi.org/10.1093/oxfordhb/9780195394733.001.0001

Gaztambide-Fernández, R. (2010). Wherefore the musicians? *Philosophy of Music Education Review, 18*(1), 65–84. https://doi.org/10.2979/pme.2010.18.1.65

Jorgensen, E. R. (2006). On philosophical method. In R. Colwell (Ed.), *MENC handbook of research methodologies* (pp. 176–198). Oxford University Press.

Jorgensen, E. R. (2001). A dialectical view of theory and practice. *Journal of Research in Music Education, 49*(4), 343. https://doi.org/10.2307/3345617

Jorgensen, E. R. (2001). What are the roles of philosophy in music education? *Research Studies in Music Education, 17*, 19–31.

McCall, C. C. (2009). *Transforming thinking: Philosophical inquiry in the primary and secondary classroom.* Routledge.

Pirsig, R. M. (1974/1999/2005). *Zen and the art of motorcycle maintenance: An inquiry into values.* HarperCollins.

Richerme, L. K. (2013). *Complicating, considering, connecting: Rhizomatic philosophizing in music education* [Doctoral dissertation]. Arizona State University. https://repository.asu.edu/attachments/110398/content/Richerme_asu_0010E_12891.pdf

Helpful Resources

American Philosophical Association Teaching Resources: www.apaonline.org/page/teaching_resources

The Fallacy Files: www.fallacyfiles.org/index.html

Lucid Philosophy, Fallacy Quizzes: https://lucidphilosophy.com/fallacy-quizzes/

Short List of Fallacies: www.fallacydetective.com/articles/read/short-list-of-fallacies

REFERENCES

Alperson, P. (2011). Music education. In T. Gracyk & A. Kania (Eds.), *The Routledge companion to philosophy and music* (pp. 614–623). Routledge.

Autry, K. (2019). *A case for the conservatory teaching style in K-12 music education violin instruction* [Master's thesis]. California State University Long Beach. ProQuest Dissertations & Theses Global (Publication No. 2307397216).

Balija, A. T. (2015). *What do I assume? An applied lesson approach integrating critical thinking and student-directed learning* [Doctoral dissertation]. James Madison University. ProQuest Dissertations & Theses Global (Publication No. 1685389348).

Bates, V. C. B. (2019). Standing at the intersection of race and class in music education. *Action, Criticism, and Theory for Music Education, 18*(1), 117–160. https://doi.org/10.22176/act18.1.117

Bell, A. P. (2015). Can we afford these affordances? Garage band and the double-edged sword of the digital audio workstation. *Action, Theory, and Criticism for Music Education, 14*(1), 44–65. act.maydaygroup.org/articles/Bell14_1.pdf

Benton, C. W. (2002). *A study of the effects of metacognition on sight-singing achievement and attitudes among students in a middle school choral music program* [Doctoral dissertation]. Shenandoah University. ProQuest Dissertations & Theses Global (Publication No. 3077263).

Bleiker, R. (2009). *Aesthetics and world politics.* Palgrave Macmillan.

Bowman, W. D. (1992). Philosophy, criticism, and music education: Some tentative steps down a less-traveled road. *Bulletin of the Council for Research in Music Education, 114*, 1–19.

Bowman, W. D. (1998). *Philosophical perspectives on music.* Oxford University Press.

Bowman, W. D. (2012). Music's place in education. In G. E. McPherson & G. F. Welch (Eds.), *The Oxford handbook of music education* (Vol. 1, pp. 21–30). Oxford University Press. https://doi.org/10.1093/oxfordhb/9780199730810.013.0003

Bowman, W. D., & Frega, A. L. (Eds.) (2012). *The Oxford handbook of philosophy in music education.* Oxford University Press. https://doi.org/10.1093/oxfordhb/9780195394733.001.0001

Bradley, D. (2007). The sounds of silence: Talking race in music education. *Action, Criticism, and Theory for Music Education, 6*(4), 132–162. http://act.maydaygroup.org/articles/Bradley6_4.pdf

Bradley, D. (2012). Good for what, good for whom? Decolonizing music education philosophies. In W. D. Bowman & A. L. Frega (Eds.), *The Oxford handbook of philosophy in music education* (pp. 409–433). Oxford University Press.

Burrage, M. L. (2013). *Jordan D. "Chick" Chavis Jr.: His legacy and role in the implementation of instrumental music education in the Nashville African American community* [Master's thesis]. Tennessee State University. ProQuest Dissertations & Theses Global (Publication No. 1461773820).

Cee, V. J. (2008). *Christopher Small and music education, 1977–2007* [Doctoral dissertation]. University of Massachusetts Amherst. ProQuest Dissertations & Theses Global (Publication No. 304578774).

Chandler, D. L. (2004). *Colleen Jean Kirk (1918–2004): Her life, career and her influence on American choral music education* [Doctoral dissertation]. Florida State University. http://purl.flvc.org/fsu/fd/FSU_migr_etd-3908

Cho, K. (2010). *A constructivist approach to studio instruction: A case study of a flute class* [Doctoral dissertation]. Columbia University Teachers College. ProQuest Dissertations & Theses Global (Publication No. 756254566).

Chudnoff, E. (2007). *A guide to philosophical writing.* Harvard Writing Project. https://philosophy.fas.harvard.edu/files/phildept/files/guide_to_philosophical_writing.pdf

Cohen, M. L. (2007). *Christopher Small's concept of musicking: Toward a theory of choral singing pedagogy in prison contexts* [Doctoral dissertation]. University of Kansas. http://hdl.handle.net/1808/29289

Countryman, J., & Stewart Rose, L. (2017). Wellbeing in the secondary music classroom: Ideas from hero's journeys and online gaming. *Philosophy of Music Education Review, 25*(2), 128–149. https://doi.org/10.2979/philmusieducrevi.25.2.03

Dale, P. (2012). Derridean justice and the DJ: A classroom impossibility? *Philosophy of Music Education Review, 20*(2), 135–153. https://doi.org/10.2979/philmusieducrevi.20.2.135

Dees, M. I. (2005). *A review of eight university clarinet studios: An investigation of pedagogical style, content and philosophy through observations and interviews* [Doctoral dissertation]. Florida State University. ProQuest Dissertations & Theses Global (Publication No. 304996546).

Dexter, J. (2014). *Making music matter: Social relevance and community engagement as a catalyst for transformation through the choral arts* [Master's thesis]. California State University Los Angeles. ProQuest Dissertations & Theses Global (Publication No. 1611895131).

Elliott, D. J. (1995). *Music matters: A new philosophy of music education.* Oxford University Press.

Elliott, D. J., & Silverman, M. (2012). Rethinking philosophy, re-viewing musical-emotional experiences. In *The Oxford handbook of philosophy in music education* (pp. 37–62). Oxford University Press. https://doi.org/10.1093/oxfordhb/9780195394733.013.0003

Eshelman, D. A. (1995). *The instructional knowledge of exemplary elementary general music teachers: Commonalities based on David J. Elliott's Model of the Professional Music Educator* [Doctoral dissertation]. University of Oklahoma. ProQuest Dissertations & Theses Global (Publication No. 304211896).

Field, S. T. (1997). *Critical thinking skills and the secondary school choral music curriculum* [Doctoral dissertation]. Columbia University Teachers College. ProQuest Dissertations & Theses Global (Publication No. 304345843).

Fieser, J., & Dowden, B. (1995). *The Internet encyclopedia of philosophy.* www.iep.utm.edu/

Freer, P. K. (2019). In dialogue. *Philosophy of Music Education Review, 27*(1), 87–91. https://doi.org/10.2979/philmusieducrevi.27.1.07

Froehlich, H. C., & Cattley, G. (1993). Language, metaphor, and analogy in the music education research process. In E. R. Jorgensen (Ed.), *Philosopher, teacher, musician: Perspectives on music education* (pp. 243–258). University of Illinois Press.

Garberich, M. D. (2008). *The nature of inspiration in artistic creativity* [Doctoral dissertation]. Michigan State University. ProQuest Dissertations & Theses Global (Publication No. 3348106).

Gaztambide-Fernández, R. (2010). Wherefore the musicians? *Philosophy of Music Education Review, 18*(1), 65–84. https://doi.org/10.2979/pme.2010.18.1.65

Goldman, A., & O'Connor, C. (2021, Spring). Social epistemology. In E. N. Zalta (Ed.), *The Stanford encyclopedia of philosophy.* https://plato.stanford.edu/archives/spr2021/entries/epistemology-social/>

Gordon, E. (1980). *Learning sequences in music: Skill, content, and patterns.* G.I.A. Publications.

Gould, E. (2007). Legible bodies in music education: Becoming-matter. *Action, Criticism, and Theory for Music Education, 6*(4), 201–223. http://act.maydaygroup.org/articles/Gould6_4.pdf

Helfer, J. A. (2003). *Susanne K. Langer's epistemology of mind as an interpretive resource for music education* [Doctoral dissertation]. University of Illinois Urbana-Champaign. http://hdl.handle.net/2142/79749

Hess, J. (2017). Critiquing the critical: The casualties and paradoxes of critical pedagogy in music education. *Philosophy of Music Education Review, 25*(2), 171–191. https://doi.org/10.2979/philmusieducrevi.25.2.05

Jensen-Hole, C. (2005). *Experiencing the interdependent nature of musicianship and educatorship as defined by David J. Elliott in the context of the collegiate level vocal jazz ensemble* [Doctoral dissertation]. University of North Texas. https://digital.library.unt.edu/ark:/67531/metadc4867/

Jorgensen, E. R. (2001). A dialectical view of theory and practice. *Journal of Research in Music Education, 49*(4), 343–359. https://doi.org/10.2307/3345617

Jorgensen, E. R. (2006). On philosophical method. In R. Colwell (Ed.), *MENC handbook of research methodologies* (pp. 176–198). Oxford University Press.

Kedem, Y. (2008). *Performance, conservation, and creativity: Mentoring for musicianship in four string music studios* [Doctoral dissertation]. University of Illinois Urbana-Champaign. ProQuest Dissertations & Theses Global (Publication No. 304626866).

Kertz-Welzel, A. (2008). Music education in the twenty-first century: A cross-cultural comparison of German and American music education towards a new concept of international dialogue. *Music Education Research, 10*(4), 439–449. https://doi.org/10.1080/14613800802547672

Krönig, F. K. (2021). Six fallacies regarding the question of whether we conceive of practices as "Musical". *Philosophy of Music Education Review, 29*(1), 102–116. https://doi.org/10.2979/philmusieducrevi.29.1.07

Kuehmann, K. M. (1987). *A theoretical model for curriculum development in general music for fundamentalist Christian elementary schools* [Doctoral dissertation]. Arizona State University. ProQuest Dissertations & Theses Global (Publication No. 303561727).

Lamb, R., Dolloff, L., & Wieland Howe, S. (2002). Feminism, feminist research, and gender research in music education: A selective review. In R. Colwell & C. Richardson (Eds.), *The new handbook of research on music learning and teaching* (pp. 648–774). Oxford University Press.

Lee, W. R. (1982). *Education through music: The life and work of Charles Hubert Farnsworth (1859–1947)* [Doctoral dissertation]. University of Kentucky. ProQuest Dissertations & Theses Global (Publication No. 303238294).

Louth, J. P. (2008). *Music, metaphor, and ideology: Toward a critical theory of forms in music education* [Doctoral dissertation]. The University of Western Ontario. ProQuest Dissertations & Theses Global (Publication No. 304350450).

Mantie, R. (2012). Bands and/as music education: Antinomies and the struggle for legitimacy. *Philosophy of Music Education Review, 20*(1), 63–81. https://doi.org/10.2979/philmusieducrevi.20.1.63

McAfee, N. (2018, Fall). Feminist philosophy. In E. N. Zalta (Ed.), *The Stanford encyclopedia of philosophy*. https://plato.stanford.edu/archives/fall2018/entries/feminist-philosophy

McPhail, G. (2018). Too much noise in the classroom? Towards a praxis of conceptualization. *Philosophy of Music Education Review, 26*(2), 176–198. https://doi.org/10.2979/philmusieducrevi.26.2.05

Mortyakova, J. (2011). *Existential piano teacher: The application of Jean-Paul Sartre's philosophy to piano instruction in a higher educational setting* [Doctoral dissertation]. University of Miami. ProQuest Dissertations & Theses Global (Publication No. 3358229).

Orrel, M. S. (1995). *The work of Grace C. Nash in music education in the United States, 1960–1990, and her influence upon members of the American Orff-Schulwerk Association in the states of Arizona and Colorado* [Doctoral dissertation]. University of Houston. ProQuest Dissertations & Theses Global (Publication No. 9611456).

Panaiotidi, E. (2002). What is philosophy of music education and do we really need it? *Studies in Philosophy and Education, 21*(3), 229–252. https://doi.org/10.1023/A:1015513807617

Parkinson, T., & Smith, G. D. (2015). Towards an epistemology of authenticity in higher popular music education. *Action, Criticism and Theory for Music Education, 14*(1), 93–127. act.maydaygroup.org/articles/ParkinsonSmith14_1.pdf

Rainbow, E., & Froehlich, H. (1987). *Research in music education: An introduction to systematic inquiry.* Schirmer.

Reeves-Johnson, P. L. (2002). *Abraham A. Schwadron: His life and contributions to music education* [Doctoral dissertation]. Florida State University. ProQuest Dissertations & Theses Global (Publication No. 276317480).

Regelski, T., & Gates, T. (Eds.) (2009). *Music education for changing times: Guiding visions for practice (landscapes: The arts, aesthetics, and education).* Springer.

Reimer, B. (2008). Research in music education: Personal and professional reflections in a time of perplexity: 2008 senior researcher award acceptance speech. *Journal of Research in Music Education, 56*(3), 190–204. https://doi.org/10.1177/0022429408322709

Reimer, B. (2012). Uncomfortable with immanence: The nature and value of music and music education as singular or supplemental. In *The Oxford handbook of philosophy in music education* (pp. 111–128). Oxford University Press. https://doi.org/10.1093/oxfordhb/9780195394733.013.0006

Revkin, L. K. (1984). *An historical and philosophical inquiry into the development of Dalcroze eurhythmics and its influence on music education in the French cantons of Switzerland* [Doctoral dissertation]. Northwestern University. ProQuest Dissertations & Theses Global (Publication No. 8411180).

Richerme, L. K. (2013). *Complicating, considering, connecting: Rhizomatic philosophizing in music education* [Doctoral dissertation]. Arizona State University. https://repository.asu.edu/attachments/110398/content/Richerme_asu_0010E_12891.pdf

Richerme, L. K. (2015). Who are musickers? *Philosophy of Music Education Review, 23*(1), 82–101. https://doi.org/10.2979/philmusieducrevi.23.1.82

Rosabal-Coto, G. (2016). *Music learning in Costa Rica: A postcolonial institutional ethnography* [Doctoral dissertation]. Sibelius Academy of the University of the Arts Helsinki. https://helda.helsinki.fi/handle/10138/235009

Russell, B. (1959). *Wisdom of the West: A historical survey of Western philosophy in its social and political setting.* Doubleday.

Saint-Andre, P. (2013). *Index of ISMS.* www.ismbook.com/ismlist.html

Scarlato, M. K. M. (2021). Go ask Alice: How is a raven like a band director? *Philosophy of Music Education Review, 29*(1), 4–23. https://doi.org/10.2979/philmusieducrevi.29.1.02

Scruton, R. (1997). *The aesthetics of music.* Oxford University Press.

Shiraishi, F. (2001). *Calvin Brainerd Cady (1851–1928): Unification of intellect and emotion in music education* [Doctoral dissertation]. University of Kansas. ProQuest Dissertations & Theses Global (Publication No. 304697235).

Small, C. (1997). Musicking: A ritual in social space. In R. Rideout (Ed.), *On the sociology of music education* (pp. 1–12). Proceedings of the Oklahoma Symposium for Music Education in April, 1995, Oklahoma University School of Music, Norman, Oklahoma.

Small, C. (1998). *Musicking: The meanings of performing and listening*. University Press of New England.

Smith, D. W. (2018). Phenomenology. In E. N. Zalta (Ed.), *The Stanford encyclopedia of philosophy* (Summer 2018). Metaphysics Research Lab, Stanford University. https://plato.stanford.edu/archives/sum2018/entries/phenomenology/

Tan, L. (2016). A transcultural theory of thinking for instrumental music education: Philosophical insights from Confucius and Dewey. *Philosophy of Music Education Review*, *24*(2), 151–169. https://doi.org/10.2979/philmusieducrevi.24.2.03

van der Schyff, D., Schiavio, A., & Elliott, D. J. (2016). Critical ontology for an enactive music pedagogy. *Action, Criticism, and Theory for Music Education*, *15*(4), 81–121. http://act.maydaygroup.org/volume-15-issue-5/act-15-5-81-121/

van Inwagen, P., & Sullivan, M. (2020, Spring). Metaphysics. In E. N. Zalta (Ed.), *The Stanford encyclopedia of philosophy*. https://plato.stanford.edu/archives/spr2020/entries/metaphysics

VanWelden, K. (2004). Racially stereotyped music and conductor race: Perceptions of performance. *Bulletin of the Council for Research in Music Education*, *160*, 38–48. www.jstor.org/stable/40319217

Whale, M. (2009). *Music as the between: The idea of meeting in existence, music and education* [Doctoral dissertation]. University of Toronto. https://central.bac-lac.gc.ca/.item?id=TC-OTU-19248&op=pdf&app=Library&oclc_number=1033108244

Whalen, M. F. (2008). *Charles L. Gary: His contribution to and perspective on music education in the United States* [Doctoral dissertation]. Catholic University of America. ProQuest Dissertations & Theses Global (Publication No. 3294711).

White-Hope, S. (2019). Elma Lewis, her school of fine arts, and her vision of arts education as cultural emancipation. *Bulletin of the Council for Research in Music Education*, *219*, 47–60. https://doi.org/10.5406/bulcouresmusedu.219.0047

Wiktionary. (2017). *Appendix: Glossary of philosophical isms*. https://en.wiktionary.org/wiki/Appendix:Glossary_of_philosophical_isms

Williams, B. J. (2010). *Music composition pedagogy: A history, philosophy and guide* [Doctoral dissertation]. Ohio State University. ProQuest Dissertations & Theses Global (Publication No. 759530017).

Williams, D. A., & Shannon, S. G. (Eds.) (2004). *August Wilson and Black aesthetics*. Palgrave Macmillan.

Williams, Y. Y. (2017). *The intellectual capital of the Black music educators of the Twin Cities (1974–1994)* [Doctoral dissertation]. University of Minnesota. https://hdl.handle.net/11299/188917

Zalta, E. N. (2021). *Stanford encyclopedia of philosophy*. Center for the Study of Language and Information. https://plato.stanford.edu/

CHAPTER 6

Historical Inquiry
Getting Inside the Process

Marie McCarthy

This chapter describes

- Historical research as a mode of inquiry.
- Contemporary trends and developments.
- Ethics and Historical Research.
- Steps for conducting a historical study.
    - exploring topics of interest and framing research questions
    - locating, selecting and verifying sources
    - crafting a proposal for a historical study
    - organizing, critiquing and interpreting sources
    - making inferences and drawing conclusions
    - organizing and writing the narrative
    - publishing the findings

Numerous studies as well as the cases presented in this book illustrate the variety of approaches common in the historical mode of inquiry.

INTRODUCTION

Doing historical research in music education takes you on a journey into the past for the purpose of collecting evidence and creating a historical narrative. The evidence comes in many forms of primary sources, from documents to photographs, oral testimonies to recordings, and other traces of the past in the present (Burke, 2001). Using primary sources, the researcher creates a critical account of the past by analyzing and interpreting the evidence in the context of social, cultural, political, and educational values of the time period.

Aware of the importance of bringing historical research to life in the classroom, *Prof. E.* frequently had students examine and evaluate primary source materials. To illustrate the value and power of visual media in historical research, he brought to class two books that included photographs and images of music education in past

DOI: 10.4324/9781003057703-9

eras: The *Music Educators Journal*, "Special Issue: The Sesquicentennial" (MENC, 1988) that marked the sesquicentennial of the introduction of music into the public schools in the United States (1838–1988), and *MENC: A Century of Service to Music Education 1907– 2007* (2007), a book that marked the centenary of the founding of the Music Supervisors National Conference, forerunner to what today is known as NAfME: The National Association for Music Education. In addition to the two sources, he shared photographs of music education in the context of racial and ethnic groups not represented in the two books.

Prof. E. presented a selection of photographs and asked the members of the class to share questions that arose from examining them. Organizing the class in groups, he then asked each group to choose a particular photograph. Reminding the class that "who, what, where, when, why, and how" questions had guided discussion in other sessions, he presented these questions:

- *Who is in the photo? Where was the photo taken, and by whom?*
- *When was it taken? What was the occasion and context?*
- *How does the content reveal the culture and values of the time period?*
- *What questions does the photo elicit?*
- *What can I learn from this photograph?*
- *How might the source be useful for research purposes?*

The discussion of the photographs spoke to the power of visual media to provide a window into the past, to stimulate questions, to impact the historical imagination, and to cause self-reflection about one's assumptions and biases.

Exploration: Thinking about History in Your Professional Life

Before proceeding to choose a topic to research, think about what "history" means to you and what you believe about its function and value in the lives of music educators, individually and collectively.

HISTORICAL RESEARCH AS A MODE OF INQUIRY

> To possess a historical sense does not mean simply to possess information about the past. It means to have a different consciousness, a historical consciousness, to have incorporated into our minds a mode of understanding that profoundly influences the way we look at the world. History adds another dimension to our view of the world and enriches our experience.
>
> (Wood, 2008, p. 11)

The word "history" has etymological roots in the ancient Greek word *historia*, translated as "inquiry" or "knowledge acquired through investigation." This meaning is resonant of the Latin meaning cited in Chapter 1 (*histor*, learned person) since both refer to someone who is intellectually curious and seeks wisdom through inquiry. The historical researcher creates a narrative by chronicling past actions and events, identifying relationships and patterns among pieces of evidence, inferring meaning from those relationships, and finding echoes of the past in contemporary trends and practices.

Historian Lawrence Stone defined narrative as "the organization of material in a chronologically sequenced order and the focusing of the content on a single coherent story, albeit with sub-plots" (1979, p. 3). Narrative is descriptive in form and provides an account of how an individual life story, community, institution, set of norms and practices, to name some examples, unfolded in time. Through narrative, the researcher connects and creates a sequence of events across time and explains and interprets the outcomes of actions and events. Several challenges and tensions can arise in presenting history in and through narrative. Among others, the researcher might make connections that are not true to what actually occurred, tell the story as he thinks it should have happened, or gather some evidence and neglect to find or include evidence that presents an alternative viewpoint or line of reasoning. As you can see, there is considerable responsibility associated with historical research and writing, a point that will be explored later in the chapter.

What kinds of narratives emerge from historical study in music education? We learn about the lives of persons who contributed in important ways to music education; the development of curriculum, pedagogy and programs at local, regional, and international levels; and the evolution of institutions and organizations. Researchers also investigate the emergence and demise of trends and practices; the participation of particular groups and sub-cultures in formal and informal music education; and the transmission of music in various contexts as it relates to political, social and cultural history.

Why Engage in Historical Research?

Research about music teaching and learning in the past in all its forms and contexts is an important task of the music education profession. Historical knowledge deepens professional understanding and knowledge. Wisdom gained from an examination of past practices and values informs present contexts. In the process, it can foster community, identity, and continuity between generations of music educators.

Coming to know the past gives us a sense of how music education today came to be—for example, how instructional practices evolved, what stimulated change in curriculum, how music in schools interacted with musical cultures outside of school, and how and why music was valued, or not, in education. This kind of professional knowledge provides a frame of reference, a source of inspiration, and an advocacy tool for music teachers and for professional organizations.

Learning about the conditions under which teachers taught in bygone times generates a sense of admiration for their accomplishments and gratitude for the resources available today. It highlights how you are part of a lineage of professionals seeking to broaden and deepen the impact of music in individual lives and in society at large. Historical knowledge also provides a foundation for understanding trends in music education and for evaluating new curriculum materials. Insights gained from historical study allow us as music educators to see who we are, where we came from, and to what we belong (Wood, 2008, p. 8), thus lending a sense of continuity and depth to our work. For these reasons, it is a professional responsibility for each generation to add to the body of research literature on the history of music education.

Overview of the Historical Research Process

Research based on historical inquiry is similar to that of other modes in some ways. All research involves systematic documentation of evidence, methodological rigor, scholarly standards of citation and sourcing, interpretation of evidence, and contextualization and evaluation of findings. Historical research also has unique processes and challenges. With the exception of oral history, the historian uses data sources from bygone times, and thus relies heavily on imaginative and intuitive strategies to make connections between pieces of evidence. The historical researcher may use multiple fields of literature in the arts, humanities and social sciences to support interpretation of evidence—for example, education, musicology, history, psychology, sociology, and cultural studies. The focus is on crafting a narrative to convey a chronological sequence of events and actions and to infer meanings from multiple layers of evidence gathered from primary sources. Collingwood (1946/1994) captured the essence of doing history when he wrote that history is a science of a special kind, whose business is:

> to study events not accessible to our observation, and to study these events inferentially, arguing to them from something else which is accessible to our observation, and which the historian calls "evidence" for the events in which he is interested.
>
> (pp. 251–252)

In examining evidence, you navigate between investigative work on the one hand and humanistic interpretation on the other. You are guided in this process by critical thinking skills which are key in moving a historical account from a mere chronicling of past actions and events to uncovering the thoughts and motivations of those whose stories are being narrated. Throughout, you recognize your own biases and assumptions, evaluate related research studies, and identify a topic that leads to a research purpose. You question the veracity of sources, examine evidence for motivation, error, and bias, corroborate pieces of evidence, and make inferences.

All of these moments of critical thought contribute to a historical narrative that is communicated to the reader in a voice that is, on the one hand, detached in the presentation of chronological facts and sequences and, on the other hand, personally engaged in description and interpretation. The manner in which you achieve this balance varies. Traditional approaches to history tend toward dispassionate reporting, whereas contemporary approaches are more oriented toward the inclusion of the author's voice, empathy, and worldview. The change resulted in part from a movement away from the idea of history as a singular set of facts and truths to a view of history as a set of perspectives that can be re-examined and revised using different lenses to view and interpret.

Visualizing the process can help to distinguish historical study from other forms of inquiry. Which of these metaphors would you likely draw upon when engaging in historical inquiry: History as a window or lens into the past; a map or a canvas on which a story is framed; a jigsaw puzzle to be solved; a sculpture not yet realized, waiting for a sculptor to chip away extraneous material and bring it to life? As you develop your topic, create your own image or metaphor for the process of doing historical research.

DOING HISTORY IN CONTEMPORARY TIMES: TRENDS AND DEVELOPMENTS

> The music educator must operate with a proper realization of his present and past place in society not only for the sense of pride that such realization brings with it but also for the fund of wisdom thus made available with which to deal with contemporary problems.
>
> (Britton, 1969, pp. 109–110)

The nature of historical inquiry has changed in recent decades, resulting in part from developments in philosophy of history, expansion of intellectual paradigms, and advancements in technology and media. Philosophy of history is part of the larger area of historiography, the study of history—its past achievements, approaches, methods and effects (Humphreys, 2015). The functions and uses of history came under scrutiny when scholars in a number of disciplines began to evaluate its political effects. Questions arose such as: Whose stories have been told? Whose voices have been heard and whose voices remain silent?

The idea that there is one universal or master narrative of the past, one story that produces a single historical truth for all time, was challenged in the latter half of the 20th century. Influenced by postmodern thinking, critical theory, and other intellectual paradigms, historians began to acknowledge the importance of documenting multiple historical narratives, using different vantage points as starting places and different lenses to examine and interpret evidence.

Revisionist Views of the Past

Revisionist approaches to history focus on bringing values and ideologies of the present to bear on investigations and interpretations of the past. Recognizing the limitations of depending on one grand narrative, revisionist historians are therefore critical of earlier interpretations of the past, particularly those written from the perspective of dominant groups that re-construct the past from their own vantage point, advancing their values and political agendas (Lee, A. H.-C., 2002). Historical study itself is dynamic and always evolving (McCollum & Hebert, 2014, esp. pp. 372–375). As social values and political ideologies change, new perspectives call us to look again into the past for new stories and new ways of re-framing and re-telling old stories. Thus, revisionist historians have expanded the paradigms used for interpretation, brought forth alternative viewpoints of marginalized groups, and created new narratives out of evidence that was previously kept silent due to neglect, or worse, oppression.

For an excellent discussion of revisionist history, read Carol Pemberton's (1987) article on the topic, in which she uses the life of Lowell Mason to illustrate how perceptions of his contributions during his lifetime contrast with those of the late 20th century. She concludes that when we recognize influences on historical writing, our own and others, "we become more perceptive readers and more insightful writers" (p. 213).

Expanding the Scope of Historical Research

Parallel to the introduction of revisionist approaches, historians have expanded the paradigms and disciplinary bases they draw on to include sociological, feminist, cultural and post-colonial perspectives (see Cox, 2002, pp. 695–706). These trends and developments have influenced historical study in music education (McCarthy, 1999, 2012; Simpson, 2019). They also have contributed to fundamental changes related to where we look for topics, what we look for, how we look, and why we are motivated to study certain topics. Thus, the scope of historical research is expanding. An increasing number of studies account for political, cultural, economic and social influences on music education (e.g., Chybowski, 2017; Goble, 2009; Volk, 2007; Sullivan, 2019). Insights from such studies enlighten our understanding of the relationships between music, society, and education.

Furthermore, studies about the history of music education in settings outside the public school serve to establish a more complete picture of music learning and teaching (e.g, Shansky, 2020). And, the lives of all music educators are under consideration, not only those who taught in public schools or held leadership positions, although such work remains important (Volk Tuohey, 2015). Similarly, the stories of all social groups and classes, ethnicities, and marginalized groups are beginning to receive the attention they deserve. Their stories are being told, some for the first time (e.g., Björkén-Nyberg, 2019; Clark, 2019; Groulx, 2018; Handel & Humphreys, 2005; Howe, 2009; Lee, 1997; May, 2005; Sullivan, 2017). Increasingly, historical researchers contextualize their studies within the social norms and cultural values of the time period under study.

Contemporary Approaches and Methodologies

When Rainbow and Froehlich (1987) were writing about historical research in the mid-1980s, they referred to a broadening of approaches from the social sciences and the natural sciences—comparative historical research, oral history, psychohistory, and quantitative (social-scientific) history. With the exception of psychohistory, these approaches are increasingly present in historical studies in music education.

Comparative Historical Research

The topic of comparative and cross-cultural research has entered the mainstream of music education in recent decades (Cox, 2002; Lepherd, 1995; Kertz-Welzel, 2015; McCarthy, 2012). Cox (2002) argued for the value of "historically grounded comparative work," and for encouraging music educators in a variety of countries and cultures "to question what they take for granted in their practice" (p. 703). After carrying out a cross-cultural historical study, Gruhn (2001) recommended further studies that engage in cross-cultural analysis, arguing that such studies "could result in better understandings of the roots of ideas and practices that are or have been implemented in another cultural context" (p. 18). Cox and Stevens (2017) adopted a cross-cultural approach in their edited volume, *The Origins and Foundations of Music Education: Cross-Cultural Historical Studies of Music in Compulsory Schooling.* This expanded second edition of national case studies can stimulate thinking about other topics to study cross-culturally. As comparative and cross-cultural historical research develops, it reveals the predominant factors that impacted music education practices internationally, in particular the spread of European music and music pedagogy across the world during various colonial periods.

Oral History

The Oral History Association (2021) defines it as "a field of study and a method of gathering, preserving and interpreting the voices and memories of people, communities, and participants in past events" (www.oralhistory.org). Those spoken firsthand memories are collected during an interview that is focused on "a specific historical topic, place, or event of interest" (Sommer & Quinlan, 2018, p. 1). An interview becomes an oral history "when it has been recorded, processed in some way, made available in an archive, library, or other repository, or reproduced in relatively verbatim form for publication" (Ritchie, 2003, p. 24). Oral history, then, can be understood as both process (the act of interviewing) and product (the record that results from the interview) (Shopes, 2011). The purpose of an interview could be either to document a person's account of his or her life or to examine a particular time frame or series of events from the perspective of those who lived through them.

The interviewee is referred to as the narrator or the informant. Interview topics focus on the interviewee's recollections of specific life experiences or events, or perspectives about what it was like to live or work with an influential figure or in a particular place or era, among others. Oral history can also document the experiences of groups, institutions, and communities. Such oral histories can serve, for example, to document traditions and cultures that are disappearing, to tell the stories of marginalized and indigenous groups whose voices have been excluded in mainstream history, or to chronicle a community's response to a major event.

Techniques for conducting interviews in oral history follow those advocated in qualitative as well as quantitative research methods (see Chapters 8 and 10 for further information). Key to good interviewing is careful preparation. Know as much as possible about the interviewee so that your questions are to the point and invite responses that open the dialogue for rich exchange. Remember that interviewees are often recalling events that took place many years ago and their memories may not be clear and accurate and need to be stimulated with, for example, a photograph or artifact related to the topic.

In sum, oral history is "both the oldest type of historical inquiry, predating the written word, and one of the most modern, initiated with tape recorders in the 1940s and now using 21st-century digital technologies" (Oral History Association, 2021). The possibilities for using oral history to research aspects of music education are many and varied. Consider how such an approach might be valuable in relation to your research topic.

Quantitative History

Records based on quantitative data (typically used to illustrate the occurrence or frequency of events, trends, etc.) have been used more frequently in recent years as a form of historical evidence. For example, Wasiak (2000) included statistical data from department of education records in his study of school bands in Saskatchewan. In her study of the inclusion of women composers in college music history textbooks, Baker (2003) presented her data in tables to show frequencies of representation. Handel and Humphreys (2005) used population statistics in their study of the Phoenix Indian School Band, while Preston and Humphreys (2007) conducted a quantitative analysis of dissertations in music education and music therapy completed in the 20th century. Sanders (2015, 2017) used a quantitative approach to categorize temperance songs that appeared in school songbooks published between 1840–1860 and 1865–1899, respectively.

In sum, quantitative data can serve different purposes in historical studies, among them: to create a picture of the size and magnitude of a trend or development, to summarize themes present in sets of data, to ground or refute other kinds of evidence, to provide precise data to complement other primary sources, to compare statistical data from one place or region with others, or to back up claims leading to conclusions.

Developments in Technology and Media

Technological advances greatly enhance possibilities for creating and re-constructing the past. For example, digital video recording of oral history interviews is a superior source for biographical study and an effective way of preserving recent history for future researchers. Digitized recordings of archival media present a clear record of the past that allows you to move closer to the historical event or action. The availability of online archival materials and serials, among other resources, provides easy access to sources. When working with archival material, the researcher can use a digital camera to capture images and later include them in a study. Such developments have impacted positively the research process, the quality and scope of images included in a published study, and the types of supplemental material that can accompany a published study.

Visual images in historical studies are coming into their own, in part because advancements in technology have facilitated their inclusion in publications. The power of visual images to bring the researcher to the heart of a historical moment, to stimulate questions and wonderings, and to reveal the values and priorities of a group and its surrounding culture cannot be underestimated.

At no other time in our professional history has there been a more dynamic and comprehensive array of topical and methodological resources available to the historian. The field of historical research in music education is vast, the task is noble, and the outcome can be fulfilling and valuable.

FRAMING A RESEARCH STUDY: TOPIC, PURPOSE AND RESEARCH QUESTIONS

The initial tasks in the research process described here do not necessarily happen one after the other. The process is cyclic, similar to the "think, read, observe, share" process described in Chapter 1. As you read sources, you refine the initial topic that interested you. As you discuss your topic with the instructor and classmates, your interest may shift and new questions may arise. Similarly, as you read sources, a gap in the research literature may be revealed.

Choosing a Topic

Sources that inspire historical questions are many and varied, such as: teaching experience, historical papers or artifacts that are close at hand and can be linked to a meaningful professional question, your cultural background, a source that you stumble upon and that piques curiosity, or a sense of professional responsibility to document a particular topic. For example, Christy's research interest originated in her extensive voice teaching: She was curious about the works of vocal pedagogues since 1800 for continuity with teaching voice today.

Similarly, Isbell's (2006) curiosity about the history of the unique Steamboat Springs High School Ski Band (a band providing entertainment for skiing festivals in Steamboat Springs, Colorado) that he conducted was his inspiration for a research study. Documenting its history, Isbell addressed these questions: "What factors contributed to the Steamboat Springs high school ski band's creation in 1935? What changes have occurred in performance practice since its creation? What is the relationship between the ensemble and the local community?" (p. 25).

Inspiration for a study often originates in our own backyard, in historical documents or artifacts that are close at hand. Ward-Steinman (2003) drew on a treasure trove of historical data that she found in family archives. Her father and grandfather managed Madura's Danceland in the greater Chicago area, and she had access to their papers and used them "to gain unique insights into big band musicians' compensation during the Big Band Era" (p. 167). Cultural background, too, can be a motivating factor in choosing a topic. Chi-Hui's research interests originated in her first point of reference for music education, her home country of Taiwan, as she compared her experience there with music education in her adopted country, the United States. She anticipated that such a study might give her insights into prevailing practices in her own country and possibly strengthen her professional philosophy and pedagogy.

Scholars also stumble upon topics that pique their curiosity and inspire them to pursue a study. For example, when McCarthy was reading Birge's *History of Public School Music in the United States* (1928/1966), she noticed a reference to an "international gathering" of music educators in London in 1928 and a forthcoming meeting in Switzerland in 1929 (p. 270). She was surprised to read this reference because prior knowledge led her to believe that organized international activity began with the founding of the International Society for Music Education (ISME) in 1953. Curious, she decided to examine further. She searched for published studies describing these earlier events and determined that they had not been documented, at least not in English-language sources. She established the need to trace the roots of international activity in music education and that led to two studies, which documented the history of international music education prior to the founding of ISME (McCarthy, 1993, 1995).

Inspiration can also arise out of a sense of professional responsibility for documenting the story of music education in a community, state or region. A striking example is the compilation of essays on music and music education in the state of Rhode Island that started out as a project in a graduate class and developed into an edited book. *Rhode Island's Musical Heritage: An Exploration* (Livingston & Smith, 2008) provides testimony to the musical and cultural diversity that comprises the state's musical heritage and confirms the value and importance of doing local history. When you choose your topic, pay similar attention to the origin of your curiosity. Such knowledge will sustain your interest and motivation to complete the study.

Until the late 20th century, historical researchers documented primarily the chronology of events, the development of music programs in public education, and the contributions of leaders in music education. Studies included questions such as: What was the rationale for introducing music into the public schools in 1838? When was the first professional organization of music educators founded and how did it develop from a small group to a national body of music educators? Why did music appreciation enter the music curriculum in the early 20th century and how did Frances Elliot Clark, leader in the development of music appreciation curriculum and media, contribute to the movement? Although questions of *who, what, when, where, how* and *why* remain relevant, contemporary researchers are beginning to interrogate patterns of thought, roots of value systems, motivations for actions, and causes for change with greater intention and focus.

A content analysis of articles in the first twenty volumes of *The Bulletin of Historical Research in Music Education*, 1980–1999 (McCarthy, 1999) yielded the following categories of topics: development of music education programs (local, national, international), biography, curriculum methods and materials, and historiography. A similar study of more recent volumes (21–30) in the newly titled *Journal of Historical Research in Music Education* resulted in the addition of two new topic categories—cross-cultural studies that focus on a topic in more than one national setting, and studies whose primary focus is the political and/or cultural context in which music and music education developed (McCarthy, 2012).

Discerning a Purpose

When you have found a topic that addresses an important aspect of music education history and is likely to hold your interest over time, you are ready to carry out some preliminary research to assess its feasibility. Begin reading secondary sources that others have written about the topic, thereby expanding your knowledge of the scholarly base. Confirm the existence of a substantial number of relevant primary sources and identify specific "holes" in current knowledge about the topic under study. Reading secondary sources and identifying primary research sources will provide the foundation for assessing the need for and feasibility of conducting a study.

Becoming familiar with the history of the time period and the people and events related to your topic will build confidence and develop a sense of ownership. Questions will arise as you engage with sources. Write them down and begin to shape a purpose statement for the study.

As *Chi-Hui* explored her topic of comparative music education in the context of Taiwan and the United States, Prof. E. suggested that she examine several books containing investigations on music education in different countries or discuss music education internationally (Cox & Stevens, 2017; Hargreaves & North, 2001; Kertz-Welzel, 2008; McCarthy, 2004). He advised Chi-Hui to focus on countries close to her homeland in East Asia (Gong, 2013; Ho, 2000; Kou, 2001; Lee, W.R., 2002). During her review of these and related sources, Chi-Hui realized that although she was educated in the Taiwanese school system, she knew little about how the system worked. She became fascinated with accounts of the educational system in Taiwan and felt she should have a formal knowledge of that system before comparing it to those of other nations. The topic of her study thus evolved: Western influences in primary and secondary music education in Taiwan since music became a compulsory subject in the curriculum. She was close to having a purpose identified.

Christy, after an initial phase of searching in secondary sources, found that the chronological scope of the topic she started out with—vocal pedagogues since 1800—was too broad, given time constraints and available resources. She was not finding literature from the 1800s, other than biographical sketches of vocal performers. Based on her initial search, she decided to focus on pedagogues of the 20th century whose works were more readily available to her. The next task was to choose which pedagogue(s) to study and to identify which aspects of their contributions she wanted to investigate.

Exploration: From Purpose Statement to Research Questions

Choose either *Chi-Hui's* or *Christy's* purpose statement (see Chapter 3) and compose 2–3 research specifications (sub-problems/questions) that would fulfill the study's intent. Compare your suggestions with those of your classmates.

FINDING SOURCES AND VERIFYING EVIDENCE

There are two principal categories of sources from which historical evidence is gathered: primary sources and secondary sources (see Chapter 2). Although the categories are presented as discrete, there can be overlap between them depending on the context of the study. For example, a dissertation can serve as a primary source when its author is the topic of a study or as a secondary source if a researcher uses its findings for a related study. A researcher often encounters secondary sources first—for example, secondary textbooks in music education, annotated bibliographies, or books and articles related to their topic of interest. Such sources serve an important role in establishing the need for and value of a proposed study. They also serve to build a case for the feasibility of the study, to refine the research purpose and question, and most importantly, to guide the researcher to relevant primary sources.

Primary Sources

Primary sources are "the gold standard of historical research" (Danto, 2008, p. 62). Generated by someone who witnessed or participated in the historical event under study, they provide firsthand evidence to the researcher. Criteria used to determine the value of a primary source include originality, veracity, relevance, and evidentiary value.

- *Originality*: How close was the witness to the subject of the study when an event was documented? As a historical researcher, you work with sources that are as close as possible in time and space to the "origin," that which is being studied—the person, institution, organization, curriculum, program or cultural group.
- *Veracity*: What is the relationship between the person providing the evidence and the subject under study? This question helps you judge a primary source from the perspective of the witness and their motivation to report the situation.
- *Relevance*: How is the content of the source related to the research questions? In historical research, it is possible for a researcher to become fascinated with interesting sources that are at best tangentially related to the purpose of the study. To establish data relevance, then, ensure that each source can be placed in some meaningful way into the collection of sources that is being assembled and that it can contribute to the story you are about to tell.
- *Evidentiary value*: How does the piece of evidence contribute to the overall collection of data? Does it contribute to increasing the variety of evidence, the multiplicity of voices, or elaborating on different dimensions of the topic under study? Evaluate the overall collection of primary sources to ensure that they represent different perspectives on the topic. In studying the life of one person, for example, multiple and sometimes contradictory perspectives may be found.

The Infinite Variety of Primary Sources

Historical study engages you in examining different kinds of evidence. Barzun and Graff (2004) categorize evidence into "the Verbal and the Mute," the verbal referring to the majority of sources which contain words and the mute consisting of "any physical object bearing no words" (p. 117). Some sources fall between or outside these broad categories. Visual media reside primarily in "the Mute" but can have elements of "the Verbal"—for example, a photograph with a caption and/or description of its contents or a plaque with an inscription. Quantitative data have numeric attributes but could be accompanied by verbal description. Perhaps a more inclusive approach to primary source categorization is as follows:

1) *Written documents* e.g., autobiographies, diaries, letters, scrapbooks, memoirs, magazines, newspapers, government documents, institutional records, quantitative records such as school music enrollment numbers, demographics, test scores, music festival ratings,
2) *Oral records* e.g., interviews, audio and visual recordings of school concerts or festivals, recordings of student compositions,
3) *Artifacts* e.g., photographs, textbooks, instructional media, musical instruments, trophies, music scores, costumes and uniforms, concert props.

Locating Primary Sources

As already stated, the scope of research topics in music education history is expansive. Thus, the primary sources related to such varied topics are deposited across several kinds of libraries and special collections, public and private. Researchers draw on primary sources from a range of public records and documents, private collections and personal papers, oral history interviews, journals, proceedings and yearbooks, concert programs, textbooks, songbooks, tune books and tutors, and autobiographies (McCarthy, 2012). Materials are accessed in public libraries and archives, for example, the Library of Congress, Special Collections in Performing Arts—University of Maryland, U.S. Government Archives, and the Naval Historical Center. While it is true to say that more and more documents and serials are available online, the majority of topics will require the historical researcher to visit archival collections.

Using Archival Material

The use of archival material (a collection of historical records) is unique to historical research and deserves special attention since it involves policies and procedures that you will typically not encounter when gathering data for other kinds of research studies. Due to the care required for accessing and handling archival materials, each institution that houses archives will have its own policies for making materials available to patrons.

The Special Collections in Performing Arts at the University of Maryland is the largest and perhaps most comprehensive repository of music education archives in the United States. The Collections most closely related to music education are: Band, Music Education, Performers/Scholars, Professional Organization, and Score Collections (www.lib.umd.edu/scpa/index-of-collections). The Special Collections website provides clear guidelines on how to get in touch with the curator and gain access to the materials.

In writing a history of the first fifty years of the International Society for Music Education (McCarthy, 2004), the author examined sources in the ISME records that are part of the Professional Organization Collection. The origin and content of a collection is described in a *finding aid*, a document that is useful in gaining an overview of the collection and identifying which records to read. Records of some individuals who held office in ISME were located elsewhere in the Special Collections (e.g., Marguerite V. Hood was active in ISME and also President of MENC, and Vanett Lawler, a key figure in the founding and early development of ISME and also Executive Secretary of MENC).

For archival research, it is frequently less convenient to access historical sources than it is to conduct research online, and this reality may challenge your patience and lead to frustration. Focus on the positive aspects: the sensory information that is afforded by handling an original piece of historical evidence; the closeness you feel to the subject of your study when you have that tactile experience with sources; or, the excitement that is found when you turn a page to find a photograph that captures an essential aspect of your investigation. Furthermore, there is the satisfaction gained when you begin to grasp the spirit of a time and place through reading newspapers and locally produced print media; the immediacy of listening to a recording and hearing the performances of those whose musical accomplishments you seek to document; and finally, the overall sense that you are touching the humanity of a bygone age by studying these historical sources.

Engaging with Primary Sources

It is vitally important to experience historical sources firsthand. This can be achieved in a number of ways—visiting a library that has an archival collection and looking at some primary sources, finding a historical artifact in your family records, visiting a historic building, or reading an old music textbook that is in your school library.

Exploration: Bringing a Primary Source to Life

Appendix C contains a reprint of John Curwen's account of observing Sarah Glover teaching music in Norwich, England. Curwen (1816–1880) is commonly known as the creator of the Curwen hand signs, a sol-fa system of hand signals that represent pitch. He based the system on a method known as Norwich Sol-fa, developed by Sarah Glover (1785–1867). Read Curwen's account and reflect in writing on the following questions: What images form in your mind as you read the document? What sounds do you hear? What emotions do you feel? What do you imagine was the intention of the writer who created the document? Do you detect any biases on the writer's part? If so, what does that tell you? Finally, what makes this source a primary source?

Reading and Recording

In advance of reading your sources, choose a method of recording data—note-taking, photocopying, scanning or whatever technology seems appropriate and is permitted for the material at hand. It takes considerable time to immerse yourself in a particular place and era in order to grasp the *zeitgeist* ("the spirit of the times"). It is necessary, then, to examine the evidence carefully. Contemplate the words and the use of language, the modes of communication, the visual images where they apply, and the underlying assumptions of the authors or creators. As you read, be prepared for the unexpected, and keep a watchful eye for inconsistencies between data sources and ambiguities that may arise. In addition to reading the sources directly related to your topic, read "around" the topic, and when possible watch movies or documentaries about the era, and when possible talk to people who lived at the time. Become an insider to the time and place you are studying just as you would when conducting other forms of qualitative research. At all times, use a journal for recording questions that arise when you read or listen to sources and for writing responses.

Verifying the Evidence

Verification of primary source material is essential to all historical investigations. Each source undergoes what historians call external and internal criticism. Both serve the purpose of establishing that evidence should be considered trustworthy.

External Criticism

The term refers to the authenticity and reliability of a source. Both qualities are ascertained by questions such as:

- When was the source produced?
- Where was it produced?
- Who produced it?
- Is it in its original form? If not, where is the original?
- Is there any reason to suspect that this source may not be genuine?
- Could it have been written by someone else?

External criticism may not be as great a challenge for documents of the 19th and 20th centuries as it is for documents of earlier time periods. There may be instances, however, when essential information is lacking because a date of origin cannot be found, information is inconsistent with other sources, or handwriting is not legible. For example, W.R. Lee (2002) used external criticism as one aspect of examining an essay by Charles Farnsworth (1859–1947), a pioneer in American music teacher education. When scrutinizing Farnsworth's papers at the Thetford Library and Archive in Thetford, Vermont, Lee found an unpublished paper with a questionable date of origin. The Thetford document was labeled as a speech titled "Music in the Secondary School," given on September 21, 1898. Lee was aware that the archive at the University of Colorado mentioned a speech of the same title, given at a meeting of Colorado teachers a year earlier, in 1897. The Thetford manuscript contained typewritten revisions pasted over the handwritten speech and was signed and dated by Farnsworth. An expert on Farnsworth's life, creative output, and scholarly work habits, Lee made the following claims about the manuscript: Since Farnsworth rarely made substantive changes in revisions of his work, the 1897 version would likely have differed little in content from the later version. Further, Lee suggested that typewritten revisions must have been added after 1899, since Farnsworth's essays and speeches were not typewritten until after his move to New York City in 1900. Since Lee based his article on this one essay, and found evidence of two speeches of the same title, it was necessary for him to provide a detailed account of its provenance.

Internal Criticism

Establishing accuracy and credibility of information contained in a source requires such questions as:

- What motivated the author of the information to produce this statement/image/object?
- What is the author's role in relation to the information provided?

- Are facts included in the piece consistent with other writings of the time period?
- Does the author show bias in the way thoughts and ideas are expressed?
- Are the stated thoughts and ideas consistent with other writings by the same author?
- What is the evidentiary value of the content? Can this evidence be corroborated with evidence from other sources?

Reading sources related to the history of African American music education requires close attention to content and awareness of unique challenges. For example, the birth of enslaved people was not officially recorded and they were named after their enslavers. When reading journals of abolitionist teachers who taught in Black communities in the mid-19th century, the researcher must take their biases into consideration when interpreting the evidence (McCarthy & Hoffman, in review). The authors also found inconsistent or incomplete information on events and individuals across multiple sources when researching African American school music in the Reconstruction Era. This author encountered similar challenges researching Black music and music education in the middle decades of the 20th century (McCarthy, 2021). Such challenges may apply to other groups who relied on oral transmission and whose stories were not included in works that formed the disciplinary literature base.

ETHICS AND HISTORICAL RESEARCH

In other research modes that involve human subjects, ethical standards are established and reported. Similar standards are applied when doing oral historical research (see Chapters 4 and 5 for discussion of ethical issues and Chapter 8 for a discussion of human subjects in qualitative research). You request the written consent of persons being interviewed and have the study approved by the Institutional Review Board at your college or university. Transcripts of interviews are shared with the interviewee who has the opportunity to make changes. In oral history, typically, the interviewees will be older and have much life experience. Their ability to recall accurately will vary, and you will sometimes need to corroborate evidence received in this way with that of other sources. Consider how the interviewee is positioned in relation to the topic and how recollections may be biased, inaccurate, or emotionally charged. Furthermore, when researching the lives of individuals or groups, some sensitive information or negative responses may come to your attention. When that occurs, you need to be diplomatic and to suspend judgment. Corroborate the evidence provided by the interviewee with other sources and evaluate its place in your study.

There are additional ethical guidelines that apply to the conduct of historical research beyond interviewing oral history participants:

1) Exercise care in interpreting sources. The persons and groups under study are no longer present to respond to how their words or actions are interpreted. Thus, care must be taken to examine the evidence with sensitivity, to corroborate evidence, and to remember that you have obligations to the individuals or groups you study.
2) Acknowledge the values of the time period and evaluate evidence accordingly. This principle is related to the idea discussed earlier that it takes considerable time to understand what it meant to live during a particular time period. Gather information related to the contextual factors that influenced the mentality and shaped the values of the people who lived at the time.

3) Honor the historical record without distorting it—for example, avoid filling in holes in the records without adequate evidence.

4) Read widely about the history of marginalized groups you are studying for contextual knowledge. Maintain ongoing dialogue with those who are insiders to the tradition or heritage being documented, including librarians or curators of special collections.

5) Present a holistic interpretation that includes both glorious achievements and painful or contentious actions. Remember that individuals and groups have memories that may contain pain and animosity caused, for example, by political suppression. As African-American novelist and political activist James A. Baldwin (1955) put it, "People are trapped in history and history is trapped in them" (p. 163). Recalling the past can bring to the surface emotion and unresolved pain and anger, or a preference to stay silent.

CRAFTING A PROPOSAL FOR A HISTORICAL STUDY

After you have framed the study and read widely on the topic, it is time to commit your plan to writing with a formal proposal. A proposal is a detailed description of what, why, where, and how you intend to conduct the study, set in the context of the work of others who have researched related topics. Prior to describing the contents of a proposal for a historical study, it is important to note that you will likely use *The Chicago Manual of Style* (2017) and use numbered footnotes rather than parenthetical references. A proposal for a historical study is usually presented in three sections or chapters: (1) Introduction, (2) Review of related literature, and (3) Methodology of study.

1)   Introduction

In Chapter 3 of this book, you identified key elements of the research plan—the topic, the rationale and need for the study, and the purpose and research questions. Now it is time to re-examine them and develop them further, integrating them with other elements to present a compelling argument for conducting the study.

a. Draw on scholarly and research literature to make a case for the need for the study and its value to the profession.

b. Use the rationale and need for study to form a clear purpose and initial research question(s).

c. Establish the category of historical study you are planning—biography, program development, examination of curriculum materials, school or institution, impact of trends and events on music education.

d. Having established the direction and focus, locate the topic in historical contexts that are likely to inform your study of the topic—for example, cultural, musical, political, and social, contexts.

e. Identify any unique challenges that may arise around the time period or individual or group that you plan to study.

f. List any special terms or language that may be specific to an era, racial or cultural group, or institution.

g. Depending on the topic, a researcher might draw on a theoretical framework to inform their reading and interpretation of sources and to provide a critical lens for making inferences from the evidence—for example, critical theory, cultural-historical theory, post-colonial theory.

2)   Review of related literature

In Chapter 2 you identified some literature sources related to your topic. In a historical research proposal, a literature review will typically contain contextual information about the topic, findings of prior studies, an overview of relevant secondary sources, and an introduction to primary sources.

a.   Re-assess items in the collection in terms of their coverage of emerging sub-themes developing around your topic. Use different keywords to identify more sources.
b.   Identify sub-headings to organize the literature.
c.   The review will include not only research studies but also secondary sources that inform various aspects of the topic. For example, in her study of the contributions of country musician Doc Williams with applications to the general music curriculum, Cover (2016) drew on related secondary literature on hillbilly music, country music, and musical life in Williams' hometown of Wheeling, West Virginia.
d.   Provide an introduction to the scope and nature of primary sources to be used in the study.
e.   The summary of the literature demonstrates your expert knowledge of the topic, your understanding of the time, place, and people, and your readiness to approach and interpret primary sources informed by perspectives gained from the literature.

3)   Methodology of Study

The methodology section of a historical study proposal has a similar goal to other modes of inquiry; you describe in clear and concise detail your plan for carrying out the study.

a.   Provide a detailed description of the exact location of primary source materials, their form and content, their relationship to the research questions, how you will access and record them.
b.   Identify the procedures you will follow to verify and evaluate the evidence.
c.   If conducting oral history is part of the plan, provide details of the informants and the proposed interview location, interview structure, and permission forms.
d.   Describe ethical issues that you anticipate and how you will account for them.
e.   Looking beyond the selection and collection of evidence, anticipate what method you will use to organize, analyze, and synthesize the content of the sources.
f.   Finally, return to the value that underpins the study and anticipate how the findings of your historical topic will inform music educators today.

INTERPRETING THE EVIDENCE

After the proposal is approved, you continue to read and take notes from primary and secondary sources. As evidence is evaluated and sources are corroborated, your understanding of the topic deepens. You begin to find connections between events and actions, see patterns within and across pieces of evidence, and organize a chronological order and thematic sequence for the narrative.

There is no history without interpretation. The mere reporting of facts in chronological order or the categorization of evidence into themes is not sufficient in order to complete a historical study. As Barzun and Graff (2004) caution: "*No piece of evidence can be used in the state in which it is found.* It must undergo scrutiny of the researcher's mind according to the rules of the critical method" (pp. 119–120, emphasis original). Criticism is integral to all interactions with historical data. Recall the discussion of internal and external criticism when verifying sources. It is particularly vital in the interpretive phase when the researcher creates a narrative of the past from the evidence examined in the sources.

Senses and Sensibilities at Work

Although the researcher is working with materials that originated in the past, doing history can be a concrete and tangible activity when sources are approached interactively. Listen for the intention of the writer, look for connections with other pieces of evidence, imagine why the writer or speaker thinks and feels as she does, and identify places where the source is silent about something and speculate why, given the setting and context. Ask numerous questions of each source and pursue answers elsewhere if necessary. Assume that human motivation is complex and that the words or visuals before you reveal only part of the story. Pemberton (1999) alludes to that complexity when she writes: "As historians, we have to look around corners, expecting circular and zigzag progressions. After all, history is the record of human endeavors, and those endeavors don't run in straight lines" (pp. 117–18). Therefore, it is necessary to read multiple sources of data, to juxtapose their insinuations and implications, and to place their meanings in the larger social and cultural contexts in which they occurred.

Acknowledging and Minimizing Bias

It is important to keep in mind that when you interpret historical evidence, you are influenced by your own background and experience. Reflect on your relationship to the topic you are studying, and the values and beliefs you bring to interpreting the sources.

> When *Christy* discussed her reading of sources with Prof. E., she tended to be overly critical of vocal teaching in the past. Prof. E. asked her several questions about what she thought it was like to be a voice teacher in the early 20th century: How were teachers educated? What was known about vocal development? What repertoire and vocal pedagogy materials were available? What was known about the physiology of the human voice in regard to singing? Responding to these questions, among others, helped Christy to construct a picture of what it was like to be a voice teacher in the past. It also helped her to critique practices with a more informed and compassionate perspective.

Similar to Christy's initial response to vocal teaching, consider the lens that you bring to investigating your topic. In what ways are you drawing on values, beliefs and experiences to critique past events? Do present-day ideas and perspectives dominate your interpretation of the past? It would be impossible to remove such bias totally, but it is important to acknowledge it. Situate yourself in the past by asking questions such as: What was it like to be a music teacher at the time being studied? Who valued the teacher's work? What was considered to be a successful music program? What kinds of music were valued at home, in the community, in society at large?

Making Inferences and Drawing Conclusions

According to some historians, the study of history is a study of causes, and Pemberton (1992) sees it as "a tangle of causes and effects diffused over time and space" (p. 96). How does one make sense out of this "tangle of causes and effects" in the process of making inferences and drawing conclusions? This is a challenging task that demands a combination of corroboration of sources, contextual knowledge, and critical thinking.

a. Review and evaluate the meanings you deduced from the evidence.
b. Ensure that the evidence is pointing strongly in the direction of the inference you are making.
c. Look for patterns of change and continuity.
d. Distinguish between events and actions that are correlated and those that have a causal relationship.
e. Isolate contradictions or ambiguities and revisit sources for enlightenment, or read additional sources to gain a different perspective.
f. Ensure that the conclusions you draw are credible within the larger context of the time period.

Bringing the Past into the Present

Recent practices in historical writing connect findings from a study with contemporary music education. This extends the value and relevance of historical research into the present. For example, both Kennedy (2000) and Nelson (2004) examined the history of creativity in U. S. music education and used historical perspectives gained from their studies to comment on the present status of creative music-making in the schools and to make a prognosis for the future. Hash's (2008) recommendation to conduct further studies into "school band contests in individual states and other parts of the world," if implemented, may contribute valuable insights into the ongoing discussion about their value and role in music education.

ORGANIZING AND WRITING THE NARRATIVE

After a phase of immersion in the sources, synthesizing the evidence and making inferences, the next phase is to write the study. A good narrative in historical research (a) has a clear structure with sub-headings to guide the reader through the manuscript; (b) engages the reader in the details of the story by including quotations from primary sources; (c) honors the chronology underlying the topic by including dates and historical facts and presenting events in chronological order; (d) elaborates on and interprets ideas that emerge from the evidence; (e) brings persons, places and events to life using active verbs, descriptive adjectives, and poetic imagery to sustain the tension of the narrative throughout; and (f) includes photographs and other images to transport the reader to the time and place of the study.

There are several ways to organize the narrative, among them chronological order, developmental phases of the topic, topical or thematic order, or a combination of both. The degree to which these approaches are employed depends on the topic under study. In a biographical study, the researcher might organize the individual's life around periods that represent distinct phases of that life. In a study that has a narrow chronological timeline, the emphasis may be on interrelated events and actions that developed simultaneously. A combination of chronological and thematic approaches is recommended in most cases; combining them effectively presents one of the challenges of writing history, moving the chronology forward while addressing the topic in a dynamic way using varied primary sources.

The following three examples show a diverse range of possibilities for organizing historical narrative. Karpf (2002) reported on William Bradbury's observations of European music educators, 1847–49, using Bradbury's letters from Europe as published in the *New York Evangelist* as primary sources. She organized the narrative around Bradbury's descriptions of teachers and schools and presented them in the order in which he wrote about them—from London, Leipzig, and Switzerland.

May (2005) studied the early musical development of African American jazz musicians in Indianapolis in the 1930s and 1940s. She presented her findings using three overarching themes: formal music education, informal music education, and the contributing political, social, and cultural influences. Her organization around themes was effective in achieving the goals of her oral history study.

W. R. Lee's (2002) study of Charles H. Farnsworth's unpublished essay mentioned earlier further illustrates the diversity of ways historical evidence can be presented. After an in-depth description of the essay's context, both internal and external, Lee presented an edited and annotated version of Farnsworth's speech. He added side notes and footnotes to provide commentary on the manuscript and suggested possible sources of influence.

In conclusion, historical writing must present a compelling story and convince the reader that evidence was collected according to the highest standards of historical scholarship. The author must present conclusions as an outcome of precise and painstaking documentation, empathetic and critical reading of evidence, and careful interpretation that is supported by multiple sources and argued by reason. Historical research demands both the rigor of the scientific method and the humanistic qualities needed to interpret the significance of events and actions of persons and groups in the context of time, place and culture.

PUBLISHING A HISTORICAL STUDY

As you consider publishing your study, it is wise to read published historical studies. The *Journal of Historical Research in Music Education* (JHRME) is devoted to the publication of historical studies (https://journals.sagepub.com/author-instructions/JHR). Other journals that publish historical music education studies include *The Bulletin of the Council for Research in Music Education*, *Contributions to Music Education*, *International Journal of Music Education*, and the *Journal of Research in Music Education*. Be sure to read the submission guidelines and adhere to them as you prepare your manuscript.

Publishing a historical study today is similar in ways to publishing articles in any mode of inquiry. Essential elements must be present—a significant topic, rationale, purpose, research questions, literature review, description of methodology, plan for data collection, analysis and interpretation, and a concluding section. The presentation of a historical study has unique expectations as well.

a. The *Chicago Manual of Style* is commonly used to format historical manuscripts. Read several articles to learn how to integrate footnotes into a manuscript. Since primary sources are important for documenting historical evidence, you can find more than 100 footnotes in an 8,000-word article, some quite extensive in order to explain, elaborate on, or provide context for the source.

b. It takes skill to integrate primary sources into the narrative. Be sure to include a variety of sources to support the narrative, when appropriate—written, visual, audio, numeric, and graphic.

c. The reconstruction of the past is done in story form. In addition to the continuity and flow we experience when listening to or reading a story, the scholar writing historical narrative brings a set of meta-skills to the task. Those skills are founded on deep knowledge of human behavior and motivation, an imagination that brings them (and the reader) back into the "tangle of causes and effects" in the historical setting, and a degree of empathy and intuition that lends credibility to the author's inferences and conclusions.

CHAPTER SUMMARY

1) Writing history is an interdisciplinary activity, drawing on the sciences and the humanities.

2) The historical process involves reconstructing the past in narrative form.

3) The values of historical research are diverse, and findings can be made relevant to and inform contemporary music education.

4) Contemporary trends and developments in historical research are influenced by changing intellectual paradigms and advancements in technology and media.

5) Primary sources represent the data of historical research. They are varied in form: written documents, oral records, and artifacts.

6) Criticism is key to historical research, especially in the examination of primary sources: external criticism to test authenticity and reliability and internal criticism to test accuracy and credibility.

7) Interpretation of sources stands at the core of the historical process.

Topics for Further Exploration

1) Compare and contrast the role and use of various kinds of primary sources (written, oral, artifacts).

2) Discuss the nature of ethics in historical research as compared to other modes of inquiry.

3) Distinguish between interviewing in oral history contexts and in qualitative research studies.

Suggested Assignments

1) Consider the following purpose statements chosen from historical studies and identify a number of research questions that would need to be asked to fulfill each respective purpose.

    a. *Title:* Political Influences on Curriculum Content and Musical Meaning: Hong Kong Secondary Music Education, 1949–1997

       Purpose: The purpose of this article is to examine the history of secondary school music education in Hong Kong, with emphasis on a period of major socio-political change: from 1949 to the transfer of Hong Kong's political sovereignty from the United Kingdom to the People's Republic of China in 1997. (Ho, 2000, p. 5)

   b. *Title:* The Use of Creativity in Music Textbook Series, 1900–1950

      Purpose: The purpose of this paper is to investigate the type of creativity included in U.S. music textbooks during the first half of the 20th century. Did students have access to music creativity in music textbooks of the first half of the 20th century, and if so, what was the nature and scope of the creative experiences presented in the textbooks? (Nelson, 2004, p. 129)

   c. *Title:* History of Illinois School Band Association: 1924–1941

      Purpose: The purpose of this study is to document the history of the Illinois School Band Association (ISBA) and the contests this organization sponsored between 1924 and 1941. It examines questions about the origin, leadership, rules and procedures, impact, growth, and decline of the organization. It also discusses how these findings can be used in modern practice. (Hash, 2008, p. 4)

2) Review a historical study of your choice. Identify the rationale, purpose statement and research questions, and critically analyze them.

3) In small groups, select two source readings from Michael L. Mark's book, *Music Education: Source Readings from Ancient Greece to Today* (2013). Choose one from Part 1 (Music Education in Earlier Times) and the other from a later period in Part II (Views of Music Education to 1950) or Part III (Views of Music Education after 1950). Compare sources in relation to authorship, time period, context of production, language and tone, and content.

4) Go to the Digital Collections at the Library of Congress website, and link to the Performing Arts page: www.loc.gov/collections/?fa=subject_topic:performing+arts.

   a. Search for a photograph or image that is of interest to you. Use Prof. E.'s questions from the second page of this chapter as prompts for examining it. Share your findings in class.

   b. Find an artifact or oral record that may be used to begin a conversation about the history of music education (e.g., musical instrument, textbook, photograph, certificate, recording). Spend time with the artifact, looking or listening with intent, interrogating the evidence and forming questions around it. Bring to class and share findings.

5) Visit an archive on or near your campus. As a class, select a historical figure for study based on materials found in the archive. Work together to compose a historical portrait that helps the reader to engage with the life story of the individual. Consider how you could include visual and/or audio media to bring the narrative to life.

6) Compare articles written about the same historical topic. (See example below.) Use these guiding questions: What is the purpose of each study? What primary sources are used? What is unique about each author's treatment of the topic? How are conclusions drawn? What did you learn about interpretation by doing this exercise?

   a. American Music Education 1941–1946: Meeting Needs and Making Adjustments During World War II (Beegle, 2004)

   b. Nationalism in United States Music Education during World War II (Goble, 2009)

   c. Women Music Teachers as Military Band Directors during World War II (Sullivan, 2017)

Helpful Websites

History of Education Society, US: www.historyofeducation.org/
History of Education Society, UK: www.historyofeducation.org.uk/

The International History of Music Education: http://music-ed.net/ihme/

History Special Interest Research Group (NAfME): https://hsrig.gcsu.edu

Oral History Association: www.oralhistory.org

Organization of Educational Historians: www.edhistorians.org/

Special Collections in Performing Arts, University of Maryland: www.lib.umd.edu/scpa

United States Library of Congress, Music Division Finding Aids Online: www.loc.gov/rr/perform/special/gd-index.html

United States National Archives and Records Administration: www.archives.gov

Recommended Reading

Barzun, J., & Graff, H. F. (2004). *The modern researcher* (6th ed.). Wadsworth/Thomson Learning.

Burke, P. (2001). *Eyewitnessing: The uses of images as historical evidence.* Cornell University Press.

Cox, G. (2002). Transforming research in music education history. In R. Colwell & C. Richardson (Eds.), *The new handbook of research on music teaching and learning* (pp. 695–706). Oxford University Press and MENC.

Heller, G. N., & Wilson, B. D. (1992). Historical research. In R. Colwell (Ed.), *Handbook of research on music teaching and learning* (pp. 102–114). Schirmer.

Howell, M., & Prevenier, W. (2001). *From reliable sources: An introduction to historical methods.* Cornell University Press.

Janesick, V. J. (2010). *Oral history for the qualitative researcher: Choreographing the story.* The Guilford Press.

Pemberton, C. A. (1987). Revisionist historians: Writers reflected in their writings. *Journal of Research in Music Education, 35*(4), 213–220.

Sommer, B. W., & Quinlan, M. K. (2018). *The oral history manual* (3rd ed.). Rowman & Littlefield.

REFERENCES

Baker, V. D. (2003). Inclusion of women composers in college music history textbooks. *Journal of Historical Research in Music Education, 25*(1), 5–19. https://doi.org/10.1177/153660060302500103

Baldwin, J. A. (1955). *Notes of a native son.* Beacon Press.

Barzun, J., & Graff, H. F. (2004). *The modern researcher* (6th ed.). Wadsworth/Thomson Learning.

Beegle, A. (2004). American music education 1941–1946: Meeting needs and making adjustments during World War II. *Journal of Historical Research in Music Education, 26*(1), 54–67. https://doi.org/10.1177/1536600604026007

Birge, E. B. (1966). *History of public school music in the United States.* Music Educators National Conference. (Original work published 1928).

Björkén-Nyberg, C. (2019). From Carl Czerny's Miss Cecilia to the Cecilian: Engineering, aesthetics, and gendered piano instruction. *Journal of Historical Research in Music Education, 40*(2), 125–142. https://doi.org/10.1177/1536600618771268

Britton, A. P. (1969). Research in the United States. *Journal of Research in Music Education, 17*(1), 108–111. https://doi.org/10.2307/3344196

Burke, P. (2001). *Eyewitnessing: The uses of images as historical evidence.* Cornell University Press.

The Chicago manual of style (17th ed.). (2017). The University of Chicago Press.

Chybowski, J. J. (2017). Selling musical taste in early twentieth-century America: Frances E. Clark and the business of music appreciation. *Journal of Historical Research in Music Education, 38*(2), 104–12. https://doi.org/10.1177/1536600616684969

Clark, R. H. (2019). A narrative history of African American marching band: Toward a historicultural understanding. *Journal of Historical Research in Music Education, 41*(1), 5–32. https://doi.org/10.1177/1536600619847933

Collingwood, R. G. (1994). *The idea of history.* Oxford University Press. (Original work published 1946)

Cover, J. (2016). *Early country musician Doc Williams (1914–2011): Contributions to the development of country music and applications for a general music curriculum, Grades 3–5* [Master's thesis]. University of Michigan. https://deepblue.lib.umich.edu/handle/2027.42/123006

Cox, G. (2002). Transforming research in music education history. In R. Colwell & C. Richardson (Eds.), *The new handbook of research on music teaching and learning* (pp. 695–706). Oxford University Press.

Cox, G., & Stevens, R. (Eds.) (2017). *The origins and foundations of music education: International perspectives* (2nd ed.). Bloomsbury Academic.

Danto, E. A. (2008). *Historical research*. Oxford University Press.

Goble, J. S. (2009). Nationalism in United States music education during World War II. *Journal of Historical Research in Music Education, 30*(2), 103–117. https://doi.org/10.1177/153660060903000203

Gong, H. (2013). Protestant missionaries and school music education in late Qing China. *Chime, 18–19,* 101–134.

Groulx, T. J. (2018). Influences of segregation and integration on the bands at Historically Black high Schools in Duval County, Florida. *Journal of Historical Research in Music Education, 40*(1), 58–78. https://doi.org/10.1177/1536600617720760

Gruhn, W. (2001). European "methods" for American nineteenth-century singing instruction: A cross-cultural perspective on historical research. *Journal of Historical Research in Music Education, 23*(1), 3–18. https://doi.org/10.1177/153660060102300102

Handel, G. A., & Humphreys, J. T. (2005). The Phoenix Indian school band, 1894–1930. *Journal of Historical Research in Music Education, 26*(2), 144–161. https://doi.org/10.1177/153660060502600205

Hargreaves, D. J., & North, A. C. (Eds.) (2001). *Musical development and learning: The international perspective.* Continuum.

Hash, P. M. (2008). History of Illinois School Band Association: 1924–1941. *Journal of Historical Research in Music Education, 30*(1), 4–20. https://doi.org/10.1177/153660060803000103

Ho, W.-Ch. (2000). Political influences on curriculum content and musical meaning: Hong Kong secondary music education, 1949–1997. *Journal of Historical Research in Music Education, 22*(1), 5–24. https://doi.org/10.1177/153660060002200102

Howe, S. W. (2009). A historical view of women in music education careers. *Philosophy of Music Education Review, 17*(2), 162–183. www.jstor.org/stable/40495498

Humphreys, J. T. (2015). Energizing the 'Birge story' of public school music in the United States: Some ideas on how to amp it up. *Journal of Historical Research in Music Education, 36*(2), 91–102. https://doi.org/10.1177/153660061503600202

Isbell, D. (2006). The Steamboat Springs High School Ski Band, 1935–2005. *Journal of Historical Research in Music Education, 28*(1), 21–37. https://doi.org/10.1177/153660060602800103

Karpf, J. (2002). "Would that it were so in America!": William Bradbury's observations of European music educators, 1847–49. *Journal of Historical Research in Music Education, 24*(1), 5–38. https://doi.org/10.1177/153660060202400102

Kennedy, M. A. (2000). Creative music making since the time of the singing schools: Fringe benefits. *Journal of Historical Research in Music Education, 21*(2), 132–148. https://doi.org/10.1177/153660060002100203

Kertz-Welzel, A. (2008). Music education in the twenty-first century: A cross-cultural comparison of German and American music education towards a new concept of international dialogue. *Music Education Research, 10*(4), 439–449. https://doi.org/10.1080/14613800802547672

Kertz-Welzel, A. (2015). Lessons from elsewhere? Comparative music education in times of globalization. *Philosophy of Music Education Review, 23*(1), 48–66. https://doi.org/10.2979/philmusieducrevi.23.1.48

Kou, M.-L. L. (2001). Development of music education in Taiwan (1895–1995). *Journal of Historical Research in Music Education, 22*(2), 177–190. https://doi.org/10.1177/153660060102200208

Lee, A. H.-C. (2002). The influence of Japanese music education in Taiwan during the Japanese protectorate. *Journal of Historical Research in Music Education, 23*(2), 106–118. https://doi.org/10.1177/153660060202300203

Lee, W. R. (1997). Music education and rural reform: 1900–1925. *Journal of Research in Music Education, 45*(2), 306–326. https://doi.org/10.2307/3345589

Lee, W. R. (2002). Charles H. Farnsworth's "Music in the secondary school." *Journal of Historical Research in Music Education, 24*(1), 39–61. https://doi.org/10.1177/153660060202400103

Lepherd, L. (Ed.) (1995). *Music education in international perspective: National systems.* University of Southern Queensland Press.

Livingston, C., & Smith, D. E. (Eds.) (2008). *Rhode Island's musical heritage: An exploration.* Harmonie Park Press.

Mark, M. L. (Ed.) (2013). *Music education: Source readings from Ancient Greece to today* (4th ed.). Routledge.

May, L. F. (2005). Early musical development of selected African American jazz musicians in Indianapolis in the 1930s and 1940s. *Journal of Historical Research in Music Education, 27*(1), 21–32. https://doi.org/10.1177/153660060502700103

McCarthy, M. (1993). The birth of internationalism in music education, 1899–1938. *International Journal of Music Education, 21*, 3–15. https://doi.org/10.1177/025576149302100101

McCarthy, M. (1995). *Canticle to Hope:* Widening horizons in international music education, 1939–1953. *International Journal of Music Education, 25*, 38–49. https://doi.org/10.1177/025576149502500105

McCarthy, M. (1999). *The Bulletin of Historical Research in Music Education:* A content analysis of articles in the first twenty volumes. *Bulletin of Historical Research in Music Education, 20*(3), 181–202. https://doi.org/10.1177/153660069902000303

McCarthy, M. (2004). *Toward a global community: The International Society for Music Education 1953–2003.* International Society for Music Education.

McCarthy, M. (2012). Developments and trends in historical research as reflected in the 'Journal of Historical Research in Music Education', Volumes 21–30 (1999–2009). *Journal of Historical Research in Music Education, 33*(2), 152–171. https://doi.org/10.1177/153660061203300204

McCarthy, M. (2021, February 25–27). *Black music and music education in the decades leading up to Brown v. Board of Education* [Paper presentation]. National Association for Music Education Biennial National Music Research & Teacher Education Conference, virtual event.

McCarthy, M., & Hoffman, A. (in review). Music in African American schooling and community life in post-Emancipation Albemarle County, Virginia, 1865–1896.

McCollum, J., & Hebert, D. G. (2014). Advancing historical ethnomusicology. In J. McCollum & D. G. Hebert (Eds.), *Theory and method in historical ethnomusicology* (pp. 361–378). Lexington Books.

Music Educators National Conference. (1988). Special Issue: The Sesquicentennial. *Music Educators Journal, 74*(6).

Music Educators National Conference. (2007). *MENC: A century of service to music education 1907–2007.* MENC: The National Association for Music Education.

Nelson, S. L. (2004). The use of creativity in music textbook series, 1900–1950. *Journal of Historical Research in Music Education, 25*(2), 128–141.

Oral History Association. (2021). *Oral history: Defined.* www.oralhistory.org/about/do-oral-history

Pemberton, C. A. (1987). Revisionist historians: Writers reflected in their writings. *Journal of Research in Music Education, 35*(4), 213–220. https://doi.org/10.2307/3345074

Pemberton, C. A. (1992). Research in music education: One historian's experiences, perspectives, and suggestions. *Contribution to Music Education, 19*, 87–100. www.jstor.org/stable/24127399

Pemberton, C. A. (1999). Unconventional wisdom: Observing how research, writing and editing fly in the face of clichés. *Bulletin of Historical Research in Music Education, 20*(2), 115–120. www.jstor.org/stable/40214990

Preston, K. Y., & Humphreys, J. T. (2007). Historical research on music education and music therapy: Doctoral dissertations of the twentieth century. *Journal of Historical Research in Music Education, 29*(1), 55–73. https://doi.org/10.1177/153660060702900106

Rainbow, E. L., & Froehlich, H. C. (1987). *Research in music education: An introduction to systematic inquiry.* Schirmer Books.

Ritchie, D. A. (2003). *Doing oral history: A practical guide* (2nd. ed.). Oxford University Press.

Sanders, P. (2015). Temperance songs in American school songbooks, 1840–1860. *Journal of Historical Research in Music Education, 37*(1), 5–23.

Sanders, P. (2017). Temperance songs in American school songbooks, 1865–1899. *Journal of Historical Research in Music Education, 38*(2), 178–208. https://doi.org/10.1177/1536600615608464

Shansky, C. L. (2020). "We are aiming for quality and good music": The Hebrew Orphan Asylum Harmonica band (NYC) and music education, 1924–1930. *Journal of Historical Research in Music Education, 42*(1), 46–70. https://doi.org/10.1177/1536600619853885

Shopes, L. (2011). Oral history. In N. K. Denzin & Y. S. Lincoln (Eds.), *The SAGE handbook of qualitative research* (4th ed., pp. 451–465). Sage.

Simpson, G. A. (2019). *Content analysis of the Journal of Historical Research in Music Education: 1980–2019* [Doctoral dissertation]. The University of Mississippi. eGrove. https://egrove.olemiss.edu/etd/1944

Sommer, B. W., & Quinlan, M. K. (2018). *The oral history manual* (3rd ed.). Rowman & Littlefield.

Stone, L. (1979). The revival of narrative: Reflections on a new old history. *Past and Present, 85,* 3–24.

Sullivan, J. M. (2017). Women music teachers as military band directors during World War II. *Journal of Historical Research in Music Education, 39*(1), 78–105. https://doi.org/10.1177/1536600616665625

Sullivan, J. M. (2019). John Philip Sousa as music educator and fundraiser during World War I. *Journal of Historical Research in Music Education, 40*(2), 143–169. https://doi.org/10.1177/1536600617743013

Volk Tuohey, T. (2015). *A musician and teacher in nineteenth-century New England: Irving Emerson, 1843–1903.* Lexington Books.

Volk, T. M. (2007). Anne Shaw Faulkner Oberndorfer (1877–1948): Music educator for the homemakers of America. *Journal of Historical Research in Music Education, 29*(1), 26–39. https://doi.org/10.1177/153660060702900104

Ward-Steinman, P. M. (2003). Musical training and compensation in the Big Band era: A case study of Madura's Danceland from 1930–1950. *Journal of Historical Research in Music Education, 24*(2), 164–177. https://doi.org/10.1177/153660060302400204

Wasiak, E. B. (2000). School bands in Saskatchewan, Canada: A history. *Journal of Historical Research in Music Education, 21*(2), 112–131. https://doi.org/10.1177/153660060002100202

Wood, G. S. (2008). *The purpose of the past: Reflections on the use of history.* The Penguin Press.

CHAPTER 7

Purposes and Questions in Qualitative Research

This chapter:

- Describes how research purposes and questions emerge from an interpretive perspective;
- Summarizes distinct characteristics of various qualitative research traditions such as basic qualitative research, ethnography, phenomenology, case study, grounded theory, and narrative research; and
- Outlines and describes the conceptual and theoretical aspects of a proposal for qualitative research.

Questions and purposes situated in qualitative research contexts come from different traditions and worldviews. Their diversity leaves open the possibility that additional qualitative research practices may be on the horizon.

INTRODUCTION

> Qualitative research is a situated activity that locates the observer in the world. Qualitative research consists of a set of interpretive, material practices that make the world visible. These practices transform the world. They turn the world into a series of representations, including field notes, interviews, conversations, photographs, recordings, and memos to the self. At this level, qualitative research involves an interpretive, naturalistic approach to the world. This means that qualitative researchers study things in their natural settings, attempting to make sense of or interpret, phenomena in terms of the meanings people bring to them.
>
> (Denzin & Lincoln, 2017, p. 10)

Researchers who use qualitative research methods do so based on a belief that reality is socially constructed, complex, diverse, and not reducible to mutually exclusive, "objective" observations. Any documented observation is also an interpretation, which cannot and should not be separated from the researcher's way of knowing the world. Such epistemological underpinning requires that researchers are aware of and acknowledge their own perceived realities along with their observations.

Because qualitative research is contextual, many researchers prefer to guide their work with questions instead of or in addition to statements of purpose. Such questions seek "to make sense of or interpret phenomena in terms of the meanings people bring to them" (Denzin & Lincoln, 2017, p. 10).

DOI: 10.4324/9781003057703-10

Descriptive questions posit: "What is happening here?" Analytic queries ask, "What does this mean?" Theoretical analyses propose new holistic ways in which observations and descriptions might be interpreted and understood within their respective contexts (Roulston, 2006, p. 156). All three analytic processes may be involved from the onset of the study. To do the data full justice, researchers visit and revisit them repeatedly throughout a project.

When we think of music education in its broadest sense, countless questions lend themselves to consideration and study. All aspects of observing music learning and instructional processes may be embedded in systematic reflection about and interpretation of the research process itself. Participation means involvement; research questions therefore mirror that involvement.

Take, for instance, the following selection of research purposes and questions. Each of the approaches reflects to varying degrees the connection between rationale, purpose, and the researcher's role in the investigative process:

"Exploring Access, Intersectionality, and Privilege in Undergraduate Music Education Courses"

Curiosity about how preservice teachers "adopt dispositions toward teaching in socially just ways" (Escalante, 2020, p. 23) led Samuel Escalante to design a qualitative study around a three-session social justice workshop "to investigate undergraduate music education students' understandings of and attitudes toward sensitive social justice issues" (p. 25). Escalante's research question addressed 1) participants' "understandings of and attitudes toward issues of equity and diversity," 2) participants' "perceptions of the workshop itself," and 3) any challenges the participants experienced "throughout the workshop" (p. 25). Escalante chose the basic qualitative approach because his purpose was "to understand how the participants made sense of their experiences" (Merriam & Tisdell, 2015). Escalante did not "seek additional methodological dimensions" (as might be found in the other traditions described in this chapter) so as to remain "open to possibilities that may not necessarily have arisen naturally with stricter parameters of other qualitative research paradigms" (p. 25).

"Mutual Learning and Democratic Action in Instrumental Music Education"

Dissatisfaction with the "false dichotomy" caused by "the disconnection between the music studied at school and the hidden or private musical world of our students" (p. 25) inspired Randall Allsup (2003) to create and study *mutual learning communities*, defined as "workable space[s] where students and educators [come] together to share and create music" (p. 25). Allsup's research questions

> were both philosophical and pedagogical: How would the participating groups evolve and define themselves through the practice of composing and analyzing music? What would our choices reflect or signify? How might this experience affect individual growth as well as community-making? And finally, how is such a project congruent with philosophies of democratic education (Dewey, 1916; Freire, 1970, 2000; Greene, 1988, 1995, 2000; hooks, 1994). (p. 25)

"Degree Perseverance Among African Americans Transitioning from Historically Black Colleges and Universities (HBCUs) to Predominantly White Institution (PWIs)"

As a female African American band director who earned degrees from PWIs (Predominantly White Institutions), Joyce McCall (2015) knew Black colleagues who faced a difficult transition between undergraduate study at HBCUs (Historically Black Colleges and Universities) and graduate study at a PWI. Using a narrative method to examine such experiences, the following questions guided her phenomenological study:

1) What are the experiences of African Americans who have transitioned from undergraduate music programs at HBCUs to graduate music programs at PWIs?
2) How do these students compare academic, social, and cultural aspects of their experience within two institutional environments?
3) What are these students' self-perceptions of their own degree perseverance?
4) What social, cultural, and academic aspects of their experience influence perseverance among African Americans who have transitioned from undergraduate music programs at HBCUs to graduate music programs at PWIs? (p. 4)

"Virtual Vocal Ensembles and the Mediation of Performance on YouTube"

Inspired initially by the work of composer Eric Whitacre (well before the Covid-19 pandemic would make virtual music-making ubiquitous in music education), Christopher Cayari (2016) sought to understand virtual music- making via "collective, collaborative, and one-person virtual vocal ensembles" (p. 13) by exploring "the complex implications of what happens when singing with others becomes an asynchronous activity produced through digital files instead of face-to-face" (p. 16). Two guiding questions directed his multiple case study:

1) "What are the musical and social implications of virtual vocal ensemble participation and creation?
2) How does a medium emerge as people create virtual vocal ensembles?" (pp. 17–18).

Sub-questions addressed who, how and why the creators crafted the videos, its impact on creator skills and identity, the emergence of community, institutional impacts, and networks "through which the medium emerges" (pp. 17–18).

"The Process of Social Identity Development in Adolescent High School Choral Singers: A Grounded Theory"

Concern with the social identity development of adolescents inspired Elizabeth Parker's 2009 study of high school choral settings. She sought to construct a theory to "more fully explicate the contextual conditions, actions/interactions, core phenomenon, intervening conditions and consequences of social identity processes that are being engaged in high school choral ensembles" (p. 5). Her main and secondary research questions included the following:

"How do high school students describe the development of their social identity within the context of the high school choir?

• What actions/interactions influence high school students' social identity development in choir?
• What strategies do high school students use to develop social identity in choir?
• What intervening conditions influence high school students' social identity development in choir?
• What consequences result from high school students' development of social identity in choir?" (p. 5)

"Navigating the Experience of an Adult Piano Student"

Piano teacher and researcher Seyeon Kang (2016) was intrigued when long-haul truck driver "Mr. K revealed that he wanted to learn the piano." She described the rationale for her narrative study this way:

> I wondered what led him to decide to [learn the piano]. . . . I became interested in how his life experiences influenced his learning piano, and how his learning piano impacted his life. . . . I also wondered how storytelling helped the teller. I took these wonderings about motivation and self-directed learning, the contexts and experiences of adult music students, and the role of storying with me as I set out on the road to research Mr. K's experience as an adult piano student.
>
> (p. 101)

Considering the topics and approaches featured in the above questions, you may notice that each of the examples reflect what philosophers call an interpretive worldview. The following section of this chapter summarizes the characteristics of the qualitative research traditions that are most frequently used to investigate topics germane to music education in its many forms (i.e., grounded theory, ethnography, phenomenology, case study designs, and narrative inquiry). Finally, we provide guidelines for the conceptual elements of qualitative research proposal (including a 'basic' qualitative project for those not committed to a particular tradition). Chapter 8 then outlines major procedural considerations for qualitative research in music education. The information provided in both qualitative chapters rely on such sources as Barrett and Stauffer (2009), Charmaz (2008a, 2008b, 2014), Conway (2020), Denzin and Lincoln (2017), Glaser and Strauss (1967/2009), and Strauss and Corbin (1990). Other sources are acknowledged where quotations are directly attributable to them. Chapter 13 addresses three related procedures: Mixed Methods Research, Practitioner Inquiry/Action Research and Arts-based Research.

RESEARCH WITH AN INTERPRETIVE PERSPECTIVE

Qualitative research questions take as a given that all research reflects a particular worldview in a specific setting. Each research participant (including the researcher) is assumed to construct a unique reality. Thus, individual understandings of experiences and knowledge can only be shared with the researcher present, or "embodied" in the space in which the phenomenon under study takes place. Many researchers who share in such a worldview reject the notion of universals of truth. Rather, they believe in the "here-and-now" of knowledge, temporary from moment to moment. This viewpoint distinguishes it from quantitative and even historical inquiry.

However, belief in the temporary nature of knowledge and perceived reality does not prevent the researcher from gaining insight into that which is being investigated. As the construction of knowledge involves continual unfolding and decision-making, change is a constant in the work of a qualitative researcher who should acknowledge, if not welcome it. Signifiers of the ongoing construction of knowledge, changes of mind and unanticipated actions are often the source of unanticipated insights. Thus, for many scholars, initial research purposes and questions are fluid and emergent. But they are necessary nonetheless, to provide direction and a basis for documenting and examining changes in knowledge.

In addition to purposes and/or questions, qualitative investigations must be framed theoretically. Such a framework argues the purpose for the investigation (see Chapter 3), presents the literature-based and/or philosophical perspectives that guide the study (see Chapters 2, 4, and 5), and articulates the researcher's reasons for design choices (see Chapter 8). Even an inductive approach requires a framework, if only to declare an intent to remain open to what transpires.

The partnership that arises when researchers ask questions as both data gatherer and participant can occur on a continuum from fully involved participant to (mostly) detached observer (see Figure 7.1).

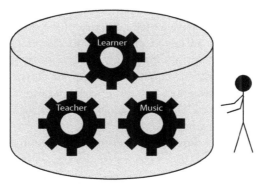

The Researcher as Bystander:
Non-Participant Observer, Involuntary
Contributor to All Observed Interactions
IMAGE A

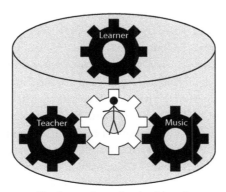

The Researcher as involved Agent:
Conscious Contributor to All Recorded Interactions
IMAGE B

FIGURE 7.1 The Researcher's Role as Participant and Non-Participant

Being aware of one's place on that continuum is part of the qualitative research process and requires written acknowledgement. Likewise, the "place" of a researcher in the research setting varies, depending on their purpose for being there. Some researchers strive to minimize their involvement in the field, whereas others make no such effort, but acknowledge and report how their presence may have interrupted or changed the situation under study. A third group purposefully becomes integral to what is being observed; such is stated in their research questions. Being thusly "situated" in the research means acknowledging one's role as an interpreter rather than reporter; this premise is assumed to strengthen rather than weaken the veracity of qualitative observations.

Exploring the duality of insider-outsider can be a particular strength of qualitative research. Campbell (2003) describes the phenomenon, referring to the Greek terms *emic* and *etic* as capturing the ongoing tension between what we know as insiders to a situation (*emic*) and what we can know as outsiders (*etic*). Derived from the Greek word "phon*emic*," the insider is "akin to the perspective of one born and raised within a culture." "Phon*etic*" reflects "the perspective of someone born outside the culture of study" (p. 23). "Emic" and "etic" always work in tandem; at times in conflict, at times living smoothly side-by-side. In certain contexts the duality can even lead to *dialectic* prose and argumentation (see Chapters 4 and 5), based on a belief that no matter how hard any of us try to understand the people we study, the best we can do is to acknowledge that reality resides somewhere in-between our outsider view and that of the insiders we study.

Qualitative writing requires imagined dialogue with readers, expanding the connection between researcher and participants by anticipating how readers might respond to and engage with the writing both thoughtfully and emotionally. Thus, the charge of the researcher-writer is to develop not only skills of observation, but also of clear and evocative writing, weaving data, analysis and interpretation together. These methodological issues are addressed, along with other more technical considerations, in Chapter 8.

The characteristics described above are markers of excellence in qualitative research (Elliott, Fischer, & Rennie, 1999; Tracy, 2010): A *coherent* study stitches all components into an interconnected and engaging whole whose parts (research questions, appropriate methods, related literature, theoretical perspectives, and interpretations) are clear yet connected. *Credibility* is demonstrated by the use of multiple data sources (also called *triangulation*, which hints at a specific number and shape [see Roulston, 2018], or *crystallization*, suggested by Richardson and St. Pierre in 2017 to signify multiplicity without constraints in shape or number). A detailed "thick" representation of observed actions, events, and related reflections also brings credibility to a research account. *Reflexivity* is demonstrated when an author acknowledges and reflects upon personal biases and preconceptions, and *rigor* is present when data are sufficiently plentiful, rich, and varied. *Resonance* can address the extent to which a writer's work evokes a response from readers; and for some studies, the degree to which findings suggest a theoretical model. Finally, *trustworthiness* speaks to the relevance and timeliness of the research. Researchers reach that goal by being honest with themselves and their readers, and ethical toward others—both participants and peers.

Several authors suggest additional quality criteria based on a summarized version of Denzin & Lincoln's (2017) "moments," mentioned earlier in this chapter, based on the epistemological underpinnings of each moment (See Ravenek & Rudman, 2013). Finally, Robinson (2020) offers these specific questions to music education researchers (summarized for space considerations). Is the goal to:

- "know a specific thing . . . or to explore a group, a phenomenon, a happening, or an occurrence so as to further our understanding . . . ?"

- "measure the effectiveness" of one thing against another, or "know more about the choices and beliefs of a group of teachers, students, or community members?"
- "test a hypothesis . . . or to work toward change when we perceive inequity, unfairness, or a lack of justice?"
- "produce a product or measure a behavior, or sometimes simply to begin a conversation?"
- "provide an answer, or to provoke a thought?" (p. 145)

Evolution of Interpretive Research

The *interpretive* perspective arose from philosophical disagreements in the late 19th and early 20th centuries about the validity and applicability of specific scientific paradigms to questions in the human sciences. In contrast to the view of positivists, interpretivists suggested that understanding of human action is best approached by observing and/or experiencing such action in the settings where they occur (rather than manipulating behavior in lab settings), and at the same time trying to "grasp the meanings that constitute that action" (Schwandt, 2003, p. 296).

Primarily inductive in nature, methods developed to systematize observations and reflections are derived from and situated more in the study of text interpretation (*hermeneutics*, see Chapter 4) than in forms of experimental empiricism common to behavioristic research models. The often-used term "thick description," brought to anthropology by Geertz (1973) exemplifies the difference between the two worldviews: Explaining a wink simply as a behavior (i.e., contracting the eyelids) ignores its meaning. To get at intention, a researcher's interpretation of human action must include the perspective of the actor(s)—in this case, the winker—and the context in which the wink is delivered.

The belief systems that undergird interpretive research questions have evolved from post-positivist roots to the vibrant and multi-faceted interpretive community of the present. Authors Denzin and Lincoln (2017, pp. 9–10) suggest that eight "moments" mark those changes:

- Traditional (1900–1950): a period "associated with the positivist, foundational paradigm" (p. 10).
- Modernist or golden age (1950–1970) and Blurred genres (1970–1980): moments "connected to the appearance of postpositivist arguments" and simultaneously to "a variety of new interpretive, qualitative perspectives" by which "the researcher became a bricoleur . . . learning to how to borrow from many different disciplines" (p. 10).
- The paradigm wars (1980–1985): a time when "qualitative researchers fought for a place at the table, resisting positivist domination from the SBR [science-based research] machine" (p. 10).
- Crisis of representation (1986–1990): Produced by the blurred genres phase, "researchers struggled with how to locate themselves and their subjects in reflective texts," and as a result moved between a variety of perspectives (p. 10).
- Postmodern experimental moment (1990–1995): "Researchers continued to move away from foundational and quasifoundational criteria" and to seek "alternative evaluative criteria . . . that might prove evocative, moral, critical, and rooted in local understandings" (p. 10).
- Post-experimental inquiry (1995–2000), methodologically contested present (2000–2004), paradigm proliferation (2005–2010), the fractured post-human present (2010–2015), and the uncertain, utopian future (2016-present): Moments that "overlap in the present" (p. 10).
    (For further discussion of these moments and their conflicts, see Clarke, Friese, & Washburn, 2015; Lather, 2006; Ravenek & Rudman, 2013; and St. Pierre & Roulston, 2006.)

QUALITATIVE RESEARCH TRADITIONS

Qualitative research traditions have evolved from many disciplines: the humanities as well as the social sciences, evaluation research, and even literary and linguistic theory. The traditions used most often for qualitative research in music education focus on methodology (i.e., ethnography), philosophy (i.e., phenomenology), research design (i.e., case study), analysis (i.e., grounded theory), and even the medium in which the researcher works (i.e., narrative inquiry). These distinctions reflect the decisions researchers make about their work.

While we encourage an understanding of the various research labels, we caution against seeing the "traditions" as fixed. Like the boundaries on a map, they are more obvious in theory than on the ground. There are many examples of "border crossings:" ethnographers who write from a phenomenological perspective, case studies that use grounded theory for analysis, and so forth. Why, then, do the distinctions matter? Because the various qualitative traditions evolved from different disciplines. Within each sub-discipline are conventions for representing knowledge, making and backing up assertions, and communicating with the community of scholars (Shulman, 1999). In Schoenfeld's words,

> The application of any research method is only as good as the match between the assumptions underlying the method and the set of circumstances being explored. And if there is a mismatch, the findings may well be either meaningless or wrong.
>
> (1999, p. 180)

Basic Qualitative Research

Interpretivism, the belief that reality is open to interpretation, is central to all qualitative research. Closely related is constructivism, the notion that individuals construct their own reality. Together, these ideas suggest that qualitative researchers have an interest in "(1) how people interpret their experiences, (2) how they construct their worlds, and (3) what meaning they attribute to their experiences. The overall purpose is to *understand* how people make sense of their lives and their experiences" (Merriam & Tisdell, 2015, p. 24, emphasis original).

While many qualitative researchers identify with one or more of the qualitative traditions described below, it is possible to do a qualitative study that does not identify with a specific tradition. Merriam and Tisdell (2015) call this the "basic qualitative" approach. In this context, the word "basic" does not address the distinction between research for the sake of advancing knowledge and research for solving practical problems as described in Chapter 1, but rather the basic underlying premises and methods for qualitative research. Studies based on specific qualitative traditions "have an *additional* dimension" (p. 24, emphasis original). For this reason, Conway (2020) encourages novice researchers and others who may not want to be "boxed in" by specifics of one of the other traditions to follow the basic qualitative approach.

Ethnographic Research

Ethnographic procedures were first developed by western anthropologists to study the culture of "other" people, a perspective that tended to privilege the Western point of view (Clifford, 1983, p. 118). Prodded by the interpretive turn along with the dissolution of colonialism and subsequent human rights and ethnic power movements that occurred in the early and mid-20th century, ethnography evolved into a more "generalized" tradition that acknowledges difference as a human invention (p. 119).

Ethnographers learn about and describe observed actions and interactions between individuals in an in-depth manner known as *immersion*. They spend extended time observing and interviewing participants in natural settings. Data are collected by way of observation, interview, document analysis, and personal reflection. Ethnographies may be written from the researcher's point of view or that of the participant(s), who are often called *informants* in this research tradition.

Doing ethnography requires identifying and approaching one or more groups who represent the researcher's purpose. Guided first by the rules of research ethics (described in Chapter 8 as well as in Chapter 3), access is often gained by contacting a member of the group who mediates between the researcher and the group members—ethnographers call this person the *gatekeeper*. Living in the research environment (known as *the field*), it is sometimes difficult for the researcher to navigate between the shared roles of researcher and participant. This challenge can compromise a study if the researcher is unreflective of its impact on their work.

Ethnographic questions in music education might ask: "What is the nature of musical culture among . . .?" Or "What cultures and sub-cultures emerge in a typical (or elite or underserved) middle school choral (or band or other musical) setting?" Allsup (2003), featured above, added what he called an "experimental" component to the ethnographic perspective by initiating the small democratic musical ensembles whose evolving cultures he studied.

Influenced by philosophy, sociology, and anthropology, *ethnomusicology* is a discipline whose data comprise music performed and/or notated along with the researcher's experience of becoming part of a musical culture. The researcher is therefore as much a "participant performer" as a participant observer (Campbell, 2003, p. 23). In addition to the traditional qualitative procedures of observation, interview, and document/artifact analysis (see Chapter 8), ethnomusicological research involves transcribing musical activities with the goal of describing the transmission of musical traditions. Contemporary researchers use modern tools such as hand-held digital recording devices, but the earliest ethnomusicologists carried such things as Edison wax cylinders and heavy battery-operated recorders (p. 23). Watch, for instance, the film called *The Songcatcher* (2000) and notice what happened as the researcher became immersed in the Appalachian sub-culture.

Like ethnographers, ethnomusicologists typically spend at least a year immersed in a musical culture, more if the study involves short visits rather than a long residency. The distinction for music educators is whether exploring the musical aspects of a given situation will provide new information about music teaching and learning.

Often music educator/ethnomusicologists begin by studying with a master teacher, using this experience to get to know a musical culture. This might mean recording and analyzing the music of a culture from a distant location, but it could just as easily be closer to home. For example, a pioneering ethnomusicological study of the musical creativity of young children was undertaken by the Pillsbury Foundation in the 1940's. Researchers Moorhead and Pond (1978/1941, 1942, 1944, 1951) investigated how children developed as musicians through musical play by observing young children in that setting. A more recent example, published as *Songs in their Heads*, is Campbell's 2010 study of the meanings young children give the music in their lives, as demonstrated by musical play at school and at home.

Phenomenological Research

As a philosophical worldview, phenomenology dates back many centuries (see Chapter 5). Scholars such as van Manen (1990) and Moustakas (1994) are responsible for bringing the phenomenological research tradition to the United States. Their application of phenomenology to mental and physical health has provided guidance to researchers in many fields.

Moustakas (1994) describes the phenomenological approach as "a process of internal search through which one discovers the nature and meaning of experience." This quest places the "self of the researcher" into the process of inquiry, thereby increasing the depth of understanding a phenomenon. The positioning in the process also leads to a researcher's "growing self-awareness and self-knowledge" (p. 17). A phenomenological researcher, therefore, seeks to get at the core of what makes a lived experience what it is, and without which it would not be the same (p. 10).

Phenomena, according to Vagle (2014) "are not constructed, designed, or defined in the autonomously-encased human mind separated from the world," a la Descartes (p. 20). Neither are they "unexplainable occurrences produced by outside forces. Rather, phenomena are the ways in which we find ourselves being in relation to the world through out day-to-day living" (p. 20).

Closely connected to dialectics, interpretivism and hermeneutics, phenomenological research allows for an open-ended research process. Its degree of scholarship rests in the rigor of carefully probing and analyzing diverse viewpoints and examining different "understandings" of the "life world." Sorting through such understandings becomes the body of knowledge from which new questions emerge. Researchers like Bernard (2015) and McCall (2015) have found the phenomenological perspective useful for understanding the lived experiences of music educators in particular circumstances.

Case Study

As much a design as a method, case studies reflect the traditions of the fields in which they are used: business, education, law, medicine, political science, psychology, and sociology, to name a few. They differ in definition, structure, and purpose but have in common the selection of one or more cases for study that represent a researcher's purpose. A "bounded" case is specific; it may be an individual, a group of individuals, or one particular setting during a prescribed period of time. It may not, however, be a process such as a relationship, a method, or a belief system—these may emerge as factors within case studies but do not themselves constitute a case.

Qualitative case studies can involve ethnographic or phenomenological procedures and be referred to as collective, intrinsic, instrumental, and comparative (Stake, 1995). Unique cases tend to be *intrinsic* or *instrumental*. An intrinsic case might be chosen because of its uniqueness (p. 3); for instance, a teacher whose background or current position is compelling and distinctive, a group of amateur or professional musicians who have found an unusual performance niche, or other one-of-a-kind examples of music teaching and learning. An instrumental case illustrates a common situation that may have transferable value beyond the case itself; it serves to make a point beyond the situation examined. Such might be the case when a researcher chooses an individual music teacher or a single music program as a "case" that exemplifies a common issue such as school reform or assessment.

Studies that involve multiple cases may be *collective* or *comparative* (Stake, 1995, p. 3–4). In the former, each case is examined descriptively without comparison to the other cases. The result is a comprehensive picture of multiple cases as they relate to the research purpose. In contrast, a comparative case study utilizes multiple cases for the purpose of looking at similarities and differences among them. Such projects can be cross-cultural and even international, although some researchers might question the wisdom behind such broad-scaled comparisons. Both Cayari's (2016) study of three *YouTube* channel video creators, and Kruse's (2014) study of hip hop as music education were multiple case studies.

Grounded Theory

Grounded theory is unique among qualitative traditions because it suggests specific guidelines for gathering and analyzing data. These guidelines were initially developed by two sociologists, Barney Glaser and Anselm Strauss (1967/2009) to provide a transparent method for inductive theorizing from qualitative data. Grounded theory procedures initially were intended to enable qualitative researchers to stake a scientific claim for their work, which was important during what Denzin and Lincoln (2017), have called the "modernist" or "golden age" moment. Although constant comparison, or concurrent data collection and analysis, is now a common qualitative procedure, it was an innovation when suggested by Glaser and Strauss in 1967 (Charmaz, 2008b).

Since then the process has been expanded and further codified by Strauss and Corbin (1990/1998), Charmaz (2008a, 2008b, 2014), Corbin and Strauss (2014), and others. These procedures enable researchers to theorize about relational questions, such as: What relationships exist between social identity development and participation in high school choir (Parker, 2014)? How does the process of including an individual with special needs in choir create change in that individual (Haywood, 2006)? The initial concern with scientific veracity has been replaced by an intentional turn toward constructivism.

Despite or perhaps because of its "modernist" beginnings, grounded theory is now used by researchers with a wide variety of worldviews, the result of which has consequences for other qualitative traditions as well. We find that its systemized nature provides concrete guidelines for novice researchers (see Chapter 8).

Narrative Research

Throughout history, people have used stories (or narratives) to construct their understandings of the world (Barrett & Stauffer, 2009, p. 7), explaining not only the facts, but also what those facts mean to them (Bowman, 2006, p. 8). The human tendency toward narrative is so strong that psychologist Jerome Bruner (1986) called it a "way of knowing" (in contrast to "logico-scientific" or "paradigmatic" knowing, which seeks universal truths). Thus, the term "narrative research" (sometimes also called narrative *inquiry*) specifically denotes "the study of experience as story" (Clandinin, 2006).

Stauffer (2020) observes that music education researchers tend to follow one of three pathways into narrative inquiry: the psychological point of view suggested by Bruner (1986), Clandinin and Connelly's narratives of personal experience, often focusing on the work of educators (e.g., Clandinin, 2006; Connelly & Clandinin, 2006; Clandinin, 2013), or Tom Barone's pathway of critical storytelling, described below.

Rooted in the philosophies of John Dewey, Clandinin (2006) posits a three-dimensional "metaphoric narrative inquiry space" (p. 47) that distinguishes narrative research from other qualitative traditions:

- Interaction, describing the personal and social elements of the situation;
- Continuity, recognizing past, present, and future implications; and
- Situation, or place, depicting the physical details of the place where the research takes place, and acknowledging its impact on the stories and their interpretation.

(p. 47)

Narrative researchers focus on a combination of *telling* stories and *living* them (Connelly & Clandinin, 2006, p. 478). A researcher focused on "telling" concentrates on stories conveyed by participant(s), or on their own interpretation (or re-telling) of those stories. They may emphasize the story or its meaning. Research from the perspective of "living" includes an ethnographic dimension, the researcher's recounting of being involved in the life or lives of the other participants. Kang (2016), whose questions are included in the examples above, merged the two in her own "wonderings about motivation and self-directed learning, the contexts and experiences of adult music students, and the role of storying" (p. 101) with stories shared by Mr. K. in an effort to "research Mr. K.'s experience as an adult piano student" (p. 101).

The line between using aesthetic tools for qualitative research and doing qualitative research for an aesthetic purpose is, like other boundaries, open to interpretation. Two sub-genres that straddle that boundary are worthy of mention. *Autoethnography* is a research method that focuses deliberately on the researcher's point of view. An "autobiographical genre of writing and research that displays multiple layers of consciousness, connecting the personal to the cultural" (Ellis & Bochner, 2000, p. 739), autoethnography focuses on the "self" within specific cultural contexts. Ellis and Bochner suggest that autoethnography is particularly pertinent when "the success of your work depends on developing some degree of intercultural understanding . . ." (p. 760). In his study of hip-hop music education, Kruse (2014) employed autoethnography as a way to translate his "personal position within larger societies and my vacillation between insider/outsider statuses in hip-hop musical settings" (p. 61).

The sub-genre known as *literary non-fiction* or *critical storytelling* (Barone, 1992) has much in common with investigative journalism (p. 145). Written from the perspective of critical theory, "the responsible story . . . adopts an openly political stance" (p. 143). A well-known example is Barone's (1989) "Ways of Being at Risk: The Case of Billy Charles Barnett." Following Sartre's claim that the writer is responsible to "speak for those who cannot speak for themselves," Barone explored the many kinds of "riskiness" that threatened the future of an adolescent boy who was failing in a rural southern school. Telling the Billy Charles' story led Barone "to rethink my tired notions about such fundamentals as, oh, the meaning of life, the purposes of schooling, and the various ways in which an adolescent can be at risk of not being educated" (p. 147). By turning a qualitative case study into a story with a beginning, middle and end, Barone reached an audience that might not otherwise have been aware "of the locations of [the] characters' thoughts, beliefs, desires, and habits, in the webs of contingencies that constitute their life-worlds" (p. 142).

In sum, curiosity and inventiveness, coupled with stamina and persuasiveness, are the factors that ultimately propel qualitative researchers. What may or may not be considered factual, what qualifies as evidence, and what deserves to be called truth are ongoing questions that have been debated for centuries and have thus triggered an ever-increasing pool of methodological possibilities.

CONSIDERING RESEARCH POSSIBILITIES

If you, like several students in RC533, sense a connection between the interpretive research described in this chapter and your own thinking, it may be time to pay attention to the details of that relationship. As you can see from the lists below, qualitative research can seek to understand human experiences across a wide variety of places, points of view, phenomena, and perspectives. We suggest examining a few that you find interesting.

Places, Points of View, Phenomena, and Perspectives

Nearly everything opens up as a research field when you consider qualitative research approaches—locations such as playgrounds (e.g., Harwood, 1993; Campbell, 2010) or prisons (e.g. Cohen, 2007; Edri & Bensimon, 2018). Research questions might suggest a focus on a music classroom from the students' points of view (e.g., Adderley, Kennedy, & Berz, 2003; Silvey, 2005; Gouzouasis, Henrey, & Belliveau, 2008; Parker, 2014), or that of the teacher (e.g., Reese, 2006; Cronenberg, 2016). Other foci might include the experience of being in a music-making family (e.g., Gingras, 2012); a children's choir (e.g., Hall, 2018; Lindl, 2018); or of virtual music-making (e.g., Cayari, 2016) or music learning (e.g., Waldron, 2013).

You might seek to understand phenomena like refugee resettlement (e.g., Crawford, 2016; Jaber, 2020); mundane or extraordinary experiences of individuals (e.g., Kang, 2016; Nichols, 2016) or groups (e.g., Berglin, 2015; D'Alexander, 2015). Even school reform policies, of interest to Michelle, has found its way into qualitative research (e.g., Craig, 2003; Frierson-Campbell, 2003; Kos, 2007; Bernard, 2015).

You might examine research questions through a construct such as gender (e.g., Legg, 2010; McBride, 2016), a theory like critical pedagogy (e.g., Bernard, 2015) or intersectionality (Berglin, 2018; Escalante, 2020), a cultural issue such as war (e.g., Walker, 2009), or a philosophical perspective such as Jorgensen's dialectics (e.g., Cronenberg, 2016), feminism (e.g., Patteson, 2013), critical race theory (e.g., McCall, 2015), or even "post everything" (see Lather, 2006; Carlson, Wells, Mark, & Sandoval, 2021; St. Pierre, 2021).

Researcher Position

The interpretive perspective requires that qualitative researchers acknowledge their own points of view as well as their position in the research at every step of the process. Thus, starting now, we encourage you to consider the make-up of your researcher lens, whether personal interest, insights gleaned from personal experience, the literature, or formal, published theories and philosophies (Scheib, 2020, p. 57). Consider also, if you are proposing research, 1) the locations and participants suggested by your research questions, and your reasons for seeing those as possibilities, as well as 2) your own imagined place in the research, and your reasons for that position. Ultimately, you will craft the perspectives that ground your work into a section of your proposal (often called a "conceptual" or "theoretical framework") that clearly communicates your own biases and subjectivities. (For a thorough discussion of theoretical framing for qualitative research, see Scheib, 2020.)

CRAFTING A PROPOSAL FOR QUALITATIVE RESEARCH

A research proposal for a degree requirement usually has four sections or chapters: (1) Introduction, (2) Review of related literature, (3) Methods and Procedures, and (4) Conclusions. Its purpose is to connect your specific view of the topic to the published body of knowledge in the field, support your claim that there is a need for your study, and communicate that you have the necessary skills and knowledge to complete the proposed project.

In this chapter we describe how to write the first two sections of the proposal. The Methods and Procedures and Conclusion sections are described in Chapter 8. Guidance for mixed methods, participant inquiry/action research and arts-based proposals may be found in Chapter 13.

Preliminary Steps

Prior to formalizing your proposal, it is helpful to re-visit your thinking about your topic and research purpose and to re-assess your literature collection.

Purpose, Rationale and Purpose Specifications

Re-examine the purpose, rationale, and research questions you wrote in Chapter 3 to confirm that they suggest qualitative research—that is, using an interpretive perspective to understand a music education phenomenon. If you have doubts, discuss with your course instructor or project advisor.

Literature Collection

Assess the literature you have collected thus far. Many experienced qualitative researchers prefer to approach the literature after their research has begun. However, new researchers— particularly those preparing formal research proposals for a degree requirement or grant proposal—should have a thorough grounding in the literature surrounding their research topic and purpose as well as that explaining the tradition(s) that align most closely to their research questions.

   If such is not the case, you may need to try additional search terms to find additional sources. Re-visiting (and possibly revising) the literature map you completed in Chapter 2 may be helpful.

Writing the Introduction

In the introduction you expand on your research purpose and rationale to present a logical argument for your proposed research. While quantitative researchers use mathematical formulas and tables, qualitative researchers paint vivid pictures with the words they use to describe their work (Richardson & St. Pierre, 2017). As such, the introductory section should evoke not only the details of your topic but also the perspectives and lenses you bring to the study and the meanings you are trying to understand and interpret. Note that the words you use in explaining your topic and rationale signals to your committee and other readers that your intention is qualitative. Specific words may suggest a particular qualitative tradition (e.g., ethnography, ethnographic, or culture; lived experience; case; grounded theory; narrative or story, among others). Conclude this section with your statement of purpose, rationale, and research questions, constructing research questions to address each element of the topic under study: places, points of view, phenomena, perspectives, and researcher position.

Writing the Literature Review

The literature review communicates to readers that your research ideas are grounded in the traditions in which you will work. This review is often organized around your research questions. As with other types of research, literature within each sub-topic or question is typically arranged from general to more specific, often with a final transitional section that suggests connections between your research questions and the procedures you will be proposing. We have chosen to separate the discussion of procedures into the next chapter, but the reality when you're making decisions about qualitative research is much more fluid.

CHAPTER SUMMARY

1) Qualitative research methods reflect an interpretive worldview, a belief that reality is socially constructed, complex, diverse, and not reducible to mutually exclusive observations.
2) Because qualitative research is contextual, many researchers prefer to guide their work with questions instead of or in addition to statements of purpose.
3) Excellence in qualitative research depends on coherence, credibility, reflexivity, rigor, resonance, and worthiness.
4) Interpretive research is done in a naturalistic setting and involves a situated research perspective.
5) The philosophical underpinnings of interpretive research have evolved from post-positivism to a multiplicity of postmodern perspectives.
6) Beyond basic qualitative research, the labels used most often by music educators for qualitative traditions focus on methodology (i.e., ethnography), philosophy (i.e., phenomenology), research design (i.e., case study), analysis (i.e., grounded theory), and the medium in which the researcher works (i.e., narrative inquiry).

Topics for Further Exploration

1) What are the similarities and differences between the worldviews behind qualitative and quantitative research traditions?
2) How can you recognize excellence based on coherence, credibility, reflexivity, rigor, resonance, and worthiness?
3) Discuss the pros and cons of doing basic qualitative research versus one or more of the traditions described in this chapter and Chapter 8. Is it better to keep the traditions separate or combine them?
4) Why are qualitative researchers expected to acknowledge their own perspective(s) and position(s) in their research?
5) How might you address your own interests using one or more of the research traditions described in this chapter?

Suggested Assignments

1) Look through published research studies that used the qualitative traditions described above. Try to find sources that address similar topics with different traditions. Write a response to each of the studies you read:
   a. To what extent does each source exemplify the shared characteristics described at the beginning of this chapter?
   b. What are the similarities and differences? The strengths and weaknesses?
2) Write a preliminary review of one of the sources listed in the section on **places, points of view, phenomena, and perspectives** to ascertain excellence based on characteristics of coherence, credibility, reflexivity, rigor, resonance, and worthiness. Report to your classmates and compare your findings to theirs.

Recommended Reading

Basic Qualitative Study

Merriam, S. B., & Tisdell, E. J. (2015). *Qualitative research: A guide to design and implementation.* John Wiley & Sons, Incorporated.

Case Study

Stake, R. (1995). *The art of case study research.* Sage.
Yin, R. K. (2021). *Case study research and applications* (6th ed.). SAGE Publications Inc. Student resources: https://study.sagepub.com/yin6e/student-resources-0)

Ethnography/Ethnomusicology

Campbell, P. S. (2003). Ethnomusicology and music education: Crossroads for knowing music, education, and culture. *Research Studies in Music Education, 21*(16), 16–30.
Wolcott, H. F. (2008). *Ethnography: A way of seeing* (2nd ed.). AltaMira Press.

Grounded Theory

Charmaz, K. (2014). *Constructing grounded theory* (2nd ed.). Sage Publishing.
Corbin, J., & Strauss, A. (2014). *Basics of qualitative research* (3rd ed.). Sage Publishing.

Narrative Research

Barrett, M. S., & Stauffer, S. L. (2009). *Narrative inquiry in music education: Troubling certainty.* Springer Science + Business Media.
Connelly, F. M., & Clandinin, D. J. (2006). Narrative inquiry. In J. L. Green, G. Camilli, & P. Elmore (Eds.), *Handbook of complementary methods in education research* (3rd ed., pp. 477–487). Lawrence Erlbaum.
Stauffer, S. L. (2020). Narrative inquiry and the uses of narrative in music education research. In C. M. Conway (Ed.), *The Oxford handbook of qualitative research in American music education* (Vol. 1, pp. 125–147). Oxford University Press.

Phenomenology

Manen, M. V. (1990). *Researching lived experience: Human science for an action sensitive pedagogy.* The Althouse Press.
Moustakas, C. (1994). *Phenomenological research methods.* Sage.
Vagle, M. D. (2014). *Crafting phenomenological research.* Routledge

Overview of Qualitative Research

Bogdan, R. C., & Biklen, S. K. (2007). *Qualitative research for education: An introduction to theory and methods* (5th ed.). Allyn and Bacon.
Bresler, L. (2010). Ethnography, phenomenology and action research in music education. *Visions of Research in Music Education, 16*(4). http://www-usr.rider.edu/~vrme/ (Reprinted from *The Quarterly Journal of Music Teaching and Learning, 6*(3), 4–16)
Creswell, J. W., & Poth, C. M. (2018). *Qualitative inquiry and research design: Choosing among five approaches* (4th ed.). Sage.

Theoretical Underpinnings of Qualitative Research

Denzin, N. K., & Lincoln, Y. S. (2017). Introduction: The discipline and practice of qualitative research. In N. K. Denzin & Y. S. Lincoln (Eds.), *The Sage handbook of qualitative research* (pp. 1–32). Sage Publications.

Lather, P. (2006). Paradigm proliferation as a good thing to think with: Teaching research in education as a wild profusion. *International Journal of Qualitative Studies in Education, 19(1),* 35–57. http://people.ehe.ohio-state.edu/plather/files/2008/11/qse-06-me.pdf

Helpful Resources

QualiQ Blog: www.qualiq.ca/blog

The Qualitative Report (open access peer reviewed journal and academic community): https://nsuworks.nova.edu/tqr/

QualPage blog, "Examining the world through qualitative inquiry": https://qualpage.com/

University of Huddersfield "open resource" lectures on qualitative research analysis: http://sre.hud.ac.uk/resources/HMB2009_QDA.htm

REFERENCES

Adderley, C., Kennedy, M., & Berz, W. (2003). "A home away from home": The world of the high school music classroom. *Journal of Research in Music Education, 51*(3), 190–205. https://doi.org/10.2307/3345373

Allsup, R. (2003). Mutual learning and democratic action in instrumental music education. *Journal of Research in Music Education, 51*(1), 24–37. https://doi-org/10.2307/3345646

Barone, T. E. (1989). Ways of being at risk: The case of Billy Charles Barnett. *Phi Delta Kappan, 71*(2), 147–151. www.jstor.org/stable/20404091.

Barone, T. E. (1992). Beyond theory and method: A case of critical storytelling. *Theory into Practice, 31*(2), 142–147. www.wilsonweb.com.

Barrett, M. S., & Stauffer, S. L. (2009). *Narrative inquiry in music education: Troubling certainty.* Springer Science + Business Media.

Berglin, J. A. (2015). "It's much more collaborative": Democratic action in contemporary collegiate a cappella. *Bulletin of the Council for Research in Music Education, 205,* 51–69. https://doi.org/10.5406/bulcouresmusedu.205.0051

Berglin, J. A. (2018). *"Behind the beautiful music is a person": The intersections of race and social class on the path to careers in music education* [Doctoral dissertation]. Northwestern University. ProQuest Dissertations and Theses (Publication No. 13419542).

Bernard, C. (2015). *Ensemble educators, administrators, and evaluation: Support, survival, and navigating change in a high-stakes environment* [Doctoral dissertation]. Teachers College, Columbia University. ProQuest Dissertations and Theses (Publication No. 3704455).

Bowman, W. D. (2006). Why narrative? Why now? *Research Studies in Music Education, 27*(1), 5–20. https://doi.org/10.1177/1321103X060270010101

Bruner, J. (1986). *Actual minds, possible worlds.* Harvard University Press.

Campbell, P. S. (2003). Ethnomusicology and music education: Crossroads for knowing music, education, and culture. *Research Studies in Music Education, 21*(16), 16–30. https://doi.org /10.1177/1321103X030210010201

Campbell, P. S. (2010). *Songs in their heads: Music and its meaning in children's lives* (2nd ed.). Oxford University Press.

Carlson, D. L., Wells, T. C., Mark, L., & Sandoval, J. (2021). Introduction: Working the tensions of the post-qualitative movement in qualitative inquiry. *Qualitative Inquiry, 27*(2), 151–157. https://doi.org/10.1177/1077800420922271

Cayari, C. (2016). *Virtual vocal ensembles and the mediation of performance on YouTube* [Doctoral dissertation]. University of Illinois at Urbana-Champaign. http://hdl.handle.net/2142/90478

Charmaz, K. (2008a). Constructionism and the grounded theory method. In J. A. Holstein & J. F. Gubrium (Eds.), *Handbook of constructionist research* (pp. 397–412). Guilford Press.

Charmaz, K. (2008b). Grounded theory as an emergent method. In S. N. Hesse-Biber & P. Leavy (Eds.), *Handbook of emergent methods* (pp. 155–170). Guilford Press.

Charmaz, K. (2014). *Constructing grounded theory* (2nd ed.). Sage Publishing.

Clandinin, D. J. (2006). Narrative inquiry: A methodology for studying lived experience. *Research Studies in Music Education, 27*(1), 44–54. https://doi.org/10.1177/1321103X060270010301

Clandinin, D. J. (2013). *Engaging in narrative inquiry*. Left Coast Press.

Clarke, A. E., Friese, C., & Washburn, R. (2015). Introducing situational analysis. In A. E. Clarke, C. Friese, & R. Washburn (Eds.), *Situational analysis in practice: Mapping research with grounded theory* (pp. 11–75). Left Coast Press.

Clifford, J. (1983). On ethnographic authority. *Representations, 2*, 118–146. https://doi.org/10.2307/2928386

Cohen, M. L. (2007). *Christopher Small's concept of musicking: Toward a theory of choral singing pedagogy in prison contexts* [Doctoral dissertation]. University of Kansas. https://kuscholarworks.ku.edu/handle/1808/29289

Connelly, F. M., & Clandinin, D. J. (2006). Narrative inquiry. In J. L. Green, G. Camilli, & P. Elmore (Eds.), *Handbook of complementary methods in education research* (3rd ed., pp. 477–487). Lawrence Erlbaum.

Conway, C. M. (2020). *The Oxford handbook of qualitative research in American music education* (Vols. 1, 2, & 3). Oxford University Press.

Corbin, J., & Strauss, A. (2014). *Basics of qualitative research* (4th ed.). Sage.

Craig, S. (2003). *Narrative inquiries of school reform: Storied lives, storied landscapes, storied metaphors*. Information Age Publisher.

Crawford, R. (2016). Creating unity through celebrating diversity: A case study that explores the impact of music education on refugee background students. *International Journal of Music Education, 35*(3), 343–356. https://doi.org/10.1177/0255761416659511

Cronenberg, S. S. (2016). *Music at the middle: Principles that guide middle level general music teachers* [Doctoral dissertation]. University of Illinois at Urbana-Champaign. http://hdl.handle.net/2142/90502

D'Alexander, C. M. (2015). *Voices from within: Perceptions of community youth orchestras and musical identities of child musicians* [Doctoral dissertation]. University of Southern California. ProQuest Dissertations and Theses (Publication No. 3704228).

Denzin, N. K., & Lincoln, Y. S. (2017). Introduction: The discipline and practice of qualitative research. In N. K. Denzin & Y. S. Lincoln (Eds.), *Handbook of qualitative research* (pp. 1–24). Sage Publications.

Edri, O., & Bensimon, M. (2018). The role of music among prisoners and prison staff: A qualitative research study. *European Journal of Criminology, 16*(6), 633–651. https://doi.org/10.1177/1477370818775295

Elliott, R., Fischer, C. T., & Rennie, D. L. (1999). Evolving guidelines for publication of qualitative research studies in psychology and related fields. *British Journal of Clinical Psychology, 38*, 215–229. www.psy.au.dk/fileadmin/site_files/filer_psykologi/dokumenter/Forskerskolen/Kurser09/Fishman/No_7-Elliott__Fischer__Rennie__1999_Standards_Qual_Research.PDF

Ellis, C., & Bochner, A. P. (2000). Autoethnography, personal narrative, reflexivity: Researcher as subject. In N. K. Denzin & Y. S. Lincoln (Eds.), *Handbook of qualitative research* (pp. 733–768). Sage Publications.

Escalante, S. (2020). Exploring access, intersectionality, and privilege in undergraduate music education courses. *Journal of Music Teacher Education, 29*(2), 22–37. https://doi.org/10.1177/1057083719873981

Frierson-Campbell, C. (2003). Professional need and the contexts of in-service music teacher identity. In H. Froehlich, D. Coan, & R. R. Rideout (Eds.), *Sociology of music education symposium III: Social dimensions of music, music teaching and learning* (pp. 199–216). Department of Music & Dance, University of Massachusetts.

Geertz, C. (1973). Thick description: Toward an interpretive theory of culture. In *The interpretation of cultures* (pp. 3–30). Basic Books.

Gingras, P. (2012). *Music at home: A portrait of family music-making* [Doctoral dissertation]. Eastman School of Music, University of Rochester. ProQuest Dissertations and Theses (Publication No. 3555024).

Glaser, B. G., & Strauss, A. L. (2009). *The discovery of grounded theory: Strategies for qualitative research*. Transaction Publishers. (Original work published 1967).

Gouzouasis, P., Henrey, J., & Belliveau, G. (2008). Turning points: A transitional story of grade seven music students' participation in high school band programmes. *Music Education Research, 10*(1), 75–90. https://doi.org/10.1080/14613800701871397

Hall, C. (2018). *Masculinity, class and music education: Boys performing middle-class masculinities through music.* Palgrave Macmillan UK.

Harwood, E. (1993). Content and context in children's playground songs. *Update: Applications of Research in Music Education, 12*(1), 4–8. https://doi-org/ 10.1177/875512339301200101

Haywood, J. (2006). You can't be in my choir if you can't stand up: One journey toward inclusion. *Music Education Research, 8*(3), 407–416.

Jaber, H. (2020). *An arts practice investigation of community music interventions in the context of post- conflict migration, with particular reference to the Syrian community in Ireland* [Doctoral dissertation]. Irish World Academy of Music and Dance, University of Limerick.

Kang, S. (2016). Navigating the experience of an adult piano student. *Bulletin of the Council for Research in Music Education, 210–211,* 101–118. https://doi.org/10.5406/bulcouresmusedu.210-211.0101

Kos, R. P. (2007). *Incidental change: The influence of educational policy implementation on music education programs and practice* [Doctoral dissertation]. University of Madison-Wisconsin. ProQuest Dissertations and Theses (Publication No. 3261425).

Kruse, A. J. (2014). *'They wasn't makin' my kinda music': Hip-hop, schooling, and music education* [Doctoral dissertation]. Michigan State University. https://d.lib.msu.edu/

Lather, P. (2006). Paradigm proliferation as a good thing to think with: Teaching research in education as a wild profusion. *International Journal of Qualitative Studies in Education, 19*(1), 35–57.

Legg, R. (2010). "One equal music": An exploration of gender perceptions and the fair assessment by beginning music teachers of musical compositions. *Music Education Research, 12*(2), 141–149. https://doi.org/10.1080/14613801003746592

Lindl, C. B. (2018). Chinese American adolescent identity in a children's choir: An exploratory study. *Bulletin of the Council for Research in Music Education, 218,* 35–48. https://doi.org/10.5406/bulcouresmusedu.218.0035

McBride, N. R. (2016). Singing, sissies, and sexual identity: How LGBTQ choral directors negotiate gender discourse. *Music Educators Journal, 102*(4), 36–40. https://doi.org/10.1177/0027432116644653

McCall, J. M. (2015). *Degree perseverance among African Americans transitioning from Historically Black Colleges and Universities (HBCUs) to Predominantly White Institution (PWIs)* [Doctoral dissertation]. Arizona State University. ProQuest Dissertations and Theses (Publication No. 3702142).

Merriam, S. B., & Tisdell, E. J. (2015). *Qualitative research: A guide to design and implementation.* John Wiley & Sons, Inc.

Moorhead, G. E., & Pond, D. (1978). *Music of young children.* Pillsbury Foundation for the Advancement of Music Education. (Original work printed in four Vols. 1941, 1942, 1944, 1951)

Moustakas, C. (1994). *Phenomenological research methods.* Sage.

Nichols, J. (2016). Sharing the stage: Ethical dimensions of narrative inquiry in music education. *Journal of Research in Music Education, 63*(4), 439–454. https://journals-sagepub-com.ezproxy.wpunj.edu/doi/full/10.1177/0022429415617745

Parker, E. C. (2009). *Understanding the process of social identity development in adolescent high school choral singers: A grounded theory* [Doctoral dissertation]. University of Nebraska-Lincoln. https://digitalcommons.unl.edu/dissertations/AAI3350454

Parker, E. C. (2014). The process of social identity development in adolescent high school choral singers: A grounded theory. *Journal of Research in Music Education, 62*(1), 18–32. https://doi.org/10.1177/0022429413520009

Patteson, A. (2013). Singing a woman's life: How singing lessons transformed the lives of nine women. *The Phenomenon of Singing, 2*(0), 184–195. https://journals.library.mun.ca/ojs/index.php/singing/article/view/674

Ravenek, M. J., & Rudman, D. L. (2013). Bridging conceptions of quality in moments of qualitative research. *International Journal of Qualitative Methods, 12*(1), 436–456. https://doi.org/10.1177/160940691301200122

Reese, J. W. (2006). *Definitions of improvisation: Perspectives of three elementary general music teachers* [Master's thesis]. University of Michigan. Proquest Dissertations and Theses.

Richardson, L., & St. Pierre, E. A. (2017). Writing: A method of inquiry. In N. K. Denzin & Y. S. Lincoln (Eds.), *The SAGE handbook of qualitative research* (5th ed., pp. 818–838). SAGE Publications, Inc.

Robinson, M. (2020). Changing the conversation: Considering quality in music education qualitative research. In C. M. Conway (Ed.), *The Oxford handbook of qualitative research in American music education* (Vol. 1, pp. 130–147). Oxford University Press.

Roulston, K. (2006). Mapping the possibilities of qualitative research in music education: A primer. *Music Education Research*, 8(2), 153–173. https://doi.org/10.1080/14613800600779592

Roulston, K. (2018, January 18). Triangulation in qualitative research. *QualPage* [blog]. https://qualpage.com/2018/01/18/triangulation-in-qualitative-research/

Scheib, J. (2020). Paradigms and theories: Framing qualitative research in music education. In C. M. Conway (Ed.), *The Oxford handbook of qualitative research in American music education* (pp. 56–73). Oxford University Press.

Schoenfeld, A. H. (1999). The core, the canon, and the development of research skills: Issues in the preparation of education researchers. In E. C. Lagemann & L. S. Shulman (Eds.), *Issues in education research: Problems and possibilities* (pp. 166–202). Jossey-Bass.

Schwandt, T. A. (2003). Three epistemological stances for qualitative inquiry: Interpretivism, hermeneutics, and social constructionism. In N. K. Denzin & Y. S. Lincoln (Eds.), *The landscape of qualitative research: Theories and issues* (2nd ed., pp. 292–331). Sage Publications.

Shulman, L. S. (1999). Professing educational scholarship. In E. C. Lagemann & L. S. Shulman (Eds.), *Issues in education research: Problems and possibilities* (pp. 159–165). Jossey-Bass.

Silvey, P. E. (2005). Learning to perform Benjamin Britten's "Rejoice in the Lamb": The perspectives of three high school choral singers. *Journal of Research in Music Education*, 53(2), 102–119. https://doi.org/10.2307/3345512

St. Pierre, E. A. (2021). Why post qualitative inquiry? *Qualitative Inquiry*, 27(2), 163–166. https://doi.org/10.1177/1077800420931142

St. Pierre, E. A., & Roulston, K. (2006). The state of qualitative inquiry: A contested science. *International Journal of Qualitative Studies in Education*, 19(6), 673–684. https://doi.org/10.1080/09518390600975644

Stake, R. (1995). *The art of case study research*. Sage.

Stauffer, S. L. (2020). Narrative inquiry and the uses of narrative in music education research. In C. M. Conway (Ed.), *The Oxford handbook of qualitative research in American music education* (Vol. 1, pp. 125–147). Oxford University Press.

Strauss, A., & Corbin, J. (1998). *Basics of qualitative research: Techniques and procedures for developing grounded theory* (2nd ed.). Sage Publications. (Original work published 1990).

Tracy, S. J. (2010). Qualitative quality: Eight "big-tent" criteria for excellent qualitative research. *Qualitative Inquiry*, 16, 837–851. Sage Journals Online.

Vagle, M. D. (2014). *Crafting phenomenological research*. Routledge.

van Manen, M. (1990). *Researching lived experience: Human science for an action sensitive pedagogy*. The Althouse Press.

Waldron, J. (2013). User-generated content, YouTube and participatory culture on the web: Music learning and teaching in two contrasting online communities. *Music Education Research*, 15(3), 257–274. https://doi.org/10.1080/14613808.2013.772131

Walker, L. N. (2009). Stories from the front. In M. Barrett & S. Stauffer (Eds.), *Narrative inquiry in music education: Troubling certainty* (pp. 179–194). Springer Science + Media Business.

CHAPTER **8**

Selected Procedures for Gathering, Analyzing, and Reflecting on Qualitative Data

This chapter:

- Emphasizes that ethical conduct should guide all procedural decisions in qualitative research;
- Describes the initial process of gathering and labeling data;
- Singles out key approaches for qualitative data analysis; and
- Provides guidance for crafting the procedural aspects of a qualitative research proposal.

Qualitative research procedures are built on assumptions of respect for those with whom you work as well as trustworthiness and credibility. Situated in naturalistic settings, simultaneous phases of data gathering and analysis guide researchers toward understanding the processes by which meanings and interpretations of music education experiences are constructed.

INTRODUCTION

When you prepare for a musical performance, your intention is to present a cohesive, finely polished product. Your repertoire selection, together with the resources you have available and the musicians with whom you work, contribute equally to that goal. While learning the music, your previous study and experience helps you to comprehend and communicate the overall essence of the work. As you rehearse, your awareness expands to include not only what your colleagues are playing, but also how and when your parts interact with theirs. In fact, the entire process— including the performance—involves weaving between the whole and the parts, attending to interactions with the music, with other performers and with the audience (Bresler, 2005).

The phases of qualitative research are similarly intertwined. Interpretation is the thread that binds them together because you, as researcher, are the *"primary instrument for data collection and analysis"* (Merriam & Tisdell, 2015, p. 16, emphasis original). You craft a plan based on your purpose and question(s). You begin the cycle of data collection, simultaneously exploring and comparing their meanings. As you come to know the people and settings, further interrogations emerge, and unanticipated themes need to be woven into the fabric. The final account, much like a performance, combines these seemingly disparate elements into a comprehensive whole. The outcome is neither fully predictable nor entirely replicable. Even when adhering to the same standards of quality and excellence, no two researchers follow the same process from beginning to end.

DOI: 10.4324/9781003057703-11

Always keep in mind the interplay between the whole and the parts of your work as well as your various interpretive roles in it. This chapter speaks to the parts one by one; from ethical conduct to planning the study, gathering and labeling data, then analyzing and reflecting on them. In reality, however, doing qualitative research is a holistic experience. It comes to life aided by your writing skills, storytelling ability, empathetic understanding, creativity, and imagination. In Chapter 15 we describe ways to invite readers to engage in that vision together with you.

PLANNING A STUDY

As described in earlier chapters, it is premature to plan research activities until you have engaged with the scholarly literature in the manner appropriate to the research tradition you will use, and developed an initial research purpose, rationale, and questions. With qualitative research, you add an interrogation of your personal motivations for developing the project (see Chapter 7). The procedural plan, which includes (1) what people and sites you wish to study, (2) the required period of time, and (3) how you will gain access, follows naturally from your research question(s).

The analytical procedures highlighted in this chapter are based on those described by Glaser and Strauss (1967/2009), Charmaz (2014, 2008a, 2008b), and Merriam & Tisdell (2015). Phases of analysis build on Glaser and Strauss' principle of *constant comparison* between collected data and analytical interpretations from the onset of the first data to the written research product. Other traditions may use only certain aspects of those described here, but the sequence of events in its entirety gives you a sense of the ongoing-ness inherent in the qualitative research process.

Analytical examples come from a study by Frierson-Campbell (2003) of music teachers whose schools (all in low-income "urban" areas) had been identified as "low performing" by the U.S. law known as *No Child Left Behind* and were part of a university-based school reform effort. The study began as a needs assessment, exploring the role played by music educators in said schools. Data were gathered from interviews and observations. Interviewees included music teachers as well as building administrators and district-level arts administrators. Analytic vocabulary has been adapted for the purpose of illustration in this chapter.

Ethical Conduct as Gauge for Research Choices

While applicable to all research situations, the individuality of philosophical and procedural choices within the qualitative research traditions makes ethical guidelines particularly important and relevant. The chapter therefore suggests ethical conduct as a major gauge by which procedural decisions of planning, data gathering, and analysis are made.

As his final degree project, *Dale* hoped to investigate college music drop-outs and self-identity. His motivation was to understand why some of his most talented college classmates had left the music profession early in their college careers. Dale saw the qualitative approach as a way to "get to the bottom" of this issue. It would be fairly easy to contact his former classmates and ask them to take part in his research project. In fact, he was concerned that participants he did not know well might be less willing to talk to him openly than his friends would.

> When he shared his concerns with the class, *Prof. E.* cautioned him about ethical concerns: "Remember that you will be asking your friends for personal information with the express purpose of sharing that information with others. Sharing personal information with a researcher can put participants at risk in their jobs, their communities, or their families. Deciding how to manage this can be awkward and even painful for everyone involved."

When you think of "risky research," medical and pharmaceutical research may come to mind. But, as Dale learned, gathering qualitative data in music education can reveal vulnerabilities in the people you study—called "dangerous knowledge" by Glesne (2016, p. 49). Formal protection of research participants regarding respect for persons, beneficence, and justice is part of the role of your institution's research ethics review board, called in the U.S. the Institutional Review Board, or IRB (see also Chapter 3). Such boards require a *research protocol*, a form they usually provide. In it you must clearly describe your intended procedures regarding observations and interviews, including procedures for gaining access and securing permission to do the study, and consideration of reciprocity, the potential benefit for those who take part in the research. All participants must be given an opportunity for *informed consent*, meaning that they are informed about the purpose of the research, acknowledge any risks (physical or mental), and consent to being part of the study. If your study involves a vulnerable population such as underage students, written permission is also required from parents or guardians. We suggest that you provide such a form even if it is not required, as it protects you and your research participants from misunderstanding your intentions.

Because complete anonymity is hard to maintain, a promise of confidentiality is more common in qualitative research. This means, to avoid the likelihood of harm to research participants, that you may not use the actual names of your participants, the location(s) of your work, or of any other identifying factors to anyone other than the IRB and the committee reviewing your proposal. The same is true for any reports or publications that follow. In your IRB protocol, research proposal, and informed consent statement you must be clear about the level of confidentiality you are promising. For further detail, see Birk and Shindledecker (2020) and consult your institutions research ethics review policy.

Making Sampling Decisions

Clear parameters make it easier to decide on the focus of a study (also known as the unit of analysis), and make detailed plans about participants, locations, and gaining access to either. Such parameters are suggested by your research questions and/or purpose. For instance, Cayari (2016) asked "What are the musical and social implications of virtual vocal ensemble participation and creation?" (p. 13). The parameters suggested by the question include "musical and social implications," "collective, collaborative, and one-person virtual vocal ensembles," and "participation" (p. 13).

Unit of Analysis

Refining your research purpose into specific questions provides clarity about the intended focus of your research: individual teachers or students, a classroom, an entire school, a school district, or a local community, and so on. Each focus suggests a different *unit of analysis*, the basis for analyzing what you see, hear, or otherwise experience through observation and participation. Be aware, however, that persons, places, and other contexts both inside and beyond the boundaries of that unit provide contextual information for your investigation.

It may be helpful to consider the units of analysis suggested by the research questions and purposes of some published studies. Regarding groups of student musicians, Allsup (2003) asked: "How would the participating groups evolve and define themselves through the practice of composing and analyzing music? What would our choices reflect or signify? How might this experience affect individual growth as well as community-making?" (p. 25). Allsup's unit of analysis was a group of musicians involved in "the practice of composing and analyzing music." He instigated and then studied two such groups. Stake, Bresler, and Mabry (1991) asked "What are the schools providing as opportunities for [arts] learning?" (p. 4). Their unit of analysis was individual schools. The unit of analysis for Cayari (2016), whose questions appear earlier, was the virtual vocal ensemble, specifically "collective, collaborative, and one-person virtual vocal ensembles," (p. 13). Haywood (2006) asked "How does the process of including an individual with special needs in choir create change in that individual?" (p. 407). Her unit of analysis was the individual special needs student, and she studied one such student in a choir setting. Once you are clear about the focus of your research, you may consider how to select and recruit participants.

Participant Selection

Making choices about research participants based on your research purpose and question(s) is called *purposeful sampling*. Most researchers begin by identifying an initial sample that meets the parameters of their purpose and questions, with tentative plans to add participants as additional issues emerge (King & Horrocks, 2010, p. 30). Merriam and Tisdell (2015) note that case studies involve two levels of purposeful sampling: 1) selecting the case(s), and 2) selecting participants within each case (p. 295). Noting the reasons for your sampling decisions is part of your data.

Other sampling options include *snowball sampling* and *theoretical sampling*. Snowball sampling entails asking participants you have already recruited to help you identify additional volunteers. Theoretical sampling involves making theoretical choices about what participants to include in a study. Either of these techniques may be used to recruit an initial sample or to find additional participants as your research evolves. It is always possible that potential participants may not agree to be part of the research. It is advisable, therefore, to make allowances for recruiting additional persons when submitting a research plan to your IRB and any other gatekeepers. Asking for more time and access than you expected at the beginning of your work is also a better strategy than asking for limited access and then having to ask for additional permission later.

Details of Engagement

At the planning stage, consider several issues regarding time. How long (weeks, months, years) do you imagine it will take to gather the data you need? (While there is no "hard and fast" rule, it is best to over-estimate rather than under-estimate.) What elements of your own or participants' calendars have to be considered? And what is the ideal length of time for each visit? Such estimates are part of the stated plan, and participants are likely to want this information as a condition of participating in a study.

It is important that the timing of visits you plan to do will be varied enough to provide a complete sense of the site as it pertains to your research purpose. For instance, New York City's

Times Square is a different place on December 31 from what it is on most other days. It would therefore be necessary to experience Times Square on many different days, including December 31, to get a realistic sense of what goes on there throughout the year. In other words, prolonged engagement and repeated observation are important for the credibility of research. Likewise, if you limit your visits to times that are convenient for your schedule, you may miss the naturalistic viewpoint that is needed to make your research trustworthy.

Gaining Access

Once your sample and site have been chosen, your timeframe estimated, and your proposal approved, the next step is to recruit participants. Known as *gaining access*, it may be as simple as speaking to one or more individuals, or it may involve going through a bureaucratic hierarchy that is controlled by "gatekeepers" or even by carefully constructed rules for conducting research. The latter is more common with schools; however, gatekeepers are not always the holders of official titles. Sometimes they are simply the people whose "okay" is needed if you want to reach potential participants in an identified sample.

Many people are suspicious of strangers coming into their daily activities. Glesne (2016) suggests creating a *lay summary* to share the details of your study in the vernacular of your participants. Such can help to allay the fears of those you work with (pp. 58–60). The information you provide should be similar to that provided on your IRB protocol. Stress in all communications that your role is not to judge or evaluate, but to understand. Even if you see yourself as an "insider" to the situation because you were (or are) a teacher, performer, or otherwise familiar with the scene under study, your participants may see you as a more distanced "outsider" whose presence changes the "normal" classroom environment.

Doing a Pilot Study

A pilot study is a "pre-study" that allows you to try out the methods and procedures you plan to use. Applicable to nearly all research methods, it follows the basic elements of research design, but has fewer formal requirements. Piloting your sampling and data gathering procedures is highly recommended. It allows you to try out your ideas prior to the official start of the project, demonstrating that you have made efforts to cultivate the skills needed for rigorous research.

Conducting a pilot study is a realistic and attainable goal for a semester research course, enabling you to prepare a well-thought-out proposal for a subsequent semester. If you are a student in such a course or a degree program, however, you should not begin a pilot study without the knowledge of your instructor or project advisor, and without securing whatever ethics approval is required by your institution. Check with your instructor or institution manager to be sure you follow the proper procedures.

GATHERING AND LABELING DATA

Gathering qualitative data involves recording interactions with participants via observations and/or interviews or by reviewing documents, artifacts, and/or electronic media that represent human action in some way. Data may be recorded electronically or in writing; audio or video recordings are usually transcribed into text for analysis.

Because data collection involves thinking analytically from the outset of a study, you begin to apply initial labels, known as *codes*, from the moment you conclude your first data gathering episode. As you transcribe, initial categories or themes emerge, and the thoughts that come to mind as you reflect on the experience become notes and memos, written in the margins of the transcript or with tools in your software program. As you continue, you create notes to examine those initial codes, revising some and combining others into focused codes and themes (Charmaz, 2014). This corresponds to rules suggested by Glaser and Strauss (1967/2009) for the reflexive process of *constant comparison*: First, continuously weigh codes used for new data against those used to label previous incidents (p. 106), and second, *"stop coding and record a memo on your ideas"* (p. 107, emphasis in original). Additional discussion of the analysis process follows later in the chapter.

Not all qualitative researchers support the use of coding. Some postmodernists and post-structuralists see the practice of coding as a carry-over from positivist conceptions of knowledge, and question its primacy in traditional qualitative research as decontextualizing and fragmenting discourse (St. Pierre & Roulston, 2006; St. Pierre, 2008). There is no question that any naming is a form of coding, albeit less structured and tested than coding for quantitative purposes.

Generating Data by Observation, Interview, and/or Document Review

Procedures related to observation, interview, and document/ artifact review may interact, or each may be considered a separate data collection tool. To assure the credibility of your research, however, data should be gathered in more than one way, and from multiple sources. The growth of digital technologies has made many additional media available for study; for instance web pages, blogs, YouTube videos, and so on. Despite their constant development, however, the basis of collecting and using information for research purposes remains similar.

During any given data gathering episode, the researcher records data electronically and/or manually, resulting in what is known as *raw data* (recordings as well as hand-written or electronic *field notes*). The episode is not complete until data are transcribed, initial labels are applied, and a memo has been written about the experience. Memos that document procedural and analytical decisions and reflections on those decisions are part of the research and are included as data. This ongoing interpretive cycle continues throughout the data gathering process. The following section describes this cycle with a discussion of observation, interviewing, document or artifact review, transcribing, naming and labeling, and memo writing.

Observation

When used in this chapter, "observation" refers to deliberately viewing and listening to human action and interaction in the context of a research study. Below we discuss qualitative observation as it typically unfolds, from the first observations in the field to determining and navigating the observer role.

The Observation Process

Whether as a teacher or student, you have experienced entering a new school for the first time. The experience can be overwhelming, as navigating between unfamiliar spaces and asking directions makes you feel out of place. Remembering the names of colleagues and of students may be similarly challenging. After a few days, however, you learn details that help you proceed through the daily schedule. You may find a schematic design that helps you to understand the layout of the building and the placement of the rooms. You may create a seating chart or develop other ways of keeping track of names and other details related to your students. What was once a sea of unfamiliar faces in a confusing space becomes a classroom full of students whose names, instruments or voice parts, and personalities are familiar.

Coming to know a research site follows a similar sequence, but instead of (or in addition to) finding your way around a building, you are getting to know the people you study both as an outsider and insider. Who do you need to talk to? Where should you look? What questions should you ask? Tentative patterns begin to emerge when you recognize and begin naming a few threads or themes that bind your observations together. Your careful notes about this part of the experience also become part of your data.

The Observer's Role

Remember how Figure 7.1 contrasted the role and view of the researcher from non-participant to participant observer? Qualitative observations exist on a continuum between those images, from *direct observation* with little interaction with the site or participants, to *participant observation*. Planning as well as reporting on your place on this continuum is part of the research. In classroom research, for instance, you may intend to be an "observer," but the teacher you observe may want you to assist in their classroom. You then have to decide whether such a role would limit or aid your research purpose. Regardless of your choice, children are likely to ask why there is a new adult in their classroom; you should be prepared with a simple explanation for them. Your deliberations, your actions, and their impacts on the research are all data that are written into your notes and memos.

Recording Observational Data

Observational data are usually recorded both with researcher notes and video recording. Some researchers develop an *observation form* to provide structure for taking field notes (see Chapter 14 and Recommended Reading). Details such as the date, time, and place of the observation, the participants involved, space for a brief schedule of activities observed, and room to jot notes and sketches are common in such a form.

Taking Notes

When taking notes, use all of your senses to grasp as much about a setting as possible. During each visit, keep records of what you hear, feel and smell (and even taste, if applicable to your research purpose). In addition to verbal notes, you may wish to draw pictures or diagrams or take photos. Make an effort to view familiar phenomena as an outsider would: How is the room organized? Why is the schedule organized one way as opposed to another? Pay attention to gestures as well as words, to tone of voice as much as what is said, and to who is not there as much as who is.

The worldviews that underlie most qualitative traditions suggest that it is not possible to truly separate your observations from your impressions of them. Thus, notes taken in the field require *narrative accuracy*—recognition that empirical perceptions (what you observe or learn through interview) reflect personal beliefs and preconceived knowledge about the situation under study. Field notes may therefore acknowledge your position in the setting, question how you may have disturbed the usual routine, and examine what personal biases have kept you from seeing some things. Reflective notes made in the field are often designated by "O.C." (observer comment) in the margin or by typing in upper case type or a different font to separate them from notes intended as descriptive.

If you gather data via video recording, note that there is no perfect camera position. A better view of the teacher may obscure students, and vice versa, but once the camera is running, "set it and forget it." Remember that the camera cannot capture everything; in fact, its placement suggests what you believe it is important to see, and you should reflect on the reasons for your choices. If possible, while the video camera is recording you should also record field notes to give context and meaning for the details that the camera will capture. Writing while observing can, however, be perceived as intrusive by research participants, so do so with caution.

Recording equipment varies from traditional video cameras to smart phones, wireless cameras, and other types of electronics. Make sure to choose equipment that will clearly record action as well as sound. Many researchers use an external microphone to assure that sounds are picked up clearly. When choosing equipment, consider how you will store the originals. Large amounts of video data can clog up a computer hard drive very quickly, so you may wish to invest in a secure digital (SD) card, external hard drive, or cloud-based storage.

Observation Ethics

Video recording and photography add additional ethical considerations to the research. Both, when used for research purposes, require written permission from authorities at the site as well as from any participants you wish to record. In the request for permission, key questions usually include how long and in what format you will store any recorded information. Typically, observational research pertaining to an adult (such as a teacher) in which children may be seen but are not part of the research, do not require parental permission. Such decisions, however, are ultimately made by the institution directing the research and the site where the research is being conducted.

Interviewing

It is difficult to get through a single day without hearing or reading about media figures being interviewed for their view on politics, entertainment, or sports (King & Horrocks, 2010). But the purpose for most media interviews is to promote entertainment or share opinions. Research interviews, on the other hand, seek to understand an experience from a variety of perspectives rather than persuading an audience toward a point of view.

The Interview Process

Research interviews may be formal (i.e., scheduled) or informal (not scheduled) (Olson, 2011, pp. 35–43). The most common approaches to interviewing include (1) informal conversations, typical in participant observation fieldwork; (2) interviews based on a *guide* or *schedule* (see Chapter 14), where you work from a set of possible topics but do not have predetermined questions, and (3) formal interviews in which respondents provide answers to predetermined questions (Patton, 2014). Open questions may enable researchers to uncover perspectives about aspects of music learning and/or teaching that formal questionnaires and structured interviews can miss. Be aware that different disciplinary perspectives and/or theoretical assumptions suggest a variety of interview procedures. For further discussion see Merriam and Tisdell (2015).

Initial interview topics are derived from four main sources: your experiences with and knowledge of the topic, the theoretical framework you develop from the literature or as the study unfolds, questions derived from any preliminary information you gathered in a pilot study (King & Horrocks, 2010, p. 37), and previously held knowledge about participants. While avoiding a linear "ask-this-then-that" process, research interviews typically include the following as part of the conversation: (1) the respondents' connection to the topic, (2) details of actions observed by or shared with the interviewer, (3) motivations for those actions, and (4) questions about (a) emotional reactions to an experience or action, (b) knowledge held by the participant, and (c) things noticed by the participant.

Interviews should be scheduled at a time and in a place that are comfortable both for you and for your participants. If possible, let the interviewee choose the setting. While interviews always involve issues of power, avoid settings that explicitly suggest a power relationship, such as an office where one of you sits behind a desk. Ideally the setting will be private with minimal possibilities for interruption. When you schedule the interview, allow additional time for introductions and parting words. Caution is in order if you are going to an unfamiliar place: For your own safety, tell someone where you are going and when you will return. Videoconferencing, which relieves some power dynamics, offers greater accessibility, and offers recording as a built-in feature, is increasingly seen as an acceptable option for interviews (particularly since the recent global pandemic).

The Interviewer's Role

As interviewer your task is to elicit responses that reflect the participant's perspective. It is an opportunity to learn from participants rather than to tell them what you think. It is important, therefore, to ask questions that "prompt," but that do not assume a particular perspective on the part of the interviewee. For instance: "How did you feel about that?" is a prompt, while "Didn't that make you mad?" is a leading question because it assumes a specific emotion. You may also wish to plan "probes" to seek additional information—possible reasons, for instance, for an action or a response (King & Horrocks, p. 40). Learning to interview without "leading" takes practice. If you plan to interview, make sure to practice first, both informally (perhaps with colleagues in your research course) and as part of a pilot study.

Empathetic listening is important in qualitative interviewing. Particularly when talking to someone who differs from you—whether by age, race or ethnicity, nationality, language, class, gender, sexuality or some other way—try to become attuned to their style and speed of speaking, and even their breathing rhythm, to put them at ease (Norkunas, 2011, para. 13). To practice this skill, set up planned, separate interviews with selected colleagues who you perceive as being different from you in some way. Ask them to tell you about an important milestone in their life. Do not respond with your own story, but instead learn to be comfortable with pauses and silences. Follow this activity by journaling about your experience as a listener, noting your reactions and assessing your skills (para. 12).

Recording Interview Data

Successful interviews require the development of rapport, and that can be difficult to do if you are trying to write or type every word of a conversation. For this reason, interviews are typically recorded electronically with manual note-taking as a back-up. In a case where the setting is particularly important, you may wish to record video, but an audio recording is generally sufficient. Using a digital device makes it possible to save the recorded interviews to your computer, allowing you to use transcription software if you wish. Digital audio recorders are relatively inexpensive, and many smart phones and tablets come with a recording function. Make sure to try out a recording device before your scheduled interview, and have both a backup recorder and a notebook and pencil in case of a technical malfunction.

Interview Ethics

As is true with video equipment, you must receive permission to use audio-recording equipment and clarify for your participants how long you will keep the recorded data. Such information is required for an IRB protocol. At the risk of being repetitive, we stress: Any audio or video recording and photography must be cleared first with your own institution (and IRB, if appropriate) and also with the institution where you will be working. These recommendations apply equally to the use of formal video equipment and seemingly informal smart phone videos, photos, and voice recordings.

If a participant asks you to stop recording when discussing a sensitive matter, or talks more freely when the device is off, you are obligated to clarify what aspects of that discussion is "on the record" or "off the record," and confirm exactly what that means. Most research reports utilize changes in names and contextual details to protect confidentiality; nonetheless, if a participant tells you not to use certain information, you may not use it—either in the research report or on other occasions. Keep those restrictions in mind from the very beginning of articulating any research questions.

Increasingly, qualitative researchers undertake "member checks" to present their interpretations to research participants before presenting any findings to the public. A first step in those member checks is providing the transcript of an interview or observation to the participant(s) described in those transcripts. A follow-up step would be to ask for specific feedback about the transcribed material. Disagreements between participants and researcher(s) must be noted and acknowledged. Such a practice ensures that the participants continue to have a "voice" in the research. It is part of doing *credible* research.

Document or Artifact Review

"Documents" include written materials, published or unpublished, electronic or print, that help to shed light on your research. "Artifacts" comprise non-written documents such as photographs, audio- or video-recordings, or memorabilia that represent your research participants. Materials in either category can provide insight into your research questions, be acquired relatively easily may and be useful data sources (see Merriam & Tisdell, 2015, pp. 175–182).

Personal documents such as diaries or a collection of letters written by a participant can reveal unique aspects of their point of view. Such primary source materials are critical for historical research, as they provide an intimate personal view of the past. Photographs and other artifacts can provide a window into present-tense data as well: Viewing a participant's collection of photographs can give you a sense of what they want to remember, or of how they want to be remembered. Research participants may not voluntarily offer them to you, so you may have to ask whether such documents exist and whether you can have access to them.

The process for reviewing documents and artifacts for research is similar to that used for observations and interviews. Begin by keeping a written record with a description of each item and the time and the location where you encountered it. If possible, copy, photograph, or scan each item. Then take notes about what you see, and reflect upon your impressions as you would with any research experience. As part of your data, these notes are treated in the same way as other field notes.

Electronic or Virtual Documents and Artifacts

Electronic media provide an interesting area for study. Web pages, for instance, can be analyzed for their content: What is their structure? How do they communicate their purpose? Beyond individual web documents, however, are questions about connections that emerge from relationships between websites (via hyperlinks, for instance). Researchers may examine associations between interactive materials people view, use, or even order on the Web.

The widespread availability of public documents online has had a major bearing on qualitative research. As Merriam and Tisdell (2015) note, when something important happens, "It's safe to assume . . . there will be some record of it somewhere" (p. 164). Whether your research questions address performance, policy, pedagogy, or something else, "locating public records is limited only by the researcher's imagination and industriousness" (p. 164).

Social media sites and online communities offer rich possibilities for researchers interested in exploring the implications of formal and informal learning online. For instance, Waldron (2009, 2013a, 2013b) has gained and shared important insights about online learning by "lurking" (observing) in online music learning communities (both social media and publicly available web communities) devoted to banjo, old-time American music, and Irish traditional music.

The recent Covid-19 epidemic expanded the use of electronic media in the form of video conference recordings, synchronous and asynchronous online teaching, and social media communications, to name only a few. Scholars are just beginning to get a grasp on the many possibilities for historical and empirical research with these tools.

Multimodal Data

The expansion of electronic media—in the classroom and the home as well as online—opens up possibilities for generating multimodal data, which can give researchers "ways to observe, analyze, and understand phenomena that might not otherwise be possible" (Tobias, 2020, p. 81). It does, however, add to researchers' responsibilities. Both Ruthman (2006) and Tobias (2020) observed multimodal music classes that involved "combinations of analog, electronic, digital, Musical Instrument Digital Interface (MIDI), and computer instruments or devices," and both found it necessary "to record multiple streams of data" (Tobias, 2020, p. 84). Analysis of multimodal data is complex and should be carefully thought through before the recordings are begun. For thoughts about this process, see Tobias (2020).

Transcribing Raw Data

Turning recorded information (observations as well as interviews) into text is known as *transcribing*. A fairly straight-forward process, it involves viewing or listening to each recording and creating a written transcript of what was recorded while it is fresh in your mind. Combining the details of the recording with your reflections on what you remember from being in that setting transforms your raw data into text that is ready for analysis. A labor-intensive process, manually transcribing a single hour of observation typically takes about four hours.

Requirements for transcription vary; some researchers transcribe only the elements of an observation that are pertinent to their research questions while others transcribe everything that occurred. We recommend doing full transcriptions in the early stages of your study; gradually moving toward transcribing only what pertains to your research purpose. While few researchers seem to use software that automatically transcribes speech, many of the data qualitative analysis packages described later in the chapter offer tools that make the process easier. Whatever procedure you follow, make sure to copy original recordings and store them in a safe place so you can return to them as the study evolves. What you define as important can change over the course of the research.

Naming and Initial Labeling

From the moment that you begin taking in information your mind begins to conceptualize and label what is going on in order to make sense of it. The first or *initial* stage of analysis involves applying names (or labels) quickly, during or immediately after transcribing data from a research experience. The qualitative researcher pays attention to those preliminary labels and notes them for later analysis.

Labels are typically devised either on your own (based on ideas that emerge from the data) or borrowed from the words of participants (known as *in vivo*). Sections, sometimes called *units of data*, may be marked word-by-word, line-by-line, paragraph-by-paragraph, or in a scheme devised by you. Choosing a specific unit for data labeling may seem arbitrary but can help assure that nothing is missed (Charmaz, 2014). Figure 8.1 displays initial labels applied sentence-by-sentence to an interview transcript used by Frierson-Campbell (2003). One of many possible ways to store and

Raw Data	Initial Label
I often think that sometimes they have grade level meetings…um…I'm not included in them.	Excluding music from grade level meetings
And–I get along with everybody around here.	Getting along with everybody
But–so I don't take it personally.	Not taking things personally
It's just that we tend not to be included.	Excluding music
And whenever we have been included…see, what they do, in here, is that they put together the music teachers, the art teachers, and the gym teachers, and we all sit together and say "What are we doing here?" and we write down some issues that nobody reads.	Isolating special area teachers
You know . . . and that's not right.	Responding to isolation

FIGURE 8.1 Initial Labeling of Interview Notes

code data, this two-column table displays interview data on the right, with each sentence placed in a different row. The column on the right holds the initial labels developed by the researcher.

The example illustrates Charmaz' advice that gerunds suggest action within labels. See, for instance, the labels "*excluding* music," "*getting* along with everyone" and others in the field notes shown in Figure 8.1. The latter phrase is also an example of *in vivo* coding, which means using participants' words to capture their interpretations of an experience. *In vivo* labels are particularly appropriate for initial coding, as they stay close to the data, but it is important to confirm their meaning with participants. For instance, probing further into another teacher's concern about "the right thing to teach" during a later interview enabled Frierson-Campbell (2003) to understand more fully the motivation behind that teacher's approach to the classroom.

Writing Memos

Scheduling specific time for notating your own thoughts is a required part of gathering data. Such notes, written after and separate from data collection instances, are known as *memos*. These comprise written reflections on what is heard and seen; questions about the parameters of promising categories and how well they fit the data as well as thoughts about what theories might be emerging as findings. As with other types of data, keep track of the time and place of any writing you do (even if the computer gives you dates as well).

The content and purpose of memos will likely change as a research project evolves. Early memos, like early labels, are exploratory. Later memos examine analytical possibilities. The following memo (condensed for illustration) was written by Frierson-Campbell early in her research. A later example is included in the section on analysis.

I need to look into research about worker productivity and morale and the like. It seems to me that it's a basic human need to talk about what you do and network with peers. What effect will simply allowing these teachers to do this have on their work?

(2–7–2001)

Memos are written quickly, to get thoughts down on paper. Editing for clarity and grammar will happen later if the notes turn out to be important for the research.

In the shared role of researcher and interpreter, one cannot help but bring one's own lived experience into the analysis of what is heard. A researcher following the *phenomenological* tradition uses memos to acknowledge and "bracket" biases and prior knowledge, setting them aside in order to fully experience the perspectives of the research participants. Because *bracketing* means different things to different researchers, part of this process is explaining in detail its meaning and how it was used it the research (Gearing, 2004, p. 1432). Vagle (2014) suggests "bridling" as a better metaphor for this process because it suggests restraining pre-understandings "so they do not limit the openness," but remaining open to tend to "the understanding of the phenomenon as a whole" (p. 76). This process is not complete until the bracketed (or bridled) data are reintegrated back into the final analysis and interpretation.

Managing Data

As a qualitative researcher, you must devise a content management strategy early in the process. Each data-gathering episode requires a transcription, often representing 45 to 60 minutes of talk or more, plus field notes and reflective memos. Add to that the collection of literature annotations and you will have a great deal of data.

Keeping a Codebook

The collection of computer files or the notebook in which qualitative data are organized and housed is traditionally called a *codebook*. Rather than an actual book, this term refers to the system you devise to keep track of various forms of data. The format and contents of the codebook differ for each researcher. Assuming the use of a computer, the codebook is likely to include the following:

1) A folder that contains raw data files in their original form. (Original audio and/or video recordings and other original media should also be copied and stored in a second location for safekeeping.)
2) A folder consisting of multiple data files that organize transcribed data by code, category, date, and participant (see Appendix D). You may wish to include a file that lists initial labels and the focused codes and groups with which they are organized.
3) A "memo" folder that holds ideas that occur to you during the research.
4) A folder to store drawings and diagrams that help explain things non-verbally.
5) A file that keeps track of all of the information described above.

Whether to use specialized or general-purpose computer software is a matter of personal preference. With a small project, you may prefer working with a familiar word processing or spreadsheet program rather than learning a complicated software program. However, if you have a lot of data to analyze, computer assisted qualitative data analysis (CAQDA or simply QDA) software packages, each of which takes on the data management function of the codebook, will make the workload much more manageable. See Silver and Lewins (2014) for a thorough review of available CAQDA packages. The companion website for their text houses links to the most up-to-date versions of the various packages as well as step-by-step guides and sample datasets for trying out the various programs (see Helpful Resources at the end of this chapter and in supplemental online materials, inquiryinmusiceducation.com). Researchers who want to use a simple spreadsheet program for data storage should see Meyer and Avery (2009).

ANALYZING AND REFLECTING ON DATA

Despite the fact that every researcher defines their own personal research path, the analytical process shares certain commonalities. The first of these, gathering and initially labeling data from individual research events (observation, interview, or document/artifact review) was described earlier in the chapter. This section describes more in-depth analytical and reflective processes, such as (1) bringing together the data from several research events, (2) re-visiting and re-coding the labels to focus them, (3) grouping similar focused codes together, and (4) seeking themes that connect codes to the original research questions or theories (inductive or deductive) that offer insight. Researchers who distrust coding as too restrictive nonetheless seek to connect their data gathering and analysis through inductive and deductive themes. How those themes come about is dependent upon the philosophical perspective of the researcher's tradition.

Focusing and Grouping Analytic Codes

After several transcripts have been coded and a relatively stable list of initial labels captures the essence of the data as you understand them, a second phase of analysis begins. Assuming you have collected data from multiple sources and in different ways, this phase typically has at least two stages: refining initial labels into *focused codes*, and *grouping* like codes together for further analysis. Frierson-Campbell's research (see Figure 8.2) is used later to illustrate the process of focusing codes.

Note that there is no "right" labeling and coding scheme; your task as a researcher is to develop a system that works for your research purpose and questions as embedded in your chosen research tradition and worldview. Our process resembles Merriam and Tisdell's (2015) description of basic qualitative research. As they note, other traditions involve additional dimensions and may use different terms and procedures for coding. See also Saldaña's (2021) coding manual for information about various coding schemes.

Focusing Codes

Charmaz (2017) uses the word focused to describe the second phase of coding. Focusing involves looking over the initial codes you devised quickly after your first few data collecting events, finding commonalities among them, and bringing together those that are similar to "focus" your ideas more clearly. For example, after reflecting on initial labels given to data from several sources, Frierson-Campbell chose the phrase "professional isolation" as a focused code because it captured the collective meaning of the various labels attached earlier to the raw data. With that

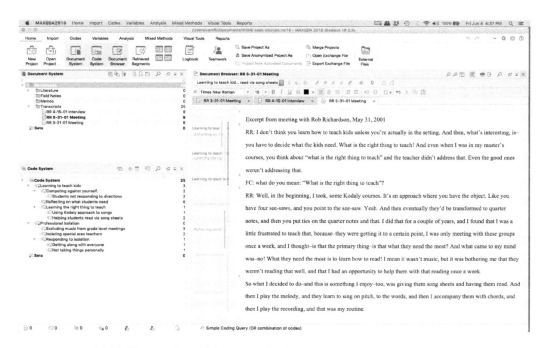

FIGURE 8.2 Initial, Focused, and Grouped Codes using MAXQDA. This illustration is used by permission of Verbi Software.

code in mind, she looked for additional instances of "professional isolation" expressed in the data. At the same time, she reviewed other initial labels, choosing "Learning to teach kids" as another focused code.

Grouping Codes

Grouping is a third level of coding, an analytical decision that should be explored in a memo, such as the one found in Frierson-Campbell's notes:

> "What other professional expectations do music teachers describe when talking about their work place? What is "professional isolation" a part of?" (4–4–2001)

As can be seen in Figure 8.2, grouping similar codes together helped her to "reduce" the data by allowing patterns to emerge across sources.

Eventually, Frierson-Campbell devised the phrase "Professional Music Teacher Expectations" to name the grouped data. The codes that fell into this group included (1) Professional isolation, (2) "Coverage teachers," (3) Discipline, (4) Enjoyment, and (5) "Neat people." (The phrases "coverage teachers" and "neat people" were used by administrators to describe the music teachers in the study. They were used by the researcher as *in vivo* codes.)

Labeling, focusing, and grouping codes continues for as long as data are collected. Once data are analyzed, however, they are usually stored in a new file so they can eventually be sorted by code and category. Appendix D displays one possible method for organizing data: using a spreadsheet or word-processed table to keep track of what files house what information (in this case, transcribed interviews and field notes) by code and group, as well as by other characteristics. Housing data in such a file enables a researcher to sort data by any column: date, file, line, speaker, role, code, or group. QDA software packages provide this feature by default.

Thematic Analysis

Inductive analysis builds themes from individual codes and groups of codes that emerge from the whole of the data. The memos by which your thoughts were documented during data collection; that is, your data interrogations, provide guidance for thematic analysis. Based on the research tradition that informs your study, codes may be examined inductively or deductively, dialectically or propositionally. Phenomenological interpretation deliberately avoids theorizing, striving instead to present the essence of the experience as communicated by the research participants themselves. A grounded theory interpretation, on the other hand, would seek to induce a new theoretical framework out of the codes emerging from the data.

To approach thematic analyses, ask yourself the following questions: When I look at the entire body of data, what relationships might exist between insights noted in my memos and the codes that have emerged most frequently from my data? Do stages uncovered in my research suggest a chronological description? Is there a particular story or incident that illuminates my findings in a particular way? Are concepts and constructs from an underlying discipline (i.e., anthropology, history, psychology, sociology) useful for explaining such illuminations? Answers to any of these questions may form the basis for your written interpretation.

Writers use a number of strategies for thematic analysis. Many write analytic memos to explore how their findings illuminate the questions that guided the research or expand upon findings from other studies. Some researchers use tools such as chart paper to list, organize, and re-organize themes. Concept mapping or mind-mapping, a process that is somewhat similar to the literature map explained in Chapter 2, is a non-linear approach that allows you to consider various organizational schemes (e.g., mindmeister.com)

The following analytic memo explores thematic connections between Frierson-Campbell's data and sociological constructs from the literature:

> If music teacher identity is realized/actualized/recognized at the intersection of musi-cianship and teachership, what can we learn from the first group about identity and/or need? Very little about musicianship—almost no mention of it. And very little about teachership or musicianship in relation to student learning. I learned more about music teachers interacting very little with their schools, but instead acting as isolated adults in a professional world that they perceive as hostile to them. Based on the first year's inter-views, it does not seem to be clear to anyone what the music teacher's roles are or what their needs are.
>
> (5–3–2001)

The terms "role" and "professional identity" are sociological constructs; this memo inspired Frier-son-Campbell to connect her thinking to sociological writers in and out of music education (i.e., Becker, 1973; Bouij, 1998).

True grounded theorists add an additional step to the process of analysis. *Theoretical* cod-ing involves conceptualizing and even hypothesizing possible relationships between codes and/or themes. This involves re-visiting codes and groups of codes in search of those that "carry the weight of the analysis" (Charmaz, 2008b, p. 164). While initial labels may reflect action, and addi-tional analysis may group common actions together, theoretical codes seek to make sense of the analysis on a conceptual level. This is a challenge for any researcher, but especially for those new to the process of qualitative analysis. If you are new to qualitative research, you may opt to focus on thematic rather than theoretical interpretation.

DESCRIBING METHODS AND PROCEDURES FOR A QUALITATIVE RESEARCH PROPOSAL

The following discussion continues with directions for crafting a qualitative research proposal that began in Chapter 7. It assumes that you have re-examined your purpose, rationale, and research questions; re-assessed your collection of related literature and begun writing the Introduction and Review of Literature for your proposal. As noted throughout this chapter, while the "steps" for doing qualitative research are recursive rather than linear; we have separated them for clar-ity. Guidance for proposing mixed methods, practitioner inquiry/action research and arts-based research proposals may be found in Chapter 13.

Describing Proposed Methods and Procedures

Begin with a summary paragraph that explains how your proposed sample, site, timeline, and methods for analysis have emerged from your purpose, rationale, and research questions. If your research is based on a specific philosophical or research tradition—such as ethnography, phenomenology, case study, grounded theory, or narrative inquiry—it is important to explain the impact of that tradition on your proposed research design.

Next, craft a paragraph or two that explains the purposeful sample you propose, and detail the connection between your proposed sample and the parameters suggested by your research purpose and questions. If you are proposing a case study, remember that you will do two levels of sampling, as described earlier. If you plan to expand your sample after you begin, provide as much detail as possible about the ways you plan to make decisions as the project unfolds. This will not only make it easier for committee members reviewing your proposal, it will make the research itself easier.

Ultimately, the following details (as applicable), described earlier in greater detail, must be included:

a. Participant selection.
b. Site selection and processes for gaining access to places, people, and other data sources.
c. Details of engagement.
d. Methods for data gathering (interview, observation, documents, etc.) and data storage. This includes the use of recording devices and other tools.
e. Processes for data analysis.
f. Acknowledgement of ethics concerns and protection for human subjects. This usually requires a sample "Informed Consent Form" that is included in an Appendix to the document.
g. Details of any preliminary study/ies you have done in preparation for this proposal.
h. How your proposed design reflects coherence, credibility, reflexivity, rigor, resonance, and worthiness (see Chapter 7).

For more information see Chapter 14 and Recommended Reading.

Writing the Conclusion

The conclusion section of your proposal usually begins by summarizing the points made in the introduction and design section. It affirms your project as a cohesive, whole that will make an important contribution to the field of music education.

CHAPTER SUMMARY

1) Qualitative research, much like performing music, involves awareness of simultaneous interactions between the whole and the parts. Interpretation by you, as the primary research instrument, is the thread that binds them together.
2) Planning a qualitative study involves making choices about the unit of analysis, participants, details of engagement, and gaining access to the chosen sample and location. A pilot study is a good way to find out whether your sample and chosen methods and procedures will address your research questions.

3) Ethical considerations demonstrate care for participants. This includes (a) approval from an Institutional Review Board, (b) written consent from participants for interview, observation and/or document review, (c) clear communication regarding confidentiality and caution in dealing with "dangerous knowledge," (d) concerns about reciprocity, and (e) special consideration of vulnerable populations.

4) In qualitative research, gathering, analyzing, and interpreting data overlap to varying degrees.

5) Three primary procedures comprise qualitative data collection: observation, interview, and document or artifact review. Combining these and having multiple data sources are important for making sure your data are credible and rigorous.

6) Qualitative observations exist on a continuum from direct observation to participant-observation. An observation guide is helpful for keeping records.

7) Documents and/or artifacts produced by participants can be a rich source of data. Because they are open to interpretation, however, they should be used in conjunction with other data gathering procedures.

8) Data analysis and interpretation begin with initial labeling in conjunction with data transcription. Once preliminary codes are stable, focusing and grouping help to organize and further reduce the data. Thematic analysis, whether inductive or deductive, helps to connect your research into a comprehensive whole.

9) Using a codebook or QDA software is necessary for managing data and data analysis.

Topics for Further Exploration

1) Perceptions of the benefits and drawbacks of qualitative methods for research.

2) Strengths and limitations of "basic" qualitative research as compared to one or more qualitative research traditions.

3) Discuss the ethics involved when a music-teacher participant in your research study shares in an interview that she is concerned about the way a certain group of students is treated in their school. What are your obligations, and how might you resolve them?

Suggested Assignments

1) Imagine how you might explore your current research idea using qualitative methods. What procedures would be most useful? What location and what participants would you choose?

2) Create an observational study using video from *YouTube* or a similar resource. For example, enter "Music in Times Square" into the *YouTube* search engine. Choose three to five videos to observe, taking field notes, and making observer comments. Create codes to analyze your data. What do your selected videos suggest about music in Times Square? How well do you think your observation represents the totality of music in Times Square? Why?

3) Interview one or more of your colleagues about their experience in graduate school, or one or more of your students about their experience studying music. Review your notes and make observer comments. Combine your data with others from your class and analyze using codes you develop together.

4) Visit the website for NAfME: The National Association for Music Education (www.nafme. org/). Take notes as if this site was a collection of documents that you were reviewing for research purposes. Create codes to analyze your data. What do your notes suggest about

NAfME's vision of music education? How well do you think your notes represent NAfME's views? Why?

5) Combine the results of your NAfME observation from Assignment 4 with those of colleagues from your class. Analyze and interpret them collectively. How similar and different are your individual and collective impressions?

Recommended Reading

Qualitative Research Overview

Creswell, J. W., & Poth, C. M. (2018). *Qualitative inquiry and research design: Choosing among five approaches* (4th ed.). Sage.

Glesne, C. (2016). *Becoming qualitative researchers: An introduction* (5th ed.). Longman.

Merriam, S. B., & Tisdell, E. J. (2015). *Qualitative research: A guide to design and implementation.* John Wiley & Sons, Incorporated.

Qualitative Observations

Emerson, R. M., Fretz, R. I., & Shaw, L. L. (1995). *Writing ethnographic fieldnotes.* The University of Chicago Press.

Emerson, R. M., Fretz, R. I., & Shaw, L. L. (2001). Participant observation and fieldnotes. In P. Atkinson, A. Coffey, S. Delamont, J. Lofland, & L. Lofland (Eds.), *Handbook of ethnography* (pp. 352–368). Sage.

Qualitative Interviews

King, N., & Horrocks, C. (2010). *Interviews in qualitative research.* Sage.

Kvale, S., & Brinkman, S. (2009). *InterViews: Learning the craft of qualitative research interviewing* (2nd ed.). SAGE.

Seidman, I. (2013). *Interviewing as qualitative research: A guide for qualitative researchers in education and the social sciences* (4th ed.). Teachers College Press.

Qualitative Data Analysis

Meyer, D. Z., & Avery, L. M. (2009). Excel as a qualitative data analysis tool. *Field Methods, 21,* 91–112. https://doi.org/10.1177/1525822X08323985

Ramey, K. E., Champion, D. N., Dyer, E. B., Keiffert, D. T., Krist, C., Meyerhoff, P., & Villanosa, K. (2016). Qualitative analysis of video data: Standards and heuristics. *Proceedings of the 12th International Conference of the Learning Sciences.* Singapore. www.christinakrist.org/uploads/7/0/0/7/70078653/qualitative_analysis_of_video_data_final.pdf

Saldaña J. (2021). *The coding manual for qualitative researchers* (4th ed.) Sage.

Silver, C., & Lewins, A. (2014). *Using software in qualitative research: A step-by-step guide.* SAGE Publications Ltd. https://doi.org/10.4135/9781473906907

Wertz, F., Charmaz, K., McMullen, L. M., Josselson, R., Anderson, R., & McSpadden, E. (2011). *Five ways of doing qualitative analysis: Phenomenological psychology, grounded theory, discourse analysis, narrative research, and intuitive inquiry.* Routledge.

Helpful Resources

A basic guide to cross-cultural research (resources for teaching and learning cross-cultural ethnographic research): https://hraf.yale.edu/cross-cultural-research/basic-guide-to-cross-cultural-research/

Companion website to Silver & Lewins (2014), *Using Software in Qualitative Research: A Step-by-Step Guide*: https://study.sagepub.com/using-software-in-qualitative-research

*Fundamentals of Qualitative Research Metho*ds (Yale University, four modules): https://youtu.be/wbdN_sLWl88

REFERENCES

Allsup, R. (2003). Mutual learning and democratic action in instrumental music education. *Journal of Research in Music Education, 51*(1), 24–37. https://doi.org/10.2307/3345646

Becker, H. S. (1973). *Outsiders: Studies in the sociology of deviance.* The Free Press of Glencoe.

Birk, J. M., & Shindledecker, C. S. (2020). Ethics and qualitative research in music education. In C. M. Conway (Ed.), *The Oxford handbook of qualitative research in American music education* (Vol. 2). Oxford University Press.

Bouij, C. (1998). Swedish music teachers in training and professional life. *International Journal of Music Education, 32*(1), 24–32. https://doi.org/10.1177/025576149803200103

Bresler, L. (2005). What musicianship can teach educational research. *Music Education Research, 7*(2), 169–183. https://doi.org/10.1080/14613800500169399

Cayari, C. (2016). *Virtual vocal ensembles and the mediation of performance on YouTube* [Doctoral dissertation]. University of Illinois at Urbana-Champaign. http://hdl.handle.net/2142/90478

Charmaz, K. (2008a). Constructionism and the grounded theory method. In J. A. Holstein & J. F. Gubrium (Eds.), *Handbook of constructionist research* (pp. 397–412). Guilford Press.

Charmaz, K. (2008b). Grounded theory as an emergent method. In S. N. Hesse-Biber & P. Leavy (Eds.), *Handbook of emergent methods* (pp. 155–170). Guilford Press.

Charmaz, K. (2014). *Constructing grounded theory* (2nd ed.). Sage Publishing.

Charmaz, K. (2017). The power of constructivist grounded theory for critical inquiry. *Qualitative Inquiry, 23*(1), 34–45. https://doi.org/10.1177/1077800416657105

Frierson-Campbell, C. (2003). Professional need and the contexts of in-service music teacher identity. In H. Froehlich, D. Coan, & R. R. Rideout (Eds.), *Sociology of music education symposium III: Social dimensions of music, music teaching and learning* (pp. 199–216). Department of Music & Dance, University of Massachusetts.

Gearing, R. E. (2004). Bracketing in research: A typology. *Qualitative Health Research, 14*(10), 1429–1452.

Glaser, B. G., & Strauss, A. L. (2009). *The discovery of grounded theory: Strategies for qualitative research.* Transaction Publishers. (Original work published 1967).

Glesne, C. (2016). *Becoming qualitative researchers: An introduction* (5th ed.). Longman.

Haywood, J. (2006). You can't be in my choir if you can't stand up: One journey toward inclusion. *Music Education Research, 8*(3), 407–416. https://doi.org/10.1080/14613800600957511

King, N., & Horrocks, C. (2010). *Interviews in qualitative research.* Sage.

Merriam, S. B., & Tisdell, E. J. (2015). *Qualitative research: A guide to design and implementation.* John Wiley & Sons, Inc.

Meyer, D. Z., & Avery, L. M. (2009). Excel as a qualitative data analysis tool. *Field Methods, 21*, 91–112. https://doi.org/10.1177/1525822X08323985

Norkunas, M. (2011). Teaching to listen: Listening exercises and self-reflexive journals. *The Oral History Review, 38*(1), 63–108. www.jstor.org/stable/41440852

Olson, K. (2011). *Essentials of qualitative interviewing.* Routledge.

Patton, M. Q. (2014). *Qualitative evaluation and research methods* (4th ed.). Sage.

Ruthmann, S. A. (2006). *Negotiating learning and teaching in a music technology lab: Curricular, pedagogical, and ecological issues* [Doctoral dissertation]. Oakland University. ProQuest Dissertations and Theses (Publication No. 3401356).

Saldaña, J. (2021). *The coding manual for qualitative researchers* (4th ed.) Sage.

Silver, C., & Lewins, A. (2014). *Using software in qualitative research: A step-by-step guide.* SAGE Publications Ltd. https://doi.org/10.4135/9781473906907

St. Pierre, E. A. (2008). Afterword: Decentering voice in qualitative inquiry. In A. Y. Jackson & L. A. Mazzei (Eds.), *Voice in qualitative inquiry: Challenging conventional interpretive and critical conceptions in qualitative research* (pp. 221–236). Routledge.

St. Pierre, E. A., & Roulston, K. (2006). The state of qualitative inquiry: A contested science. *International Journal of Qualitative Studies in Education*, *19*(6), 673–684. https://doi.org/10.1080/09518390600975644

Stake, R., Bresler, L., & Mabry, L. (1991). *Custom and cherishing: The arts in elementary schools*. Council for Research in Music Education, School of Music, University of Illinois.

Tobias, E. S. (2020). Generating and analyzing multimodal and multimedia data. In C. M. Conway (Ed.), *The Oxford handbook of qualitative research in American music education* (Vol. 2, pp. 80–98). Oxford University Press.

Vagle, M. D. (2014). *Crafting phenomenological research*. Routledge.

Waldron, J. (2009). Exploring a virtual music community of practice: Informal music learning on the Internet. *Journal of Music, Technology and Education*, *2*(2), 97–112. https://doi.org/10.1386/jmte.2.2-3.97_1

Waldron, J. (2013a). User-generated content, YouTube and participatory culture on the Web: Music learning and teaching in two contrasting online communities. *Music Education Research*, *15*(3), 257–274. https://doi.org/10.1080/14613808.2013.772131

Waldron, J. (2013b). YouTube, fanvids, forums, vlogs and blogs: Informal music learning in a convergent on- and offline music community. *International Journal of Music Education*, *31*(1), 91–105. https://doi.org/10.1177/0255761411434861

CHAPTER 9

Quantitative Research in Music Education

Letting Numbers Speak

Setting the stage for the next three chapters on understanding descriptive statistics, interpreting correlations, and designing *ex post facto* and experimental research projects, this chapter:

- Illustrates the importance of labels, counts, and measures for communicating about research through numbers; and
- Introduces basic concepts of measurement theory that impact how questions are asked and hypotheses formulated.

Quantitative research uses mathematical formulas known as statistics to examine differences and commonalities (physical, biological, sociocultural and/or socio-psychological traits) across large numbers of individuals or groups. The ultimate goal is the testing of theory by means of reliable and valid evidence that results in the ability to generalize findings, predict performance outcomes, and provide empirical guidelines for making informed conceptual and practical decisions.

INTRODUCTION

Music educators use numbers to report counts of students in their ensembles and classes, calculate student grades, and prepare budgets for the coming year. Like other professional musicians, they also use mathematics to tune instruments, contract for gigs, or estimate audience size for a grant. However, in both teaching and research contexts, counts are most meaningful when they are clearly labeled and used with measurements of equal intervals.

As an example, imagine two choir teachers: one experienced (Teacher 1) and one quite new (Teacher 2). They have been paired to work together for professional development. In the course of observing, it seems that Teacher 2 says "okay" very frequently, while Teacher 1 says "okay" hardly at all. What additional information is needed to determine whether this word is being over-used, and by whom? Certainly we could start with counting: Perhaps Teacher 1 says "okay" 3 times while Teacher 2 says "okay" 12 times. But we need more detail. Were the counts done over the same period of time? Similar teaching contexts? Comparable age groups? More information is needed before we can make a judgment about the differences between the two teachers' use of the word "okay."

In both teaching and research contexts, counts are most meaningful when they are used with measurements of equal intervals. A measure common to this kind of question is time. If both

DOI: 10.4324/9781003057703-12

teachers were observed for the same period of time, then Teacher 2 uses "okay" four times as often as Teacher 1. If Teacher 1 was observed for 10 minutes and Teacher 2 was observed for 40 minutes, however, there may be no difference in the frequency of their use of the word. If, on the other hand, Teacher 1 was observed for 40 minutes while Teacher 2 was observed for 10 minutes, what conclusion might you draw?

The example above uses labels, counts, and measures to describe and compare the issue under study; that is, the teacher's use of a specific mannerism in the choral rehearsal. The labels (Teacher 1, Teacher 2) replaced the teachers' names; the counts recorded the occurrences of the mannerism, and the measure (time) offered an agreed-upon standard (number of minutes) against which to consider the counts. Without measurement, the counts alone would have been meaningless.

A similar dilemma occurs when you observe that Teacher 1 spent 45 minutes rehearsing the same piece, or that Jamie received a test score of 120. Both observations report measurements: Time for rehearsal length and a test score that reflects certain measured values. But a test score by itself means little if you do not know the test that provided the score. Once the content of the test and the overall range of scores become known, then Jamie's score takes on meaning because you can place his score within the range of all possible scores. The story behind the data becomes concrete to you.

Similarly, saying only that Teacher 1 spent 45 minutes of rehearsal time on the same composition relays little information. Far more details need to be known before the statement becomes meaningful. Those details, when studied by a researcher, might include the content of the rehearsal or the actions/behaviors exhibited by the director and/or the students, the type of ensemble, the students' age, the school setting, the time of year (e.g., "crunch" time before the winter concert), or other contextual information important to tell the story.

What story it is, of course, depends on your research purpose, which can be derived from many different angles, rehearsal strategies being just one of them. The more details you have identified, the more likely it is that your study accounts fully for what you want to know. Knowing what details to look for is greatly enhanced by engagement with extant studies in the field (as described in Chapters 2 through 4). One goal of Chapters 9–12 is to provide you with the background to understand quantitative studies so that you can examine (rather than skipping over) the statistical symbols, tables, and graphs that represent the story each investigation has to tell. Equipped with this knowledge, you can make their meanings come to life so that they become the basis for your own research questions. One investigation builds on the other; each part by itself means much less than all of them together. As Phillips and Burbules (2000) suggest:

> Science does not attempt to describe the *total reality* (i.e., *all* the truths) about, say, a classroom; rather, it seeks to develop *relevant* true statements—ones that can serve to explain the situation that is of concern or that describe the causal relationships that are the focus of interest.
>
> (p. 39)

Seen in this light, questions that initially may seem inconsequential can yield meaningful information when viewed as a smaller piece in the much larger mosaic of knowledge to which all research questions, quantitative and qualitative, contribute. In all cases, however, knowing how numbers function as labels, counts, and measures helps you determine whether your observations were more than chance occurrences.

BASIC ASSUMPTIONS UNDERLYING EMPIRICAL MEASUREMENTS

Researchers who do quantitative research use mathematics to *"mirror relevant relations"* among the phenomena under study (Tal, 2020, para. 13, emphasis original). Measurement, then, is "a method of assigning numbers to magnitudes" (para. 11). Choosing what value works best for any given observation requires repeated efforts of defining, clarifying, and testing what you have selected as your particular phenomena of interest. These occurrences, once operationalized as mutually exclusive classes, rubrics, or categories, are called *variables*.

After an appropriate and meaningful operational definition has been attached to a variable, its presence can be documented, compared across individuals or groups of individuals, and tested for any possible effects it may have on other variables. For the results of such purposes to be valid, some background knowledge about statistical assumptions underlying quantitative research designs is necessary. Here, the following four issues are singled out:

- the nature of a normal curve,
- the difference between population and sample,
- the concept of probability, and
- hypothesis testing.

These concepts are important for visualizing how a stated research purpose and planned methods fit a particular design. The next three chapters give you selected hands-on procedures necessary to reach such a goal. The following discussion introduces some of the underlying principles guiding those procedures.

The Normal Curve

According to the German mathematician Carl Friedrich Gauss (1777–1855), repeated independent measurements of an infinite number of human characteristics, objects, and/or behaviors are distributed over a continuum in a predictable way. That continuum is called the normal curve (also known as the bell curve, see Figure 9.1). Its main characteristic lies in the relationship between

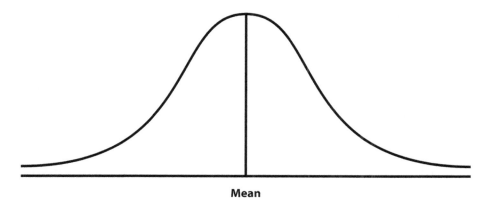

Mean

FIGURE 9.1 The Normal or Bell-Shaped Curve

all measured individual scores and how they are distributed around the mean (the mathematical average of all scores).

The following assumption guides the model of a normal curve: If a population of interest, such as every female child born in 2021, is measured on a specific characteristic—for example, weight—and if these measurements are plotted on a histogram (a type of two-dimensional chart) with the weight on the horizontal base line in ounces and the frequency (number of female children) on the vertical line, the distribution of these various measurements would resemble a standard normal curve model, representing the spread of individual measurements from an infinite number of people in relationship to the average of those measurements.

The concept of averages, or *measures of central tendencies*, is an important aspect of the normal curve. It is described further in the next chapter, with visual examples and explanations of when, how, and why to use different types of averages with different types of observations. Here it suffices to say that an average calculated from the sum of all measures, divided by the total number of measurements, is called a *mean*. The mean tells you where to find the center-point of all scores on the curve. Knowing the location of the mean does not, however, tell you how all scores are dispersed, or spread around the mean score.

Research questions that suggest the use of quantitative methods often assume the use of the normal curve: Does a certain score come close to the average of all measures or does it deviate greatly from that average? If an individual score falls repeatedly far away from the average, why does it do so? If someone measures consistently close to the average, is there some reason for that? Are there discernible and consistent patterns among all scores? A few of them? Answers to these and similar questions rely on and require repeated measures of the same observations to be certain that the measured values were not obtained by chance.

The Relationship of a Population to Its Sample

In the technical language of measurement theory, the words *population* and *sample* carry precise meanings. A population represents the entire group a researcher is interested in knowing about; in our earlier example of female children born in 2021, the population is literally *every* child born during that time.

Fortunately, music education researchers are usually interested in much smaller populations. Nonetheless, it can be difficult to access an entire population of interest, even when limited to music teachers within a single state or children within a single school district.

Measurement theory suggests that researchers can approximate a full population by choosing a representative sample from that population and using that subset "to gain information about the whole" (Moore & Notz, 2020, p. 3). The ideal for such a sample is that its members are chosen at random; that is, selected in such a way that every member of the population of interest has a chance of being chosen. Before computers were widespread, randomization procedures were tedious and somewhat prone to researcher mistakes. Fortunately, readily accessible Internet-based randomization procedures such as *Research Randomizer* (randomizer.org) are convenient to use.

Based on the assumption that measurements from a carefully drawn sample will approximate those of the full population, researchers use statistics to generalize the results from an examination of a sample to the population from which the sample was extracted. (Note that any generalizations of results may not exceed the population that generated the sample.) The realities of the sampling process are more complex than this simple description allows; however, more advanced explanations are included in future chapters and in recommended reading.

The Concept of Probability

Probability is a concern in all research but is expressed differently in the various modes of inquiry. Philosophers account for it with the process of inductive argumentation, in which arguments corroborate only the validity of a conclusion (see Chapters 4 and 5). Historians (Chapter 6) establish the probable truth of evidence with procedures of verification, such as consulting public records, documents, or manuscripts. Documentation of such evidence allows the reader to trust the researcher that such consultations were carried out. In other words, the reader's own knowledge of the subject and the reader's perception of the researcher's integrity—together with documented evidence—are factors that lead to confidence in data accuracy.

Measurement theory assumes that it is possible to estimate the mean and distribution of a population from that of a representative sample. The confidence a quantitative researcher has in the accuracy of that estimate is expressed as *probabilities of chance*, known informally as the *p value*, and represented by a lowercase p. The p value represents the chance of error; that is, the likelihood that the data may not accurately represent what the researcher intended them to represent. Of course, there is also a chance that the data may accurately describe what was being observed. It is conventional in social science research to accept a p value that is less than or equal to .05, meaning that the researcher is 95% certain that the results of their statistical analysis were not due to chance. Results that meet or exceed that cutoff are considered *statistically significant*.

It is important to make considerable efforts for all possible observations to have an equal chance of occurring. This effort is called *controlling for bias*. The more your observations are free of bias, the better the probability that your findings will not be due to chance. Since it is nearly impossible (other than in a laboratory situation) to eliminate all unwanted bias, be aware that the chances for findings to be in error may be rather great. Strong quantitative research designs reflect that possibility from the moment the research purpose is articulated. Statistical tests tell you how successful you were in that regard.

Hypothesis Testing

A *hypothesis* is an educated guess about the outcome of a problem. In research, hypotheses predict the outcomes of research purposes or purpose specifications (sub-purposes, questions, etc.). Whether or not it is feasible to make such an educated guess depends on whether the purpose of your investigation is descriptive, relational, or experimental in nature. Hypothesis testing is most often called for when you have reason to assume a relationship between two or more variables, such as with correlational research (see Chapter 11) or ex post facto or experimental research (see Chapter 12).

Investigations that focus on the detailed enumeration and description of specific variables in particular contexts should be referred to as descriptive quantitative. Language to articulate the research purpose should be restricted to such terms as describe, observe, or survey. Such studies do not usually utilize hypotheses. Projects whose variables are believed to be related but not causal might be called relational. Their hypothesized relationship should imply nothing more than that statistical connections between variables might be possible.

Unless you have access to a research lab where you can control the environment, true causation is difficult to establish in music education. Naturalistic settings like a classroom or rehearsal hall are not ideal for controlling for unwanted bias due to the many intervening variables that make instruction enjoyable on the one hand and unpredictable on the other. This is why research in the behavioral sciences relies heavily on what is known as *ex post facto* (Latin for "after the fact") and so-called *quasi-experimental* designs.

To illustrate causal hypothesis testing, we offer the following fictitious experimental research purpose (which you will re-visit in the chapter on ex post facto and experimental designs): "to investigate the relative effectiveness of two procedures for teaching movement to first grade students during music class." To address this purpose, the researcher proposes to draw two random samples of 65 students, each from the larger population of first graders in a metropolitan school district.

One group (group A) will be taught using large-muscle movement (method X); the other (group B) will be taught with small-muscle movement (method Y). Otherwise, the lesson content and the teacher will be the same for both methods. Prior to instruction (what researchers call the treatment), students in both groups will be tested for their rhythmic steadiness. If both groups have similar scores, they will be considered comparable for the purposes of the study.

The researcher hypothesizes that the treatment will result in differences in rhythm steadiness scores between the two groups, making the relative effectiveness of the two methods evident. The sub-purposes are to (1) determine the learning outcomes for each of the methods, and (2) compare their relative effectiveness. Following an equal time of instruction, each group will be administered the same rhythmic steadiness test a second time to assess the changes that have taken place with each teaching method. Statistical tests will be used to estimate the effect of the two treatments by comparing the means of the two sets of scores.

The researcher suggests three possible outcomes (or hypotheses): (a) There will be no difference in the relative effectiveness of the two methods; (b) Method Z will be more effective than Method Y; and (c) Method Y will be more effective than Method Z. The researcher hopes to find support for one of the three possibilities. Note that the study had one purpose, two sub-problem/questions, and three (statistical) hypotheses.

As can be seen in this example, research hypotheses may be stated non-directionally, to suggest general difference; or directionally, to suggest more or less difference. For example, hypotheses (b) and (c) above suggest a directional outcome. Had the hypothesis stated only that students using the two methods would experience different outcomes, it would not suggest direction.

Based on a tradition of believing that scientific theories must be falsifiable (see Miksza & Elpus, 2018, pp. 10–11), statisticians prefer to test a counter-factual, or *null hypothesis* (p. 48). The null hypothesis essentially suggests the opposite of the intended outcome: that any differences measured would be within the range of chance occurrence, meaning that the treatments did not have a significant effect on the outcome. If the null hypothesis *cannot* be rejected, further statistical tests are not warranted and are therefore unnecessary. Further testing takes place only when the null hypothesis *is rejected*.

In general, a researcher rejects a null hypothesis if the probability of its occurrence suggests that it was not due to chance. Thus, the result of testing a null hypothesis does not offer irreversible proof for the acceptance or rejection of the hypothesis; it merely provides a probability of acceptance or rejection within set and restricted limits. The researcher has control over these limits of accepted probability levels.

Statistical Assumptions and Design Decisions

In order to use statistical research procedures correctly, you must test whether your sample meets the assumption of normality; that is, their scores on the tested variables are "normally" distributed. In cases where that assumption is met, you may use what are called *parametric* statistics, which are based on the assumption that you are working with samples or populations that exhibit similar characteristics, or *homogeneity of variance*.

The information provided in the next three chapters deals mostly with parametric statistics because these are more powerful and more commonly selected than distribution-free, or *non-parametric*, statistics. The latter are applicable when you do not know the shape of the curve under which a sample of scores or a set of observations may fall, or when you know for a fact that the data do not meet the required assumptions. You will learn in Chapter 12 how to test for normality and can find in Appendix E a list of *parametric and non-parametric* statistics, excerpted from Motulsky (1995), corroborated by information in Miksza & Elpus (2018) and Russell (2018), that can be used in cases where that assumption is not met.

Most researchers prefer to use parametric tests whenever possible because of the greater variety of tests available and because the tests are better able to discern small differences between samples. The ability to assess small differences within a sample or between several samples mandates parametric statistical tests because they are more likely to lead the researcher to reject the null hypothesis when, indeed, it *should* be rejected. Parametric tests are also able to assess larger samples and to "squeeze" more information out of the data.

To make sure that other researchers can yield comparable results for a particular investigation, all decisions related to research design and analysis are painstakingly detailed in published reports of quantitative research. This is because full disclosure of all data is essential for any replication. However, it must be acknowledged that while "real world" experiences in music education may be very much alike, no two will ever be exactly the same. As noted by Heraclitus' famous maxim, "No one steps in the same river twice." The passing of time causes all experiences to be unique even if they closely resemble each other. In addition, new knowledge gained by an individual during an interim period of time, as well as changes caused by natural or man-made events, are likely to produce conditions that effect all moments of life and, therefore, all experiences. Even under the best of circumstances, therefore, evidence obtained through measured observations can never be fully verified but only *corroborated* against repeated, similar observations.

In the following chapters you are introduced to a few of the many statistical tests available to quantitative researchers. If you are completing a final project for a graduate degree, you can obtain additional (and more advanced) information from sources in recommended reading; doctoral level researchers will want to take at least one additional course in quantitative research design and analysis, if not statistics in the social sciences or education. A researcher interested in questions requiring quantitative analyses should do no less.

CHAPTER SUMMARY

1) Numbers convey meaning when their characteristics as labels, counts or measurements are understood.

2) You must address several assumptions before using statistics to analyze quantitative data. They derive from knowledge about the nature of a normal curve, the difference between population and sample, the concepts of probability and hypothesis testing, and the parametric or non-parametric distribution of scores.

3) Quantitative research reports require detailed explanation of all design considerations, including whether and how assumptions were addressed.

Topics for Further Exploration

1) Why researchers distinguish between numbers used as labels, counts, and measures.
2) What is meant by the word *assumptions* in the context of statistics.
3) Possible variables in class members' research ideas.
4) Hypothesis testing and the null hypothesis.

Suggested Assignments

1) Return to the observations of Times Square you made early in the research class. Select five observations and break them down into *measurable* variables. Select five of those variables to operationalize. Determine how you might express the essence of that definition numerically so that you can record the occurrence of each variable in a systematic way.
2) Find a recent quantitative research article in *Update: Applications of Research in Music Education* or another music education research publication. Summarize in writing the descriptions of and/or relationships between variables discovered in the research report.
3) Compile a list of rationales for and against grading as a valid measure of student achievement. Sort out for yourself which purposes of grading seem valid to your goals as a teacher.
4) Make a list of ratings other than grading that you use in your professional life as musician-teacher. What do they mean to you? In what context would you consider them well-used, or in contrast, abusive?

Recommended Reading

Bandalos, D. L. (2018). *Measurement theory and applications for the social sciences*. The Guilford Press.
Cronk, B. C. (2020). *How to use SPSS: A step-by-step guide to analysis and interpretation*. Routledge.
Moore, D. S., & Notz, W. J. (2020). *Statistics: Concepts and controversies* (10th ed.). MacMillan Learning.
Navarro, D. J., Foxcroft, D. R., & Faulkenberry, T. J. (2019). *Learning statistics with JASP: A tutorial for psychology students and other beginners*. https://learnstatswithjasp.com/
Shultz, K. S., Whitney, D. J., & Zickar, M. J. (2020). *Measurement theory in action: Case studies and exercises* (3rd ed.). Routledge.

Helpful Resources

Analyse This!!! Learning to analyse quantitative data: http://archive.learnhigher.ac.uk/analysethis/main/quantitative.html
Companion website for Russell's (2018). *Statistics in music education research:* https://global.oup.com/us/companion.websites/9780190695224/
MASH (Mathematics and Statistics Help, University of Sheffield): www.sheffield.ac.uk/mash/resources/statistics-resources
Normal distribution: www.mathsisfun.com/data/standard-normal-distribution.html
StatSpace (University of British Columbia): statspace.elearning.ubc.ca

REFERENCES

Miksza, P., & Elpus, K. (2018). *Design and analysis for quantitative research in music education*. Oxford University Press.

Moore, D. S., & Notz, W. J. (2020). *Statistics: Concepts and controversies* (10th ed.). MacMillan Learning.

Motulsky, H. J. (1995). *Intuitive biostatistics*. Oxford University Press.

Phillips, D. C., & Burbules, N. C. (2000). *Postpositivism and educational research*. Rowman and Littlefield.

Russell, J. A. (2018). *Statistics in music education research*. Oxford University Press.

Tal, E. (2020, Fall). Measurement in science. In E. N. Zalta (Ed.), *The Stanford encyclopedia of philosophy*. https://plato.stanford.edu/archives/fall2020/entries/measurement-science/

CHAPTER 10

Understanding Descriptive Statistics

Debbie Rohwer

This chapter highlights the following concepts:

- Numbers in descriptive research
  - level of measurement
  - central tendency and variability
- Types of descriptive studies:
  - survey research
  - frequency count studies
- Inputting data into a statistical program
- Using descriptive statistics in the classroom
- Crafting a proposal for descriptive quantitative research

INTRODUCTION

While there are many types of research studies that describe phenomena, they can be simplified into those that describe what exists through an in-depth, contextual, "picture-in-words" (i.e., qualitative research, see Chapters 7–8) and those that describe what exists through numbers (i.e., quantitative research). In addition to descriptive studies, there are also other types of quantitative studies. Correlational studies look at the relationship of one observed phenomenon to another (see Chapter 11), and ex post facto and experimental studies look at differences between groups (see Chapter 12). All quantitative studies, however, use descriptive statistics to provide context to the overall picture of the data before using relationship or difference statistics.

Teachers commonly use numbers as a part of their classroom activities: rating or ranking students based on a playing test, or reporting to the administration the number of students accepted for all-state band, or asking students to respond to questions about their own understanding of classroom content. Researchers who use numbers do so for some of the same basic reasons: coming up with information on such things as skill level, or knowledge level, or frequency of an activity, or perceptions of musical learners. All of these data gathering and reporting scenarios start with a large data set that is then distilled into a descriptive, concise, manageable and comparable format: a number.

The most important point is that the purpose of the research must guide (1) the questions asked, (2) the way that the answers are obtained, and (3) the form of those answers. If your goal is to get at a contextual understanding of a setting, then numbers may not be appropriate to the

DOI: 10.4324/9781003057703-13

purposes of that study. If, however, you have 1,000 responses to a specific question, and want to find one answer that can summarize the 1,000 responses best, then a number and specifically, a descriptive statistic, may be very appropriate.

NUMBERS IN DESCRIPTIVE RESEARCH

Descriptive, quantitative studies gather data to answer questions such as "how often" or "how much." Understanding how to obtain answers to these types of questions, as well as to relationship and difference questions in other types of research, necessitates a basic understanding of numerical concepts and the limitations that exist when choosing certain question formats. This chapter focuses on two basic numerical concepts: (1) Level of measurement and (2) Central tendency and variability.

Level of Measurement

As a PhD student who specializes in studio voice, *Christy* was wondering how she could learn more about the practice habits of collegiate vocalists. As she discussed her ideas with *Prof. E.*, she learned that the wording of questions and the formatting of response options had important consequences for data analysis and interpretation. For instance, the question "Did you know how to practice before arriving at the university?" suggested a yes/no response. But re-wording the question to "How much has your practice routine changed during your college career?" suggested a Likert-type range of responses from "not at all" to "a great deal." A question such as "Which practice techniques do you find most useful?" (with descriptors gleaned from the research literature) could be organized with check boxes so students marked each of the techniques they used. But she might get more detailed information if she asked respondents to rank their preferences in order. Finally, the question "How much time do you normally spend practicing each day?" would provide concrete answers with a specific number.

Suggesting Baughman's survey research (2014 and 2017) or that of Rohwer and Svec (2014) as possible models, Prof. E. told Christy that she would have to weigh which question format would best address her research question and also to consider the best way to organize the questions and decide how she wanted to analyze the data. In order to understand data analysis choices, Prof. E. then described the basic number-related issues involved in item format decisions.

This conversation helped Christy understand the many possible ways a question can be constructed (see Chapter 14 for more information about constructing data gathering tools). Christy's first question has response options that are called *nominal* (and later, in Chapter 12, we will also use the synonymous term, *categorical*). The first question has two response options: yes or no. These options have no inherent order; students would mark one answer and leave the other answer blank.

If Christy asks respondents to *rank* a list of practice techniques, she would then use an *ordinal* level of measurement. Such ordered responses have a hierarchy, but the space between the numbers that represent preference is not equidistant; that is, someone who ranks vocalization first and breathing exercises second is only documenting order, not saying they prefer vocalization twice as much as breathing exercises. And lastly, Christy employs a third level of measurement when she asks the students to enter the number of minutes they practice on a typical day. With measures such as minutes, the specific distance between response options is considered to be equal; that is, daily practice of 60 minutes is twice as much as daily practice of 30 minutes. This question would yield data at the *ratio* level of measurement. Both *interval* and *ratio* level measurements have equivalent values; ratio data also has a true zero point.

Each of these *level of measurement* options leads to a choice about how the data can be analyzed. While the purpose of the study and the pragmatics of the respondents' ability to answer the questions have to be the primary guiding principles in question choice and design, it can be useful to weigh the amount of information you can obtain through the format of your question. Just as Christy demonstrates in her pondering, all of these questions may address the same topic, but the level of detail in the responses will differ.

Central Tendency and Variability

Taking an average of the responses in order to represent the complete data set with one representative number is a common way researchers analyze data. These "averages" are called *central tendencies*, and while they all provide a representative number, they do so in different ways. The *mode* is calculated for a nominal question by finding the most common response from the complete data set. The *median* is calculated for an ordinal question by ordering the responses from smallest to largest and taking the "middle" response. The *mean* is calculated for an interval or ratio question by using a traditional average: adding all responses together and dividing by the number of responses in the data set.

For Christy's nominal question of yes or no, if 47 people answer yes and 32 answer no, the mode would be yes (the most common response). The median documents the middle response of the data set, so Christy's question about ranking practice techniques might result in a subset of responses that documents the ranking of vocalization, such as: 1, 3, 4, 4, 5. The middle response for these data would be 4. The mean could be used to document the answers for Christy's rating question. If, for instance, students were asked to respond as to how much they liked the technique of vocalization using a 1–10 scale, a subset of their responses might be 1, 2, 5, 8, 9. Adding these responses (total = 25) and dividing by the number of responses (5) would provide a mean value of 5.

The strength of the mean is that it represents all numbers in the data set through the averaging procedure. That being said, there are cases where there may be extreme scores in the data set that can artificially skew the central tendency. This can happen, for instance, if you are asking salary information of respondents and almost all respondents are middle class, but you have one multi-millionaire. The multi-millionaire will artificially raise the salary average for the group. Instead of the mean, the median might be the more appropriate central tendency to use in this case, since it documents the middle number instead of averaging all the numbers. If your question is asked at the interval or ratio level of measurement, you always have the choice of using a central tendency other than the mean (i.e., the median or mode), if it best represents the data. If your question is at the ordinal level, you can choose the median or mode. If your question is at the nominal level, your only central tendency option is the mode.

Level of Measurement	Central Tendency	Variability
Interval or Ratio	Mean	Range & Standard Deviation
Ordinal	Median	Percentile
Nominal	Mode	–

FIGURE 10.1 Summary: Level of Measurement, Central Tendency, and Variability

In addition to central tendency measures, *variability* statistics are calculated to represent the extent to which responses vary across the participants. For nominal level questions, no variability statistic is documented, because the number that is used for the computer analysis of nominal level data is only a coding mechanism. For instance, yes might be coded 1 and no might be coded 0 for Christy's study, but the number itself is meaningless. For questions with ordinal level response formats, *percentiles* can be added that show the point where 25% of the ordinal responses lie, and the point where 75% of the ordinal responses lie so as to give more detail as to how the responses spread.

For questions with interval or ratio level response formats, *range* is added to document the distance between the highest and lowest scores, and the *standard deviation* is added to give context as to how much the scores vary around the mean. A large standard deviation relative to the mean indicates that there is more spread (or deviation) to the scores, while a small standard deviation relative to the mean indicates that the scores tend to group together around the mean; a standard deviation of 0 means that all the scores are the same as the mean (see Figure 10.1).

A large standard deviation, then, means more variability and less agreement in responses. So, for instance, with Christy's subset of scores as listed above (1, 2, 5, 8, 9) the standard deviation is 3.5, while a different subset of scores (4, 5, 5, 5, 6) has the exact same mean of 5, but the standard deviation is much smaller at .7. Thus, Christy's scores show a much greater spread than the second set of scores.

The following descriptive research example from Dale's master's thesis demonstrates the use of descriptive statistics.

Dale was interested in knowing how students and parents perceived the instructional choices in the school district's music programs. He had found that parents and students alike were positive about scheduling (M = 4.98, SD = .10), trips (M = 4.82, SD = .23), and uniforms (M = 4.79, SD = .19), but the students (M = 2.10, SD = .86) perceived the classroom technology less favorably than did the parents (M = 4.01, SD = .35).

In Dale's findings, the means provide a strength order to the responses, with the most positive responses on average being reported for scheduling (mean of 4.98) and the least positive responses on average being reported by the students for technology (mean of 2.10). In this scenario, the smallest standard deviation (i.e., the most agreement in responses) was found for scheduling (standard deviation of .10) and the largest standard deviation (i.e., the least agreement in responses) was found for student technology responses (standard deviation of .86).

Behavioral Likert:

I practice using a metronome.

Always   Frequently   Sometimes   Rarely   Never

Affective Likert:

I feel that the ensemble uniforms in our school are attractive.

Strongly Agree   Agree   Neutral   Disagree   Strongly Disagree

FIGURE 10.2 Behavioral and Affective Likert-type Questions

Researchers have to consider level of measurement as an issue related to the clarity and purpose of questionnaire items. *Likert-type scales* are a type of question structure, demonstrated below, that is commonly used, easy to construct and easily answered by respondents. While the level of measurement for Likert-type scales has been debated (see discussions in Ghiselli, Campbell, & Zedeck, 1981; Kline, 2005; Lubke & Muthen, 2004; Spector, 1976, 1980), textbooks tend to document affective response options (such as strongly agree, agree, neutral, disagree, strongly disagree) as being ordinal in nature. If used with behavioral response categories (such as always, frequently, sometimes, rarely, and never) there may be greater justification to accept Likert-type questions as interval level data, and with interval level questions, a mean, range and standard deviation can be calculated. As a side note to add to the debate, universities across the country provide individual item means for teacher evaluation items using affective Likert-type scales. Suffice it to say that you may see studies in the field of music education that analyze Likert-type questions as ordinal or interval level data (see Figure 10.2).

TYPES OF DESCRIPTIVE STUDIES

Survey research and frequency count investigations are two common types of descriptive studies found in the field of music education. Both types of studies aim to describe, with survey research describing by obtaining responses from individuals, and frequency count investigations describing by coding behaviors or actions of individuals.

Survey Research

Researchers wishing to learn about the backgrounds, experiences, practices, and beliefs (Miksza & Elpus, 2018) of a group of people often sample a feasible number of participants and then administer a questionnaire to that sample in the hope of generalizing the results to a larger group of individuals who are much like those in the sample. This procedure works well when you have a complete list of all people in the group to which you as a researcher would like to generalize (called the *target population*), or have access to the listing of a group that represents that population (called the *sampling frame*), and then use a sampling procedure that allows everyone on the list to have a chance of being in the sample (called *probability sampling*).

Choosing the Sample

Examples of probability sampling procedures are *simple random sampling* where individuals are chosen from a list at random, or *stratified sampling* where individuals are randomly sampled from subgroups that need to be represented (such as voice part, gender, or zip code in a state-level population). Sometimes probability sampling is not feasible because of pragmatic issues such as a population list not existing, and if that is the case, then alternative procedures may need to be considered, such as *purposeful sampling*, where you make a professional judgment concerning which individuals should be in the sample, or *convenience sampling*, where you take those participants who are readily available to you. Both of these non-probability sampling procedures, however, greatly impact readers' ability to generalize to a larger population beyond those in the study itself. Whether you choose to conduct a study through mailed questionnaire or online survey software systems such as *Qualtrics* or *SurveyMonkey*, you should carefully weigh your sampling procedures so that generalizability to the target population of interest is feasible.

Validity and Reliability

Before sending the questionnaire out to the sample, you must ensure that the items on the questionnaire are appropriate, clear, and cover the content well (i.e., valid), and that respondents answer the questions without excessive error (i.e., consistently/reliably). Types of validity found in music education studies are: *content validity*, *criterion-related validity*, and *construct validity*, and types of reliability are *internal consistency*, *test-retest*, and *interjudge reliability*. Test development and checking for reliability and validity are further discussed in Chapter 11.

Designing a Questionnaire

When designing a viable survey research instrument, it is important that the purposes of the study align specifically with the questions being asked. One way to learn to do this is to pay close attention to how survey items are worded in published studies inside and outside of the field of music education. If you are proposing survey research, include several survey-based sources in your literature review, and be sure to consult the additional sources in Recommended Reading. Further information about data gathering tools can also be found in Chapter 14.

Ensuring the comfort as well as anonymity and/or confidentiality of the participants is important in the process of planning how questions will be asked of the participants and how results will be reported. For institutions in the United States, the Institutional Review Board (IRB) serves as an external set of eyes to ensure that procedures are ethical and that the protocols inform research participants of their rights in the study; institutions in other countries have similar review boards. Researchers who plan their studies with clarity and ethics in mind will be far ahead in their efforts to make a quality measurement tool.

Once questions are written, the most common procedure for ensuring that a questionnaire (or other "test") will be useable and appropriate is to send it to a panel of experts for feedback on its content. You might include feedback prompts asking something like "Which questions are superfluous to the topic that is being measured: teacher perceptions of technology?" and "What questions should be added so as to address more completely the topic that is being measured: teacher perceptions of technology?" The panel then offers subjective feedback that is used to improve the content validity of the questionnaire.

Field Testing

Following the content validity procedure, it is common to ensure the clarity of items on the questionnaire by asking a small group of individuals to discuss the item content with the researcher. This process is called a *field test*. It is best if the participants in the field test are of the same basic age and demographic as the respondents planned for the main study. This ensures the greatest potential for generalizability to the main study sample. The discussion with field test participants often centers on issues such as the clarity of the instructions or whether certain terms or acronyms might be understood by the respondents. After the questionnaire has been adjusted based on content validity and field test input, the next step is to estimate the reliability of the questionnaire through a *pilot test*.

Pilot Testing

For reliability, you chose a group of individuals who are of the same basic age and demographic as the respondents who will be in the main study and ask these individuals to answer the questions on the questionnaire. A researcher may choose to give the questionnaire to the same pilot group of individuals twice to check for consistency of individual responses over time (called *test-retest reliability*). This procedure would be valuable if the questionnaire results were going to document responses on individual items. For instance, on a questionnaire of perceptions of technology, a researcher may want to provide means for individual questions, such as perceived value of smartboard, or Finale, or other technological devices or applications.

On a questionnaire where the items are summed to get one number as an overall score of, for instance, perception of technology, the summed number could be used to describe the extent of support for a general topic. In this case, a higher summed score would mean that the respondent valued technology more than someone who had a lower summed score; this type of reliability check is called *internal consistency*, with the most common type of internal consistency being *Cronbach's alpha*.

Administering the Questionnaire

After a researcher has "tested the test" (in this case, a questionnaire) thoroughly to ensure that it is as valid and reliable as possible (see Chapter 11), the next step is administering the questionnaire to the main study sample. Once responses to the questionnaire have been obtained, you as the researcher would need to determine the coverage of the information that was received: From those to whom the questionnaire was sent, how many responded? Unless an extremely high response is garnered, some form of *follow-up* should be considered in order to be able to describe the complete picture. If, for instance, only half of those who are sent a questionnaire respond, how do you know that their responses represent the full sample? What if those who do not respond are very much against the topic and those who do respond are in favor of the topic? In such a case, the incomplete information that is obtained from the initial half of the participants will not accurately represent the opinion of the whole.

Authors such as Dillman, Smyth, and Christian (2014) advocate a series of follow-up reminders, further followed by a sampling of the non-respondents. This sub-group can be used to compare the non-respondent answers to the respondent answers. If the responses do not differ across the non-respondents and the respondents, then you have a more defensible stance that the results can be defended as representing the complete sample.

Frequency Count Studies

In addition to survey research studies, there are also descriptive studies that describe how often behaviors occur. These studies use *frequency counts* to document the extent of behavior.

> As an experienced teacher interested in effective teaching, *Michelle* decided to investigate the amount and type of feedback that expert teachers provided to their students. She observed 10 expert teachers and found that the teachers most commonly gave many short, specific feedback statements that were directive for improvement, and then notified the students when they had achieved the goal. Over the rehearsals Michelle viewed, the expert teachers demonstrated an average of 15 of these directive-followed-by-notification cycles in each 45-minute rehearsal (range of 9–23, SD = 4.88).

In this example, Michelle noted that the expert teachers in her sample had a common trend in completing directive-followed-by-notification teaching cycles. The data from this study were tallies of the number of times that each teacher completed a cycle in a class period. The number of cycles documented in this study ranged from 9 to 23, with two teachers demonstrating 12 cycles. Table 10.1 shows the data for the frequency of complete teaching cycles from the 10 expert teachers.

Before conducting the study, Michelle checked whether her measurement tool (in this case a coding sheet designed to document how often her phenomenon of interest occurred) corresponded to the teaching cycles reported in the relevant literature. She also had a panel of experts evaluate her coding sheet for its representativeness of teaching cycles. Checking against relevant literature and obtaining expert evaluations were steps to ensure that her *operationalization* of the construct she was coding was accurate and complete; in short, that the tool had content validity. Next, she did a pilot test of the measurement tool by observing and coding a set of teacher behaviors using two observers: herself and a second qualified observer. The

TABLE 10.1 Frequency Count of Complete Teaching Cycles

Cycles	Frequency	Percent
9.00	1	10.0
11.00	1	10.0
12.00	2	20.0
13.00	1	10.0
14.00	1	10.0
19.00	1	10.0
20.00	1	10.0
21.00	1	10.0
23.00	1	10.0
Total	10	100.0

pilot showed her if there was agreement across the two sets of observations. This procedure assessed *interjudge reliability*, a measure that documents the consistency of a measurement tool across observers.

If you, like Michelle, wish to do a frequency count study, you must first be clear about what you wish to observe. You must detail the particulars of "what" and "who" in your research proposal via your purpose specifications as well as in the body of your introduction, literature review and methods description. Michelle *operationalized* the "what" in her proposal by describing her phenomenon of interest with characteristics (researchers call them *indicators*) that could be measured. Often such indicators are distilled from the literature (sometimes in combination with expert opinion) or borrowed from an existing theory. Miksza and Elpus (2018) suggest that operational definitions should be clear enough that other researchers would recognize them as "an authentic representation of the ideal construct, and . . . independently observe the phenomenon with consistency" (p. 19).

Other considerations include the perspective and focus imagined in earlier chapters, which resemble what researchers call *units of analysis*. Will you be measuring the behaviors of individuals, groups, classrooms, or schools? Will your measures occur over minutes, hours, or existing teaching cycles, like Michelle's? The setting and procedures for the research should logically follow your purpose as well. For Michelle, who wished to observe teacher behavior in a classroom setting, a naturalistic setting was best. However, if the behavior itself had been the phenomenon of interest—for instance, individual students' practice strategies—a controlled setting might have been more appropriate (Miksza & Elpus, 2018). Like Michelle, you will also need to create and test a measurement tool (researchers call them *instruments*) or use a previously developed one from the research. The measurement strategies most commonly used by music education researchers designing such instruments include coding and analysis (chosen by Michelle), force-choice tests, open-ended descriptions, and ratings of music performance or of teaching (Rutkowski, Thompson, & Huang, 2011). Finally, you need to decide whether to do in-person or video-recorded observations. While there are pros and cons to each, video (or audio) recording offers the possibility of multiple viewings at your own convenience, as well as better opportunities for interjudge reliability.

INPUTTING DATA INTO A STATISTICAL PROGRAM

Once data have been obtained from a sample, you need to input the data into a statistical program to calculate the appropriate statistics. One of the most commonly used statistical programs in the field of music education is SPSS Statistics (version 27, as found at ibm.com/products/spss-statistics). SPSS is only one option from the many statistical programs that are available, but by seeing the input process for one example program, you will be able to envision the numerical and format issues that may transfer to any program. Readers who do not have an institutional subscription to SPSS or another similar program may want to try the open-source program JASP (jasp-stats.org).

The example below takes a small sample of questionnaire data and describes the input process for illustration purposes.

Question 1, Demographic: What is your gender?
Answers: Male, Male, Female, Female, Female

Because the data for this question are nominal level, you assign a number to represent male and female (perhaps 0 and 1). Note that such a number is for grouping only and has no mathematical meaning. Don't be alarmed if your program adds decimals to the numbers; the coding of male and female remains the same. The inputted data for these 5 responses would look like the following, with each person's response to the gender question being a row (so Bob may be #1 across and Michael may be #2 across, etc.):

Gender

1.   0.00.
2.   0.00.
3.   1.00.
4.   1.00.
5.   1.00.

The next step with this nominal level question would be to choose a central tendency and variability statistic from the descriptive choices. To do this, go to the "analyze" drop-down and then choose frequency with mode, minimum, maximum, and range as the statistic choices (see Table 10.2).

From this readout, then, you can ascertain that there were 5 valid responses and no missing data. The most common response was female (1). While the table documents that the responses ranged from the minimum numeric response of 0 (male) to the maximum response of 1 (female), range is not listed for nominal level data since the number is simply a place marker for grouping purposes.

Question 2, Behavioral Likert-type: I use a metronome when I practice my band music.
Possible Answers: Always, Frequently, Sometimes, Rarely, Never

Because the data for this question may be considered interval level, a number represents the strength of the responses from positive to negative: always (5), frequently (4), sometimes (3), regularly (2), never (1). The input data for these 5 responses would look like the following, with each person's response to the question being a row (so Sasha's "Always" response would be #1 across, and Flora's "Frequently" response would be #2 across, etc.):

TABLE 10.2 SPSS Results for Nominal Data Input of Five Responses

Statistics

Gender

Number	Valid responses	5
	Missing data	0
Mode		1.00
Range		1.00
Minimum		.00
Maximum		1.00

TABLE 10.3 SPSS Results for Interval Data: Central Tendency and Variability

Descriptive Statistics

	N	Range	Minimum	Maximum	Mean	Std. Deviation
Band	5	3.00	2.00	5.00	3.8000	1.30384

Practice

1. 5.00.
2. 4.00.
3. 5.00.
4. 3.00.
5. 2.00.

The next step with this interval level question would be to choose a central tendency and variability statistic from the descriptive choices. To do this, go to the "analyze" drop-down and then choose "descriptive" with mean, standard deviation, minimum, maximum, and range as the statistic choices (see Table 10.3).

From this readout, you can ascertain that there were 5 valid responses and no missing data. The central response was 3.8 with the most negative response being 2 (Rarely) and the most positive response being 5 (Always), and a spread around the mean of 1.3.

DESCRIPTIVE STATISTICS IN THE CLASSROOM

An understanding of how data can be obtained, structured and analyzed is useful when publishing a research study, but it can also help teachers to analyze their own teaching behaviors. With a descriptive quantitative study, you can measure time use in music classes, perhaps to compare how experienced and novice teachers use instructional time. Informal questions can be asked, such as, "How much time do I spend talking?" and "Is the content of my teacher talk serving an instructional purpose?" Descriptive inquiries can serve as important research-based questions that every teacher can ask and investigate in their own classroom.

Teachers can also use descriptive statistics to analyze and improve teacher-constructed tests, not necessarily for research study publication, but for developing a better understanding of their teaching and of student progress. This analysis can help them determine whether certain test items are successful in assessing who knows the content and who does not. If, for instance, a test question is missed by the high scoring people on the test, but the low scorers on the test happen to get that test question correct, then the test item may not be serving the test well, and may not be giving the teacher accurate information about what the students know; for example, the low scorers may have guessed extremely well on that item, and/or the high scorers could have been distracted by one of the other possible responses.

You can investigate how easy or how difficult an item on a test is by using the formula as shown in Figure 10.3:

$$\text{Difficulty value for an item} \quad = \quad \frac{\text{\# of persons answering item correctly}}{\text{Total \# of persons taking the test}}$$

FIGURE 10.3 Formula for Determining Item Difficulty

The closer to 1 the difficulty value is, the easier the item; conversely, the closer to 0 that the difficulty value is, the more difficult the item. So if 100 students took a test and all 100 of them got the first question correct, then the difficulty value for that item would be 1 (easy), whereas if only 10 out of the 100 got the second item correct, the difficulty value would be .10 (difficult). The variability of test scores is maximized when the difficulty values of a test average .5. In other words, mid-level difficulty items usually have the highest power to *discriminate* between those who know and those who do not know the content.

How well an item discriminates between high and low scorers on the test can be checked by analyzing the responses to individual questions for the high scorers and for the low scorers. You put the tests in order from highest to lowest score and then choose one item to analyze. Then, you tally the number of test takers who answered the item correctly. Lastly, you subtract the number of correct responses for the lower half tests from the number of correct responses for the upper half tests, and divide by the number of test takers in one of the groups (i.e., half of the class). This analysis is completed for each item on the test. The formula for this procedure for each item (see Figure 10.4), is:

$$\text{Discrimination value for an item} \quad = \quad \frac{\text{\# correct from upper half - \# correct from lower half}}{\text{\# of half of the respondents}}$$

FIGURE 10.4 Formula for Determining Item Discrimination

If there are many more high scoring test takers who get the item correct than lower scoring test takers, then the item will discriminate well (ideally with a discrimination value above .4). If, however, more lower scoring test takers get the item correct than the high scoring test takers, then the item will not distinguish well between the knowledgeable and the less knowledgeable (with the poorest items in need of elimination having values below .2).

If the test items are, for instance, multiple choice items on a music theory test, you can further analyze how the students responded to each possible option out of the 4 choices provided. An ideal question would have those who knew the answer choosing the correct response and those who did not know the answer choosing randomly between the possible responses. When looking at the spread of how enticing the wrong answers were to test takers, you can divide the number of *distractor* (wrong) item choices by the total number of those answering the item incorrectly. For instance, if 30 people got number 1 wrong and there were 3 incorrect options, then ideally the 30 would be equally spread, with 10 on each incorrect response. If that is not the case, you can analyze which response options are, perhaps, distracting too many test takers, and conversely, which response options are not distracting enough test takers for the response options to be useful.

The most important next step would be to see how many upper-half, high scoring test takers and how many lower-half, lower scoring test takers were torn away from the correct answer by each incorrect choice. If only lower-half test takers were drawn to the incorrect responses, and those lower-half test takers were drawn equally across the 3 wrong answers, then that is ideal. If however, a large number of upper-half test takers were drawn to a wrong choice item, then that incorrect response may be too close to the correct response, thereby distracting too well the test takers who knew the material.

A close analysis of teacher-designed test items can lead to an improved understanding of the classroom content that needs more explanation, as well as a more complete understanding of the quality of the test itself. The task of making a useful test and refining it so that it does the best possible job of helping teachers help those who are struggling with the course content, should be a primary goal for all teachers.

CRAFTING A PROPOSAL FOR DESCRIPTIVE QUANTITATIVE RESEARCH

A proposal for quantitative research is usually presented in four sections or chapters: (1) Introduction, (2) Review of related literature, (3) Methods and Procedures, and (4) Conclusions. Its purpose is to connect your specific view of the topic to the published body of knowledge in the field, support your claim that there is a need for your study, and communicate that you have the necessary skills and knowledge to complete the proposed project.

Preliminary Steps

Prior to formalizing your proposal, it is helpful to re-visit your thinking about your topic and research purpose.

Purpose, Rationale and Purpose Specifications

Re-examine the purpose, rationale, and purpose specifications (i.e., sub-purposes, hypotheses, or research questions) you wrote in Chapter 3 to confirm that they suggest descriptive quantitative research—that is, using numbers to describe what exists or is happening. If you have doubts, discuss with your course instructor or project advisor.

Literature Collection

Assess the literature you have collected to this point. Your literature collection should represent your perspective on the topic and your understanding of its lineage, address your research purpose and any specifications, justify the approach you propose to follow, and clarify any theoretical or philosophical lens(es) that guide your thinking. If this is not the case, you may need to try additional search terms to find additional sources. Re-visiting (and possibly revising) the literature map you completed in Chapter 2 may be helpful.

Writing the Introduction

In the introduction you expand on your research purpose and rationale to present a logical argument for your proposed research. It begins with background on the lineage of your topic using concepts drawn from the literature. Typically it is organized from general to specific, and may be further organized according to your purpose specifications (i.e., sub-purposes, hypotheses, or research questions) and any theoretical lenses that are pertinent to your perspective.

Following that, you present your argument in the form of a problem statement: purpose statement, rationale, and research specifications (see Chapter 3). **Note that the way you word your purpose—for instance, using the terms** *describe,* **or** *explore* **in your purpose statements—signals to your committee and other readers that your intention is descriptive (Rohwer, 2018; Miksza & Elpus, 2018).** If there are specific terms to be defined, those may follow the problem statement. Although the introduction is the part of your proposal that will be read first, you may wish to complete it after writing your literature review.

Writing the Literature Review

Quantitative researchers use the literature to explore concepts and constructs, offer definitions, provide a theoretical basis, and suggest methods—including new and existing measurement tools. Quantitative literature reviews are organized according to purpose specifications. The literature within each specification is organized from general to specific, often with a final section that discusses sources that influenced the research design. If your research is influenced by a particular theory, include a section with sources that explain and utilize that theory. This same organizational scheme in summarized form may be used for the introduction to your proposal and your final report.

Describing Proposed Methods and Procedures

Earlier in this chapter, we summarized the steps for designing two types of descriptive studies: a survey and a frequency count study. These steps can be the basis for a detailed yet concise description of your research design. The following details must be included:

a. The people involved (target population, sampling frame, and sample).
b. The way you will collect data (including constructing, checking for validity and reliability, pilot testing and distributing any instruments), the variables you will examine, and your timeframe.
c. The way you will analyze the data you collect.
d. The way you will manage research ethics (including IRB submissions, if applicable).
e. Any field testing or pilot testing, and preliminary results, including validity and reliability.
f. Note that copies of data collection instruments such as questionnaires or checklists should be included in Appendix/ces at the end of the proposal.

For more information see Chapter 14 and Recommended Reading.

Writing the Conclusion

Your conclusion summarizes the proposal and reiterates the logical argument put forth in your introduction. Begin by re-stating your purpose, purpose specifications and rationale—preferably with slightly different wording to avoid redundancy. Next, provide a brief review of your methods and procedures, organized according to your purpose specifications. End with a preliminary "so what" statement that explains what you expect to find and why those findings matter to the field of music education. Your conclusion must communicate to the committee reviewing your proposal that your expectations are reasonable and do-able.

CHAPTER SUMMARY

1) Designing and analyzing questions for research purposes requires an understanding of the numerical concepts of level of measurement (nominal, ordinal, interval, and ratio), central tendency (mode, median, mean) and variability (percentile, range, standard deviation).
2) Survey research and frequency count studies are common descriptive studies in the field of music education.
3) Sampling is an important consideration when choosing participants for a study.
4) All measurement instruments should be assessed for issues of validity and reliability.
5) Teachers and students can benefit from having classroom tests analyzed for difficulty and discrimination.
6) Designing procedures for a research study begins after you have re-considered your purpose and rationale for the research and re-assessed your literature collection.

Topics for Further Exploration

1) How to use descriptive statistics to summarize the home practice behaviors of your students.
2) What real-world scenarios may place constraints on ideal research studies? For instance, how might you deal with issues of sample size, sampling choices, and test design in the real world?
3) Imagine how your current research idea could be explored with descriptive quantitative research.

Suggested Assignments

1) Individually and as a class, design a questionnaire on the topic of practice or study skills. What types of questions seem to suggest nominal, ordinal, interval, or ratio data? If possible, administer and analyze your questionnaire using the statistics in this chapter.
2) Analyze a test you have given to your own students using difficulty and item analysis concepts, as appropriate to the type of test.
3) Review a published descriptive study and determine the connection between the purpose, rationale, literature, and research design.

Recommended Reading

Cohen, R. J., & Swerdlik, M. E. (2017). *Psychological testing and assessment: An introduction to tests and measurement* (9th ed.). McGraw-Hill.

Dillman, D. A., Smyth, J. D., & Christian, L. M. (2014). *Internet, mail, and mixed-mode surveys: The tailored design method* (4th ed.). Wiley.

Fraenkel, J. R., Wallen, N. E., & Hyun, H. (2018). *How to design and evaluate research in education* (10th ed.). McGraw-Hill.

Huck, S. W. (2012). *Reading statistics and research* (6th ed.). Pearson.

Miksza, P., & Elpus, K. (2018). *Design and analysis for quantitative research in music education*. Oxford University Press.

Navarro, D. J., Foxcroft, D. R., & Faulkenberry, T. J. (2019). *Learning statistics with JASP: A tutorial for psychology students and other beginners*. JASP Team. https://learnstatswithjasp.com/

Rea, L. M., & Parker, R. A. (2004). *Designing and conducting survey research: A comprehensive guide* (4th ed.). Jossey-Bass.

Rohwer, D. (2018). Comments from the editor: Best practices for using questionnaires. *Update: Applications of Research in Music Education*, *37*(2), 3–4. https://doi.org/10.1177/8755123318810110

Russell, J. A. (2018). *Statistics in music education research*. Oxford University Press. https://global.oup.com/us/companion.websites/9780190695224/

Helpful Resources

Learning statistics with JASP: A tutorial for psychology students and other beginners. JASP Team: https://learnstatswithjasp.com/

MASH (Mathematics and Statistics Help, University of Sheffield): www.sheffield.ac.uk/mash/resources/statistics-resources

StatSpace (University of British Columbia): statspace.elearning.ubc.ca

Survey Design (Pew Research Center): https://youtu.be/eFzGdQrr2K8

Understanding Descriptive Statistics (from Toward Science): https://towardsdatascience.com/understanding-descriptive-statistics-c9c2b0641291

Sample Size Calculators

Survey Monkey: www.surveymonkey.com/mp/sample-size-calculator/

Qualtrics: www.qualtrics.com/blog/calculating-sample-size/

REFERENCES

Baughman, M. (2014). *An examination of methods used to teach effective practice strategies in the college voice studio* [Doctoral dissertation]. University of Missouri-Columbia. ProQuest Dissertations & Theses Global (Publication No. 10157617).

Baughman, M. (2017). An examination of methods used to teach practice strategies in the college voice studio. *Update: Applications of Research in Music Education*, *35*(2), 15–22. https://doi.org/10.1177/8755123315593325

Dillman, D. A., Smyth, J. D., & Christian, L. M. (2014). *Internet, mail, and mixed-mode surveys: The tailored design method* (4th ed.). Wiley.

Ghiselli, E. E., Campbell, J. P., & Zedeck, S. (1981). *Measurement theory for the behavioral sciences*. Freeman.

Kline, T. (2005). *Psychological testing: A practical approach to design and evaluation*. Sage.

Lubke, G. H., & Muthen, B. O. (2004). Applying multigroup confirmatory factor models for continuous outcomes to Likert scale data complicates meaningful group comparisons. *Structural Equation Modeling*, *11*, 514–534. https://doi.org/10.1207/s15328007sem1104_2

Miksza, P., & Elpus, K. (2018). *Design and analysis for quantitative research in music education*. Oxford University Press.

Rohwer, D. (2018). Comments from the editor: Best practices for using questionnaires. *Update: Applications of Research in Music Education*, *37*(2), 3–4. https://doi.org/10.1177/8755123318810110

Rohwer, D., & Svec, C. (2014). Perceived value of research preparation opportunities for future music education professors. *Update: Applications of Research in Music Education*, *33*(1), 57–64. https://doi.org/10.1177/8755123314540666

Rutkowski, J., Thompson, K. P., & Huang, Y.-T. (2011). Cited quantitative research articles in music education research journals, 1990–2005: A content analysis of selected studies. In P. M. Ward-Steinman (Ed.), *Advances in social psychology and music education research* (pp. 169–183). Ashgate.

Spector, P. E. (1976). Choosing response categories for summated rating scales. *Journal of Applied Psychology*, *61*, 374–375. https://doi.org/10.1037/0021-9010.61.3.374

Spector, P. E. (1980). Ratings of equal and unequal response choice intervals. *Journal of Social Psychology*, *112*, 115–119. https://doi.org/10.1080/00224545.1980.9924303

CHAPTER 11

Interpreting Correlations

Debbie Rohwer

This chapter highlights the following concepts:

- Components of a correlation coefficient
  - direction and strength of a correlation
  - measurement assumptions that can impact correlations
  - significance of the correlation coefficient
- Validity and reliability coefficients
  - assessing validity and reliability with correlations
- Inputting data into a statistical program
- Crafting a proposal for correlational quantitative research

Correlations look at relationships between variables. This chapter focuses on the parametric statistic called Pearson "r," appropriate when both sets of data are from interval or ratio level tests. It concludes with guidelines for crafting a proposal for correlational research.

Teachers commonly ask correlational questions concerning their students, such as "I wonder if students who score well in music also tend to have high scores on reading tests?" or "I wonder if those who practice the most also tend to receive the highest music performance scores?" Research studies document similar questions in the form of correlational investigations.

This chapter specifically addresses bivariate correlations. For example, you may have two sets of scores for one group of individuals and notice that those individuals scoring well on one of the tests also tend to score well on the other. To determine exactly how closely related the results from one test are to the results from the other, you calculate what is called a correlation coefficient. The statistic most commonly used to investigate the relationship between two scores for one group of people is called the Pearson product moment correlation coefficient. For a description of other possible types of correlations, consult Miksza and Elpus (2018) or Russell (2018) (see Related Reading).

COMPONENTS OF A CORRELATION COEFFICIENT

A first step in investigating a correlation is to view the data on a graph called a *scatterplot*. You could start by plotting both the music score and the reading score from a single student on a graph as illustrated in Figure 11.1. The horizontal axis shows the music test score, the vertical axis the

DOI: 10.4324/9781003057703-14

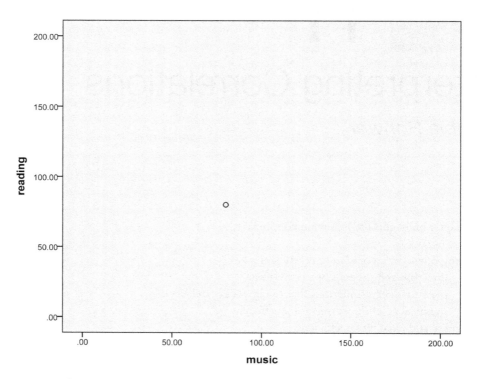

FIGURE 11.1 One Individual's Scores on a Music and a Reading Test

reading score. Joe received a score of 80 on both the music and the reading test, so you can plot Joe's reading score on the vertical axis and his music score on the horizontal axis. Going up from the music score and over to the right from the reading score, the scores meet at the dot shown in the figure.

A single point on a graph does not provide much information, but if you follow this same procedure for an entire class, you get a picture that illustrates the relationship between two tests for one group of individuals. Figure 11.2 represents a perfect positive correlation between our hypothetical music and reading tests. Here you can see particular characteristics of the scores on the graph, such as the *direction* of the relationship and its *strength*, as described below.

Direction and Strength of a Correlation

When two sets of scores exhibit a *perfect positive correlation*, you can use one score (a student's score on one test), to accurately predict the second score (the same student's score on the other test). With a perfect positive correlation, students who scored high on the music test also scored high on the reading test, and if you follow a straight path on the scatterplot, you would see the other extreme: students who scored low on the music test also scored low on the reading test. Thus, even if you did not know a student's score on the reading test, you could predict the student's reading score based on your knowledge of the music score. The linear path in Figure 11.2 shows a positive direction to the line (upper right to bottom left). If an *inverse* relationship exists between music and reading test scores for a group of students, the opposite situation might occur. Figure 11.3 illustrates the case of a *perfect negative correlation*.

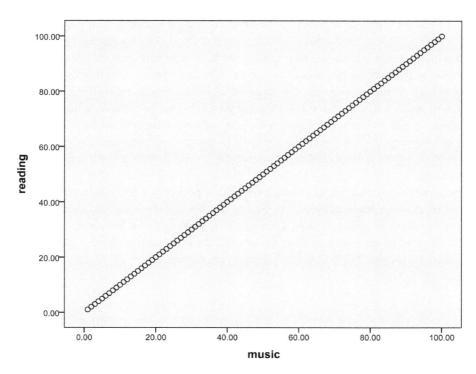

FIGURE 11.2 Scatterplot of a Perfect Positive Correlation

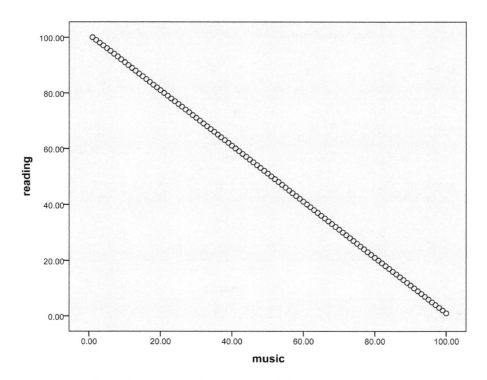

FIGURE 11.3 Scatterplot of Perfect Negative Correlation

In the case of a perfect negative correlation, knowing a student's score on the music test would make it possible to predict the student's reading score; those who scored high on the music test also scored low on the reading test, and if you follow a straight path on the scatterplot, you come to the other extreme that would document that those who scored low on the music test also scored high on the reading test. This linear path shows a negative direction to the line (bottom right to upper left). Note that the term "negative" in this case does not imply judgement. Researchers as well as teachers might expect and want negative relationships. For instance, a negative relationship could document that those who practice *more* also tend to make *fewer* errors. That would clearly be a positive educational outcome, even though it is a negative relationship between scores.

Results of correlations fall somewhere between a perfect positive relationship ($r = +1.00$) and a perfect negative relationship ($r = -1.00$). As the relationship becomes less strong, then the line fattens, making its path less clear. Consequently, you would be less accurate in predicting scores on the reading test based on your knowledge of the music test: there is more *static* (a less clear line) in the picture. For instance, a less strong correlation of $r = .80$ or $r = -.80$ might look like Figure 11.4:

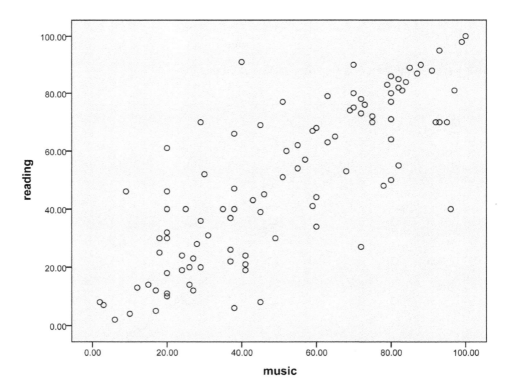

FIGURE 11.4 Scatterplots for r = +.80 and r = -.80

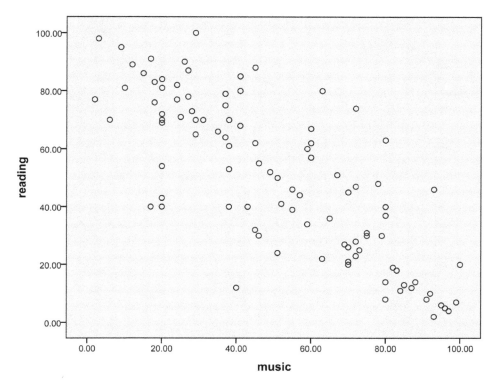

FIGURE 11.4 (Continued)

When looking at *strength* of the correlation, the *absolute value* of the correlation coefficient is used; that is, $r = .80$ and $r = -.80$ are equally *strong*; these two correlations simply have a different *direction*, with one correlation being positive and the other correlation being negative. A weaker correlation of $r = .40$ or $r = -.40$, with even more static, is shown in Figure 11.5.

A complete lack of a linear trend, a correlation of r = .00 might look like Figure 11.6.

Correlation and Causation

Establishing that a relationship between variables exists does not mean that one variable *causes* the other. A finding that those who score high on a music performance exam also tend to have high reading scores simply documents that these two phenomena may be related. It does not imply that being in music *causes* students' reading scores to be higher. Any of a number of possibilities could have been the third-party variable that is embedded within a positive relationship between performance scores and reading scores. Correlation, then, does not imply causation; it only documents trends between variables.

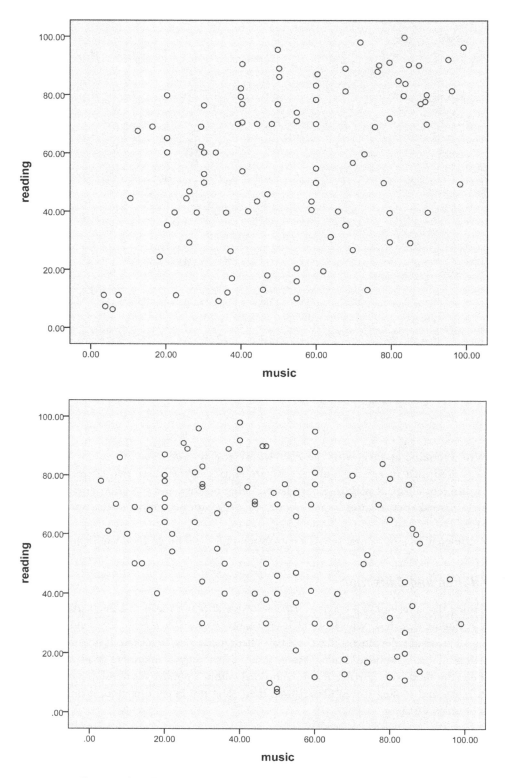

FIGURE 11.5 Scatterplots for r = +.40 and r = -.40

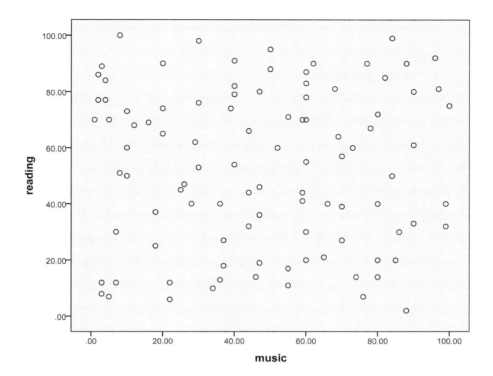

FIGURE 11.6 Scatterplot of r = .00

Note that when a correlation equals zero, you have no ability to predict one score based on another score.

Measurement Assumptions That Can Impact Parametric Correlations

In addition to making sure that your two data sets use interval or ratio level data (see Chapter 10), the Pearson product moment correlation requires investigation of three other assumptions, or rules: linearity, outliers, and restriction of scores. Before deciding to calculate a correlation, a scatterplot (as shown earlier) can tell you whether the assumptions are met. One of the assumptions of the Pearson product moment correlation coefficient is that the two data sets must form a linear distribution.

Linear and Nonlinear Score Distributions

When data follow a straight path, they are considered to be linear distributions. The data gathered to investigate one of Christy's research questions, however, resulted in a distribution that was non-linear.

As a master's performance student, *Christy* had been surrounded by friends who experienced performance anxiety. Curious about possible relationships between music performance and anxiety, she asked her friends if she could measure their anxiety and correlate those scores to their jury scores. When she plotted the correlation data, though, she noted that its shape documented a non-linear trend (see Figure 11.7). Students with moderate anxiety tended to have the highest

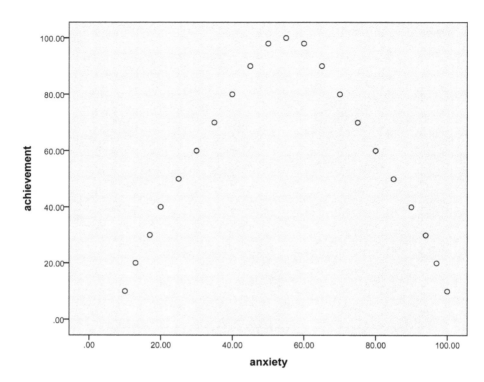

FIGURE 11.7 Scatterplot Depicting a Curvilinear Score Relationship

performance achievement, while those with a small amount or a great deal of anxiety tended to have lower achievement. Christy knew that she would need to take special steps with this data set since the data points were in the shape of a curve.

A different statistic is needed to represent relationships that have a curvilinear shape. If Christy had not looked at the scatterplot, she would not have known that this situation existed. She might have calculated the wrong statistic and come up with an inaccurate, very small linear correlation instead of the very strong curvilinear relationship that should be documented. (Using Pearson for the calculation would result in a correlation of $r = .00$, whereas using a correlation coefficient for curvilinear distributions, such as eta, the correlation calculated would be $r = .74$). Christy took the correct step by viewing the scatterplot so that she could avoid the problem of using an inappropriate statistic.

Outliers

A scatterplot can also advise you of an *outlier*—an additional data point that is distant from the rest of the distribution—that may be present in the data. Figure 11.8 shows two correlations, one without and the other with an outlier.

In the first picture, the relationship between music and reading is $r = .80$, but the relationship documented in the second picture, with the addition of the outlier in the upper left-hand

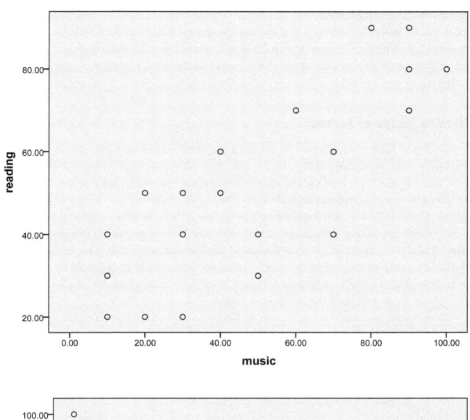

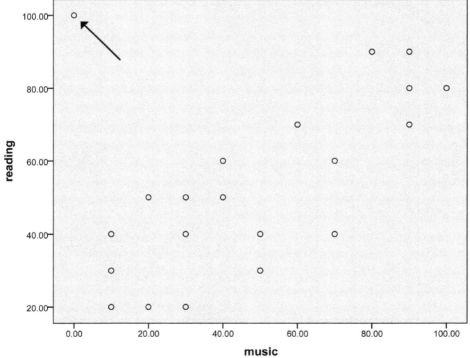

FIGURE 11.8 Scatterplot with Outliers

corner, lowers the correlation between music and reading to $r = .53$. In the case of an outlier, it is important to document its presence and provide the reader with the calculated correlation coefficient with and without the outlier in the data set. If you include this information in your report, the reader will better understand why decisions were made the way they were for the results of the study.

Restriction/Range of Scores

Lastly, you should look at the range of scores that are obtained before a correlation is calculated. Too narrow a range of scores can lead to an inaccurate, attenuated (lowered) correlation coefficient, such as the one shown in Figure 11.9, because there may be no high scores in the chosen sample that lead to a clearly discernible line.

Trying to obtain scores that represent a continuum of high to low scores will help you represent the overall population correlation that would exist if every person in the population were measured. This is an important factor in designing any correlational study. The scatterplot in Figure 11.10 demonstrates the change of correlation coefficients that occurs simply by the inclusion of one additional point that increases the range of scores and the look of the line. In this case, the addition of one score increased the correlation from $r = .12$ to $r = .90$.

In this example, the one extreme score would most likely be documented as an outlier and taken out, but the basic issue is still important: a great variability of scores is necessary in order to accurately document a linear trend. If you did a pilot test and found a restriction of scores to

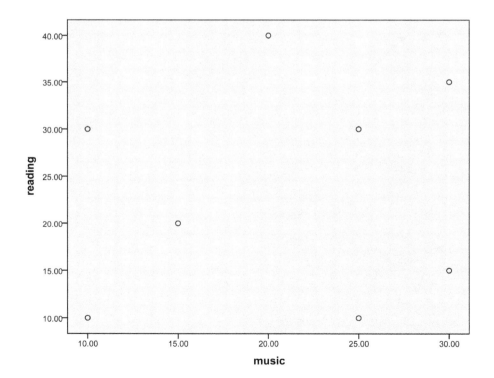

FIGURE 11.9 Scatterplot with a Narrow Range of Scores

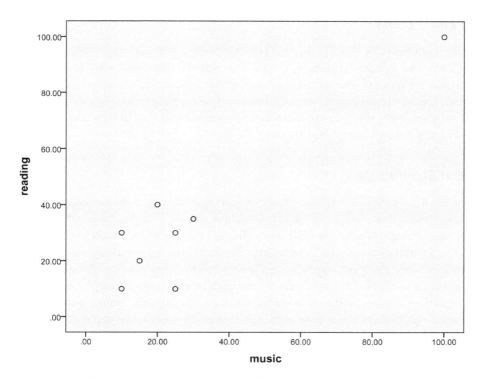

FIGURE 11.10 A Narrow Range of Scores with One Score Added

be apparent in the data, it would be advisable to find a greater spread of individuals to give as complete of a picture of the linear possibilities of the variables as possible. You might consider rethinking your purpose or expanding the sample. Insufficient sample size has been the downfall of many quantitatively conceptualized projects.

Significance of the Correlation Coefficient

As demonstrated above, the correlation coefficient describes basic issues of strength and direction. In addition, most researchers report the statistical significance of the correlation. In layman's terms, statistical significance means the level of risk, or probability, of the result happening by chance. This is expressed by the *p-value*. Music education researchers tend to choose a *p* value, or *significance* cutoff of .05, meaning that they are willing to take a 5% risk of the result happening by chance; or conversely, being 95% sure that the result is not occurring by chance.

In the case of a correlation, you are specifically testing the null hypothesis (see Chapter 9) that the correlation is different from .00 (or no relationship). When setting the significance threshold at .05, you are documenting that a p value *below* .05 is within your chance/risk comfort zone. A calculated significance (*p*) value of .03 says that you are 97% sure that the calculated correlation is different from *r* = .00 (or no relationship) and not by chance. Conversely, a calculated significance (*p*) value of .99 says that you are only 1% sure that the calculated correlation is different from *r* = .00. This is not a bet that most people would be willing to make.

Type I and II Errors

It must be cautioned that there is always a risk of making a wrong decision when you accept a result as occurring or not occurring by chance. If you find a significant result in a study, there is a chance that the result should actually be a non-significant finding; your result, then, would be inaccurate to what the population would document if you had access to everyone. This is called a *Type I error*. Conversely, if you do not find a significant result even though the result should actually be significant, you have made a *Type II error*.

Practical Significance

A concern with significance testing is that statistical significance is relatively easy to obtain in a correlational study if the sample size is big enough. A sample of approximately 100 people will produce a significant result for a correlation coefficient of only $r = .19$, which is relatively close to $r = .00$. For a correlation that may be statistically significant but not practically meaningful, it may be necessary to state that the statistically significant correlation found in a study may be related to the large sample size, but is not practically meaningful. In such a case, it may be important to go beyond significance testing as the only determining factor to gauge the "importance" of a finding.

Practical significance can be estimated with a statistic known as the *coefficient of determination* (r^2), which calculates the percent of variance explained between the two tests. This information can be added to significance testing to get beyond the statistical issues associated with significance testing in isolation. For instance, if you take a correlation of $r = .19$ and square it, you can then discuss this number as the percent of information that is understood from this correlation; in this case, the correlation represents a 4% ($r^2 = .04$) overlap of information across the two tests. You understand 4% of the variance in one test based on information from the other test. For an extensive discussion of the coefficient of determination, see Grissom and Kim's (2012) *Effect Sizes for Research*. A visual example of "information in common" that could be represented by r^2 can be seen in the darkened middle part of the Venn diagram depicted in Figure 11.11.

The coefficient of determination has been called a conservative estimate of practical significance (Cohen, 1988). An alternate form of documenting practical significance can be found in Cohen's more liberal effect size estimate for correlations, where the calculated correlation itself is

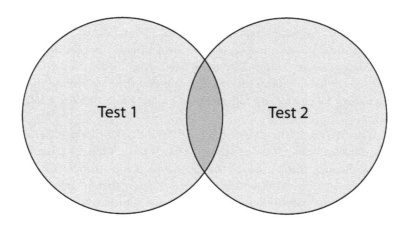

FIGURE 11.11 Venn Diagram for r²

used to determine practicality; Cohen (1988) documented a .1 correlation to be *small*, a .3 correlation to be *medium*, and a .5 or larger correlation coefficient to be *large*. Which decision (conservative or liberal) to favor has been the subject of debate among statisticians for many years. Your own choice, ideally, is a matter of informed judgment about that debate and your understanding of the context of meaningful correlations from the past literature in the content area being studied

Statistical Inference

Another related caution with significance testing of correlations is the assumption that if a correlation is significant then the result from the sample can automatically be generalized to the population. Known as *inference*, this complicated concept requires careful consideration of statistical issues such as probability sampling procedures and test reliability. For a thorough discussion of inferences and inferential statistics, please see Huck (2012) and Miksza and Elpus (2018).

The following example highlights how Greg used some of the concepts addressed in this chapter to investigate a correlational question. By reviewing Greg's procedures, you can check your understanding of these concepts.

Greg, an orchestra director, noted informally that students in his class who are highly skilled performers also tend to have had more years of piano lessons. He decided to investigate this trend formally. At the first round of All State orchestra auditions in one state region, he asked the organizers if they could have auditioning students answer one question as part of their application materials: How many years have you taken piano lessons? After receiving the data and before running the correlation, Greg checked the scatterplot to assess the viability of the correlation in terms of linearity, outliers, and restriction of scores. He found all assumptions to be tenable (acceptable) for using the Pearson product moment correlation coefficient. The result of the correlation between years of piano lessons and audition score was positive and strong (N = 178, r = .84, p = .001, r2 =.71) with higher audition scores tending to align with more years of piano study, and lower scores tending to align with fewer (or no) years of piano instruction.

Greg documented that he checked the data for the assumptions of the statistic (linearity, outliers, and restriction of scores) before calculating the correlation. He used a Pearson product moment correlation, which is justifiable with two sets of interval level data. The correlation coefficient of .80 documents the positive trend toward the data with relatively little static. Prior to doing the calculation he determined that a significant p value would be set at below .05. Greg's findings actually had a p value of .001, which means that he could be 99.9% sure that the correlation was different than .00 and that the finding was not by chance. While the sample size was large, the correlation coefficient itself was also large, documenting less concern that the large sample size was the sole cause for the significance in this case. To document practical significance, Greg added the coefficient of determination ($r2$ =.71) to the description. Based on this correlation, therefore, Greg's research suggested that 71% of the variance across the two tests was understood.

VALIDITY AND RELIABILITY COEFFICIENTS

In addition to documenting the results of a research question, sometimes the correlation coefficients found in a method section of a study describe how one or more tests were assessed for appropriateness (*validity*) and consistency (*reliability*). Many of the statistical possibilities for checking appropriateness and consistency of a test use validity or reliability coefficients (which are correlation coefficients).

ASSESSING VALIDITY AND RELIABILITY WITH CORRELATIONS

Checking for validity and reliability is especially important when constructing tests. If, for example, you were designing a test that measured music aptitude, but your test was shorter than many of the music aptitude tests on the market, you could check to see whether students' scores on your new test lined up with (or were correlated to) scores on the longer, standardized test. If the scores on the shorter version documented a strong, positive correlation to the scores on the longer, standardized test, and the standardized test was considered to be valid, you could say that your test had strong *criterion-related validity*. The coefficient that would be obtained by correlating the two tests would then be called a *validity coefficient*.

If you were constructing a test that measured not just one small concept like rhythmic accuracy, but a large construct like musicianship, you would first define the sub-components of the construct (see *operationalization* in Chapter 10), and then use advanced correlation statistics and other statistical procedures to document that while the subcomponents are not related to each other, the subcomponents do relate to the overall construct of musicianship. So for instance, you might use factor analysis to see whether items on a performance rubric, an ability to improvise test, and a theory test all link to the topic of musicianship, but do not overlap excessively with each other. This would be one way that you might document *construct validity*. Procedures related to construct validity are beyond the scope of this text, but if you would like more information concerning this topic, please see Miksza and Elpus (2018), Russell (2018), or other sources in Recommended Reading.

On the reliability side, if items on a rubric (such as rhythmic accuracy, tonal accuracy, etc.) were added together to obtain one performance achievement score, you would want to estimate whether these items "grouped together" well. You could assess this by correlating each item to every other item to make sure that people who are the best performers tend to consistently score high on these items, and people who are the lowest skilled performers tend to consistently score low on these items. This type of reliability is called *internal consistency*. (The statistic used for this calculation is often *Cronbach's alpha*.) You would also want to make sure that judges using this rubric were consistent in their own scoring and across the other judges; this type of reliability is called *interjudge reliability*. (The statistic used for this calculation is often the same one used by Greg, above: a Pearson's product moment correlation coefficient, but it does depend on the level of measurement of the tests.)

As a teacher or researcher, you may want to improve common errors in musicians' performances through a treatment. But in order to measure the skill level of the students, you would need to know that the etude used to test them lends itself to consistent performances, and that the errors are not random. For instance, if Imani plays the etude twice and each time she plays a certain rhythm incorrectly, but she plays it the same way both times, then that etude is estimated to have high *test-retest reliability* for people of the same skill level as Imani. You can then determine if a type of treatment causes improved scores on Imani's performance, knowing that if the scores at the end show improvement, that the improvement is not from variability in the performance of the etude, but due to the treatment itself. All of these types of reliability checks are done by calculating correlation coefficients, called *reliability coefficients.*

As you have read in this chapter, there are several uses for correlations in music education research. With the statistics in this chapter you might investigate whether a relationship exists between two variables across a single group of people, or estimate the validity or reliability of an etude or written test. (As you will read in Chapter 12 and in sources in Recommended Reading, more advanced statistics allow for the investigation of relationships across a larger number of variables and/or groups.)

If you, like Christy or Greg, wish to do a correlational research study, you must first confirm that your purpose, purpose specifications, and rationale provide a logical explanation as to why the relationship you seek to explore is both credible and consequential. As with descriptive research, you must be clear about the "who" as well as the "what" via your purpose specifications as well as in the body of your introduction, literature review and methods description. But without an equally clear "why," there is no point in looking for a relationship.

Other considerations include the target population, sampling frame, and sample; note that it is advisable to use a minimum of 30 participants. You will also need to determine how you will collect data, making certain that scores are carefully paired as they are collected. As was demonstrated by both Christy and Greg, you will need to check the data for linearity, outliers, and restriction of scores before calculating the correlation, and seek alternative statistics if your data do not meet those assumptions. In addition, you will need to decide on an acceptable level of risk; as described above, a *p* value set at .05 is common in social science research.

INPUTTING DATA INTO A STATISTICAL PROGRAM

As in Chapter 10, the following SPSS input process is provided as a way for you to envision the numerical and format issues that may transfer to any program. (Readers without an institutional subscription to SPSS may want to try JASP: jasp-stats.org or another online resource.) The example below provides a small set of data for a correlation study between the variable of "Practice time" and "Audition score" and describes the input process for illustration purposes.

Test 1: total practice time as documented on a practice card the week before auditions
Test 2: audition performance score

Because the data for this question are both at the interval level of measurement, the Pearson product moment correlation will be used. The data shown below represent two data sets for five individuals, with each row being an individual's score on the two tests (so Jasmine may be #1 across and Khalil may be #2 across, etc.), and with the amount of time in hours in the first column and the audition performance score in the second column. The variable names are therefore *practice* and *audition*, which can be seen in Table 11.1.

The next step would be to check basic assumptions for correlation statistics: linearity, outliers, and restriction of scores. These issues can be weighed by looking at a scatterplot. To do this, go to the "Graphs" dropdown and then choose "Legacy dialogs," "Scatter/dot," and "Simple

Scatter." By entering *practice* for the Y axis and audition for the X axis, you will get what is shown in Figure 11.12:

TABLE 11.1 Practice and Audition Scores (N = 5)

	Practice	Audition
1.	10.00	88
2.	4.00	87
3.	8.00	72
4.	3.00	35
5.	2.00	52

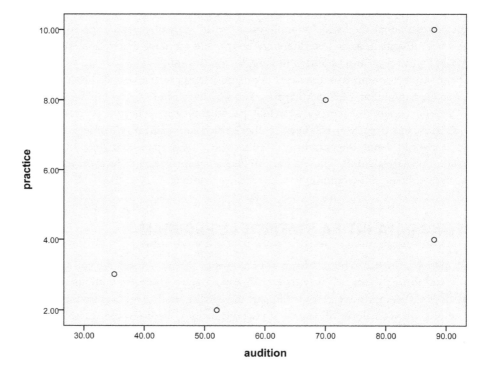

FIGURE 11.12 Scatterplot for Practice and Audition Correlation (N = 5)

From the picture you can see the general positive, linear trend of the data (not curvilinear), no clear outlier cases, and a lack of restriction of scores (especially for this example of 5 data points; any real study would have a far larger sample size).

Next, a correlation coefficient can be calculated by going to the "Analyze" dropdown and choosing "Correlate," and "Bivariate" (for two sets of scores) and checking "Pearson" (provided your data are interval or ratio level). The readout, shown in Table 11.2, documents the sample size of 5 respondents, the correlation coefficient of r = .663 and the calculated significance of .222 (not significant; i.e., not less than .05, but would be significant if the sample size were larger):

TABLE 11.2 Readout Example: Practice and Audition Correlation (N = 5)

Correlations

		Practice	Audition
Practice	Pearson Correlation	1	.663
	Sig. (2-tailed)		.223
	N	5	5
Audition	Pearson Correlation	.663	1
	Sig. (2-tailed)	.223	
	N	5	5

Do not be confused by the duplication inherent in the table. Any test will be perfectly correlated to itself with a score of 1, and the .663 is presented in mirror image for the correlation between the two tests. Even though there are many numbers in the table, if you were including this result in a research study, the numerical part of the result statement would look like this: ($N = 5$, $r = .66$, $p = .22$).

To conclude, correlations serve the purpose of establishing relationships between observed phenomena that can lead researchers and teachers alike to ask further questions about the strength of such relationships. For instance, music teachers can weigh trends, even informally, with their own students by considering correlation questions of interest, such as "Do students who tap their feet also tend to play more steadily?" These questions can lead to an analysis of the possible reasons that might exist for a seeming relationship: Is it the tapping or is there a third-party variable that may be causing students to play more steadily? Did the steady performers also have an extensive amount of musical experiences when they were young; or are the steady performers all highly coordinated? Learning how to weigh situations may help teachers make instructional decisions in a more carefully considered and informed manner. Clearly, a basic understanding of correlations can make real the possibility that answers will come from teachers in the field who have important, pragmatic questions that can advance the profession of music education as a whole.

CRAFTING A PROPOSAL FOR CORRELATIONAL QUANTITATIVE RESEARCH

A proposal for quantitative research is usually presented in four sections or chapters: (1) Introduction, (2) Review of related literature, (3) Methods and Procedures, and (4) Conclusions. Its purpose is to connect your specific view of the topic to the published body of knowledge in the field, support your claim that there is a need for your study, and communicate that you have the necessary skills and knowledge to complete the proposed project.

Preliminary Steps

Prior to formalizing your proposal, it is helpful to re-visit your thinking about your topic and research purpose.

Purpose, Rationale and Purpose Specifications

Re-examine the purpose, rationale, and purpose specifications (i.e., sub-purposes, hypotheses, or research questions) you wrote in Chapter 3 to confirm that they suggest correlational quantitative research—that is, investigating the relationship between two or more characteristics with a single group of people.

Literature Collection

Assess the literature you have collected to this point. Your literature collection should represent your perspective on the topic and your understanding of its lineage, address your research purpose and any specifications, justify the approach you propose to follow, and clarify any theoretical or philosophical lens(es) that guide your thinking. If this is not the case, you may need to try additional search terms to find additional sources. Re-visiting (and possibly revising) the literature map you completed in Chapter 2 may be helpful.

Writing the Introduction

In the introduction you expand on your research purpose and rationale to present a logical argument for your proposed research. It begins with background on the lineage of your topic using concepts drawn from the literature. Typically it is organized from general to specific, and may be further organized according to your purpose specifications (sub-purposes, hypotheses, or research questions) and any theoretical lenses that are pertinent to your perspective.

Following that, you present your argument in the form of a problem statement: purpose statement, rationale, and research specifications (see Chapter 3). Some correlational researchers use hypotheses to state their research specifications. **Note that the way you word your purpose— for instance, using the terms** *relationship* **or** *predict*— **signals to your committee and other readers that your intention is correlational (Mertler, 2019, p. 102).** If there are specific terms to be defined, those may follow the problem statement. Although the introduction is the part of your proposal that will be read first, you may wish to complete it after writing your literature review.

Writing the Literature Review

Quantitative researchers use the literature to explore concepts and constructs, offer definitions, provide a theoretical basis, and suggest methods, including new and existing measurement tools. Quantitative literature reviews are organized according to purpose specifications. The literature within each specification is organized from general to specific, often with a final section that discusses sources that influenced the research design. If your research is influenced by a particular theory, include a section with sources that explain and utilize that theory.

Miksza and Elpus (2018) suggest using a theoretical framework to guide quantitative research specifications and organize literature reviews (pp. 71–72). Such a framework may be based on the experience of experts, on previous research, or on one or more existing theories. Examples of the latter include Brown's (2020) use of existing measures of vocal health and job related stress and Bley's (2015) use of existing measures of management and work-life balance.

Describing Proposed Methods and Procedures

Earlier in this chapter, we summarized two uses for correlational research: investigating the existence of a relationship between two or more measured variables for a single group of people, or examining the validity or reliability of an etude or test to be used for research. Detailing the steps described in those summaries can form the basis for a section that explains your research design. The following details must be included:

a.   The people involved (target population, sample, and intended participants) as well as your method for recruiting participants. As noted above, the ideal is a sample drawn at random from the target population but it is possible to use alternative procedures if such is not feasible. The minimum number of participants recommended for a correlational study is 30 (Mertler, 2019, p. 103).

b.   Your procedures for collecting data (including the construction, testing, and distribution of any instruments), the two variables you will examine, and the timeframe.

c.   The way you will analyze the data you collect, recognizing that differences in nominal, ordinal, and interval or ratio levels of measurement require different statistics. For guidance in choosing statistics for parametric and non-parametric data, see Appendix E; you may also wish to consult Miksza and Elpus (2018) or Russell (2018).

d.   The way you will manage research ethics (including IRB submissions, if applicable), and

e.   A discussion of any field testing, pilot testing, and preliminary results.

f.   Copies of data collection instruments such as questionnaires or checklists should be included in Appendix/ces at the end of your proposal.

For more information see Chapter 14 and Recommended Reading.

Writing the Conclusion

Your conclusion summarizes the proposal and reiterates the logical argument put forth in your introduction. Begin by re-stating your purpose, purpose specifications and rationale—preferably with slightly different wording to avoid redundancy. Next, provide a brief review of your methods and procedures, organized according to your purpose specifications. End with a preliminary "so what" statement that explains what you expect to find and why those finding matter to the field of music education. Your conclusion must communicate to the committee reviewing your proposal that your expectations are reasonable and do-able.

CHAPTER SUMMARY

1)   Correlation research questions investigate statistical relationships between two sets of scores for a group of individuals.

2)   You interpret correlation coefficients according to (a) direction and strength, and (b) statistical significance.

3)   To use correlation statistics appropriately, you must check for the underlying measurement assumptions of linearity, outliers and restriction of scores.

4) Scatterplots are valuable for assessing whether assumptions for parametric correlations have been met.

5) Correlations are useful in estimating the validity and reliability of measurement tools.

6) Designing procedures for a research study begins after you have re-considered your purpose and rationale for the research and re-assessed your literature collection.

Topics for Further Exploration

1) Research examples that reinforce the idea that correlation does not imply causation.

2) The difference between the terms significant and important.

3) Choosing useful measures for research purposes.

4) Recruiting well-balanced, representative samples for correlational studies.

5) Imagining how your current research idea could be conceptualized as a correlational study.

Suggested Assignments

1) Calculate the correlation for two easily gathered interval or ratio-level variables such as height and undergraduate GPA for students in your class. Discuss.

2) Correlate scores on a classroom test to the age or other quantitative variable of the students in your class. Discuss.

3) Gather chair placement performance test score data or other test data on a group of music students and correlate those data to the students' practice or study time.

4) Describe how Christy's research topic described in Chapter 10 might be re-designed as a correlational study.

Recommended Reading

Cohen, J. (1988). *Statistical power analysis for the behavioral sciences* (2nd ed.). Lawrence Erlbaum.

Ghiselli, E. E., Campbell, J. P., & Zedeck, S. (1981). *Measurement theory for the behavioral sciences*. W. H. Freeman.

Huck, S. W. (2012). *Reading statistics and research* (6th ed.). Pearson.

Miksza, P., & Elpus, K. (2018). *Design and analysis for quantitative research in music education*. Oxford.

Mitchell, M. L., & Jolley, J. M. (2020). *Research design explained* (8th ed.). Wadsworth.

Russell, J. A. (2018). *Statistics in music education research*. Oxford.

Helpful Resources

Learning statistics with JASP: A tutorial for psychology students and other beginners. JASP Team: https://learn-statswithjasp.com/

MASH (Mathematics and Statistics Help, University of Sheffield): www.sheffield.ac.uk/mash/resources/statistics-resources

StatSpace (University of British Columbia): statspace.elearning.ubc.ca

Sample size calculators

Survey Monkey: www.surveymonkey.com/mp/sample-size-calculator/

Qualtrics: www.qualtrics.com/blog/calculating-sample-size/

REFERENCES

Bley, S. (2015). *An examination of the time management behaviors and work-life balance of K-12 music educators* [Master's thesis]. Bowling Green State University. ProQuest Dissertations & Theses Global (Publication No. 1703023886).

Brown, E. P. (2020). Music teacher self-perceived vocal health and job-related stress. *Bulletin of the Council for Research in Music Education, 224*, 46–60. https://doi.org/10.5406/bulcouresmusedu.224.0046

Cohen, J. (1988). *Statistical power analysis for the behavioral sciences* (2nd ed.). Lawrence Erlbaum.

Grissom, R. J., & Kim, J. J. (2012). *Effect sizes for research: Univariate and multivariate applications* (2nd ed.). Routledge.

Huck, S. W. (2012). *Reading statistics and research* (6th ed.). Pearson.

Mertler, C. A. (2019). *Introduction to educational research* (2nd ed.). Sage.

Miksza, P., & Elpus, K. (2018). *Design and analysis for quantitative research in music education*. Oxford University Press.

Russell, J. A. (2018). *Statistics in music education research*. Oxford University Press.

CHAPTER 12

Designing Ex Post Facto and Experimental Studies

Debbie Rohwer

This chapter highlights the following concepts:

- Types of difference studies
- Internal and external validity
  - design options
- Analysis of Variance
  - the F statistic
  - statistical issues with the ANOVA
- Inputting data into a statistical program
- Using difference studies in the classroom
- Crafting a proposal for ex post facto or experimental research

Trying to understand differences between groups is familiar to music education researchers. Research that investigates differences uses *ex post facto* (Latin for "after the fact"; sometimes called causal–comparative) and/or *experimental* designs. This chapter describes and distinguishes between these two types of research designs, and concludes by providing guidelines for crafting a proposal for a research question investigating differences between groups.

INTRODUCTION

As a high school music teacher, *Isaac* noted a trend in his band classes over the last two years. Of the current students, male percussionists seemed to play at a higher level than female percussionists. He wondered if this was just an issue with this group of students or whether the issue was more widespread. To answer this question, he arranged for all high school percussionists in his school district to take a performance test. He found that the difference between males and females was statistically significant, favoring males (M = 87.6, SD = .65) over females (M = 73.1, SD = .80). He pondered the clarity of this result. Maybe it wasn't gender, but something else that caused the result. What other variables might he consider? It was challenging to know for sure.

DOI: 10.4324/9781003057703-15

Isaac's dilemma—trying to understand differences between groups—is familiar to music education researchers. Research that investigates differences uses *ex post facto* (Latin for "after the fact;" sometimes called causal-comparative) and/or *experimental* designs. The distinction between ex post facto and experimental research is determined by the *independent variable* (sometimes called the *predictor variable*), which is a nominal level grouping variable. Since the independent variable in Isaac's study is the pre-existing category of gender (with distinct levels of male and female), his study would be *ex post facto*. Studies in which the researcher is in control of the independent variable are called *experimental*. The *dependent*, or *outcome variable* in both ex post facto and experimental studies is a test. In Isaac's case, the dependent variable was an interval level test of performance ability. The following section details considerations for both types of studies.

TYPES OF DIFFERENCE STUDIES

In ex post facto studies the independent variable is pre-existing (as in Isaac's study). Such variables can also be described as self-selected or non-manipulated. Examples relevant to music teachers may include gender (male, female), instrument family (woodwinds, brass, percussion), voice part (soprano, alto, tenor, bass), aptitude groupings (high, medium, low scorers), grade level (middle school, high school), and so forth.

As an example, consider an article titled: "The effect of grade level on motivation scores." Here, the independent variable (the nominal level grouping variable) is grade level (middle school and high school), and the dependent variable (the interval level test) is motivation scores. Because the nominal-level independent variable is pre-existing—the participants are already in middle school or high school—the study is ex post facto.

In an experimental design, the independent variable is manipulated (or controlled) by the researcher. Examples might include treatment groups (block chord accompaniment versus arpeggiated accompaniment) or conditions (sight-singing with Curwen hand signs, and also without hand signs). A researcher can also design a study that combines the two, one independent variable being manipulated (in the treatment groups) and one independent variable being pre-existing (e.g., gender).

As an elementary music teacher, *Keisha* was interested in measuring the difference between those students who receive large-muscle movement training and those who receive small-muscle movement training. She had learned that large movements may help flow and feel related to rhythm, while small movements may be more transferrable to the Orff instrument techniques she used. She wondered if small-muscle movements would also help rhythmic feel. She designed an experiment where she tested the rhythmic steadiness of all four of her classes of third graders. Then she took two of the classes and taught them rhythms using small motor movements specific to Orff mallet technique. The other two classes learned the same rhythms but used large motor movements. She then measured all students at the end and found no significant differences in steadiness across the two treatment groups (large motor: M = 36.1, SD = .20; small motor: M = 35.8, SD = .39).

In contrast to Isaac, Keisha designed a study using two different treatment groups (large motor training in one group and small motor training in the other group). Her study was experimental because as the researcher, she was in control of the independent variable.

Notice that in both of these examples, the independent variable is a *grouping* or *categorical variable* (at the nominal level of measurement, as discussed in Chapter 10), which places participants into families or subgroups of people. The independent variable is better able to differentiate between scores on the test (the dependent variable) if the groupings maximize variance. This concept is the first component of Kerlinger's (1986) MAXMINCON principle, wherein studies ideally MAXimize variance, MINimize error, and CONtrol extraneous variables.

Maximizing variance (MAX) can be done by choosing independent variable groupings that allow for differences to be apparent. For instance, if you were trying to give clear examples to a young child of what the words "short" and "tall" meant, you would most likely choose people who could maximize the difference, thereby clarifying the terms: Someone 4 feet tall might represent "short" and someone 7 feet tall would represent "tall." In the case of an experiment, then, instead of choosing neighboring test score groupings of high and low groups as an independent variable (low: scoring 25-49, and high: scoring 50-74), you could have a more extreme spread of representative scores that would maximize the groupings, such as low scores between 1 and 25, and high scores between 75 and 100.

Minimizing error variance (MIN) can be accomplished by doing a validity check to make sure (1) the testing instrument is appropriate for the age level of the test takers, (2) the items represent the concept being measured, and (3) the test does not have superfluous content or missing items. After a validity check and a field test to check for clarity, you can do a pilot test to assess the reliability of the instrument (see Chapters 10 and 11), with the goal of this three-step process being to lessen the impact of error variance.

The CON (CONtrol extraneous variables) in Kerlinger's principle can be accomplished by careful design and implementation to assure that factors other than the independent variable were not the cause of the results. In order to control for extraneous variables, researchers must analyze, redesign, and discuss any research-related issues that could question the claim of the independent variable being the most likely cause of the study's results. For instance, a community activity such as a competitive drum line for boys could account for the strong performance of the boys in Isaac's band. Likewise, children who participate in family music programs such as Music Together might confound the results of Keisha's study. To control for such, both researchers would need to add an additional independent variable to their studies, or assure that participants participating in the potentially confounding activity were not part of the study.

INTERNAL AND EXTERNAL VALIDITY

Campbell and Stanley (1963) published a seminal list of what they called *threats to internal validity*. Such threats, detailed further below, are factors that could weaken a study by causing readers to question whether the independent variable or some other extraneous variable caused the results to happen the way they did. Since 1963, there have been further expansions of the initial list of threats to internal validity (Cook & Campbell, 1979; Shadish, Cook, & Campbell, 2001), but the issue is the same: Studies should be designed and conducted in such a way that the likelihood of any extraneous variables causing the findings can be ruled out to the greatest extent possible.

Design Options

Threats to internal validity have to do with whether causal findings are trustworthy (Miksza & Elpus, 2018, p. 98). Such threats may arise from choices made when designing a study as well as choices made while the study is underway. Design considerations, for instance, include (1) whether to have a comparison group, (2) whether to use a pretest, and (3) whether to use random assignment. *Pre-experimental* (or less controlled) designs use fewer control options than true experimental designs.

A common middle-ground design, called a *quasi-experimental design*, uses a realistic combination of the three issues mentioned; it has a treatment and comparison group, each of which was intact (already formed) before the study began. Individuals in each group are given a pretest at the beginning of the study to see if the groups score equally on the test. Then each group receives "a level of the independent variable," technical language for saying that, for instance (using Keisha's study as an example), one class receives large-muscle movement training whereas the second class is instructed in small-muscle movement. After some period of training, members of both groups take a posttest. This design is called the *non-equivalent control group design* due to the use of non-randomly assigned, intact groups, similar to how Keisha used intact classes that were pretested, then "treated," and then posttested. (For a detailed discussion of design issues, see Miksza & Elpus, 2018, *Design and Analysis for Quantitative Research in Music Education*.)

Threats to Internal Validity

Designs that do not have a pretest or that do not use randomization have a potential *selection* threat. This means that the groups could be different from the start without the researcher knowing it. Consider the challenge faced in the following scenario:

A researcher has two groups, one receiving "hand/sign and solfege" training and the other receiving "solfege alone" training. At the end of the treatment, all students take a sight singing performance exam. The "hand/sign and solfege" group had a mean score of 47.3 on the posttest and the "solfege alone" group had a mean score of 71.4 on the posttest. No pretest was given before the treatment. The results are shown in Table 12.1:

TABLE 12.1 Scores on a Posttest-Only Design

Pretest Score	Treatment	Posttest Score
?	hand/sign and solfege	47.3
?	solfege alone	71.4

The posttest information alone may lead you to conclude that the training caused the "solfege alone" group to score higher than the "hand/sign and solfege" group. We do not know, however, whether the groups were equal at the beginning. It could have been that the "solfege alone" group actually might have *decreased* from an initial pre-treatment mean of 88.7 and the "hand/sign and solfege" group actually might have *increased* from an initial pre-treatment mean of 21.3.

Now think about the finding reported in Table 12.2:

TABLE 12.2 Pre and Posttest Scores on Sight Singing With and Without Solfege

Pretest Score	Treatment	Posttest Score
21.8	hand/sign and solfege	47.3
88.7	solfege alone	71.4

Based on this example, you can see that a pretest is pivotal to understanding whether groups differ at the start of a study. If they do differ, you would then need to undertake further statistical solutions to analyzing the data, perhaps using an advanced statistic to control for initial differences between groups. Or you could change the design of the study, for instance, reorganizing the original groups into equivalent groups based on pretest scores. Either way, interpreting results without pretest information may be incorrect. Therefore, researchers need to weigh the pretest variable carefully in order to avoid a selection threat.

The selection threat is only one of a number of possible challenges that researchers face when trying to determine cause and effect. Other examples are:

- *Implementation threat:* The researcher treats the two groups differently, for instance giving highly positive feedback to one treatment group and less positive feedback to the other group, when feedback is not the measured independent variable (i.e., the treatments are not being implemented consistently across the groups).
- *Instrumentation threat:* The individuals in the performance judging panel tire as the day goes on and become more lenient in their scoring (i.e., the scoring is not being conducted consistently across the participants).
- *Location threat:* One treatment group is in a well-lit room and the other is in a room that is poorly lit (i.e., the environment/setting is not consistent across groups).
- *History threat:* The students in one of the treatment groups get together outside of the treatment sessions to do extra study/work, while the other treatment group participants do not meet (i.e., students' study/work activities outside of the treatment are not consistent across groups).

Especially in ex post facto studies, almost anything in addition to or in place of the independent variable may have caused the results of the study:

> In *Isaac's* study of male and female percussionists, the independent variable was out of his hands, and anything may have worked in conjunction with the independent variable to confound the clarity of the findings. This led him to wonder: "Maybe the difference has to do with something other than gender? Perhaps how long they've played, or taking private lessons, or even how they practice?" Isaac would need to consult the literature to find additional causes.

Threats to External Validity

While possible threats to internal validity make you consider the clarity of the independent variable as a cause for the study's results, *threats to external validity* lead to questions about whether a given study's design or methodological choices may be generalized to other settings. Having an expert provide instruction for the treatment groups in a study may not be problematic for determining cause and effect (i.e., the internal validity), but it could make the results ungeneralizable to other settings. Or, a study that compares two treatments with a group of students who have participated in many different experiments may not call into question the internal validity of the study, but due to the students' experimental savvy, the results may not be generalizable to other, less savvy student samples. In fact, simply having students know that they are part of an investigation may make its results less generalizable to settings where the treatment is being implemented in an ordinary, non-research classroom setting. Both internal and external validity issues need to be weighed so that the best choice for determination of cause, issues of generalizability, and considerations of feasibility can be considered.

If you, like Isaac and Keisha, wish to investigate differences between two or more groups, you must first be clear about whether your research purpose and specifications suggest a type of difference study. With that decided, consider whether you will use an independent variable that is pre-existing or one (or more) that you will manipulate. (Note that this choice may also involve practical and ethical considerations.) Next, you must develop familiarity with research literature related to your purpose, your theoretical framework, and the specific methods and procedures you will use. In fact, you may learn from the literature about existing measures that will help you do the study.

As discussed in Chapter 11, Miksza and Elpus (2018) suggest using or creating a theoretical framework to develop purpose specifications and to organize related literature (pp. 71–72). For an example using an existing theory, see Alexander and Henry's (2015) ex post facto examination of "The Effect of Pitch and Rhythm Difficulty on High School String Sight-Reading Performance." Examples that crafted theoretical frameworks around their purpose specifications include Rohwer and Polk's (2006) ex post facto study of "Practice Behaviors of Eighth-Grade Instrumental Musicians," and the experimental study of "The Effect of Wearing Foam and Etymotic Earplugs on Classical Musicians' Pitch Perception" by MacLeod, Geringer, and Miller (2021).

As your research plan progresses, you will have to decide "what" and "how" you will measure, "who" will participate, and "how" you will sample, recruit and study the participants. These details are communicated in your proposal via your purpose and purpose specifications as well as in the body of your introduction, literature review and methods description. Keep Kerlinger's (1986) MAXMINCON principle in mind, as it will remind you to assure that 1) your independent variable is set up for differences, 2) you have checked the validity of any testing or other measurement instruments you will use, and 3) you have controlled both internal and external validity to the extent possible. Note that Keisha's study, described above, was quasi-experimental because she worked with intact classrooms. Randomizing the treatment for individual students would have increased the internal validity of the study, but it could have been unwieldy and difficult to execute in the school setting. Thus, a quasi-experimental non-equivalent control group design was an appropriate and feasible choice for her.

ANALYSIS OF VARIANCE

The most common statistical method for analyzing data in difference studies (i.e., ex post facto studies or experimental studies) is the inferential statistic known as *analysis of variance* or *ANOVA*. In this chapter, the principles of the ANOVA will be explained as the main statistic by which you compare means of subgroups to determine the extent of difference between them.

In an ANOVA, the number of independent variables determines the naming of the ANOVA: A study with one independent variable is called a 1-way ANOVA; a study with two independent variables, such as "treatment" and "gender," is called a 2-way ANOVA.

Both Isaac's and Keisha's research efforts (described earlier in this chapter) were 1-way ANOVAs with 2 levels or subgroups to the independent variable. Gender was the independent variable in Isaac's case, with male and female as the levels. In Keisha's study, treatment was the independent variable, with large motor and small motor treatments as the levels.

A 2-way ANOVA with two levels to each independent variable (such as having both of the variables "treatment and gender" in the same study) can also be called a 2 X 2 ANOVA ("two by two"). This term describes the number of levels or subgroups in each independent variable. In the case of a 2 X 2 ANOVA, then, the variable "treatment groups" has 2 levels (such as moveable do training and fixed do training) and the variable "gender" also has 2 levels (male and female). This terminology changes according to the number of levels of each independent variable. For instance, you would call the statistic a 3 X 2 ANOVA for a study with 2 independent variables where the first independent variable (treatment group) had 3 levels (such as Eastman counting system training, Gordon counting system training, and Kodaly counting system training) while the second independent variable had 2 levels. This design is illustrated in Figure 12.1.

The F Statistic

The result of an ANOVA is documented as an *F statistic.* The larger the F, the greater the calculated difference between groups. Also, the larger the F, the smaller the calculated significance, or *p* value will be, documenting a smaller likelihood that differences were due to error or chance. Results of an ANOVA are listed together with significance. A *p* value equal to or less than .05 indicates a low probability that differences between the means for the subgroups were found in error.

For example, if a group of females and males was assessed for differences on a theory test, the ANOVA would be used to assess if the theory scores for the males (seen in the first graph of Figure 12.2) differed from the theory scores for the females (seen in the second graph of Figure 12.2). The height of the bars on the graphs below displays the number of people with that score; for instance, there were 12 females who scored 80 on the second graph below, which makes up the tallest bar on the graph. Just by looking at the middle of each graph (a mean of 40 for the males and a mean of 80 for the females) you can envision that the means are probably going to be different enough not to be attributable to error or chance.

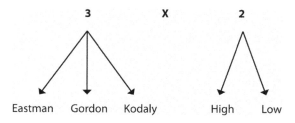

FIGURE 12.1 Illustration of a 3 X 2 ANOVA Design

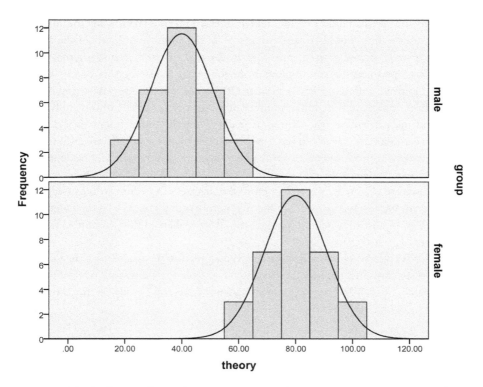

FIGURE 12.2 Music Theory Score Distributions for a Sample of Male and Female Students

The ANOVA calculated for this data set documents a significant difference for the variable gender, $F(1, 62) = 220.44$, $p < .001$, favoring females ($M = 80.00$, $SD = 1.91$) over males ($M = 40.00$, $SD = 1.91$). The p value being smaller than .001 in the result sentence tells us that we are at least 99.9% sure that the groups differ, and not by error or chance. The large F value aligns with the small p value. The numbers in the parenthesis after the F are part of the calculation of the F; you would see these numbers in the ANOVA table if you looked at the degree of freedom column.

Whether you are looking at an ANOVA table or reading results embedded in an article's results section [for instance, $F(1, 62) = 220.44$, $p < .001$], it is important to know what the numbers mean so that you can be an educated reader. The numbers in the parentheses are called the *degrees of freedom* (abbreviated as *df*). They serve as part of the calculation of the F statistic, but also tell you important information about the choices the researcher made. The first number is the *df* for the independent variable, gender. If you add 1 to this number, it tells you the number of levels to the independent variable (note that this only works for independent variables). In this example, then, there are two levels to the variable gender (male and female). The second number in the parenthesis is the degree of freedom for error, and if you add this number (62) to the degree of freedom for the independent variable (1+62) and add 1 more, you will get the sample size for this 1-way ANOVA. This study, therefore, had 64 people in it. The result that would be stated in the article would be that there was a significant *main effect* for gender, favoring females. You know that females outperformed males by looking at the original means for both subgroups. The term main effect is commonly used when discussing the results of independent variable findings.

Both Isaac and Keisha could provide degree of freedom information for the results of their studies. Such information would remind the reader of the number of levels of the independent variable in each study as well as the sample size. In the case of Isaac, comparing male and female percussionists on a performance test resulted in the following: F (1, 92) = 27.3, p =.02. He found a statistically significant difference between male and female percussionists, favoring males.

To determine sample size as well as number of subgroups (or levels) in this study, look at the first number in the parenthesis, the degree of freedom for the independent variable (1). The 1 (plus 1) states that there are 2 levels to the variable gender (males and females). Add the degree of freedom for gender (1) to 92 and add 1 more and you get the sample size: 94 students.

In Keisha's experiment with two treatment groups, no significant differences across the two groups were found: F (1, 78) =.03, p =.92. From the degrees of freedom, you can determine that she had two treatment levels (you add 1 to the first number, in this case 1, in the parenthesis). Her sample size can be obtained by adding together the two numbers in the parenthesis and then adding an additional 1, which equals 80.

The ANOVA table listed in many research articles provides the reader with the same information you can glean from the parenthetical statistic. The table for a one-way ANOVA with the ex post facto variable "voice part" being the independent variable in a study of choral musicians, for example, may look like Table 12.3:

TABLE 12.3 Summary Table of a One-Way ANOVA

Tests of Between-Subjects Effects
Dependent Variable: score

Source	Type III Sum of Squares	Df	Mean Square	F	Sig.
Voice part	1403.750	3	467.917	4.984	.003
Error	7135.000	76	93.882		

The finding shown in Table 12.3 documents that for the variable voice part there is a significant main effect or difference (p = .003) that is below the normal significance cutoff of .05. In the example shown in Figure 12.2, there were only two levels to the independent variable "gender" (male and female), and just by looking at the original subgroup means (80 and 40) you could say that females outscored males. In this example, however, there are 4 levels to the independent variable "voice part" (i.e., soprano, alto, tenor, bass). You can discern this information by looking at the degree of freedom for the variable "voice part" (3) and then adding 1, which equals 4. You can also tell from this table that the degree of freedom for error is 76 and if you add 76 to 3 and add 1 more you will get the sample size for this study, which is 80. For a discussion of how degree of freedom information works in all forms of ANOVAs and other statistics, see Miksza and Elpus (2018).

Because the example deals with 4 levels to the variable "voice part," the basic ANOVA cannot describe the specifics of "where" the difference(s) lie; it only documents that there is a difference. After obtaining a significant ANOVA finding for a study that uses a variable with more than two levels, you could calculate a *post hoc* (Latin for "after this") test to determine information on the specific subgroup differences. Another option would be to calculate planned comparisons based on suggestions in the literature. However, do so with caution. Conducting further statistical tests like post hocs can sometimes be like data mining. The debate of data mining versus specified comparisons is a topic that needs to be purposefully and philosophically weighed.

Returning to the data set represented in Table 12.3: Descriptively, the sopranos had the lowest overall mean (49.00), with the altos (51.00), tenors (58.00), and basses (58.50) having higher mean scores. If a post hoc statistic were calculated, you could document that the lowest mean from the sopranos (49.00) was not significantly different from that of the altos (51.00), but the sopranos (49.00) were significantly different from both the tenors and basses (58.00 and 58.50). The alto, tenor and bass means did not significantly differ from each other (51.00, 58.00, and 58.50).

If a study has more than one independent variable, then the table will document results for each independent variable, and will also document an *interaction* result, which highlights whether the findings need to be qualified or not. If there is a significant interaction between the independent variables, then the results are in some way hazy and need to be clarified. For instance, a researcher might find a significant main effect for gender favoring females, but females in one of the treatment groups actually scored lower than the males in both of the treatment groups. It would then be misleading and incomplete to say that there was a significant main effect for gender, favoring females. The significant *interaction* helps clear up that misinterpretation by qualifying the main effect result. An interaction qualification statement may read:

> ". . . while there is a significant main effect for gender favoring females, the main effect was caused by females in treatment group one who outscored all other subgroups. Females in treatment group two, however, scored lower than both male treatment sub-groups, so it may be wise to consider the interaction of gender and treatment groups when making instructional decisions."

Table 12.4 displays findings from a study with two independent variables (treatment and age) and one interaction result. The table has degree of freedom (*df*) information, the *F* statistic, and the *p* values (significance). The other table information (i.e., Sum of Squares and Mean Square) is used as part of the calculation of the *F* statistic.

Once Table 12.4 has been analyzed to determine significance or non-significance, the original descriptive means of each subgroup could be looked up, a graph could be made, and then the following description could be written as results of the study:

1) There is no significant main effect for the variable treatment groups [F (1, 96) = .038, p = .85], with the visual group scoring: $M = 50.0$, $SD = 11.43$, and the auditory group scoring: $M = 50.0$, $SD = 21.55$.

TABLE 12.4 Summary Table of a Two-Way ANOVA

Tests of Between-Subjects Effects
Dependent Variable: score

Source	Type III Sum of Squares	Df	Mean Square	F	Sig.
Treatment	4.000	1	4.000	.038	.846
Age	23104.000	1	23104.000	217.791	.000
Treatment * age	23104.000	1	23104.000	217.791	.000
Error	10184.000	96	106.083		

2) There is a significant main effect for age [F (1, 96) = 217.79, $p <$ .001], favoring younger students (M = 65.0, SD = 18.65) over older students (M = 35.0, SD = 17.34).

3) There is a significant interaction between treatment and age [F (1, 96) = 217.79, $p <$ .001], showing the need to qualify the significant main effect for age. While younger students in the auditory group scored higher than all other subgroups (M = 80), younger students in the visual group achieved lower scores (M = 50), with those scores being equal to the scores of the older students in the visual group (M = 50). Also, older students in the auditory group scored the lowest of all subgroups (M = 20). This interaction is illustrated in Figure 12.3:

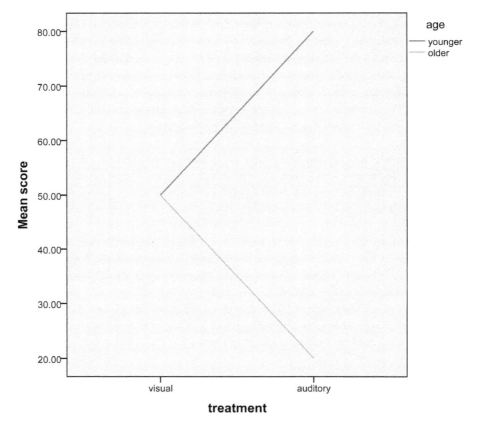

FIGURE 12.3 Graph of Interaction of Two Independent Variables

Any time a significant interaction exists, you need to examine the subgroup means to determine where the non-parallel lines are occurring so that an explanation can be made of the qualifying information.

Statistical Issues with the ANOVA

The Analysis of Variance (ANOVA) is a *parametric* statistic (see Chapter 9) that has certain rules, or assumptions, governing its use. Most importantly, you need to be concerned with issues of *normality* (normal distribution of all scores) and *homogeneity of variance* (equal spread of scores). If these assumptions are not met, then non-parametric statistics (see Appendix E) or some other choice, (such as transforming the data) must be used.

In order to calculate the results of a study by using an ANOVA, you first must establish that the distribution of the scores resembles the bell-shaped or normal curve (see Figure 12.4).

Distributions that are asymmetrically skewed (as shown in Figure 12.5) or too peaked (Figure 12.6), do not meet the assumption of normality and would not be appropriate for an ANOVA.

It is also important that the spread of scores across each subgroup is similar, documenting "*homogeneity of variance*." Figure 12.7 displays a pair of *box and whisker* plots wherein the medians (represented by the horizontal line in the center of each box) are equal at 80. The equal picture sizes show an equality of variability.

The medians represented by the pictures shown in Figure 12.8 are similar, but the size of the box and whisker shows a difference of spread (or variability). This discrepancy documents a problem with homogeneity of variance that would need to be solved in some way before an ANOVA could be calculated.

In general, it helps to have group sizes that are large in order to achieve a normal curve and to have enough *power* (see Cohen, 1988) so that the statistic can detect differences if they exist. A

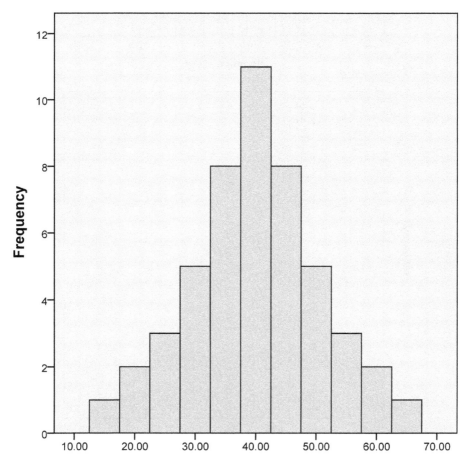

FIGURE 12.4 Normal Curve Histogram Based on Frequency of Scores in a Range from 0 to 70

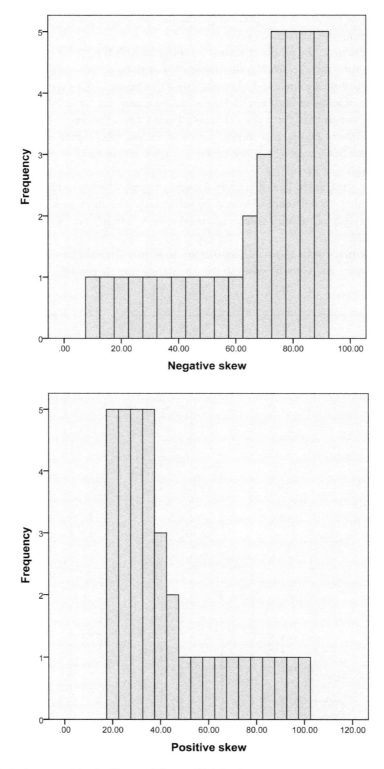

FIGURE 12.5 Asymmetrically Skewed Score Distributions

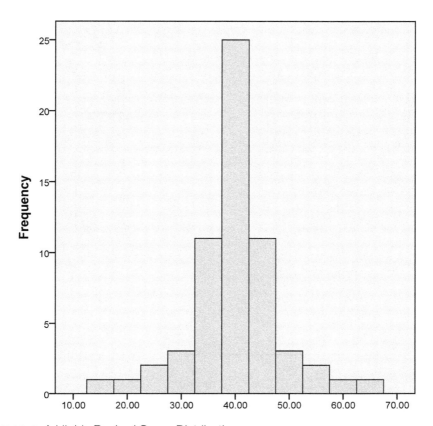

FIGURE 12.6 A Highly Peaked Score Distribution

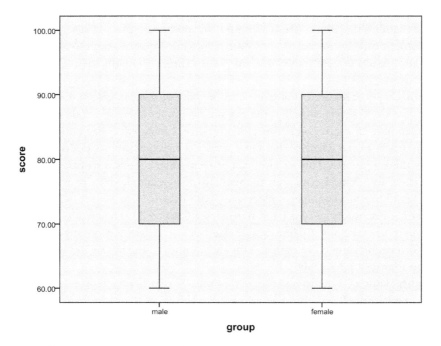

FIGURE 12.7 Box and Whisker Plots Suggesting Equality of Variability Between the Scores of Two Independent Variables

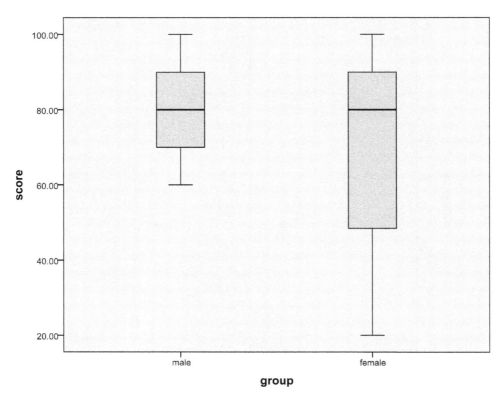

FIGURE 12.8 Box and Whisker Plots Suggesting Difference in Variability

basic rule of thumb is that 30 people in a group is an appropriate place to start for the purpose of meeting assumptions. Also important, however, is looking at past research to analyze sample size and significance results to determine how large your sample size might need to be to find differences if they exist.

As in other types of research, doing one or more pilot studies can help you estimate the power of a test to detect differences as well as the magnitude of the differences (called *effect size*). Since sample size can have an impact on statistical significance, adding effect size estimates can help the reader of an article gauge whether the stated statistical significance was positively or negatively impacted by the sample size. This scenario can be seen when a result is statistically significant but has a small effect size (Type I error: can happen with a large sample size), or when a result is not statistically significant but has a large effect size (Type II error: can happen with a small sample size.) For further discussion of Type I and II error, see Chapter 11. Hence, it is important to plan a study's sample size carefully. Online sample size calculators (see Recommended Reading) are available to determine sample size estimates for a main study, using power and effect size data that can be gathered from a pilot study.

One other statistical issue to consider is that the .05 significance level is appropriate to calculate only one statistic. If you plan to run multiple ANOVAs, then you need to correct the .05 cutoff so that there is not an overuse of the data set. Statisticians sometimes describe studies that calculate multiple statistics with the same grouping variable but different dependent variables as "fishing" to find results, because there is a possibility that by just casting a line a great number of times (running statistics), you might catch a fish (find something significant). The fishing scenario might be seen in studies that use an independent variable such as gender to determine the effect on individual questions in a questionnaire (30 questions). In this case, there are 30 ANOVAs calculated. To counter this concern, the researcher can sum questions on a questionnaire and calculate one ANOVA instead of 30 or divide the .05 cutoff by the number of statistics to be calculated (in this case 30), thereby providing a more conservative cutoff that takes into account the multiple statistics being calculated (.05/30 = .002).

As a final note, there are many types of ANOVAs, such as an ANCOVA (analysis of covariance) where you can control for initial differences in group scores by weighting them on the post-test scores, or a repeated measures ANOVA where the same participants are measured multiple times. The text *Statistics in Music Education Research* by Russell (2018) is a valuable resource that covers each of these advanced ANOVA options.

INPUTTING DATA INTO A STATISTICAL PROGRAM

The example below explains how to use SPSS (Statistical Package for the Social Sciences, available from www.spss.com) to examine data from an ex post facto study. The example provides a small set of data with the independent variable being instrument family (woodwinds and brass) and the dependent variable being scores on a performance anxiety measure. (Readers without an institutional subscription to SPSS may want to try JASP, jasp-stats.org or another online resource.)

An ANOVA will be used to compare the scores of the woodwind and brass instrumentalists on a performance anxiety test. The inputted data for the example set of 4 woodwind and 4 brass instrumentalists shown in Table 12.5 would have two columns: one to demonstrate the independent variable groups and another to demonstrate the dependent variable scores. The independent variable column will have nominal level data: a number to represent those in the woodwind group (labeled 0 in this case) and a number to represent those in the brass group (labeled 1 in this case). Each row shows one person's group affiliation label and that same person's score on the performance anxiety test (so Lucia the bassoonist may be #1 across, scoring 91 on the test, and Jamal the trombonist may be #2 across, scoring 51, etc.).

TABLE 12.5 Example Data for One Independent and One Dependent Variable (N = 8)

	Group	Score
1.	0	91
2.	1	51
3.	0	83
4.	0	71
5.	1	70
6.	1	60
7.	1	61
8.	0	82

The next step would be to check basic issues for calculating an ANOVA. These issues can be weighed by looking at histogram and box and whisker graphs. To do this in SPSS, go to the "Analyze" drop-down and then choose "Descriptive Statistics" and "Explore." Place the variable "score" in the Dependent List and the variable "group" in the Factor list and then click on the "Plots" button. From there mark "Factor levels together" under "Boxplots" and "Histogram" under "Descriptive." Then click "Continue."

Viewing the box and whisker graph, as shown in Figure 12.9, the spread, or *homogeneity of variance* across both groups appears consistent.

The histogram graph as shown in Figure 12.10 indicates that the distributions of the subgroup samples look like normal curves (display normality), especially for this example of 8 data points. (Note that any real study would have a far larger sample size).

You next calculate an ANOVA by going to the "Analyze" drop-down and choosing "General Linear Model" and "Univariate." Place the variable "score" in the dependent variable box and the variable "group" in the fixed factor box. Then click "OK."

The readout will look like what is shown in Table 12.6, documenting that the difference between groups was statistically significant [$F (1, 6) = 13.12$, $p = .01$]. The original means can be obtained from the options button, showing that group 0 (woodwinds: mean of 81.75) had a higher overall mean score than 1 (brass: mean of 60.75).

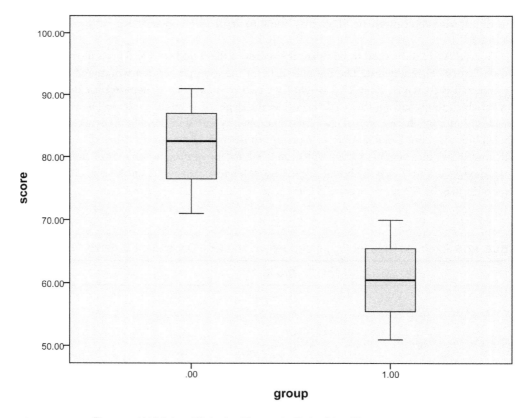

FIGURE 12.9 Box and Whisker Plots for Example Data (N = 8)

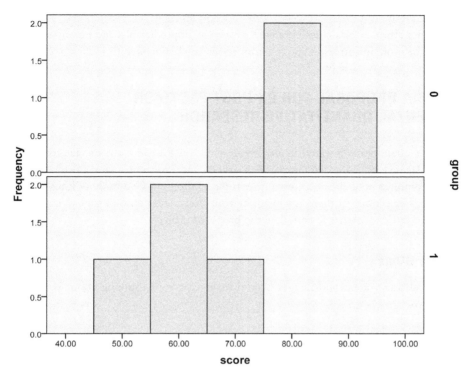

FIGURE 12.10 Histogram of Example Data (N = 8)

TABLE 12.6 Summary Table for Example ANOVA Results (N = 8)

Tests of Between-Subjects Effects
Dependent Variable: score

Source	Type III Sum of Squares	Df	Mean Square	F	Sig.
group	882.000	1	882.000	13.115	.011
Error	403.500	6	67.250		

Testing for differences among variables is at the core of many quantitative research designs. However, music teachers, too, can benefit from the procedures outlined in this chapter. For instance, when measuring differences in performance among students, an action-research-oriented teacher might consider such ex post facto difference questions as "Do my students perform at different skill levels based on what instrument they have chosen to play, or their reading grades (high/low), or the amount of practice they reported last week (none/some/much)?" Music teachers can also use these procedures in action research to weigh experimental difference questions of interest, such as "If I tried one method book format to introduce sight singing with one of my sections of students and another method book to introduce sight singing with the other section, I wonder which method book format would help the students perform better?" The possible list of questions is indeed numerous but always contextual to each teacher's interests and areas of expertise. It is always important to weigh, carefully and logically, all instructional choices so that decisions are not arbitrary or are not clouded by external, unpredictable, and potentially meaningless factors. (For more information about action research, see Chapter 13.)

CRAFTING A PROPOSAL FOR EX POST FACTO OR EXPERIMENTAL QUANTITATIVE RESEARCH

A proposal for quantitative research is usually presented in four sections or chapters: (1) Introduction, (2) Review of related literature, (3) Methods and Procedures, and (4) Conclusions. Its purpose is to connect your specific view of the topic to the published body of knowledge in the field, support your claim that there is a need for your study, and communicate that you have the necessary skills and knowledge to complete the proposed project.

Preliminary Steps

Prior to formalizing your proposal, it is helpful to re-visit your thinking about your topic and research purpose.

Purpose, Rationale and Purpose Specifications

Re-examine the purpose, rationale, and purpose specifications (i.e., sub-purposes, hypotheses, or research questions) you wrote in Chapter 3 to confirm that they suggest ex post facto or experimental research—that is, examining differences between two or more groups of people, either with an independent variable that is pre-existing or one (or more) that you will manipulate.

Literature Collection

Assess the literature you have collected to this point. Your literature collection should represent your perspective on the topic and your understanding of its lineage, address your research purpose and any specifications, justify the approach you propose to follow, and clarify any theoretical or philosophical lens(es) that guide your thinking. If this is not the case, you may need to try additional search terms to find additional sources. Re-visiting (and possibly revising) the literature map you completed in Chapter 2 may be helpful.

Writing the Introduction

In the introduction you expand on your research purpose and rationale to present a logical argument for your proposed research. It begins with background on the lineage of your topic using concepts drawn from the literature. Typically it is organized from general to specific, and may be further organized according to your purpose specifications (sub-purposes, hypotheses, or research questions) and any theoretical lenses that are pertinent to your perspective.

Following that, you present your argument in the form of a problem statement: purpose statement, rationale, and research specifications (see Chapter 3). As with other types of research, the words used in your purpose are important. **Whether posed as a question or a declamatory sentence, your wording should clearly denote an attempt to examine differences in**

groups. Often words like "effect" or "impact" are used in difference studies. If there are specific terms to be defined, those may follow the problem statement. Although the introduction is the part of your proposal that will be read first, you may wish to complete it after writing your literature review.

Writing the Literature Review

Quantitative researchers use the literature to explore concepts and constructs, offer definitions, provide a theoretical basis, and suggest methods—including new and existing measurement tools. Quantitative literature reviews are organized according to purpose specifications. The literature within each specification is organized from general to specific, often with a final section that discusses sources that influenced the research design. If your research is influenced by a particular theory, include a section with sources that explain and utilize that theory. Miksza and Elpus's (2018) suggestion to use a theoretical framework to guide your research (pp. 71–72) is also important for difference studies.

With ex post facto research designs the literature can offer information about possible causes of the phenomenon(a) under study (Mertler, 2019, p. 105). With quasi-experimental and true experimental designs, the literature can help you determine which variables to measure and how to "control for extraneous influences" (p. 113). With both methods, the literature can help you identify measurement instruments and other research tools.

Describing Proposed Methods and Procedures

Earlier in this chapter, we summarized the steps for designing two types of difference studies—an ex post facto study or an experimental study. These steps can be the basis for a section that explains your research design. The following details must be included:

a. The people involved (target population and sample) and the reasons for your choices. Note that the sampling decision for the independent variable differs between ex post facto and experimental research; however, it is advised in either case to have a minimum of 30 people in each group.

   i. For **ex post facto research**, remember MAXMINCON: *Maximize* the difference in your grouping variable, *minimize* error, and/or *control* for the impact of other variables as much as possible.

   ii. The ideal for **experimental research** is random selection of the sample and random assignment of individuals to treatment groups. However, quasi-experimental research where intact groups (but not individuals) are assigned to treatments at random is more common in music education research. It may be possible to suggest causation without randomization (for instance, in action research, see Chapter 14) but this threatens the generalizability of the results.

b. Your methods and procedures for collecting data (including constructing, testing, and distributing any instruments) and the proposed timeframe. For *experimental research* you should describe (if applicable) your pretest procedures (including checks for validity and reliability) and the design of the intervention you are testing.

c. The way you intend to analyze the data you collect. Note that the analysis of both ex post facto and experimental research includes descriptive as well as inferential statistics. This section is often organized according to your purpose specifications (sub-purposes, research questions, or hypotheses). For guidance in choosing statistical procedures for parametric and non-parametric data, see Appendix E; you may also wish to consult Miksza and Elpus (2018) or Russell (2018).

Writing the Conclusion

Your conclusion summarizes the proposal and reiterates the logical argument put forth in your introduction. Begin by re-stating your purpose, purpose specifications and rationale—preferably with slightly different wording to avoid redundancy. Next, provide a brief review of your methods and procedures, organized according to your purpose specifications. End with a preliminary "so what" statement that explains what you expect to find and why those finding matter to the field of music education. Your conclusion must communicate to the committee reviewing your proposal that your expectations are reasonable and do-able.

CHAPTER SUMMARY

1) Ex post facto and experimental designs are types of difference studies found in quantitative music education research. The distinction between them is determined by the independent variable (sometimes called the predictor variable).
2) Analysis of variance measures differences between groups. Researchers need to check whether the assumptions of the ANOVA are met before using this statistic.
3) It is important for researchers to consider how a study is designed and implemented in order to avoid threats to internal validity. External validity issues can impact the generalizability of a study's finding.
4) Designing procedures for a research study begins after you have re-considered your purpose and rationale for the research and re-assessed your literature collection.

Topics for Further Exploration

1) Types and levels of variables of interest to music educators.
2) Research designs and corresponding statistics.
3) How power, effect size and sample size work together.
4) Possible difference studies based on the research ideas of members of your research class.

Suggested Assignments

1) Compare males and females on a self-assessment of performance anxiety. Then construct a measure to document the severity of performance anxiety experiences, such as sweaty palms, quickened pulse, and so on. Sum together responses on the questions for each individual to get an overall score. Using the SPSS instructions above, calculate an ANOVA, with gender being the independent variable, and performance anxiety being the dependent variable.
2) Design an experiment, such as jumping large/small, heavy/light origami frogs as described in *Activity-Based Statistics* (Schaeffer, Watkins, Witmer, & Gnanadesikan, 2004). Using the SPSS instructions above, calculate an ANOVA with the student-gathered data.

3) Describe how Christy's research topic (see Chapter 10) or that of Isaac or Keisha in this chapter (or any of the other students in RC533) might be re-imagined as a difference study. In each case, decide whether ex post facto or experimental research would best address the research question and explain your answer.

4) Descriptively or through the use of an ANOVA, use a demographic grouping variable of your choosing (such as grade, instrument, or gender) to compare the achievement of your students on an achievement or classroom test.

Recommended Reading

Alexander, M. L., & Henry, M. L. (2015). The effect of pitch and rhythm difficulty on high school string sight-reading performance. *String Research Journal, 6*(1), 71–85. https://doi.org/10.1177/194849921500600005

Fraenkel, J. R., Wallen, N. E., & Hyun, H. (2018). *How to design and evaluate research in education* (10th ed.). McGraw-Hill

Huck, S. W. (2012). *Reading statistics and research* (6th ed.). Pearson.

MacLeod, R. B., Geringer, J. M., & Miller, D. S. (2021, February). The effect of wearing foam and etymotic earplugs on classical musicians' pitch perception. *Journal of Research in Music Education.* https://doi.org/10.1177/0022429421989993

Mertler, C. A. (2019). *Introduction to educational research* (2nd ed.). Sage.

Miksza, P., & Elpus, K. (2018). *Design and analysis for quantitative research in music education.* Oxford University Press.

Rohwer, D., & Polk, J. (2006). Practice behaviors of eighth-grade instrumental musicians. *Journal of Research in Music Education, 54*(4), 350–362. https://doi.org/10.2307/4139756

Russell, J. A. (2018). *Statistics in music education research.* Oxford.

Helpful Resources

Learning statistics with JASP: A tutorial for psychology students and other beginners. JASP Team: https://learn-statswithjasp.com/

MASH (Mathematics and Statistics Help, University of Sheffield): www.sheffield.ac.uk/mash/resources/statistics-resources

StatSpace (University of British Columbia): statspace.elearning.ubc.ca

Sample Size Calculators

Survey Monkey: www.surveymonkey.com/mp/sample-size-calculator/
Qualtrics: www.qualtrics.com/blog/calculating-sample-size/

REFERENCES

Alexander, M. L., & Henry, M. L. (2015). The effect of pitch and rhythm difficulty on high school string sight-reading performance. *String Research Journal, 6*(1), 71–85. https://doi.org/10.1177/194849921500600005

Campbell, D. T., & Stanley, J. C. (1963). *Experimental and quasi-experimental designs for research.* Houghton Mifflin.

Cohen, J. (1988). *Statistical power analysis for the behavioral sciences* (2nd ed.). Lawrence Erlbaum.

Cook, T. D., & Campbell, D. T. (1979). *Quasi-experimentation: Design and analysis for field settings.* Rand McNally College.

Kerlinger, F. N. (1986). *Foundations of behavioral research* (3rd ed.). Holt, Rinehart and Winston.

MacLeod, R. B., Geringer, J. M., & Miller, D. S. (2021, February). The effect of wearing foam and ety-motic earplugs on classical musicians' pitch perception. *Journal of Research in Music Education*. https://doi.org/10.1177/0022429421989993

Mertler, C. A. (2019). *Introduction to educational research* (2nd ed.). Sage.

Miksza, P., & Elpus, K. (2018). *Design and analysis for quantitative research in music education*. Oxford University Press.

Rohwer, D., & Polk, J. (2006). Practice behaviors of eighth-grade instrumental musicians. *Journal of Research in Music Education, 54*(4), 350–362. https://doi.org/10.2307/4139756

Russell, J. A. (2018). *Statistics in music education research*. Oxford University Press.

Schaeffer, R. L., Watkins, A., Witmer, J., & Gnanadesikan, M. (2004). *Activity-based statistics: Instructor resources* (2nd ed.). Key College.

Shadish, W. R., Cook, T. D., & Campbell, D. T. (2001). *Experimental and quasi-experimental designs for generalized causal inference*. Wadsworth.

Exploring Mixed Methods, Practitioner, and Arts-Based Inquiry

This chapter:

- Introduces mixed methods research, practitioner inquiry/action research, and arts-based research;
- Summarizes how all three approaches use both qualitative and quantitative procedures;
- Discusses history and evolution, describes defining qualities, and features examples from the three approaches; and
- Provides guidelines for expanding on previous textbook materials to propose a project for one or a combination of the three approaches.

In this chapter we introduce methods for inquiry that go beyond the qualitative and quantitative traditions noted in Chapters 7 through 12. Following a continuum from the most to the least conventional, mixed methods involves combining quantitative and qualitative methods in a single study. Practitioner inquiry, rooted in what is known as action research, sees teachers, teaching artists, and community music facilitators as experts in their own right, and uses quantitative and/or qualitative practices as tools for understanding and improving practice. Arts-based and arts practice research put forth the arts as valid ways of knowing and doing research.

INTRODUCTION

At one of Prof. E.'s coffee talks, Muna, Michelle, Carlos, and Liam were discussing their final projects. Each wanted to meet the requirement with original research, but neither the qualitative nor quantitative methods they had learned about seemed to fit what they had in mind.

Having recently become supervisor of music in the large inner city school system where she worked, *Michelle* was curious about hybrid methods developed during the Covid-19 pandemic to combine in-person and online teaching for music instruction. She considered distributing a survey, either in her district or statewide, to learn what hybrid teaching practices were being used by music teachers, but she also wanted to know how such practices had been developed by teachers. A qualitative study would allow her to gather that kind of information, but it would

DOI: 10.4324/9781003057703-16

limit the number of teachers she could hear from. Might it be possible to combine a quantitative survey with interviews of selected music teachers?

Carlos had a different idea. Still very practical, he was interested in connecting his school's new requirements for student assessment with the questions he had asked at the beginning of the semester. He wanted to implement "a concert band learning environment that is self-guided and allows students to explore new approaches to mastering required musicianship skills." But he was not really interested in studying anyone else's classroom. Could he adapt some quantitative methods to examine what was going on in his own music program?

Working in a community music program that offered arts-based outreach to recent refugees, *Muna* also wanted to examine her own practice. But rather than assessing the music learning of the people in the community program, Muna wanted to see how participants' music-making expressed their needs. She also wanted to examine and improve her own practice as a community music facilitator.

Liam, who worked as a teaching artist rather than in a traditional classroom, wondered out loud: "Why should the hard-core sciences, or Internet or library searches, be the sole purveyor of knowledge? Isn't music-making an equally valid form of knowledge? I'd like to take what I've learned about the development of scat singing to design a performance, and build on that with an interdisciplinary unit where students improvise and create songs that interpret their social realities, as Armstrong and others did with their singing."

The research ideas expressed by Michelle, Carlos, Muna, and Liam suggest different uses for the tools and practices of quantitative and qualitative research discussed in Chapters 7 through 12. Michelle's wonderings suggest a mixed methods approach that combines quantitative and qualitative methods to address a research question more fully than could be done with a single approach. Carlos, who wishes to improve his own practice, might consider practitioner inquiry. Muna's research idea also suggests practitioner inquiry. However, since some of her data would be musical, it crosses into what is known as arts-based or arts practice research. This is also the tradition suggested by Liam's research idea. Researchers working in arts-based traditions may use qualitative tools and practices to gather and analyze data, but their research output typically takes an artistic form.

The remainder of this chapter provides a brief introduction to each of these types of inquiry with categories of history and evolution, defining qualities, contexts and applications, and advice for developing a project. The chapter concludes with guidelines for crafting the procedural aspects of a proposal for a mixed methods, practitioner inquiry, or arts-based/arts practice study.

MIXED METHODS RESEARCH

History and Evolution

Combining quantitative and qualitative techniques for research is not a new notion. Maxwell (2016) presents evidence that scholars in the so-called hard sciences of astronomy, geology, medicine and epidemiology were combining qualitative and quantitative data prior to the emergence of the practice in the social sciences. The practice seems to have emerged in European social science research in the mid-1800s and then "filtered into the research landscape in the United States by the beginning of the 20th century" (Hesse-Biber, 2010, p. 2). For instance, members of the famed Chicago School of Sociology employed mixed methods, finding "quantitative data particularly valuable as a marker of social processes" for studies of urban life in the inner city (p. 2). African American sociologist W. E. B. DuBois' report *The Philadelphia Negro*, published in 1899, seems to pre-date the multi-method work of the Chicago School by at least a decade (Maxwell, 2016, p. 15).

It was not unusual for social science researchers in the early 20th century to combine quantitative and quantitative data to address specific questions more thoroughly than they could with one or the other approach alone. However, the so-called paradigm wars in the early 1980s that questioned the validity of qualitative research in the social sciences (see Chapter 7) seems to have forced scholars to consider whether the philosophical underpinnings of quantitative and qualitative research were compatible (Bryman, 2015; Creswell & Plano Clark, 2017). Toward the end of the 1980s and continuing into the present, Creswell and Plano Clark (2017) document a response to that period: intentional uses of what has become known as a mixed methods approach.

Defining Qualities

To be considered mixed methods research, findings from both quantitative and qualitative approaches must be integral to the results (Fitzpatrick, 2014, p. 172). Creswell and Plano Clark (2017) describe core characteristics of mixed methods research in their definition of the practice:
    In mixed methods, the researcher

- collects and analyzes both qualitative and quantitative data rigorously in response to research questions and hypotheses,
- integrates (or mixes or combines) the two forms of data and their results,
- organizes these procedures into specific research designs that provide the logic and procedures for conducting the study, and
- frames these procedures within theory and philosophy.

(p. 5)

Mixed methods studies are typically designed according to priority and sequence (Bryman, 2015). Priority has to do with deciding whether one of the approaches will be dominant in a given study, and sequence has to do with the order in which the approaches will be used. Both choices should be made according to what will best address the research question(s). "Thus, when deciding whether to use a mixed methods design, the research questions are of primary importance, and the method utilized to answer them secondary" (Fitzpatrick, 2014, p. 176).

Hesse-Biber (2010) suggests five reasons for using mixed methods. *Methods triangulation* refers to using more than one method so that you can examine a research problem from more than one perspective. *Complementarity* "allows the researcher to gain a fuller understanding of the research problem and/or to clarify a given research result" (p. 4). Mixed methods research can assist researchers in the *development* of their research, much as Michelle might use the results of a large-scale descriptive survey to identify participants for the qualitative phase of her research about hybrid approaches to teaching general music. *Initiation* and *expansion* are the fourth and fifth reason noted by Hesse-Biber, the former to invite "questions or contradictions that will require clarification, thus initiating a new study" and the latter to assist the researcher in expanding their ideas (p. 5).

Fitzpatrick (2014) summarizes the most common design categories for mixed methods research, encouraging scholars to "thoughtfully develop other designs that best serve the purposes of their individual studies:"

1) Sequential studies, which consist of two consecutive phases of research—one quantitative and one qualitative;
2) Parallel/simultaneous studies, in which both quantitative and qualitative phases are conducted at the same time;
3) Equivalent status designs, which utilize the qualitative and quantitative approaches equally to investigate the same phenomenon;
4) Dominant/less-dominant studies, in which most of the study is undertaken with either a quantitative or qualitative approach, but the other method is used supportively;
5) Designs with multilevel use of approaches, which utilize both methods at different levels of data integration.

(p. 178)

Of particular note in music education research are Creswell and Plano Clark's (2017) exploratory sequential and explanatory sequential designs, described further in the context discussion later in this section.

Two cautions are in order if you are considering the use of mixed methods for your research project. First, you or your research team must have the requisite skills and knowledge to do quantitative as well as qualitative research and then combine them into a coherent mixed project. In the quantitative realm this means not only understanding how to use descriptive and inferential statistics (see Chapters 10–12) but also how to design, administer, and analyze results from quantitative measurement instruments while meeting expectations of quantitative rigor. A similar level of qualitative research skills is also necessary. This means gathering and approaching textual data with a constructivist mindset, seeking to understand the meanings participants give to the phenomenon under study. You must be comfortable doing interviews and observing, and able to code developing themes (Chapter 8), all while keeping in mind the rigor, resonance, and worthiness demanded by qualitative research conventions (Chapter 7). Finally, you must have an understanding of mixed methods research itself. The second caution has to do with time. Not only does it take additional time to become fluent in quantitative and qualitative methods, it takes time to develop and implement both kinds of procedures, and the analysis and subsequent combining of those data takes still more time. Thus, you should give careful consideration to whether you—alone or in combination with a research team—have the skills as well as the requisite time that is necessary for implementing such a study. For additional information, see Creswell and Plano Clark (2017), Hesse-Biber (2010), and Bryman (2015).

Contexts and Applications

Music education researchers use mixed methods to address questions like those asked by Michelle at the start of this chapter. She wanted to know more about the "big picture" of hybrid music teaching (combining face-to-face and online teaching) adopted by music teachers in her large inner-city school district, but also to gain a micro-level understanding of exactly how a small number of teachers developed expertise and implemented hybrid practices in their teaching. To address these questions, she might use what Creswell and Plano Clark (2017) call an exploratory sequential mixed methods design. Her initial survey of music teachers could inform her understanding of the big picture and at the same time identify possible participants for a qualitative exploration of the ways teachers develop and use a hybrid approach.

Albert (2016) used what Creswell and Plano Clark (2017) call an explanatory sequential mixed methods design for his dissertation research. Inspired by the need to "break the cycle of self-perpetuation of repeating practices that have been in place for decades" (p. 28) in collegiate music education curricula, Albert sought to explore "which structural components of a music teacher education program" and what other "significant 'disruptive' influences" (pp. 29–30) were most impactful for challenging the pre-existing professional beliefs and attitudes of a cohort of undergraduate music education majors from a large school of music within a comprehensive university, and then to understand how and why the identified phenomena were disruptive. Albert used a quantitative survey to address the "what" questions, and used findings from the survey to "identify specific classes and experiences that students indicated most 'disrupted' their ideas of music education." He then created cohort groups that let him 'dig' more deeply using qualitative methodology into the forces behind the disruptions (p. 78) to address "how" and "why" questions. Other graduate projects that have utilized mixed methods procedures include a master's thesis by Furiani (2018), and doctoral dissertations by Cronenberg (2016), West (2011), and Fitzpatrick (2008).

Developing a Mixed Methods Research Project

If you, like Michelle, believe you have a need as well as the requisite resources to complete a mixed methods study, you must first confirm that your research specifications cannot be addressed with quantitative or qualitative methods alone, and develop a rationale that clearly explains your reasoning. Do you need mixed methods to triangulate your study? Or do you believe the two complimentary approaches will provide a clearer picture of the research problem than either alone? Perhaps, like Michelle, you see mixed methods as a way to develop your research. Or maybe mixed methods will help you to initiate new ideas or expand existing ones.

As you craft your rationale, assess your own skills and resources, especially the time you have available to devote yourself to the study. If your assessment is positive, it is time to consider the design of your study. Which of your research specifications will be addressed with qualitative methods, and which with quantitative? Will one or the other take priority? What order is suggested by your research specifications for implementing the quantitative and qualitative aspects of the study? What methods, techniques, and instruments will you use for each? Re-visit the directions for proposing qualitative research (see Chapters 7 and 8) and quantitative research (see Chapters 10 through 12) for further details. And finally, you must address the key requirement for mixed methods research: How and where will you bring the findings together?

PRACTITIONER INQUIRY

History and Evolution

Practitioner (or teacher) inquiry, part of a tradition broadly known as action research, represents a convergence of methodological and theoretical traditions that are used to systematically examine practice. Having initially developed in the social sciences to involve community stakeholders in research to improve the circumstances for marginalized communities, action research has spread into additional fields of study and developed into a means of democratizing knowledge and research. In many ways the approach was a response to the notion that research, in order to be valid, must reflect a detached, objective form of scientific knowledge.

The original iterations of action research included community organizers as well as stakeholders in the research process with the intention of enacting social change. Over time, teachers and teacher educators adopted the principles for the purpose of classroom inquiry and self-study.

Perhaps because it evolved across several different realms of practice, it is known by many different names. We have chosen the term practitioner inquiry, believing that term best reflects the needs and interests of our readers.

Current practices have been influenced by three lineages: that of German-American social-psychologist Kurt Lewin, Latin American activists and scholars influenced by the work of Paolo Friere, and social scientists influenced by critical theory and critical race theory (Zeller-Berkman, 2014). Action research found a place in the field of education during the 1970s and 1980s as a way for scholars to collaborate with teachers, administrators, and parents to improve educational practices. However, the earliest proponents were met with resistance, as action research was not valued by the academy as "real" research. Resurgence during the 1970s was further bolstered by the growing influence of postmodern perspectives among academics.

More recently, authors Cochran-Smith and Lytle (1990) put forth a vision of educational research driven by the knowledge and experiences of P-12 teachers. They felt that much of university-based educational research disenfranchised "those most directly responsible for the education" (p. 2). Their version of teacher research and inquiry includes collaborative forms of research that resemble earlier iterations of action research in education, but also encompass teacher-led empirical studies and teachers engaging in conceptual and theoretical scholarship (see also Cochran-Smith & Lytle, 1993).

Defining Qualities

Practitioner inquiry has the potential to help music teachers and other practitioners make immediate and concurrent changes in daily practice. This emerging way of thinking about research—some consider it a paradigm—encompasses empirical research but also includes theoretical and conceptual writings based on teacher knowledge and experience. Within the field of education, practitioner inquiry rejects the divide between the researcher and the researched as a false dichotomy. Teachers, as "the agents and sources of educational reform and not the objects of reform" (Pine, 2008, p. 30), are seen as the experts in their own classroom, and thus the most qualified to engage in systematic inquiry about teaching and learning. Thus, knowledge gathered and generated by practitioners based on daily experiences in the field is viewed as equally valid, if not more so, to university-based research findings and other forms of expert knowledge.

The "action" in action research is the implementation of findings within the teaching setting (Pine, 2008). Thus, the intention driving practitioner inquiry is the desire to learn about one's own practice in order to act—to make informed changes and improvements. Unlike "traditional" research studies, designed to imitate scientific inquiry, the nature of action research is "recursive, iterative, spiraling, and cyclical" (Pine, 2008, p. 249). You therefore envision the stages of "think/ ask questions, read, observe/document, and share" described earlier in this textbook as a continuous cycle, which can be seen in Figure 13.1.

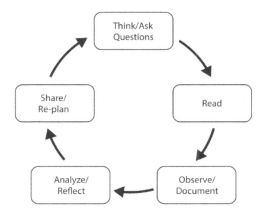

FIGURE 13.1 The Participant Inquiry/Action Research Process

The dynamic process of data collection, implementation, and analysis is flexible to the everyday spontaneity of teaching, and is therefore subject to shift based on emerging findings. It is this dialogic nature that makes practitioner inquiry a paradigm rather than a research method (Robbins, 2014). Because research questions are derived from practice, the process itself as well as the collected and analyzed data has the potential to impact practice in real time. Practitioner-researchers have the flexibility to alter the implementation of interventions based on early observations during the process. Relevant findings continue to emerge as researchers analyze and reflect upon data. Practitioner inquiry/action research does not assume generalizability. While the nature of the research problem is highly contextual, data analysis may yield *transferable* findings that resonate with teachers in other settings.

Contexts and Applications

Music educators, community musicians, and others have employed practitioner inquiry to better understand a phenomenon within an instructional space, implement and document an idea for improving practice or student achievement, and examine the process of music-making as a means of social intervention. Dana and Yendol-Hoppey (2019) have identified eight "passions" that often serve as entry points for practitioners seeking to explore and improve their work (pp. 27–65):

- Helping an individual child
- Improving or enriching curriculum
- Developing content knowledge
- Improving or experimenting with teaching strategies and techniques
- Exploring relationships between beliefs and classroom practice
- Examining intersections between personal and professional identities
- Advocating for equity and social justice
- Understanding the teaching and learning context

Practitioner inquiry and action research in general have been slow to take root in music education despite support by a number of prominent scholars within the field (e.g., Conway & Borst, 2001; Conway & Jeffers, 2004; Regelski, 1994/1995; and Robbins, 2014). Although practitioner inquiry is increasingly popular for master's level research projects, and gaining interest among scholars, there are few published examples of practitioner inquiry in the music education literature. Those that do exist tend either to examine the nature of an observed phenomenon in the classroom or document the implementation of a new teaching method or classroom procedure. Below we include a few exemplars.

The process of implementation was the focus of inquiry for Barlow (2018), an Australian music teacher who used practitioner inquiry to address a perceived conflict between government requirements for assessment of her school music ensembles and the emphasis on "student engagement through active participation" emphasized by the Australian Curriculum. She asked: "Can we track progress in a broader and more meaningful way and still adhere to the ethos of a practical, student-driven and engaging classroom?" (p. 20). In response, she implemented a systematic data collection process, using running records and multi-point rubrics, using tools from both quantitative and qualitative research. This approach assured "adherence to the rationale of the Australian music curriculum (ACARA, 2018)" and also produced "consistent measurable and equitable data for all stakeholders (Government of Australia, 2013)."

The mixed methods practitioner inquiry project designed by American music teacher Lisa Tiano (2019) was also inspired by demands for student assessment. Tiano wondered whether music composition could improve her students' music literacy while also having a "minimal impact on performance preparation time" (p. 10). Using a mixed-methods approach, Tiano used existing pre-/posttest evaluations and added student surveys, recordings of student compositions, and field note observations of student behavior and in-class discussions. Tiano found only a slight overall improvement in student sight reading, but students indicated on surveys that they experienced increased confidence in performance and wanted to engage in more musical exploration. Tiano therefore suggested that gains in student enthusiasm and engagement counteracted the potential negative impacts of "lost" rehearsal time. Other projects that have utilized participant inquiry/ action research include published research by Reynolds and Beitler (2007), Campayo-Muñoz, Cabedo-Mas and Hargreaves (2019), and Schmidt-Jones (2020).

Developing a Participant Inquiry/Action Research Project

If you, like Carlos, find that your research purpose and specifications seem geared toward practitioner inquiry, you should clearly identify an issue in your classroom, studio, or workplace, or an aspect of your teaching practice that you would like to address. Pine (2008) suggests that practitioner inquiry should be . . .

- meaningful and important for professional growth,
- manageable within your setting and context,
- relevant and beneficial to your learners or participants, and
- capable of providing actionable implications for your practice.

(p. 239)

For Carlos, as for Sarah Barlow (2018), whose work is featured earlier in the chapter, the inspiration was a perceived conflict between his desire to explore student-centered teaching and workplace demands for formal student assessment. Your inspiration may be similar, or you may wish to examine a phenomenon you have observed, improve an aspect of your practice, or create space for advocacy and activism.

As you transition from a research idea to a research purpose, be sure to consult exist-ing literature to learn what is known about your topic and consider how your study could contribute to a more robust understanding. A good rule of thumb for practitioner inquiry is to begin with about the same number of trade and scholarly publications and bring their ideas together as you craft your research design. Given the cyclical nature of practitioner inquiry, you should also build time into your research design for accessing additional literature throughout the project.

Although you will make adjustments throughout the action research process, thoughtful plan-ning will ensure that your project will provide valuable findings. In general, practitioner inquiry does not involve recruiting participants in a traditional sense because it relies on a pre-existing setting (your classroom, for instance). However, other details must be included. Your plan should describe the forms of data you will collect, and your procedures for data collection. You should select multiple data sources so you can access different kinds of insight whenever possible; Pine (2008) recommends making a comprehensive list of all potential forms of data and settling on a combination that best addresses your research question. Your plan must also include a rough time-line that acknowledges possible contingencies for obstacles or disruptions that might arise during the process.

During the planning phase, you must also obtain any necessary approvals for completing your project. According to the U.S. government's "Federal Policy for the Protection of Human Subjects" (2018), "research conducted in established or commonly accepted educational settings that specifically involves normal educational practices" is eligible for exemption status from the Institutional Review Board (IRB). However, teachers planning research for the purpose of earn-ing a degree are still required 1) to apply to their college or university IRB to confirm exemption status so that their research can be recognized as exempt, and 2) to confirm approval procedures with building or district administrators.

The continuous cycle of inquiry illustrated in Figure 13.1 means that your plans should include a process for keeping notes and reflections on the research process itself. In the qualitative tradition, these notes are referred to as "memos" and can be helpful in guiding any adjustments to your plan as well as informing your data analysis (Charmaz, 2014). Because action research is a way of thinking about research (some consider it a paradigm) rather than a specific design or method, our discussion of how to implement a study focuses primarily on contextual considerations. Spe-cific details pertaining to qualitative or quantitative tools and practices that may be used to meet the goals of your inquiry can be found in Chapters 7–12 in this textbook.

ARTS-BASED RESEARCH

History and Evolution

In response to questions like those asked by Liam at the beginning of this chapter, educationist-scholar Elliot Eisner articulated a theory of *arts-based educational research* (ABER, now more often simply ABR) that draws on artistic as well as scholarly practices. Arts-based researchers do not oppose the underlying assumptions of scientific research, but believe that science may not tell the whole story. Their "ambition is to broaden the conceptions not only of the tools that can be used to represent the world but even more to redefine and especially to enlarge the conceptual umbrella that defines the meaning of research itself" (Barone & Eisner, 2011, p. 2).

Defining Qualities

Arts-based research is undertaken by scholars who wish to use an artistic medium to express their work. Working to obfuscate traditional boundaries between scholarship and artistry, such "schol-ARTists" (Cahnmann-Taylor & Siegesmund, 2008, p. 6) believe the arts "stretch a researcher's capacities for creativity and knowing, creating a healthy synthesis of approaches to collect, analyze, and represent data" (p. 4). Leavy (2018) acknowledges a tension between those who believe ABR is a "methodological field within the qualitative paradigm, and others [who] assert that it is its own paradigm" (p. 4). Leavy supports the latter view because "ABR is based on *aesthetic knowing*" (p. 5, emphasis original) and as such, "requires a novel worldview" (p. 4).

A similar approach, known as practice as research (PaR) or arts practice research, is more common in Britain, Europe and Australia.

> PaR involves a research project in which practice is a key method of inquiry and where, in respect of the arts, a practice (creative writing, dance, musical score/performance, theatre/performance, visual exhibition, film or other cultural practice) is submitted as substantial evidence of a research inquiry.
>
> (Nelson, 2013, p. 4)

As such, the proposed inquiry must entail "practical knowledge which might primarily be demonstrated in practice—that is, knowledge which is a matter of doing rather than abstractly conceived and thus able to be articulated by way of a traditional thesis in words alone" (p. 4).

Hannula et al. describe the practice of artistic research as a "process of bringing forth" (p. 109). As such, the aesthetic possibilities for arts-based and arts practice research are virtually unlimited, ranging from photography to art-making to song-writing, musical and dramatic performance, to a host of literary and multi-media applications (Chilton & Leavy, 2014). In practice, arts-based music education research tends towards literary forms. Some arts-based researchers use the artistic element as part of the data collection and analysis, such as turning narrative data into poetry. Others share their findings in an interactive or artistic way, such as ethno-drama or even painting. Thus, arts-based research may stand alone as art, or its artistic nature may be sandwiched between sections of social science prose. Even when ABR appears in the guise of formal social science research, its evocative nature draws the reader into an experience much as a story or poem or play would do. We present, as examples, the work of Johnny Saldaña (2008) and Hala Jaber (2020).

Our first example features Saldaña's (2008) autoethnodrama, entitled "Second Chair." In it, the author (now a successful professor and playwright) explores and expresses "the underlying symbolic and metaphoric significance of first and second chair's status" (p. 188). Saldaña's rationale, stated in commentary after the script:

> If musicians can understand the feelings accorded to someone of "second chair" status, they can hopefully understand the feelings of the marginalized individual in a competitive mainstream society: ". . . it's always feeling and sometimes being treated as lesser than, second best, like playing a cheap-ass plastic Bundy when you'd rather be playing an ebony wood Selmer with a glass mouthpiece."
>
> (p. 188)

Another example is Jaber's arts practice investigation. Based on her experiences as a community music facilitator in Syria and Palestine, Jaber (2020) was interested in examining "the potential found in music-making as a tool to promote integration, and the musical approach needed to facilitate this interaction" (p. 18). Her project explored the role of "music-making within the community music workshop" (p. 4) for helping Syrian refuges in Limerick, Ireland process the trauma and conflict they experienced. Jaber utilized a variety of research methods that allowed her to capture the artistic processes, performances, and experiences shared by her participants, and also meaningfully interpret findings in order to improve her practice as a community music facilitator.

Developing an Arts-Based or Arts Practice Research Project

The process for designing or producing arts-based research begins with considering your own artistic skills and goals in light of what you want to communicate. Arts-based research is judged by "the appropriateness of the fit between research aims and methodology," how well the "aesthetic power" of the research serves the research goals, and the usefulness as well as the "participatory and transformative" nature of "the resulting representation" (Chilton & Leavy, 2014, pp. 414–417). Thus, if you, like Liam and Muna, wish to develop an arts-based or arts practice research project, you must imagine not only the people and the media with which you wish to work, but the pedagogical, artistic, and research procedures you will follow and/or the artwork you will produce. In the process, you envision a project that is true to who you are as a musician-teacher and to the context in which the work is anchored.

Nelson (2013) offers specific recommendations for PaR projects; these guidelines may also be helpful for other arts-based researchers. According to Nelson,

> a PaR submission is comprised of multiple modes of evidence reflecting a multi-mode research inquiry. It is likely to include:
>
> - a product (exhibition, film, blog, score, performance) with a *durable record* (DVD, CD, video);
> - documentation of process (sketchbook, photographs, DVD, objects of material culture); and
> - "complementary writing" which includes locating practice in a lineage of influences and a conceptual framework for the research.
>
> (p. 14, emphasis original)

CRAFTING A PROPOSAL FOR MIXED METHODS, PRACTITIONER INQUIRY/ACTION RESEARCH OR ARTS-BASED RESEARCH

A research proposal, particularly for a degree requirement, usually has four sections or chapters: (1) Introduction, (2) Review of related literature, (3) Methods and Procedures, and (4) Conclusions. Its purpose is to connect your specific view of the topic to the published body of knowledge in the field, support your claim that there is a need for your study, and communicate that you have the necessary skills and knowledge to complete the proposed project. However, as the specifics for each of the research traditions described in this chapter are quite different from each other, expectations may vary according to which tradition(s) you plan to follow. We therefore suggest reviewing details of your chosen tradition from earlier in this chapter as well as the qualitative and/or quantitative chapters that are most relevant to your research questions, and conferring with your course instructor, project advisor, and institution.

Preliminary Steps

Prior to formalizing your proposal, it is helpful to re-visit your thinking about your topic and research purpose.

Purpose, Rationale and Purpose Specifications

Re-examine the purpose, rationale, and purpose specifications (i.e., sub-purposes, hypotheses, or research questions) you wrote in Chapter 3 to confirm that they suggest the type of research or inquiry you are planning to undertake. Also note whether the way you describe your research topic to friends and colleagues reflects one of the traditions described in this chapter. For instance, mixed methods research is often based on pragmatism or "'paradigm relativism,' which encourages the use of whatever methodological approach works for the particular problem under study" (Tashakkori & Teddlie, 1998 in Fitzpatrick, 2014, p. 175). Practitioner inquiry first and foremost is about using research practices to test and enact ways to improve your practice—as a teacher, community music facilitator, arts manager, and so on—in the setting where you work. And arts-based and arts practice research is based on the belief that artistic practice is itself a valuable way of knowing.

Literature Collection

Assess the literature you have collected thus far. Regardless of the type of research or inquiry you plan to do, you need a literature collection that represents your research purpose and each specification, the approach you propose to follow, and the theoretical or philosophical lens(es) that guide your thinking. If such is not the case, you may need to try additional search terms to find additional sources. Re-visiting (and possibly revising) the literature map you completed in Chapter 2 may be helpful.

Writing the Introduction

In the introduction you expand on your research purpose and rationale to present a logical argument for your proposed research. It should evoke not only the details of your topic but also the perspectives and lenses you bring to the study. Begin with background on the lineage of your topic using concepts drawn from the literature. Typically, it is organized from general to specific, and may be further organized according to your purpose specifications (sub-purposes, hypotheses, or research questions) and any theoretical lenses that are pertinent to your perspective.

The section concludes with your statement of purpose, rationale, and research specifications (i.e., sub-purposes, hypotheses, or questions), constructed to address each element of your research purpose: people, places, points of view, phenomena, perspectives, and researcher position. If pertinent, add definitions of important terms and acknowledge any limitations of your study.

Writing the Literature Review

The literature review communicates to readers that your research ideas are grounded in the traditions in which you will work. While the contents and style of literature reviews differ across the three traditions in this chapter, the organization is similar as is its intended outcome. The review itself is often organized around your research specifications. Literature within each sub-topic or question is typically arranged from general to more specific, often with a final transitional section that suggests connections between your research questions and the procedures you will be proposing. Be sure to consult examples, both in the scholarly literature and from projects completed at your institution, ideally those under the guidance of your advisor.

Specific considerations include the following: If you plan to do mixed methods research, your literature collection should demonstrate a solid grounding in mixed methods literature. This will show that you understand the unique perspective offered by mixing and are familiar with "the best procedures and the latest techniques for conducting a good inquiry" (Creswell & Plano Clark, 2017, p. 15). If you see yourself as a practitioner-inquirer, your literature review should reflect your research purpose and specifications across a selection of practitioner and scholarly literature, and also suggest a need for your proposed project. Literature use is highly variable across arts based and arts practice research. An exhaustive collection of literature is less important than a collection that illustrates your knowledge of and perspective on the topic, your understanding of the medium in which you will work, and the lineage of the practice under study (Chilton & Leavy, 2014; Nelson, 2013).

Describing Proposed Methods and Procedures

Certain elements of research design are similar across the three types of inquiry discussed in this chapter. As was true in chapters 8 (qualitative) and 10–12 (quantitative), these include participant selection and recruitment, site selection and approval, details of engagement, methods of data gathering and data storage, processes for analysis, acknowledgement of ethics considerations, and discussion of the connection between your purpose and research specifications, your proposed research design, and your expected findings or outcome.

As you craft your research design, we suggest re-reading the descriptions in this chapter as well as the section on "Describing Proposed Methods and Procedures" in Chapters 8 (qualitative) and 10–12 (quantitative) as they relate to the inquiry tools that best fit your research needs.

If you plan to do mixed methods research, prior to describing the quantitative and qualitative elements of your design, you should specify your priority for quantitative or qualitative approaches, and the order in which the approaches will be used. See suggestions by Bryman (2015), Fitzpatrick (2014), and Creswell and Plano Clark (2017), as well as in Recommended Reading. If your intention is to examine your work as a practitioner, be clear about the process by which you expect the project to unfold, and how each element of the project relates to the others. Build in "interludes" for reflection and any recalibration that is necessary. If you will do arts-based or arts practice research, the artistic as well as the practical and technical elements of your inquiry must be clear in your proposed research design. Hannula, Suoranta, & Vaden (2005) suggest addressing practical methods, means of expression, and interactions between the two (p. 110).

Writing the Conclusion

The conclusion section of your proposal usually begins by summarizing the points made in the introduction and design section. However, beyond that point this section of the proposal is quite different across the three traditions because of their distinct philosophical underpinnings. The most conventional of the three methods in this chapter, mixed methods research is rooted in pragmatism and paradigmatic relativism. As such, mixed methods researchers seek to address research problems from multiple angles. Based on the belief that practical knowledge is as valid as scholarly knowledge, practitioner-inquirers and action researchers seek to address practical problems in the contexts in which they are manifest. Arts-based and arts practice researchers may utilize artistic processes to do their research, and they may create art as an outcome of their research. The concluding section of your proposal should likewise reflect all points made in earlier sections of the proposal, ultimately affirming to your readers that your project will make an important contribution to the field of music education.

CHAPTER SUMMARY

1) Mixed methods research, practitioner inquiry/action research and arts–based research utilize tools and procedures from quantitative and qualitative traditions to address different types of inquiry in varied ways.
2) Mixed methods research involves intentional combinations of quantitative and qualitative research methods that expand researcher perspectives and offer insights beyond what either approach can do on its own.
3) Practitioner, or teacher inquiry, originating in action research, rejects the divide between the researcher and the researched as a false dichotomy. It offers a way to systematically study and make informed changes to one's own practice.
4) Arts-based research and Practice as Research puts forth artistic processes and artistic creation as valid forms of knowledge production. Researchers in these traditions view artistic processes as research, and art as a valid research outcome.

Topics for Further Exploration

1) Pro's and con's of combining qualitative and quantitative methods to address a research purpose in a single study.
2) The idea that educational research should be driven by the knowledge and experiences of P-12 teachers.
3) Barone and Eisner's (2011) suggestion that the "conceptual umbrella that defines the meaning of research itself" must expand because "science may not tell the whole story (p. 2).
4) Possible artistic methods to address the research ideas of members of your research class.

Suggested Assignments

1) Annotate an article or chapter related to your research interest that describes research based on mixed, practitioner-inquiry, and arts-based or arts practice perspective. (See examples in Recommended Reading below or inquiryinmusiceducation.com) How did the author(s)' approach impact what they learned from the research?
2) Describe how your current research purpose might expand or change if you approached it from a mixed, practitioner-inquiry, and arts-based or arts practice perspective. Stretch your thinking and consider all three, one-at-a-time:
   a) Mixed
   b) Practitioner-inquiry
   c) Arts-based or arts practice

Whether or not you adapt your research procedures, how does considering such an approach make you think differently about your research?

Recommended Reading

(See inquiryinmusiceducation.com for additional resources)

Mixed Methods Research

Creswell, J. W., & Plano Clark, V. L. (2017). *Designing and conducting mixed methods research*. Sage.
Hesse-Biber, S. N. (2010). *Mixed methods research: Merging theory with practice*. Guilford Publications.

Practitioner Inquiry/Action Research

Alber, S. M. (2010). *A toolkit for action research*. Rowman & Littlefield.
Dana, N. F., & Yendol-Hoppey, D. (2019). *The reflective educator's guide to classroom research: Learning to teach and teaching to learn through practitioner inquiry* (4th ed.). Corwin.
Mertler, C. A. (2020). *Action research: Improving schools and empowering educators* (6th ed.).

Arts-based and Arts-practice Research

Laprise, R. (2017). Empowering the music educator through action research. *Music Educators Journal, 104*(1), 28–33. https://doi.org/10.1177/0027432117708012
Leavy, P. (2020). *Methods meets art: Arts-based research practice* (3rd ed.). The Guilford Press.
Mulvihill, T. M., & Swaminathan, R. (2020). *Arts-based educational research and qualitative inquiry: Walking the path*. Routledge.
Nelson, R. (2013) *Practice as research in the arts: Principles, protocols, pedagogies, resistances*. Palgrave Macmillan. Google Books edition.
Vallack, J. (2021). *Changing art into research: Soliloquy Methodology*. Routledge.

Helpful Websites

Mixed Methods Research

Mixed Methods International Research Association: https://mmira.wildapricot.org/
Resources page, Michigan Mixed Methods Program: www.mixedmethods.org/resources.html

Practitioner Inquiry/Action Research

Action Research Tutorials, Center for Collaborative Action Research: www.actionresearchtutorials.org/
Brown Education Alliance Action Research Handbook: www.brown.edu/academics/education-alliance/publications/action-research
Educational Action Research [Journal]: www.tandfonline.com/toc/reac20/current

Arts-based and Arts-practice Research

OAR: Oxford Artistic and Practice Based Research Platform: www.oarplatform.com/
PRAG-UK: Practice Research Advisory Group: www.tcd.ie/trinitylongroomhub/research/themes/creative-arts-practice.php
(See inquiryinmusiceducation.com for additional resources)

REFERENCES

Albert, D. J. (2016). *Disruptions and transformations: The influences of culture and community on pre-service music educators' occupational identities* [Doctoral dissertation]. Michigan State University. ProQuest Dissertations and Theses Global (Publication No. 10142666).

Barlow, S. (2018). Assessment and engagement in music classes: Are they mutually exclusive? *Australian Journal of Music Education, 52*(1), 19–27.

Barone, T., & Eisner, E. W. (2011). *Arts based research.* Sage.

Bryman, A. (2015). *Social research methods.* Oxford University Press.

Cahnmann-Taylor, M., & Siegesmund, R. (2008). *Arts-based research in education: Foundations for practice.* Routledge.

Campayo-Muñoz, E., Cabedo-Mas, A., & Hargreaves, D. (2019). Intrapersonal skills and music performance in elementary piano students in Spanish conservatories: Three case studies. *International Journal of Music Education, 38*(1), 93–112. https://doi.org/10.1177/0255761419873782

Charmaz, K. (2014). *Conducting grounded theory* (2nd ed.). Sage.

Chilton, G., & Leavy, P. (2014). Arts-based research practice: Merging social research and the creative arts. In P. Leavy (Ed.), *The Oxford handbook of qualitative research* (pp. 403–422). Oxford University Press.

Cochran-Smith, M., & Lytle, S. L. (1993). *Inside/outside: Teacher research and knowledge.* Teachers College Press.

Cochran-Smith, M., & Lytle, S. L. (1990). Research on teaching and teacher research: The issues that divide. *Educational Researcher, 19*(2), 2–11. https://doi.org/10.3102/0013189X019002002

Conway, C. M., & Borst, J. (2001). Action research in music education. *Update: Applications of Research in Music Education, 19*(2), 3–8. https://doi.org/10.1177/87551233010190020102

Conway, C. M., & Jeffers, T. (2004). Parent, student, and teacher perceptions of assessment procedures in beginning instrumental music. *Bulletin of the Council for Research in Music Education, 160*, 16–25. www.jstor.org/stable/40319215

Creswell, J. W., & Plano Clark, V. L. (2017). *Designing and conducting mixed methods research.* Sage.

Cronenberg, S. S. (2016). *Music at the middle: Principles that guide middle level general music teachers* [Doctoral dissertation]. University of Illinois at Urbana-Champaign. http://hdl.handle.net/2142/90502

Dana, N. F., & Yendol-Hoppey, D. (2019). *The reflective educator's guide to classroom research: Learning to teach and teaching to learn through practitioner inquiry* (4th ed.). Corwin.

Fitzpatrick, K. R. (2008). *A mixed methods portrait of urban instrumental music teaching* [Doctoral dissertation]. Northwestern University. ProQuest Dissertations and Theses Global (Publication No. 3303647)

Fitzpatrick, K. R. (2014). Mixed methods research in music education. In C. M. Conway (Ed.), *The Oxford handbook of qualitative research in American music education* (Vol. 1, pp. 171–187). Oxford University Press.

Furiani, D. M. (2018). *Informal teaching and learning practices in a traditional jazz ensemble: A case study* [Master's thesis]. California State University, Long Beach. ProQuest Dissertations and Theses Global (Publication No. 2213580386).

Hannula, M., Suoranta, J., & Vaden, T. (2005). *Artistic research: Theories, methods, and practices.* Helsinki Academy of Fine Arts.

Hesse-Biber, S. N. (2010). *Mixed methods research: Merging theory with practice.* Guilford Press.

Jaber, H. (2020). *An arts practice investigation of community music interventions in the context of post- conflict migration, with particular reference to the Syrian community in Ireland.* [Doctoral dissertation]. Irish World Academy of Music and Dance, University of Limerick.

Leavy, P. (2018). Introduction to arts-based research. In P. Leavy (Ed.), *Handbook of arts-based research* (pp. 3–21). Routledge.

Maxwell, J. A. (2016). Expanding the history and range of mixed methods research. *Journal of Mixed Methods Research, 10*(1), 12–27. https://doi.org/10.1177/1558689815571132

Nelson, R. (2013). *Practice as research in the arts: Principles, protocols, pedagogies, resistances.* Palgrave Macmillan. Google Books edition.

Pine, G. J. (2008). *Teacher action research: Building knowledge democracies.* Sage.

Protection of Human Subjects, 45 C.F.R. §46.104(d)(1) (2018). www.hhs.gov/ohrp/regulations-and-policy/regulations/2018-req-preamble/index.html#46.104%28d%29

Regelski, T. A. (1994/1995). Action research and critical theory: Empowering music teachers to professionalize praxis. *Bulletin of the Council for Research in Music Education*, *123*, 63–89. www.jstor.org/stable/40318693

Reynolds, A. M., & Beitler, N. S. (2007). Reflective practice in a middle-school instrumental setting. *Bulletin of the Council for Research in Music Education*, *173*, 55–69. www.jstor.org/stable/40319470

Robbins, J. (2014). Practitioner inquiry. In C. M. Conway (Ed.), *The Oxford handbook of qualitative research in American music education*. Oxford University Press. https://doi.org/10.1093/oxfordhb/9780199844272.013.011

Saldaña, J. (2008). Second chair: An autoethnodrama. *Research Studies in Music Education*, *30*(2), 177–191. https://doi.org/10.1177/1321103X08097506

Schmidt-Jones, C. A. (2020). The promise and challenge of online action research: Notes from a study of self-motivated online music learners. *Action Research*, *18*(3), 372–386. https://doi.org/10.1177/1476750317698026

Tiano, L. (2019). *Integrating composition into the performance ensemble and its effect on music literacy* [Master's thesis]. University of Massachusetts Lowell. ProQuest Dissertations and Theses Global (Publication No. 2243721414).

West, C. L. (2011). *Teaching middle school jazz: An exploratory sequential mixed methods study* [Doctoral dissertation]. University of Michigan. ProQuest Dissertations and Theses Global (Publication No. 3459081).

Zeller-Berkman, S. M. (2014). Lineages. In P. Levy (Ed.), *The Oxford handbook of qualitative research*. Oxford University Press. https://doi.org/10.1093/oxfordhb/9780199811755.013.026

Tools for Data Gathering
Basics of Content and Construction

This chapter:

*   Describes essential characteristics of commonly used data gathering devices suitable in various modes of inquiry.
*   Discusses methodological details involved in planning and designing specific tools, namely interview schedules and questionnaires, tests for doing research, and systematic observation protocols.

The purpose of this chapter is to supplement information provided in previous chapters. It describes selected methodological tools and procedures that cross or straddle qualitative and quantitative research paradigms, sometimes even bridging conceptual differences between the two. Additional "how to" sources, recommended at the end of the chapter, offer further guidance.

INTRODUCTION

This book began with what we call the spiral of inquiry—a process characterized by thinking, reading, observing, and sharing newly found information with others. In subsequent chapters, we often used the term "observe" broadly, referring to many forms of data gathering and analysis. You have learned that different forms of observation—leading to the gathering of data and, at times, their simultaneous analysis—require devices, or tools, of varying kinds. Such tools can become useful in nearly any mode of inquiry.

Because of the diversity of available choices and the importance of carefully crafting data gathering devices, introductory research courses are often accompanied by a lab or an additional class dedicated to the specifics of tool development. In places where that is not an option, this chapter is intended to help out. It describes a few of the methodological procedures that cross or straddle qualitative and quantitative research platforms, sometimes even bridging conceptual differences between the two.

Guidelines for planning and constructing tests, observation forms, surveys, and other devices useful for the collection and analysis of both quantitative and qualitative evidence may be found in textbooks in the fields of education, psychology, and sociology (see Recommended Reading at the end of the chapter). *Rating scales* and *tests* are used to make thoughts and behaviors visible, to assess how well someone performs musically or academically in comparison to others, or to set performance standards of varying kinds. They can also ascertain how participants feel about

DOI: 10.4324/9781003057703-17

specific issues you present to them. *Questionnaires* and *interviews* can provide similar information but might focus on how an individual or groups of individuals express their opinions. *Observation forms* of various kinds help to catalogue overtly visible actions and behaviors of individuals in groups or of entire groups.

The vast array of choices may make it difficult to decide what kind of information is most suited for your own research purpose. Consider the progress of Jeannette, Carlos, and Isaac in that regard:

Jeannette had begun working on a questionnaire with which she might compare perceptions of Black undergraduate music education majors at university students at historically black colleges and universities (or HCBUs) and predominantly White institutions (PWIs), While drafting items for the questionnaire, she realized that she perhaps should first talk informally with some classmates and other colleagues about the topic to give the questionnaire a contemporary "feel" by using language used "today" rather than nearly twenty years ago.

In the course of reading how other researchers kept track of operationalized behaviors in frequency count studies, *Isaac* learned about software called *Scribe*, available from the University of Texas at Austin (Duke, 2020). Perhaps this software would give him an efficient way to tally student responses in his study of expert high school band conductors. Isaac planned on contacting the Center for Music Learning at the university's Sarah and Ernest Butler School of Music for further details.

As may be clear from these examples, developing the kind of data gathering and analysis devices that Jeannette and Isaac were thinking about for their respective projects requires foresight and good planning. The items to be included and the instructions (if applicable) to the research participants should undergo careful scrutiny to assure that the tool yields reliable, valid, and/or trustworthy data. Although statistical criteria of reliability and validity may be applicable only to quantitative research designs, comparable standards of excellence in research should be the goal of any qualitative researcher employing such tools. When the researcher is "the instrument," the level of preparation should be as stringent as it is for tools designed to obtain quantitative data.

ESSENTIAL CHARACTERISTICS OF COMMON DATA GATHERING TOOLS

The litmus test for the construction of any data–gathering device is that the data you seek accurately represents the research question(s) that inspired them. By accurately, we mean they are *reliable* and *valid* in the case of quantitative data (see Chapters 10 and 11); in the case of qualitative work, they must be *coherent, credible, reflexive, resonant, rigorous*, and *worthy* (Tracy, 2010; Malterud, 2001; Elliott, Fischer, & Rennie, 1999; see also Chapters 7 and 8). The terms should not be considered mutually exclusive but, instead, as being complementary to each other.

The Constructs of Reliability and Validity Revisited

Establishing indicators for measurement reliability and validity was discussed in Chapter 11. It might be helpful, however, to recall the following: A requisite to the validity of a tool is its reliability, although a tool can be reliable without being valid. You could use a pencil to repeatedly measure your own body length and get close to the same number of pencil counts with repeated measures. But such would be a foolish undertaking because there are better (more valid) ways to accurately obtain your body size.

Information can be considered reliable when repeated measurements yield the same results—whether obtained by two or more persons at the same moment or by one person over a specified period of time. Validity is a broader term with a wider array of definitions, all of which relate to the purpose for which a study is undertaken. This means that the validity of a data gathering tool is intrinsically linked to the data analysis itself; in other words, the focus of your research questions is either addressed by the particular theory with which the research purpose originated, or your research leads to the formulation of a theory.

At times, the best way to obtain valid data is to use more than one tool. Jeannette's plans, for example, involved combining several data gathering devices. The development of rating scales of any kind always benefits from prior conversations (both informal and formal, that is, unstructured and structured) with potential study participants. Qualitatively obtained information would then lead to quantitative data gathering devices and any subsequent analysis.

It may appear that having only one tool to think about and to prepare for in a study is more efficient than having to plan several different ways to collect data. Such thinking is not necessarily accurate because "putting all your eggs in one basket" can be risky when it comes to determining a tool's validity or trustworthiness. On the other hand, if you try to use observation, interview, and performance ratings in a single study, you may face a different kind of challenge. Quantitatively, you need to make sure that the numbers in each tool are comparable to each other; qualitatively, you will have a large amount of verbal data to analyze—a time-consuming and demanding process. This means that reliability, validity, and trustworthiness of data are more closely connected to each other than terminologies in quantitative and qualitative research approaches might suggest.

Working with Trustworthy and Useful Information

For data to be useful, they must be trustworthy. This is the case whether they are expressed numerically, verbally, or in images; and whether the research is about the past or the present. Empiricists, philosophers, and historians alike look for trustworthy and useful data when talking to informants, analyzing documents, systematically examining worldviews and belief systems, or seeking to obtain deep insights into ways of living and being in a particular sub-culture. Through transparency of procedures and interjudge consensus (see Chapter 11), researchers seek to establish respectively, internal and external validity. Skills of analytic reflexivity are judged by their degree of "credibility, dependability, and confirmability" (Elliott et al., 1999, p. 218).

Many terms beyond those documented here have been used to describe what in quantitative research has become known as reliability and validity. Always at stake is the extent to which one can believe in the accuracy of the data collected and in the likelihood that the data analysis is honest and accurate. Thus, ethical conduct as a researcher does not only mean showing respect to your research participants and honoring institutional guidelines but also acting according to expected research conventions in your efforts to produce credible data and results. In the next section of this chapter we single out a few additional tools that have not been addressed in previous chapters.

CONSTRUCTING SELECTED DATA GATHERING TOOLS

This section describes aspects of constructing interview schedules and questionnaires, rating scales, tests specifically designed for research purposes, and observation forms of various kinds. Like the tools spoken to in previous chapters, many of them may be used across quantitative and qualitative research traditions.

Interview Schedules and Questionnaires

In Chapter 8 you learned about the importance of interviews (both formal and informal) in qualitative research. Informal interviews (also called unstructured) are open-ended conversations between you (the researcher) and your participant(s). You have an overall purpose, but ideas are allowed to develop freely in a chat-like atmosphere in which no topic is off limits. Such interviews often are the first step in the development of a formal or structured interview.

Structured interviews are organized ahead of a conversation and follow a particular train of thought conceptualized for the purpose of your study. To prepare for such an interview, you develop an *interview schedule*; that is, an outline of leading questions you want to ask each of your participants. Interview schedules ease data analysis later because hardly any unexpected topics come up—they are built into the schedule from the beginning.

Structured interviews keep you and your participants "on-task" but also may stifle the conversational atmosphere. Unstructured interviews, on the other hand, allow you to "feel out" how each participant thinks about a particular issue. Most useful during the early, exploratory stages of a project—be it qualitative or quantitative—unstructured interviews can be beneficial in the planning stages of writing items for questionnaires and can help when examining your thoughts on research projects and ideas for future work. Their advantage lies in their openness—you can explore topics as the need arises. The disadvantage lies in not knowing when to end the conversation and making sure that all important aspects of your research purpose are equally addressed by all participants. It can be easy to get off track and hard to get back on.

Drafting a Questionnaire

Planning for and working out a questionnaire (or other survey instrument) requires detailed steps, many of which are addressed by Dillman, Smyth, and Christian (2014), referenced in Chapter 10. Note that we do not distinguish between *survey* and *questionnaire*. In daily life, the term survey is more commonly used, although the tool used for a survey is the questionnaire—a collection of written questions to which, in most cases, specific answers are expected. In either case, think of a questionnaire as a well-crafted, concise inventory of questions about either personal opinions or factual information.

The questionnaire is a communicative tool between you (the researcher) and the population/ sample in the study. The respondents should be at ease with the issues addressed and be able to understand the questions without having to guess their meaning. Unstructured interviews may be helpful for this aspect of questionnaire development because they can help you discover the language used by your target respondents. Simplicity and short sentences in which to couch the questions should be your goal—whether you develop a paper-and pencil or a web-based format. This means that some technical terms might have to be "translated" into words that make sense to the respondents.

If an item cannot be readily justified in the context of a given purpose statement, eliminate the question from the draft. Your motto should always be to "keep it short" and to avoid questions that are ambiguous, rhetorical, or negative. Also, watch out for any questions that have "loaded" words or double meanings.

The first pilot draft of any questionnaire should contain open-ended answers that give respondents an opportunity to point out issues you may have missed or stated unclearly. You should distribute the next draft to a group of respondents who resemble or are a sub-sample of the targeted population/sample you have in mind. Discussing their views on specific issues and learning about the perceptions they harbor regarding your topic may bring new aspects of importance and even unanticipated variables to light.

When building the sequence of the survey, group questions according to response type; for instance, open-ended, multiple choice, census-type and checklist items. Census-type questions usually center on participants' demographics, but be careful to avoid questions whose answers you could have found on your own by checking public records or other publicly available documents. In Figure 14.1 you see an example for each of the other three question types worded for a survey about job satisfaction among music teachers.

Whichever formats you choose, order the items in each group from broadest to most specific. We call that process *filtering* because it allows the respondent to move from one section

The Issue: Job Satisfaction of Music Teachers

Type of question	*Possible wording*
Open-ended:	What do you find most satisfying about your chosen profession?
Yes-No:	Do you feel that reason(s) for enjoying your work outweigh your reason(s) for not enjoying it?
Multiple Choice	Yes---Most of the time---Not sure---Seldom---Not at all
Checklist:	Of the 10 reasons given here, please check [or rank by importance] up to five:

    __ I love to perform with the children
    __ The pay is adequate
    __ I love working with children
    __ I feel valued in my work
    __ I like being off in the summer
    __ I like my weekly schedule
    __ My non-music colleagues and I work well
      together
    __ I always strive for improving the quality of
      my work
    __ My work gives me opportunities to be creative
    __ I can adequately manage my professional
      and family duties

FIGURE 14.1 Various Response Formats to One Questionnaire Item

to the next without having to read all items that are not applicable to his or her situation. An example might be:

"Have you purchased a musical instrument within the last 12 months?"

The researcher-provided responses should be:

"Yes _, No_. If yes, please continue with the following questions. If no, go to Section B."

Computerized surveys, such as those available from *Qualtrics* or *Survey Monkey* allow for more expedient ways of moving from one item to the next than a paper survey.

Pilot-testing not only your complete survey but also the cover letter is paramount. Check with your advisor and your institution's ethics policy to determine what information is required. The letter should include detailed instructions about how to respond to the survey and offer to share the results with any interested respondents. (Make sure to remember that promise once your project has been completed!)

Rating Scales

> To develop a self-rating scale for her students to record their practice habits (similar to a Likert scale, see Chapter 10), *Christy* talked to each student individually. After each session, she summarized the conversation in her research log book, planning to incorporate those reported habits in the self-rating tool. For consistency, she talked to each student during two lessons, scheduled approximately a month apart, so that she could note inconsistencies or differences in comments by the students. She would have preferred more than two conversational sessions per student but was afraid of student burn-out or boredom.

Likert-type scales are used in questionnaires to enable respondents to numerically value specific tasks. You might, for instance, ask music teachers to rate their level of job satisfaction. Another kind of rating scale is the criterion-referenced scale, in which each ranking is defined according to specific, pre-set criteria. Such a scale is used for judging how close a performance comes to an established standard. Those standards should be based on evidence from the literature if possible; if not, setting and testing them would be one of your tasks as both a researcher and a teacher who wants to improve performance rating or adjudication scales for classroom use only.

Begin by ranking a large number of recorded student performances from highest to lowest by category (i.e., pitch, rhythm, style, technique, tone quality). Listen for the spread of performance levels and qualities and come up with clearly stated *descriptors* (words or phrases) that detail performance criteria within each category from highest to lowest. Check your descriptors by selecting several of the recorded student performances by chance and rate them according to the scales you developed. Establish a rating consistency score for yourself (see *interjudge reliability*, Chapter 11).

A low score indicates that your criteria are not very clear. Continue to adjust the criteria until you reach a satisfactorily high consistency score with yourself. Then create a recording of "anchors" that represent performances at each of the levels described in your scale. Use this to teach any additional reviewers about the criteria for each performance level. Make sure, however, that the examples you use as anchors are not drawn from the sample you intend to use.

The reliability of the ranking scores in your study is dependent upon how well your judges consistently apply the defined performance criteria to a given performance. It is preferable that you as the researcher are not involved as a judge. This means that your judges need to learn to consistently and in agreement with each other apply the criterion rankings as you set them. Plan a sufficient number of training sessions and prepare enough examples so that a judge's own ratings become consistent over time (internal consistency) and generally agree with other judges' ratings (for external consistency or interjudge reliability, see Chapter 11).

Tests Designed for Use in Research

At least three types of items are commonly used in written tests for research purposes: (1) open-ended long responses, such as essays, (2) open-ended short answer responses, and (3) closed choice options. Essay tests, best in small classes or for small groups, allow research participants to respond to a question freely and in their own words. This form of assessment can be either qualitatively or quantitatively analyzed but favors those respondents who like to write and are at ease with expressing themselves verbally. It also has several drawbacks: (1) There seldom is time allotted for proper contemplation and for organizing the content into a well-structured essay; and (2) applying a score to essays tends to be more a matter of personal preferences than adherence to *a priori* established criteria. You could minimize the subjectivity of scoring by providing the respondents with a list of anticipated topics that should be covered in the essay and describing how those would be weighted within the overall essay.

Closed choice items such as true-false, multiple-choice, matching, and rank-ordered responses are more easily quantifiable than open choice items. As you are likely aware, multiple-choice test items are the most commonly used and are suitable for large group testing. The items are relatively easy to score and the presence of several alternative answers reduces the chance of guessing. For the purpose of this book, we describe below how you may plan items in a quantifiable music achievement test for the purpose of assessing music students' entry level of music knowledge and skills in an introductory college music class.

Planning the Test

Greg, a teaching fellow in the music department of the university, instructs an introductory music education course for elementary education majors. The purpose of the course is to prepare pre-service teachers in basic classroom music skills, a requirement for teacher certification. A prerequisite for developing these skills is the development of basic musicianship skills as defined by the music education faculty of the department.

Musicianship as defined by the faculty involves the successful execution of tasks in specific content areas at various levels of comprehension and conceptualization. The music content areas are:

- Pitch: Notation, melodic patterns, intervals
- Rhythm: Note values, rhythmic quality, rhythmic patterns
- Timbre: Instruments, voices, tone color
- Harmony: Polyphony, homophony

The four levels of comprehension and conceptualization are that the student:

- knows basic terms,
- identifies same-different,
- compares concepts, and
- applies concepts to improvisation and the analysis of student compositions.

Greg wants to find out how much and at what level of conceptualization his students exhibit this type of musicianship when beginning the class. He believes they would more easily demonstrate many of the prerequisite musicianship skills valued by the music faculty if the music examples were drawn from popular songs they were already familiar with.

To examine his assumption, Greg designed a musicianship test to be given to the students early in the semester. He began by determining how many test items he needed in light of the definition of musicianship as provided by the faculty. A so-called specification table allowed him to do that (see Figure 14.2). It tallies the objectives for a specific group of learning tasks in such a way that you can determine how many tasks you would need per rubric to cover the objectives.

Across the top of the table are the categories of instructional objectives or types of learning to be tested. In the left-hand column is a listing of the content areas to be covered. The numbers in the cells state the projected quantity of questions for each area, if the test is not to exceed 60 items. Greg decided on that number in light of the time he had available for each student and considering that she wanted half of the tasks to be paper-and-pencil items and the other half performance items.

Note that the relative number of questions in each category relates to the importance of each rubric. A blank cell means no testing task. How to weigh particular items in the overall scheme of

	Instructional Objectives				
Content Areas	Knows basic terms	Identifies same-different	Compares concepts	Applies concepts to the analysis of compositions	Total
Pitch					
Notation	3		3		6
Melodic patterns		3	3	3	9
Intervals		3			3
Rhythm					
Rhythmic quality			3	2	5
Rhythmic patterns		3		2	5
Note Values	3				3
Tone color					
Instruments	3	2	2	2	9
Voices	2		2	2	6
Harmony					
Polyphony	2	2	2	2	8
Homophony		2	2	2	6
Total	**13**	**15**	**17**	**15**	**60**

FIGURE 14.2 Two-Way Specification Table

Source: (Note. Adapted from Anastasi, 1988, p. 431)

class content depends on the purpose of the research. If this was an achievement test to be given at the end of a semester, for instance, you would need to tell students where you placed your instructional emphasis throughout the semester.

The totals of each column represent the relative importance of each conceptual task, and the total on the right-hand side of the table represents the relative weight attached by him to each of the content areas. While this is not the only way to develop an examination or a test, it is a good way to lay out the tasks before you begin designing them.

Judging from the table, Greg tried to be even-handed about which tasks to focus on but perhaps favored instrument knowledge and the issue of polyphony a bit more than he should have if he wanted to use familiar examples from popular music for the tasks. This point was raised by two of his classmates when Greg asked for critical feedback about the table prior to administering the test.

Designing Tasks and Writing Items

Many general sources on writing test items are available; several are listed in Recommended Reading at the end of this chapter. Principally, sources on test development and other achievement measures stress that a test should be constructed as efficiently as possible so as to minimize error and bias. At the same time, you should include a minimum of two items for each tested learning task so as to establish a measure of reliability.

When designing test items for conducting research, bear in mind the following points:

1) Because items must be brief, the intention of questions can be easily misunderstood. To avoid that problem, strive for clarity in your statements and avoid ambiguous or double-meaning phrases.

2) Eliminate all "Either-Or" questions because any one answer can only respond to one of the two choices.

3) All response possibilities must not only be grammatically correct but also grammatically consistent and of approximately the same length. Test constructors tend to spend more time in phrasing the correct answer than in phrasing the wrong options. This can lead to respondents guessing an answer by appearance rather than by knowledge of its content.

4) Performance-based items should draw on musical tasks with which your participants are familiar—unless, of course, your objective is to find out how a respondent handles unfamiliar musical tasks. But even those must be within the range of skills that can be reasonably expected from participants.

5) Depending on the purpose of your study and connected to the previous point, you should provide your respondents with enough time to practice what you expect them to do. You also should make sure that your instructions are clear and that the respondents can ask for clarification before commencing the task.

6) Accept feedback for as long as possible. When you revise a drafted test, have it examined again by another group of individuals you trust. Once the test is used for research, corrections cannot be made anymore. Include calculations of the revision of drafts when setting your time schedule.

Tools for Observations of Many Kinds

There are many possible purposes for classroom observation; of those Waxman, Tharp, and Hilberg (2004, p. 3) emphasize four: (1) describing instructional practices, (2) investigating instructional inequities for different groups of students, (3) improving teacher education programs, and

(4) improving teachers' classroom instruction based on feedback from individual classroom profiles. Each of those purposes impacts your questions as well as choices of methods by which to observe.

Purposes that lead to quantifying the data require coding and tallying procedures on pre-designed observation forms (see Chapter 10). Qualitative researchers might seek less rigid process for reasons described in Chapters 7 and 8. Either choice, *a priori* codes or *a posteriori* interpretative analysis, takes time and diligence when you want to assure that your data are valid and reliable or trustworthy and honest.

Systematically gathered observational tools are useful for keeping track of specific actions and behaviors you see and hear in the presence of others as well as for interpreting complex relationships. You already know about narratives, portfolios, checklists, tallies, and ratings scales and their uses in research (see above and Chapters 7–12). Additional possibilities include so-called running records, anecdotal records, narrative event sampling, portfolios and third-party testimonies, tally event sampling, and time sampling description, among others. (This terminology is freely adapted from Nicolson & Shipstead, 2002, pp. xv-xviii.) The approaches can stand on their own, or in some cases, in combination—be it in qualitative or quantitative research designs.

Running records are those in which you write in the present tense and for a specified length of time or designated activity what specific persons say, do (Nicolson & Shipstead, 2002, p. 114), or even omit to do. Anecdotal records are "more than something interesting, emotional, or amusing to share." Rather, they are "directly observed incident[s] written in a short, concise, nonjudgmental narrative" (p. 136). The terms narrative and tally as applied to event- as well as time-sampling refer to choices of situations created by particular individuals with consequences for behaviors and actions by other individuals. From all behaviors and actions possible you select those that directly speak to the topic of your research.

In narrative sampling, for instance, you isolate incidents in which one action causes subsequent ones to occur and describe verbally those situations in which you see causally related actions or behaviors (Nicolson & Shipstead, 2002, p. 203). Tally event sampling is similar. For example, you might choose to observe only those students who have been identified by a teacher as "difficult to handle" and tally such observed incidents. In that case you are interested in their frequency of occurrence, rather than their specific characteristics. In time sampling, real time durations become the measure for sampled incidents. It is done either by notating observed actions according to equal time intervals or by recording the time lapse between the action that caused subsequent ones to occur and the action that concluded the incident.

Any of the sampling techniques described in the previous paragraph require the skill and/ or experience of drawing inferences from one observed action or event to another. For instance, when you observe a choir singing solfège and see the singers' eyes uniformly directed to the front, you may infer that the director is using hand signs even if you yourself cannot see them (Standley & Madsen, 1991, p. 7). This is an inference that differs from judgments in which you summarize observations by describing a teacher as "excellent" or a student as "lazy." In both cases, the actions from which an observer might have drawn such evaluative judgments would need to be documented to allow for the rendered interpretive "summary." Without such documentation, the judgment would not meet standards of systematic observation as a research tool.

In Person and Recorded Observations

In person observations occur in real time while classroom activities are proceeding; if an event is not noticed at the moment that it occurs, it is therefore lost for all time. That is problematic for any kind of research, but especially so for quantitative analysis, which requires observer reliability. To establish reliability, either more than one observer is needed in the classroom or one trained observer conducts all observations over a specified length of time. When recording equipment is used, there generally is no other person in the classroom than the one handling the equipment. But even that need may be eliminated if the camera is stationary and can be controlled remotely. Recorded observations have the advantage that events can be reviewed and studied repeatedly. Reliability may therefore be higher for video- or audio-based observation than when observers are stationed in the classroom. The disadvantage of observing recorded lessons is that the positioning of the camera in the classroom (whether hand-held or stationary) dictates to some degree what you may study. This is especially the case in large classes or performance group settings.

Both types of direct observation, "live" and recorded, carry with them a certain degree of intrusion into what otherwise would be assumed to be a normal setting. This makes it highly advisable for any researcher interested in the use of systematic observation techniques to minimize the appearance of intrusion by allowing those under observation to get accustomed to the recording equipment and/or the observer(s). That process, however, takes time and should be considered carefully. It might be just as important to conduct carefully planned observations that focus on the actions and behavior of students who are directly engaged with music-making and listening outside of school.

Observer Training

Often, specific research plans and designs require you to serve as the observer as well as the researcher. But if you plan to observe teachers and/or students in different schools, you might consider recruiting some additional observers for your project. Whichever option you choose, observer training is important. Its purpose is to help observers become comfortable with the setting(s), the participants, and the focuses of the research. Most importantly, however, practice is necessary to get fully "in tune" with the purpose of the project: Are you interested in observing student actions outside or inside the classroom? Do you address questions concerning classroom management and expectations of "good" classroom conduct? Does your focus lie on issues concerning your own actions as the teacher? Or, are you looking for causality between teacher actions and learning gains? Is your research directed at behavioral issues, teacher self-improvement, effectiveness, or non-guided/tutored learning?

Know the Purpose

In *behavioral research*, specific beliefs about the relationship between motivation and action have resulted in many studies on so-called "on-task" and "off-task" behavior, how students react to specific teacher actions, and what instructional (motivational) strategies might yield the most consistently positive pupil behavior (as operationalized by the researcher). Research on *teacher self-improvement* can also be situated in behaviorist theories but does not have to be. Methodologically, such research may include tallying the frequency and quality of cueing, phrasing, and modeling in conducting situations as well as the giving of cut-offs, the beating of time, inflection of voice, and facial expressions throughout rehearsals. Such functional *effectiveness research* is based on the assumption that it is possible to define, observe, and measure those variables or actions that make one teacher more "effective" than another.

Possibly in response to behavioral and effectiveness research traditions in music education, observational research on *informal learning in music* has been purposefully open-ended and contextually flexible (see Chapters 7 and 8). It clearly has steadily grown since the middle of the 20th century (see, among others, Abrahams & Head, 2005; Clements, 2010; DeNora, 2000; Green, 2001, 2011; Shehan-Campbell, 2010). Whatever your project's focus, be prepared to spend a good deal of time to internalize its purpose and rationale in very tangible terms.

For instance, in the psychological theory of *behaviorism* (going back to psychologists I. Pavlov [1849–1936] and B.F. Skinner [(1904–1990]), causality is central. What is or is not appropriate in a particular context can be "corrected" by giving immediate rewards and/or punishments (known as *reinforcement*) as deemed appropriate in the situation at hand. As an observer you therefore would need to take into consideration the teacher's interpretation of pupil conduct. Quantitatively spoken, the criterion measure for, respectively, on-task or off-task or positive or negative behavior, depends on the teacher's expectations toward "good behavior" in the classroom. You therefore would need to make contextually valid judgments about teacher and student actions (both verbal and nonverbal) as they are observed either "live" or as tape recorded lessons.

As a spin-off from effectiveness research and due to increased emphasis on school accountability across districts, states, and even nations, the last twenty years have seen a trend to morph direct observation forms into evaluation forms. Many such forms exist, usually specific to a particular state and/or school district. With the help of checklists, rating scales, and open-ended commentary about desirable and undesirable teaching strategies (according to the interpretations of school officials who serve as observers), the forms make evaluative and inferential judgments for the purpose of creating individual profiles of teacher effectiveness over time.

Teacher self-improvement studies (discussed above) use similar techniques as those common in behavioral research, but often for a different purpose. Checkmarks, observational categories, and rating scales assess clarity of communication along with patterns of verbal versus nonverbal interaction in the classroom, sequencing of instruction, and other pedagogically important constructs (Gumm, 2003; Price, 1992; Price & Yarbrough, 1993/1994; Sink, 2002). Negative and positive reinforcement, the degree of eye contact with the performers, and the relationship of individual coaching to sectional work vis-à-vis the entire ensemble are also frequently included. Focus, however, is less on testing theory than gaining insights into the superiority of one teaching method and/or style over another. The research is practice-oriented, as a result of which observation protocol and observer training may differ from case to case. In some instances, descriptive qualitative narratives are added to explain, illuminate, and otherwise enhance any quantitatively analyzed data, an approach that is sometimes called "mixed methods."

From whichever perspective you approach observational tasks, you can use pre-existing forms and templates or develop new ones. If you make use of available forms, be sure the content matches your project purpose fully. Re-examine reported reliability scores and establish new ones for your own project. Plan on doing at least one pilot study in which you take a recorded lesson or segment thereof and watch what you see while using the form. If you find that the items on the form consistently match what you see and hear, your initial judgment may be proven valid. If for some reason you find that you have to write into the form many additional observations and comments or that you or other observers have serious disagreements, you should either adjust the existing form or develop new observational guidelines, in the form of a tally sheet or checklist, categorical roster, or any other means by which you can systematically document and analyze observational data.

Awareness of flaws or mistakes does not necessarily weaken a project as long as either gives you the motivation to think of new and possibly better ways to address such weaknesses in the future. Think back to the spiral of inquiry mentioned at the beginning of this book: The ongoing-ness of the process itself is the driving force that allows you to make mistakes and learn from them. Furthermore, not everything that seemingly "goes wrong" in a study is your fault. Rather, it is the inevitable fact that life has its own rules. We may be able to anticipate and even work around them, but we cannot always control them, no matter how hard we try to expect the unexpected.

CHAPTER SUMMARY

1) The purpose of your study guides all decisions concerning any particular data gathering tool suitable for your study.
2) Knowledge about details involved in the development of data gathering tools can impact decisions about the kind of questions you choose to answer.
3) Among the many tools commonly found in music education research, surveys, tests, rating scales, and observation forms are used most frequently. Although computer programs may ease the step-by-step procedures of documenting all reliability and validity scores, continue to focus on trustworthiness and usefulness as additional quality indicators.
4) The development of any one of the tools mentioned above takes time and should be repeat-edly pilot tested. Even pre-existing tools require the re-examination of previously reported scores of reliability and validity.
5) Expect the unexpected.

Topics for Further Exploration

1) Which students in RC533 might be interested in one the tools described in this chapter? Which tools, and why?
2) Which of the tools described in this chapter might be useful for one or more of the colleagues in your research class? Why is that?

Suggested Assignments

1) Find a recent research study that details the development of a specific research tool. Summa-rize and evaluate the author's description of that process.
2) Design and test a short (20–25 item) achievement test on factual knowledge suitable for a music appreciation class or one of your own classes.
3) Compose three essay questions to assess conceptual knowledge in music education and describe your criteria for scoring them.
4) Develop a criterion-related rating scale to evaluate a music teaching situation of your choice.
5) Draft a questionnaire to obtain information on how non-music students view music students'
   a. Attitudes toward the rest of the university.
   b. Attitudes toward social position within the university.
   c. Abilities in non-music subject matters.
6) Assess and evaluate existing published tests or inventories for use in:
   a. Music education (i.e., music aptitude, music achievement, or music teaching style)

b. General education and social science (i.e., learning style, ethnic identity, or another of your interest)

7) Select two methodologically different articles on a comparable topic (see References or the supplemental online appendices in inquiryinmusiceducation.com). Abstract both studies and determine the relative strength of the data gathering tool(s) used in each.

Recommended Reading

Guerra-López, I. J. (2017). *Performance evaluation: Proven approaches for improving program and organizational performance.* Wiley.

Gumm, A. (2003). *Music teaching style: Moving beyond tradition.* Meredith Music.

Kubiszyn, T., & Borich, G. (2016). *Educational testing and measurement* (11th ed.). Wiley.

Simister, N. (2017). *Basic tools for data collection. Intrac for civil society.* www.intrac.org/wpcms/wp-content/uploads/2017/01/Basic-tools-for-data-collection.pdf

Thorndike, R. M., & Thorndike-Christ, T. (2010). *Measurement and evaluation in psychology and education* (8th ed.). Pearson.

REFERENCES

Abrahams, F., & Head, P. D. (2005). *Case studies in music education* (2nd ed.). GIA Publications.

Anastasi, A. (1988). *Psychological testing* (6th ed.). Macmillan Publishing Company.

Clements, A. C. (Ed.) (2010). *Alternative approaches in music education: Cases in the field.* Rowman and Littlefield.

DeNora, T. (2000). *Music in everyday life.* Cambridge University Press.

Dillman, D. A., Smyth, J. D., & Christian, L. M. (2014). *Internet, mail, and mixed-mode surveys: The tailored design method* (4th ed.). Wiley.

Duke, R. A. (2020). *Scribe 5* (for observation and assessment). Learning & Behavior Resources.

Elliott, R., Fischer, C. T., & Rennie, D. L. (1999). Evolving guidelines for publication of qualitative research studies in psychology and related fields. *British Journal of Clinical Psychology, 38*(3), 215–229. https://doi.org/10.1348/014466599162782

Green, L. (2001). *How popular musicians learn: A case for music education.* Ashgate.

Green, L. (Ed.) (2011). *Learning, teaching and musical identities: Voices across cultures.* Indiana University Press.

Gumm, A. (2003). *Music teaching style. Moving beyond tradition.* Meredith Music Publishing.

Malterud, K. (2001, August 11). Qualitative research: Standards, challenges, and guidelines. *Lancet, 358*(9280), 483–488. https://doi.org/10.1016/S0140-6736(01)05627-6

Nicolson, S., & Shipstead, S. G. (2002). *Through the looking glass. Observations in the early childhood classroom* (3rd ed.). Pearson.

Price, H. E. (1992). Sequential patterns of music instruction and learning to use them. *Journal of Research in Music education, 40*(1), 14–29. https://doi.org/10.2307/3345771

Price, H. E., & Yarbrough, C. (1993/1994). Effect of scripted sequential patterns of instruction in music rehearsals on teaching evaluations by college nonmusic majors. *Bulletin of the Council for Research in Music Education, 119*, 170–178. www.jstor.org/stable/40318627

Shehan-Campbell, P. (2010). *Songs in their heads: Music and its meaning in children's lives* (2nd ed.). Oxford University Press.

Sink, P. E. (2002). Behavioral research on direct music instruction. In R. Colwell & C. Richardson (Eds.), *The new handbook of research on music teaching and learning* (pp. 327–347). Oxford University Press.

Standley, J. M., & Madsen, C. K. (1991). An observation procedure to differentiate teaching experience and expertise in music education. *Journal of Research in Music Education, 39*(1), 5–11. https://doi.org/10.2307/3344604

Tracy, S. J. (2010). Qualitative quality: Eight "big-tent" criteria for excellent qualitative research. *Qualitative Inquiry, 16*, 837–851. https://doi.org/10.1177/1077800410383121

Waxman, H. C., Tharp, R. G., & Hilberg, R. S. (Eds.) (2004). *Observational research in U.S. classrooms: New approaches for understanding cultural and linguistic diversity.* Cambridge University Press.

CHAPTER 15

"So What?" Interpreting and Sharing Your Findings

This chapter addresses how to:

- Interpret and report your findings with the help of the "so what" query;
- Share your findings with different audiences; and
- Continue the spiral of inquiry by thinking about further research in light of the work accomplished.

The spiral of inquiry is incomplete until you publicly share the findings from your investigation with the profession at large. This chapter focuses first on completing the report required for a degree, and then suggests ways of using that report as the springboard for future projects. Although different modes of inquiry bring with them a variety of formats and expectations toward how a completed research document might look, the chapter focuses mostly on common elements among them.

INTRODUCTION

As *Prof. E.* walked into class, *Dale* and some of the other students were discussing the process of completing a research project. As the only student in RC 533 who had written a master's thesis, Dale was seen by his classmates as a bit of an expert. What was really involved, they wondered, in writing a research document and submitting it for approval to a committee for approval?

Dale organized his master's thesis according to the conventions of descriptive quantitative research: Chapter 1 contained rationale, purpose, questions, delimitations, and definition of terms. Chapter 2, the literature review, reported the content of studies that were pivotal to Dale's rationale and methodology. Chapter 3 detailed the methods and related procedures used in the study, and Chapter 4 presented results in the order of the research questions. Chapter 5—called Summary, Discussion, Conclusions, and Recommendations for Future Research—was just what it said: A brief version of the entire work with additional interpretations and comments about the findings.

DOI: 10.4324/9781003057703-18

Dale recalled that interpreting his findings was tougher than he had expected. Only repeated rewrites of the last chapter in his thesis eventually satisfied his committee members. Dale also remembered dragging his feet when it came to drawing conclusions beyond the specific findings. But what was most difficult (yet ultimately most satisfying) was articulating what the findings meant—what Prof. E. called the "So What?"—both in terms of practical significance for music teachers, and in applications for future research.

Prof. E. was pleased to see that the students were thinking ahead—not only about finishing their projects, but also about continuing the spiral of inquiry by sharing their findings in writing, Professor E. spent the remainder of the evening explaining the basic processes for writing up research, and encouraging the students to consider sharing their research findings beyond their course and degree requirements.

Ultimately, your research—whether for a course or degree requirement or part of a long-standing scholarly agenda—is incomplete until you publicly share the findings from the investigation with the profession at large. The spiral of inquiry requires no less. In fact, some universities require doctoral students to submit a scholarly article to a peer-reviewed journal or apply to present their research at a conference, believing this to be an integral part of becoming a scholar.

There are several reasons why it is necessary to explain to others what you did and why it matters. One, it forces you to interpret your findings in light of the literature you engaged with. Two, it helps your audience understand how your findings fit into the body of knowledge in the field. And, three, writing helps you articulate for yourself (as well as for your readers) where the spiral of inquiry might lead you intellectually as well as professionally.

BASIC REQUIREMENTS FOR GRADUATE STUDENT RESEARCH REPORTS

Requirements for formatting and organizing written research reports, theses, and dissertations vary from institution to institution. Modes of inquiry as well as research traditions and disciplinary conventions also bear on the way a research report is organized. Nonetheless, the following elements must be present in some form: (1) An introduction that provides background, mentions influential streams of thought, and offers your rationale, along with your purpose and any specifications; (2) a reiteration of key ideas and relevant research that led to your rationale, purpose, and choice of method; (3) a description of how you actually carried out your study and analyzed your data; (4) your results or findings, and (5) conclusions relative to your stated purpose, rationale, and research specifications—your interpretation of the meaning of your work. Often the latter section includes speculation about how the topic might be expanded into new questions that deserve further study. You may recognize this list as the scholarly process in its broadest form. A full list of all references included in the report is included at the end of the document.

Theses and dissertations in the quantitative realm of empirical research tend to follow the arrangement described by Dale; deviations are possible but seldom occur. A greater degree of flexibility and organizational liberties are the norm for philosophical, historical, and qualitative research. For instance, you may find purpose, rationale, and literature in the first chapter, followed by several chapters that deal with different elements of the study. Examining the literature that most closely resembles your study will help you determine the narrative style and organization of your final document.

The remainder of this chapter is divided in two parts. The first describes the basic requirements for a research report for a course or degree (i.e., master's thesis or doctoral dissertation). The second section suggests additional ways to share your research beyond course or degree requirements: a conference presentation, article in a trade or scholarly publication, or workshop. The chapter assumes that you have completed the steps outlined in the various methods chapters for proposal writing (see Chapters 5, 6, 8, 10, 11, 12, and 13). If that is not yet the case, you should still be aware of the philosophical underpinnings, technical procedures, and writing conventions for the mode of inquiry and methods you have used or will use to do the research.

Writing Up your Findings

The first step in writing the final report for your research is re-visiting your proposal. You will be able to use much of that material in the final report. If your thesis or dissertation will be organized in chapters, the introduction, review of literature, and methods section from your proposal will become chapters 1, 2, and 3, with minimal editing. Conventions for communicating your findings differ, as noted earlier, according to the mode of inquiry and methodological conventions you followed.

Writing Up Philosophical Inquiry

Having a philosophical study (or any study) unfold in exactly the way suggested in a proposal or writing plan is unusual. With philosophy in particular, it is more likely that following your intended path led you on compelling intellectual "side trips." Part of the philosophical journey, however, is returning to your initial map (in other words, your proposal), documenting where and why you deviated (if you did) and the meaning of the journey—for you, and for the profession at large.

You began developing your argument when you submitted the proposal for your project (or wrote up your writing plan, if your project is not part of a degree). As you conclude the project, returning to the point where you started is an important step. Here, you examine not only any changes in your ideas, but also the process by which those changes emerged. Once those thoughts have been written, you are ready to begin the report.

The first three chapters of philosophical reports, when written for degree requirements, tend to follow the scheme described earlier in this chapter and in Chapter 5. The first chapter presents your argumentation, premises, and definitions of terms, building on what was written in your proposal. Likewise, your second chapter builds on what you wrote in the proposal about the foundational ideas that make up your argument. In the third chapter you describe the process of your inquiry. Following that, you will expand on the premises offered in your proposal, often each into their own chapter. As both analysis and interpretation are part and parcel of a philosophical inquiry, they are stitched throughout the narrative.

Organizing and Interpreting Your Thoughts

Writing philosophy involves the creative process of designing and constructing the scaffolding or structure of an argument. Finding the "tack" one will take in a particular project is an exhilarating enterprise because an argument constitutes a new creation (Jorgensen, 2014, p. 10).

Organizing your thoughts in preparation for writing a philosophical narrative may be intimidating, but it is ultimately one of the most rewarding aspects of philosophical writing. It is the organization process that ultimately propels your thinking into a form that can be shared with, understood, and critiqued by your peers.

As was true for your argument, the organization of your narrative began with your proposal. Much of what you presented at the start of the study should still be applicable as you conclude the study. In fact, if this is not the case, you should consult with your project advisor before moving forward with a substantive re-organization. It may be, however, that the "side trips" we earlier referred to require some organizational imagination. It will be important not only to tell your readers about those journeys but also why you felt they were worthwhile.

Writing Up Historical Findings

For guidance in writing up an historical narrative, please refer to Chapter 6. That chapter offers excellent advice for completing an historical research report.

Writing Up Qualitative Findings

The qualitative research report weaves data analysis and interpretation together, bringing the layers of meaning uncovered by the research into a cohesive whole. You might compare it to composing a fugue, a musical structure in which different voices are connected by a theme (or two) and yet function independently. Musicians experience a paradox when performing a fugue in ensemble— asserting independence as a soloist and yet attending to the voices of fellow musicians—more inter-dependent than autonomous. Composing a qualitative research report is similarly contrapuntal, as the multiple voices from your fieldwork come into view via analysis and interpretation. Even unresolved dissonances become important parts of the composition, making the work both intriguing and unique.

Assuming your analysis is done or mostly done, return to your proposal and review your introduction and research questions, related literature, and proposed methods. However, do not start writing with the introduction (which will become Chapter 1). Instead, begin with the description of your methods (likely now Chapter 3). Add to this section by writing about how your proposed methods unfolded during the course of your research. How did you come to know your participants, see your role as investigator, and understand the phenomenon under study from multiple vantage points? Be clear about the analysis processes and tools you used at each stage of the study, and how they relate to specific research tradition(s). All of these details add to the credibility of your report.

Organizing and Interpreting Your Findings

Each qualitative study is distinct, meaning that it is up to you to devise an organizational scheme beyond the methods chapter. Certainly, your structure should reflect the research tradition that guided your work. But other considerations are also important.

What have you found and why does it matter? To whom does it matter? How can you best communicate to that group of people? Your answers to these questions guide you in crafting the body of your report. What possibilities for large-scale organization are suggested by the research itself? Perhaps each of your research questions, or each of your cases, or each place you visited, becomes a separate chapter. For organization within chapters, think about what categories each chapter might have in common, and where each one will be distinct. Those may become your sub-sections.

Choosing what to include in the report (and therefore what to leave out) is one of the most difficult tasks in writing up qualitative research. It is much more rewarding to talk to participants and look for themes in the data than to try to navigate through the entire project to interpret the findings for your readers. Yet without this process, the research has no possibility of impacting the field.

Once you've re-imagined your message and the organizational scheme for your findings, return to the literature review and then the introduction from your proposal. Depending on the tradition you followed, these may remain as separate chapters or be merged into one. As you revisit the literature review, reflect on how the topics, points of view, methods described, and styles of writing used in the studies you read, both before and during your research, impacted your work. Now you are ready to return to your introduction, re-crafting it to reflect the "whole" of your study.

Writing Up Quantitative Findings

Quantitative research reports adhere more closely to the organization of the research proposal than other styles of research. Thus, while philosophical, historical, and qualitative reports use a variety of organizational schemes beyond the first three chapters, quantitative reports tend to follow the conventional format described by Dale at the start of this chapter.

One common-sense difference between the proposal and the report is a change in the verb tense used to describe the methods and procedures in the methods chapter, usually the third chapter of the report. In addition, details related to actual (as opposed to proposed) numbers of participants and the percentages represented by those totals, as well as any changes in your proposed procedures for testing (if applicable), measuring, and data analysis, should be described in this chapter.

Results or findings are discussed in the fourth chapter of a quantitative research report. After a brief introduction, findings are usually presented in the order of your research specifications. Typically descriptive data are presented first, followed in order by correlational and then inferential data—see Chapters 10, 11, and 12 respectively for more information about data presentation. You may present data in narrative or graphic form, depending on which will be easier for readers to understand. The *Publication Manual of the American Psychological Association* (2020), known colloquially as the *APA Manual*, offers helpful guidelines for expressing numbers in written form. Also, Russell (2018) provides "Writing Hints" at the end of most chapters for describing statistical procedures and results.

FROM SUMMARY TO DISCUSSION/INTERPRETATION TO CONCLUSION

Consider accompanying the closing interpretation of your work with the rendition of Miles Davis' popular tune "So What?" as recorded live in 1958 for the famous Kind of Blue album. (You can find it on *YouTube* or your favorite streaming service). Davis' tune is driven by a two-note motive that hints at the title ("So What?"), moving between instruments and frequent key changes. The motive should play like a loop in your brain, reminding you to think about why your research matters, and to whom . . . potentially readers beyond the members of your research class or your thesis or dissertation committee.

Most final research documents completed by graduate students in music education (i.e., theses and dissertations) conclude with a chapter, often simply called "summary and conclusions," in which the author interprets their findings. Writing that chapter feels like the end of the project, and in many ways it is. But interpreting your findings within that chapter actually launches your communications with the profession. Subsequent publications will stem more from this chapter than from the others, because it is here that you go from summary to interpretation to conclusion.

Begin your conclusion with an abridged version of your introduction that includes purpose, purpose specifications, and the theoretical context(s) within which you placed them. Some research conventions prefer a verbatim re-statement of the problem statement; others prefer that it is re-worked. Refer to the work of previous students or check with your advisor about this if you are unsure. This section should be substantive yet succinct—more than an outline, but much less than is included in earlier chapters.

Next, describe your data gathering and analysis methods and provide an abridged review of your findings. Describe your findings in the same order in which you asked your research questions, and bring into the discussion the references that most helped you articulate the questions. Highlight similarities and differences between yours and previous findings, and conclude from such highlights how your research may have impacted the body of knowledge about music learning and teaching. Worded differently: Share with your readers how you believe your work contributes to what others in the field are thinking and writing about.

Finally, remind readers about the functions of your research in the overall scheme of the learning and teaching of music (see Chapter 1). For instance, do you interpret your findings as contributing a solution to a practical problem or to establishing "better" approaches than those generally practiced? Did you contribute to improving pedagogical "engineering," that is, tangible adaptations to instructional tools? Did you intend to illuminate further what happens in particular classrooms? Did you uncover evidence that illustrates the life or career of an influential music educator? Or, did your findings aim at re-defining music instructional contexts and point to the importance of investigating such contexts systematically?

When you address the application of your findings to extant knowledge, further distinguish between direct, practical applications and possible questions for future research. Do not overreach in such speculations; instead, couch your thinking in question format to avoid making claims you cannot support. At the same time, do not shy away from speculating about the consequences of future investigations on the subject. If appropriate, acknowledge ways to improve your own research design and method. Nearly all studies, like most performances, leave room for improvement, and recognizing this fact is the trademark of a good researcher.

General Writing Considerations

Titling your thesis or dissertation

When someone asks what your research is about, you probably wish for a short, catchy answer. That, unfortunately, does not work with original research projects because their purposes are expected to be precise and to the point. The best solution is perhaps the least creative one; that is, to let the title reflect the purpose statement as closely as possible. A common practice in dissertations and theses, it can make the title cumbersome and sometimes questionably long. If you digress from that practice, avoid claiming more in the title than what you addressed in the study; beware of exaggerations and promises your findings cannot keep.

Titles of scholarly reports tend to be declarative, descriptive, or question based (Silvey, 2021), and the best titles are both accurate and engaging. For instance, titling a study "The effect of [variable A] on [variable B]" is inaccurate when you only *observed* both variables together rather than *investigating the causality* of one on the other. The issue of accurate wording is also important in historical as well as descriptive (qualitative and quantitative), correlational and grounded theory studies. Make sure, therefore, that the methods as well as the data (facts, figures, dates, and/or verbatim quotations) in your text fully support the wording of your title.

Paying Attention to Details

Theses and dissertations are lengthy documents. This means that most readers are less knowledgeable about your topic than you are. Keep this in mind when you work on the conclusion and interpretation of your research, whether it appears first or last in your work. Tell readers exactly what you did when, and also give reasons for the conclusions you draw; otherwise, they may form different deductions and interpretations.

Remember that the same number of sentences, placed in different order, can lead to more than one interpretation. Keep this in mind for any writing task but especially when writing your final chapter. You may think you have said it all and that everyone follows your way of thinking. Consider that in the course of your research, you have come to know your topic very well. Do not assume that your readers are equally as well informed. Provide signposts to help readers connect the dots in the way you see them connected.

To avoid miscommunication, lead the reader through your thought processes from the beginning to the end of your work—even at the risk of being a bit repetitive. Only if you tell your readers what they are to take away from your work can you be sure that it is understood in the way you intended. In doing so, keep your problem statement or articulated problematic intact so that you do not claim more in the final chapter than you addressed in the body of the research. The same applies to any key definitions you used.

In several chapters throughout this book, we have referred to other elements of clear writing, and we reiterate them here. First, as noted above, be cautious about making causal inferences when you should only talk about relationships. Also be careful when using the term "significant." As you have learned, statisticians have very precise definitions for when to refer to significant and not-significant differences in linking measurements to each other, be it causally or relationally. If you do use the term in a quantitative study, be sure to draw clear distinctions between practical and statistical significance, interpreting any numbers in the context of sample size and numbers of variables. In qualitative research, avoid the term unless you have provided a definition (stipulated or operational) before making use of it. Better and more descriptive words can be easily found in the thesaurus in your word processing program.

When you have attended to the issues described above, it is time to celebrate! But it is also time to think future possibilities and consider the next steps in your spiral of inquiry. This is why we urge you to think of the final chapter of your thesis or dissertation as a springboard for further activities, such as those described in the next section. In all cases, the "so what" factor earlier highlighted should now become the driving force for such projects.

MAKING YOUR WORK ACCESSIBLE TO DIFFERENT AUDIENCES

Consider the summary chapter of an officially accepted dissertation or thesis as raw material for reaching many different audiences within the field of music education. Adjustments to title and modifications in layout will be necessary, however, if you want to bring your work to the attention of audiences beyond your thesis or dissertation committee.

Editorial boards, professional organizations, publishing houses, and/or funding agencies each have specific policies and guidelines for format of publication. Such guidelines, usually found on the publication's or publisher's website, include specific details about writing style, contents, and descriptions of methodological-technical aspects of a project; such as the target audience and other relevant information.

What follow are suggestions for preparing the content of your first research report and turning its content into material for public dissemination. Consider certain key issues when, for instance:

- proposing a paper presentation for an academic conference,
- preparing a manuscript for submission to a peer-reviewed scholarly, professional or trade journal, or book chapter,
- seeking internal or external funding, or
- proposing a professional workshop or clinic.

We present these options in the order in which they most likely occur in the career of a novice researcher. It should be noted that the procedures described here refer to high normative standards; deviations from the norm are possible.

Proposing a Paper Presentation for an Academic Conference

Presenting papers at professional conferences is an important activity for any scholar, but is especially useful for novice researchers. You get to know fellow researchers from different parts of the country (and/or world) and can discuss matters of mutual concern. Observing scholarly discourse in action can be exciting and a lot of fun, especially if you go to the same conferences on a regular basis. Most professional societies sponsor paper reading sessions whenever the society has a formal meeting, notices of which (in the form of calls for papers) are generally announced in professional journals and on the Internet.

Organizers of large conferences also include so-called poster sessions as an alternative to paper reading sessions. Rather than paper presentations, these sessions feature a selection of posters, usually displayed in a large room where interested scholars peruse them and discuss them with presenters. As a presenter, you create a large poster that visually presents key aspects of your study. The more attractive the poster, the more likely viewers will stop and want to talk about your work. Your poster may be constructed by hand, but most researchers create and then enlarge a slide from PowerPoint or a similar program or even project video. Such sessions expect presenters to provide a summary handout and/or full version of your paper (by web link or QR code) to interested colleagues if they so request.

Poster sessions and paper reading session are both important for making your work known to the profession at large. In music education, poster sessions tend not to have specified topics while "calls for papers" generally have a theme, albeit broadly worded. Such calls include the conference language(s) if it is an international meeting and may include such details as maximum length of the proposal or full paper, number of copies to be submitted, number of accepted tables or graphs, curriculum vitae of the author, and due date.

Most of the time, proposals in the form of 200–500 word abstracts are sent to the chairperson of the event, who then distributes applicants' papers on an anonymous basis for review to researchers in the field. As is the practice in most peer reviews, the referees recommend to the chairperson those proposals most appropriate because of overall purpose, specificity of questions, and methodological excellence.

The researchers whose abstracts or actual papers are deemed most worthy of presentation are invited to read the paper to the attending membership. In some instances, papers are distributed ahead of time to all participants so that more time is available for discussion. Most paper reading sessions do provide some question and answer (Q & A) time. The papers are often published— either in revised form or as presented—in proceedings of the sponsoring organization or in its journal, which provides you, the novice researcher, with an excellent (possibly first) opportunity of becoming a published author.

Even the longest research paper is shorter than an entire dissertation, but not necessarily shorter than a dissertation's summary chapter. Thus, after just having completed a one- to two-hundred page document, the challenge of reducing the information to approximately fifteen to twenty typewritten pages is formidable. It is a process, however, that teaches you to economize your writing style and organization.

Make use of your summary chapter by shortening your original research rationale and highlighting your key sources. Follow that section with the purpose/sub-purposes/questions of the study. If it is a quantitative study, describe next your methods and procedures. In a historical study, the bulk of the report should be devoted to a description of the process of data collection and verification. Reports of philosophical studies should focus on the presentation of the sequence of arguments in the complete line of argumentation. Generalizations and speculations about findings might be reserved for the Q&A session that typically follows a paper presentation.

Preparing an Article for Submission to a Peer-reviewed Journal

From the beginning of the book, we have asked you to direct your critical reading of related literature to scholarly rather than trade articles. As you may recall, the request was motivated by the fact that scholarly journals are refereed by a panel of experts whereas trade articles may not be. Furthermore, we wanted you to pay attention to methodological details that allow researchers to separate documented evidence from personal opinion and speculation. Such is not necessarily the case in trade articles, even when they are refereed, because they are often too short to contain bibliographic and procedural information. In such publications, the "so what" factor tends to matter more to readers than how you reached that point.

Most refereed journals, whether aimed at scholars or a professional/trade audience, have a webpage on which contributions are solicited. There, you commonly find a brief section outlining the steps prospective contributors should follow in preparing an article to submit for publication. These instructions normally include the maximum length of the article, specific manuscript style, placement of bibliography, graphs, tables, and figures, and the process for submitting the manuscript to the editor for consideration.

Although the advent of e-journals has made page limitations less important, always consult the publication guidelines—whether it is an e-journal or one published in print. Also pay attention to a journal's code of ethics; it spells out the prevailing policy about (1) submitting an article to several journals, (2) publishing an article that has appeared or been presented elsewhere, (3) verifying the authorship of a publication, (4) making several articles out of one primary document, (5) and verifying copyrights.

Once you have completed your manuscript and forwarded it to the editor, it enters a review process that varies from journal to journal in terms of time, rigor of review, and suggestions for revisions. First, the journal editor reviews the manuscript and decides if it meets the journal's publication guidelines. If the editor decides the manuscript does not meet the minimum criteria for publication, it will likely be immediately returned without even entering the peer review process.

Manuscripts that pass the initial screening are sent to members of the editorial board for evaluation. Normally, three or four members of the editorial board review each manuscript. Reviewers are generally instructed to return their evaluations to the editor within a reasonable period of time and to recommend whether the manuscript should be (a) accepted and published as received (a very rare occurrence!); (b) returned to the author for revision and corrections, with the opportunity to resubmit the manuscript to the review board; or (c) rejected as not suitable for the journal, perhaps with recommendations for a more appropriate publication.

Most journals provide a standard rating form for referees to use in evaluating a manuscript. The form includes such items as quality of writing style (use of appropriate grammar, correct spelling, punctuation, etc.) and clarity of writing. It is common procedure that reviewers also offer anonymous suggestions for improving the manuscript. The editor generally reserves the right to serve as the final arbiter in any dispute over a manuscript, and ultimately is responsible for the final decision to publish or reject a submitted manuscript.

Once your manuscript is accepted, it may be a while before it appears in print. Most journals publish in intervals of one to four times a year, and they are usually in the process of preparing two or more future issues for distribution. This means that even a manuscript without any revisions can experience a delay from acceptance to publication. Although the entire review process is time consuming, the peer evaluation process resembles the democratic process: It is perhaps slow and cumbersome, but preferred by many scholars over the alternative—a non-refereed process in which an editor makes all decisions single-handedly.

Regardless of the mode of inquiry or space limitations, include your rationale for the study and discuss the pivotal references that helped you in articulating your theoretical perspective and purpose. From there on, the formats of articles may differ according to mode of inquiry and research method. In quantitative research, the methods and procedures for gathering data must be described in detail and the results of the analysis should be presented in tabular form, followed by a section titled "Conclusions." Similar approaches may be true in qualitative research articles, but authors have some latitude, depending on the conventions of the methods or methodologies followed, in determining how to combine methods of data gathering with analysis and discussions of findings. Consult a variety of journal articles before settling on how to organize your material.

If the study is historical in nature, you must list the major primary sources for the investigation of all questions. When and where applicable, you should also describe procedures for the verification of your research questions. Because of the limited space available in a journal article, it is likely that you will have to limit the discussion of your findings to a small number of key questions, with a second article possibly following later. The process used to answer your research questions should be described in detail with reference to all primary evidence collected. For more information, consult Chapter 6 as well as sources listed in Recommended Reading.

For philosophical inquiry, a clear and precise statement of your thesis should precede a discussion of the form of argumentation your discourse will follow. Subsequently, the most important points in the argumentation should be summarized and adequately documented. As is the case with all other research articles, philosophical writings should make room for a conclusion section in which the points made are consistent with the purpose and specific problematic addressed in the study. For more information, consult Chapter 5 as well as sources listed in Recommended Reading.

Scholarly Articles

For scholarly articles, reviewers evaluate more than just the quality and clarity of the writing style. They also look for those elements you considered in your own assessment of literature: a logically argued rationale and research purpose; clearly defined research specifications (questions, sub-purposes or hypotheses); appropriate methods for the chosen mode of inquiry; and conclusions that address the research purpose based on the findings of the inquiry. If these points are judged by the referees to be clearly described and of interest to readers, the manuscript is usually accepted with minor revisions. But referees may not see "eye to eye" with each other on certain issues. Be prepared, therefore, to receive a variety of opinions on your work, meaning that you may have to navigate comments that appear to disagree with each other. In such a case, respond to suggested revisions as best as you can and stay in close touch with the editor about any questions or unresolved concerns.

Trade Journal Articles

Think back to the scientific elements in your research: The rationale, the questions, the related literature, the methods, and the findings/interpretations. Ask yourself which of these would be useful for practitioners in the field, as some of these sections almost certainly contain useful and rich material for colleagues teaching in the field.

You may want to start with a story that illustrates how your findings and interpretations might work in the classroom or rehearsal hall. Or perhaps to explain how what you learned from your work could impact the profession at large? Has your research led you to question previously taken-for-granted principles of instruction? Could you envision doing things differently in the future? Might you even ask your teacher-colleagues for feedback on your insights and see how they think about what you bring up as possibilities for the future?

Alternatively, take a look at your related literature section. Might some of the specific studies you reviewed be useful beyond scholarly circles? Have you encountered particular investigations that a larger audience of readers might find interesting and/or beneficial for their own work? Could you make such information relevant by simplifying wording that might sound complicated and technical in its original form?

To answer those questions, put on your "teacher hat" and think back to when you started the research process: What intimidated you? What intrigued you? Now you have an opportunity to take the intimidation factor out of research. How could you motivate others to think about research as "thinking again" or "looking again?" What, specifically, do you propose for others to think about or look at again? Can you come up with interesting ways to describe situations where you did that and, as a result, improved your own teaching skills? If so, how did you know that they had improved? Such questions and the stories around them make excellent material for general-interest articles that would be suitable for publication in a variety of refereed and non-refereed journals. Such are needed in our profession for the purpose of ongoing communication and clarification of practice.

Seeking Internal or External Funding

Even small amounts of funding can make a big difference for a research agenda. For this reason, many colleges and universities and even some school districts offer competitive research grants. Outside agencies and institutions also offer funding on a competitive basis. Grants awarded by foundations and the federal government have very strict evaluation standards and often also have predetermined funding priorities. To apply for any type of funding, you must respond to the funding agencies on their terms. Universities have offices to help you seek outside funding.

Research opportunities are often announced with what is known as a Request for Proposals (or RFP), and they can be as complete and detailed as a dissertation proposal or as brief as a single, bulleted page. To expedite the reviewers' speed of reading, however, funding proposals often request that researchers re-order the particular elements common to the scientific process. Typically, a one-page summary of the benefits of the research for the funding agencies as well as for specific target groups precedes any methodological or budgetary details. A summary of the proposed budget often follows next, sometimes coupled with a record of your previous research. A narrative description of method and design, again with budgetary specifics, goes before any detailed description of the project itself. Generally a lengthy discussion of related research is not necessary; instead you are expected to say in a few sentences or paragraphs how your research is or is not different from what is already available and known, and provide parenthetical or footnoted references that indicate your familiarity with influential related research.

A caveat: There are perhaps as many different application formats as they are funding agencies. The RFPs tell you what to do; follow them painstakingly, using their language and terminology. Make sure to obtain such forms early in the process, just as you obtained the IRB forms from your university early in your first research project.

Be aware that grant funding can actually limit your creativity. This is because both private and public agencies may call for research whose findings support a result they favor. Usually, only experienced researchers obtain those grants because it takes advanced research skills and a track record of completed projects not only to design and carry out other people's agendas but also to compete nationally and/or internationally with other researchers.

Proposing Workshops, Clinics, and Seminars

Like foundations and funding agencies, professional organizations such as NAfME, ISME, and state music education associations accept applications for presenting clinics, workshops and seminars at national or regional conferences. To apply to give a presentation during such a conference, locate the announcement for the coming event, and seek out the "Call for Proposals" on the event webpage. That will give you information about the requirements for presenting at the event, and also about any themes the event features. You might propose a workshop by yourself, but should also consider teaming up with one or two colleagues to plan a panel discussion with input from the public, take research findings and turn them into general-interest material as described earlier, or present interesting topics you encountered in your critical reading. Always thinking of yourself as the teacher you are, engage the attending public in exercises, discussions, and activities that are pertinent to the issues you examined in your original research. You may or may not refer to that research explicitly. Have handouts ready for distribution (in hard copy or electronically) in which you list a small selection of sources that are easy to obtain and easy to read. Comprehensive bibliographies should be reserved for more scholarly meetings.

CONTINUING THE RESEARCH JOURNEY

True to the spiral of inquiry, reaching different audiences with the results of your first research project may take you deeper into the "ongoingness" of research than you probably ever expected. And true to what you likely described as possible new projects within the "so what" factor embedded in your results, you have future work already outlined. We urge you to follow up on that path, beginning with a replication of your first work. That step will help you in establishing yourself as a researcher, a choice you may never have envisioned before but may find quite "doable" and even intriguing after you have learned about the new challenges inherent in becoming a music teacher-researcher.

Replicating a Study

To replicate a study is an important scientific practice, even requirement, in many fields, especially for those disciplines that rely on experimental designs in lab settings. While such studies exist also in music education, they are not as numerous as studies in natural settings. This makes replication more difficult, if not nearly impossible. However, conducting a second study based on an existing model, such as your dissertation, has great benefits and a few, albeit smaller, drawbacks.

The benefits are that you have organized, written out and described all required methods and procedures, know exactly what to do when questions arise, and have a template for the text you need to write—even if in a much more limited number of pages. The drawbacks include the following. It may be necessary to change design and procedures either because circumstances have changed or because they did not work very well in the first place. Any criticisms of design or methodology that were expressed by you in the conclusion of the original project or voiced by others should be responded to in the new study. Without the guidance of a mentor, you need to learn to become your own best critic, a role you already know well as a performer. You might also consider co-authoring your work together with your former mentor or other trusted colleagues. Who knows, some new projects as well as life-long friendships may spring up from such collaborations.

The most important drawback of replicating a study might be that the term "replication" itself can present conceptual as well as methodological challenges. Historical and philosophical questions cannot be fully replicated but, instead, need to be modified to allow for new angles to be examined. If you carry out new historical or philosophical data analyses, however, you do not replicate but produce a new study because new data lead to new questions. In both qualitative and most quantitative research, it also is quite possible that institutional contexts change too much for findings to be comparable across different school, sociocultural, or geographic settings. Once you incorporate that knowledge into your new study, you may not want to call it replication but simply indicate that you stayed close to the original study design.

Professional Aspirations as a Researcher

Whether you plan on continuing in the spiral of inquiry as suggested depends on your professional and life goals, a topic with which we began this book. Several factors generally motivate a person to engage in research: (1) Seeking a terminal graduate degree; (2) hoping to obtain financial support from institutional grants; (3) satisfying job requirements, especially if employed by institutions of higher education (the so-called "publish-or-perish" syndrome); (4) taking pleasure in being professionally visible and recognized by one's peers; and (5) simply enjoying the research process itself.

A word about the "publish-or-perish" syndrome: If you are motivated to do research for any of the other reasons mentioned above, chances are that you do not feel pushed to publish, but that you want to publish because you would like for your voice to be heard. The study of the learning and teaching of music reaches into so many research avenues that finding a niche in the vastness of the field should not be too difficult.

Rainbow and Froehlich (1987) stated in their *Coda* to the 1987 edition:

> There is some hidden benefit for all who undertake the study of music. Likewise, there is hidden benefit for all who study the research process. This benefit begins with the discovery of skepticism as a positive force in the search for truth. That skepticism, if applied to one's own work, leads to self-criticism, an important ingredient in the search for quality. Finally, skepticism and self-criticism can also cause one to seek solutions to some of the problems [and challenges] observed in one's work and environment. Although such an attitude is the essence of research, it must not be confined to those who actually conduct research. Instead, that attitude should be applied to musical performance, the writing of music, or the teaching of music to learners of any age group. To conclude, and at the risk of being repetitive: Being inquisitive, self-critical, and seeking solutions to perceived problems are traits needed in all music educators who search for quality in their work as musician-performers, teachers, and researchers.
>
> (p. 282)

We concur that research is an attitude rather than an obligation, a process rather than a product. Once you have taken to that process, ongoing curiosity and a spirit of critically examining accepted truths will become second nature. Sharing the results of those attitudinal characteristics will then guide you in all further steps that lie ahead.

CHAPTER SUMMARY

1) Sharing your research findings and new insights with the profession should be considered integral to the research process itself.
2) In theses and dissertations, that sharing happens in the form of an interpretative summary and conclusion chapter that, dependent on the mode and methods used in your work, is likely to appear first or last in your original research document.
3) Interpreting your findings means presenting them in light of the literature that helped you formulate your research question and rationale.
4) Be careful about using terminology that suggests causality between observed events and/or actions when your study was about description rather than causality.
5) Let the summary and conclusion chapter become the "raw material" for subsequent work: Replications and extensions of the original research, poster and paper presentations, scholarly and general interest articles, grant proposals, general workshops, and conference sessions.
6) Let an attitude of ongoing curiosity and a spirit of critically examining accepted truths become second nature in everything you undertake as a musician, teacher, and/or researcher.

Recommended Reading

Belcher, W. L. (2019). *Writing your journal article in twelve weeks: A guide to academic publishing success* (2nd ed.). University of Chicago Press.

Locke, L. F., Lawrence, R., Spirduso, W. W., & Silverman, S. J. (2013). *Proposals that work: A guide for planning dissertation and grant proposals* (6th ed.). Sage.

Rankin, J. G. (2020). *Increasing the impact of your research: A practical guide to sharing your findings and widening your reach*. Routledge.

Walker, B. L. E., & Unruh, H. E. (2018). *Funding your research in the humanities and social sciences: A practical guide to grant and fellowship proposals*. Routledge.

REFERENCES

American Psychological Association. (2020). *Publication manual of the American Psychological Association* (7th ed.). American Psychological Association. https://doi.org/10.1037/0000165-000

Jorgensen, E. R. (2014). Values and philosophizing about music education. *Philosophy of Music Education Review, 22*(1), 5–21. www.proquest.com/docview/1529044826/abstract/1035B892331F4731PQ/2

Rainbow, E. L., & Froehlich, H. C. (1987). *Research in music education: An introduction to systematic inquiry*. Schirmer Books.

Russell, J. A. (2018). *Statistics in music education research*. Oxford University Press.

Silvey, B. A. (2021). Comments from the editor: The effects of bourbon drinking on creating manuscript titles. *Update: Applications of Research in Music Education, 39*(2), 3–4. https://doi.org/10.1177/8755123320985086

Recapitulation

Placing Your Research Experience in the Bigger Picture

THE JOURNEY SO FAR

Think about the journey so far: You began the research journey as a virtual visitor to Times Square. Illustrated in part by what peers in a fictionalized research class experienced, the steps involved in your inquiry then spiraled into reading, observations of many kinds, and ongoing reflection into specific projects, which most likely continue at varying levels of specificity. Regardless of where you stand right now in terms of completing your envisioned project, you already know much more about what it takes to use available information as a springboard for future actions. You also may have learned that it is not always easy to ask questions or, more importantly, to address them comprehensively. In fact, your journey most likely generated more questions than it answered.

You also encountered situations in which answers were not always right/wrong, yes/no, either/or; instead, they lay in the gray area of "maybe." They emphasized uncertainty over certainty and ambiguity over a sense of clarity. What started as a "fact," became instead a "construct" subject to revision based on newly found evidence. As such, you discovered that experts do not know everything and that even the best-informed person can be wrong.

In the *Preface* to this edition we stated our task for this book to be threefold: (1) expand what we mean by music education and by research, (2) help you find your niche in that definition, and (3) teach tangible research skills that are useful for musicians, music educators, community musicians and others with diverse instructional goals and career aspirations. You alone can determine the extent to which those goals fulfilled your own expectations. Whatever your response, we hope that as a result of using this textbook, you have begun to place your own personal experiences with research into the larger frame of music education as a field of study.

It was our intention that this book would take you from your own research project to the larger picture of inquisitiveness as a state of mind, asking you to think about, engage in, and work with:

- modes of inquiry and worldviews as important contributors to how you generate and evaluate knowledge, and
- means by which to find evidence in the support of producing new knowledge or examining old truths.

We see these two bullets related to each other as illustrated in Figure 16.1.

DOI: 10.4324/9781003057703-19

RESEARCH FORMS

Experimental	Descriptive	Interpretive	Speculative
Cause-Effect Studies			
Quasi- Experimental			
Non-Experimental	Case Studies	Grounded Theory_____	
Relational Studies	Clinical Research	Life History	Narratives
Casual-comparative &		Ethnobiography	Critical-Ethnobiography
Descriptive-comparitive Studies		Oral History	
			Text & Document Analysis
			(Hermeneutics)
			Interpretivism
			Phenomenology
	Action Research_____		
			Artifact Analysis
			Conversational Analysis

From ABSOLUTISM	TO	RELATIVISM
Absolutism	Empiricism	Existensialism
Formalism	Modernism	Postmodernism
Idealism	Pragmatism	Relativism
Materialism		
Modernism		
Naturalism		
Rationalism		

FIGURE 16.1 Connections Between Research Forms and Worldviews

As you select your research methods in response to your research purpose, you inevitably place yourself somewhere within that illustration. Be sure it is where you want to be philosophically as well as methodologically. The choices you make have ramifications for what is to follow; that is, how your research agenda weaves through your life's work. You may compare this process to taking up a particular instrument early in life and staying with that choice throughout your life, thereby perfecting the art and craft of performing on that one instrument. There are also those among us who have learned to play many different instruments (hardly any music educator can do without those experiences).

You may similarly opt to test the research waters by asking questions that are philosophically far apart from each other, situated in different modes of inquiry, and requiring a variety of methods and research tools. Whichever choices you make, avoid favoring one approach over any other simply because one method seems easier than another. Do not let methodologies be the "tail that wags the [research] dog."

If you choose not to generate new research but wish to continue to evaluate current literature pertinent to your own area of interest, it is similarly important to make a connection between modes of inquiry and belief systems. Such insights provide you with an important tool for critically examining the choices made by researchers as well as teachers. Understanding the reasons behind such choices makes it easier to determine how a particular study actually contributes to the body of knowledge as a whole.

MODES OF INQUIRY AND WORLDVIEWS AS FORCES FOR GENERATING KNOWLEDGE

In the course of reading this text, you learned that physical observations alone do not create knowledge. Instead, the power of reasoning puts into context that which has been observed. With your ability to differentiate between reasoned logic and common sense, avoid relying on just one source of knowledge. Rather, examine as many sources as possible, weighing one against another.

Why and how we search for knowledge through different forms of evidence depends on our beliefs about what constitutes perceived and factual reality. If you believe, for instance, that right and wrong are relative to context and therefore not necessarily absolute values even in classroom management issues, you are not likely to begin a study with an inflexible set of observational variables. Conversely, if you believe that the purpose of education is to instill in all young people absolute values of socially accepted "rights and wrongs," you might wish to study the extent to which one set of rules was observable in many classrooms across several school districts. The two beliefs might yield very different research questions and, thus, modes and methods of inquiry concerning classroom management.

Clearly, it is not easy to pinpoint exactly how or what one thinks. Understanding theoretical definitions of different worldviews tends to be easier than figuring out where one stands on particular issues and how consistent one is in applying them—to everyday living, to professional life, or to research. An absolutist in ethical questions of right and wrong may be a relativist when it comes to choosing repertoire for a particular group of students. Professing the unalienable right of students for self-expression does not fit easily with formalism and functionalism when it comes to the disciplinary authority of the teacher. The difficulty lies in navigating between who you are in your private role as person and who you are in your public role as musician-educator.

A similar duality of roles might occur when you make research decisions. From the viewpoint of the practitioner-teacher you are or wish to become, you might want to generate knowledge that is immediately applicable to your own instructional actions. From the vantage point of commencing a research career, however, following a sequential path of planning for a battery of studies within the descriptive-relational-causal loop may be a more promising option. Or, as the practically minded person you are, you may want to be seen as an educational "engineer" who devises technological improvements for sight-reading software rather than testing hypotheses about musical taste.

The above examples suggest that decisions about what questions to ask, which methods to employ, and how to design a study can generate markedly different pieces of information in the puzzle called the body of knowledge of music education. Which pieces you contribute as a researcher may also lead to different career paths. Questions, methods, and designs within the purview of funding agencies and institutional research agendas lead to different opportunities than the active pursuit of research interests outside those typically funded or supported by interested agencies.

KNOWLEDGE, TRUTH, AND EVIDENCE IN THE RESEARCH PROCESS

Ongoing and systematic inquisitiveness leads to what one group of scholars calls truth, another knowledge, and yet another evidence. For the most part, we have used the term evidence, but distinguished between overtly discernible patterns of actions, behaviors and thought and covert, intuitive feelings and sensations. Whatever word you use, any evidence is always time-bound, thus requiring renewed examination.

Both overt actions and covert sensations are subject to change because the knowledge base that triggers those actions and sensations gets altered. Rapid advances in science and technology affirm, question, or advance accepted laws, paradigms, and theories on an ongoing basis. Research in the humanities, music education included, may be slower, that is, seemingly less "speedy" and subject to change. Especially the arts seem to rely on time-tested and long accepted practices to a much larger degree than appears to be the norm in the sciences.

However, thanks to advances in the fields of psychology, education, sociology, anthropology, and many other social and applied sciences, improvements in music pedagogies of many kinds continue to be researched and recommended by scholars in music, education, and music education. Although such improvements might make you feel confident about the validity of current instructional approaches, an inquiring and critical mind remains vigilant about new thoughts, ideas, discoveries, and insights. What seems true and agreed-upon practice today might change tomorrow.

The best way to determine which laws, paradigms, and theories require scrutiny by means of testing and ongoing examination is to remain engaged as a researcher. Continuously probing deeper by means of the spiral of inquiry allows you to stay abreast not only of the ever changing (if not growing) body of knowledge about music, education, and music education but also of latest research methods, procedures, and designs that generate new insights into what music education practices are or should be.

This book, then, can be summed up as follows:

1) Through inquisitiveness an area of interest develops. Efforts at finding answers to specific questions result in connections to a field of study in which knowledge is accumulated. Through the process of challenging and testing the answers to any given question, knowledge in the form of facts and beliefs are obtained. The more observations confirm either one of the forms of knowledge, the greater the certainty of its validity. Although both may, over time, undergo change, they are the working body of knowledge in the field of study on which all its operations are based.

2) No single answer gives the full truth. Any one answer to a question serves not so much the purpose of "knowing something once and for all" but of stimulating additional questioning. What matters is becoming engaged in continuously searching for more complete answers to the questions that are already out there or waiting to be asked.

3) There is no guarantee that either accepted facts or beliefs remain the same over time. New technologies and investigative methodologies, different perspectives and new information from external fields, may contribute to a reevaluation of once-held convictions. One task of a researcher is to determine what evidence is outdated and which continues to stand scholarly scrutiny.

4) Methods of seeking evidence by means of logic, observation, and/or experimentation are all valid approaches in the search for answers to specific questions. However, the method employed in seeking to establish facts as truth carries with it inherent limitations that must be acknowledged in the evaluation of such facts.

5) Because sole reliance on any one source of evidence may put blinders on one's inquiry, the most convincing research projects may be those that use multiple sources of evidence, thereby examining a question from many angles.

6)   An obstacle to the spirit of any form of inquiry may be one's own limitations, not only in terms of time and other resources, but also in separating what one would like to be true from what well-researched evidence suggests as being true.

MOVING FORWARD WITH THE SPIRAL OF INQUIRY

The above six points may serve you well not only in your research endeavors but in whatever else you may choose to do professionally. To that end, we distill the following possibilities for moving forward with the spiral of inquiry: (1) the skeptic, (2) the technology expert, (3) the experimenter/entrepreneur, and (4) the hands-on researcher. The order follows what we believe to be the most likely sequence within which you can take on any or all of those roles.

The Skeptic

To be a skeptic means to be informed and to understand the nature of the sources from which you get your information. Accessing professional publications (both scholarly and trade-orientated) on the web or in hard copy, therefore, would be an important first step. Make a point of not only reading what is of immediate interest to you but also looking at information from outside your own area of expertise. Even if you do not have time to read a journal from cover to cover, get a sense of the issue as a whole. This applies also to articles you may at first find difficult to understand: Do not reject them right away. The more you read, the easier it is to understand even seemingly convoluted sentences. On the basis of such reading, you may wish to engage your colleagues in conversations about pedagogical issues that concern you, and to participate in conversations similarly instigated by others.

Examine what you read and hear from as many angles as you can. Weigh common sense against possible counter-arguments and be open to the gray areas of "maybe." Accept that there are always two sides to an issue and that any seeming solution to a problem has another side to it—the side effect not always counted on. Keep track of such observations: Put them into words, write them down, and share them.

Invite colleagues to observe you, preferably after suggesting specifics you want them to focus on. Ask them whether you may also learn from them by observing their work. Spend time talking about issues of concern and do not be afraid of constructive criticism. It is hard to receive at first, but you will soon discover the benefits of being open to peer comments that are not intended to judge, but to expand professional knowledge.

The (Technology) Expert

You alone know what type of technologies and teaching methodologies your workplace sanctions, has available, endorses and encourages. Keep abreast of what is "out there," ready to use by those who can afford it. Consider writing research grants that require the use of such new developments.

If you believe you are technologically challenged, find someone who can teach you or guide you in finding out where to go or whom to contact. Begin small by asking for inexpensive items first, similar to how you may have gone to your local music merchants to obtain instruments for rent or discounted sheet music. But this time, do the asking in writing, adhering as much as possible to the guidelines for grant proposal as previously described (Chapter 14). Keep the proposal short but be sure it contains all necessary, scientific components.

Find a way to turn what you have started in partial fulfillment of your research class into a project that benefits your long-term work. Reflect on long-held beliefs and practiced methods or look for new tools (electronic or mechanical) that would make your ideas concrete. Find ways by which to share your ideas with colleagues that might be receptive to your ideas. Ask for feedback and constructive criticism. Consider preparing a general-interest article for a state or national journal that describes your ideas, especially when you have begun examining them historically, empirically, or philosophically.

The Experimenter/Entrepreneur

Without worrying too much about upholding proper research protocols, engage in some action research by which you assess pros and cons of particular instructional methods you favor, technological learning devices you use, or both. Video record and take notes about what you observe about yourself and your students, and identify questions that you think are worth pursuing further. Begin looking at pertinent literature as described earlier as the starting point of the research spiral. Consider what you might be able to do to identify specific research topics and questions.

Ponder the possibility of turning the action research into a well-designed study by engaging a colleague to help you collect data. Plan a visit to your local university to discuss your thoughts with the music education faculty there. They very likely stand ready to help you with the overall approach, appropriate research protocol, and—possibly—with locating grant opportunities. The faculty might refer you to design experts or even get personally involved. Cooperation between universities and schools continues to be a much-needed component in nearly all research agendas typical of music education as a field of study.

The Hands-on Researcher

It certainly is difficult to combine the many duties of a full-time music educator with those of a *bona fide* researcher. But it can and has been done and that is why it is included here. Admittedly, however, it seems there should be little to say at this point because one purpose of the book was to lead you down this very path. We therefore hope that following the steps described in the book will guide you from here on, always keeping in mind the context of your own realities, and we wish you well in your efforts.

When all is said and done, a researcher's mind should be more than a grant-producing fact seeker or technological expert. Instead, the research mindset should be seen as an attitude that goes beyond music education and applies to life in general. As the first edition was being completed, an article written by Isaacson, biographer of the late Steve Jobs appeared in the *New York Times Sunday Review* (October 30, 2011). In it, Isaacson stated better than we could have what seems to be at stake: " . . . the world of invention and innovation . . . means combining an appreciation of the humanities with an understanding of science—connecting artistry to technology, poetry to processors" (Isaacson, 2011, pp. 1 & 8).

Being at home with both scientific and imaginative thinking, and feeling comfortable with the language of the humanities and the language spoken in the sciences, may be a requisite for understanding what lies ahead not only for music education but also for music and education as discrete fields. Such understanding requires what Isaacson called "experiential wisdom" coupled with analytic rigor (p. 8).

The field of music education demands both qualities of us—whether we teach small children, older adults, facilitate learning in unconventional settings, or conduct band, choirs, orchestras, or folk- and other popular music ensembles. A well-developed research mind adjusts to change, understands the need to do so, and looks at the world with a sense of curiosity, imagination, and excitement. Much is to be discovered; much remains to be done.

REFERENCE

Isaacson, W. (2011). The genius of Jobs: Steve Job's biographer reflects. *The New York Times Sunday Review*, October 30, p. 1 & 8.

Working out a Course or Project Timeline

Research as Coursework

- Determine the instructor's goals in the context of the course.
- Consider commitments during the semester that might keep you from making progress; discuss with instructor early in term.
- Look over the syllabus for assignments. Plot them on a calendar. These may include:
  - Proposal requirements and due date.
  - IRB submission, if separate.
  - Other permissions (i.e., school district, etc.) if required.
  - Comprehensive exam, if related to final project.
  - First and subsequent drafts.
  - Copyright permissions, if applicable.
  - "Fair copy" (the copy you defend).
  - Scheduling of defense.
  - Final copy.
- A term project for a research course takes the full term. The project begins with the first assignment. Keep track of your work. Consider keeping a journal.
- Stay in touch with your instructor about steps you are taking and thoughts that move you forward.
- Work ahead with reading and drafts.

Research for Thesis or Dissertation

- Remember that everything takes longer than expected. Consider allowing yourself an extra term.
- Begin with the endpoint: Find out your institution's requirements for the submission of final project materials in relation to a realistic graduation date. These requirements may include:
  - Proposal requirements and due date.
  - IRB submission, if separate.
  - Other permissions (i.e., school district, etc.) if required.
  - Comprehensive exam, if related to final project.
  - First and subsequent drafts.
  - Copyright permissions, if applicable.
  - Schedule for final defense.
  - "Fair copy" (the copy you defend).
  - Article submission, if required.
  - Defend thesis or dissertation.
  - Prepare and submit final copy.
- Look into obligations you have outside of thesis/dissertation work.
- Build in time for your advisor and committee to respond to drafts.
- Communicate with your advisor and committee about their availability during the process of completing the work.
- Take a hard look at the calendar. Consider monthly, weekly, and daily installments for your work, including at least 2–3 hours' writing time every day. If you do not have that kind of time, lengthen the time allotted to the project.
- Schedule ongoing (i.e., weekly) consultation with your advisor.
- Plot your tasks on a calendar and hang it by your desk. Checking them off will give you a sense of accomplishment!

APPENDIX B

Selected "Isms" as found by Rainbow & Froehlich, 1987

Sources

AHDEL: The American Heritage Dictionary of the English Language. (1970)
Angeles: Angeles, P. A. (1981). Dictionary of Philosophy.
Flew: Flew, A. (1984). A Dictionary of Philosophy (rev. 2nd ed.).

Absolutism

AHDEL
1) A political form of state in which all power is vested in the monarch and his advisers.
2) The political theory reflecting this form.

Angeles:
1) Truth (value, reality) is viewed to be objectively real, final, and eternal.
2) Only one unchanging and correct explanation of reality exists.
3) Political theory: Unquestionable allegiance to a ruler or ruling class in a political system.

Flew:
1) Politically, exercise of unrestricted power.
2) Philosophically, juxtaposed to *relativism*.

Relativism

AHDEL
Truth is viewed to be relative to the individual and to the time or place in which he or she acts.

Angeles:
Re: value theory. Values differ from society to society, person to person, are not universally applicable at all times or in all places, are correct or incorrect only relative to their conformity with accepted norms or values; opposite to *absolutism*. (Re: protagorean). Relativity of knowledge and the *relativity of sense perception* . . .

Flew:
Variety of meanings:
1) The social environment is considered important in the determination of beliefs of what is and what ought to be.
2) Because of the diversity of social environments, there are no universal standards of good and bad, right and wrong.
3) Relativism regarding factual knowledge: the belief that there is objective knowledge of realities independent of the knower.

Existentialism

AHDEL:
A body of ethical thought, current in the 19th and 20th centuries, centering around the uniqueness and isolation of individual experience in a universe indifferent or even hostile to man, regarding human existence as unexplainable, and emphasizing man's freedom of choice and responsibility for the consequences of his acts.

Angeles:
As a modern philosophical view incepted by Søren Kirkegaard and Friedrich Nietzsche (historical roots of the view go back to the Greeks and medieval philosophy). Selected points: *existence* precedes *essence*. . . . Truth is subjectivity. The reality of individual existence cannot be communicated by abstractions. Individuals have complete freedom of the will and can become completely other than what they are. "The universe has no direction or scheme. It is meaningless and absurd."

Flew:
Not a dogma or system of thought but a philosophical attitude. Its origins: Attributed to Kierkegaard, . . . View opposite to rationalism and empiricism. There are no natural laws that govern all beings. Reason is not necessarily the power that guides human activity . . .

Rationalism

AHDEL:
The exercise of reason, rather than the acceptance of empiricism, authority, or spiritual revelation, provides the basis for action or belief. Reason is the prime source of knowledge and of spiritual truth.

Angeles:
Reason is the primary source of knowledge and independent of sense perception. Some points:
1) By abstract reasoning (thinking), fundamental truths can be obtained.
2) Reality is knowable and knowledge is independent of observation and experience (empirical methods).
3) Some truths about reality are known prior to any experience.
4) The principal origin of knowledge is reason, and science is basically a result of that reasoning.
5) "Truth is not tested by sense-verification procedures, but by such criteria as logical consistency."
6) Rational method can be applied to any subject matter whatsoever and can provide adequate explanations.
7) "Absolute certainty about things is the ideal of knowledge."

Flew:
1) The doctrines of philosophers like Descartes, Spinoza, and Leibniz. Some characteristics: (a) Reason alone can provide knowledge of what exists; (b) knowledge forms a single (deductive) system; and (c) everything can be brought under a single system of knowledge.
2) Term refers to those philosophers who accept only (b) and (c).
3) Religious belief is rejected as being without rational foundation. A commitment to reason means opposition to faith, prejudice, habit or any other source of conviction that is considered irrational.

Empiricism

AHDEL:
1) Experience, especially of the senses, is the only source of knowledge.
2) (a) The employment of empirical methods, as in an art or science. (b) An empirical conclusion.
3) The practice of medicine without scientific knowledge.

Angeles:
1) Ideas are abstractions formed by "compounding (combining, recombining) what is experienced (observed, immediately given in sensation)."
2) Experience is the sole source of knowledge.
3) Knowledge is dependent on sense data and directly derived or indirectly inferred from the sense data. . . .
4) Reason cannot be the sole source of knowledge of reality. Reference to sense experience and the use of the sense organs are necessary in the use of reason. . . .

Flew:
All knowledge or "at least all knowledge of matters of fact as distinct from that of purely logical relations between concepts is based on experience." Empiricism has taken several forms "but one common feature has been the tendency to start from experimental sciences, as a kind of prototype or paradigm case of human knowledge." Should be contrasted to rationalism which assigned a similar role to mathematics. . . .

Idealism

AHDEL:
1) The action of envisioning things in an ideal form.
2) Pursuit of one's ideals.
3) An idealizing treatment of subject in literature or art.
4) The theory that the object of external perception, in itself or as perceived, consists of ideas. . . .

Angeles:
(Also referred to as mentalism or immaterialism.)
1) "The universe is an embodiment of a mind.
2) Reality is dependent for its existence upon a mind and its activities."
3) Reality is mental (spiritual, psychical) matter. . . .
4) Knowledge exists only in the form of mental states and processes. Reality expresses itself as ideas and thoughts. The external world is not physical. (Angeles continues with a discussion of idealism in various forms.)

Flew:
A group of philosophical theories with the common view that "the external world" is created by the mind. "Idealism does not quarrel with the plain man's view that material things exist; rather, it disagrees with the analysis of a material thing that many philosophers have offered, according to which the material world is wholly independent of minds." Three principal types of idealism are acknowledged: *Berkeleian idealism*, *transcendental idealism*, and *objective idealism* (may also be called *absolute idealism*). . . .

Formalism

AHDEL:
"Rigorous or excessive adherence to recognized forms. The mathematical or logical structure of a scientific argument, especially as distinguished from its content."

Angeles:
"Any system that stresses form (principles, rules, laws) as the significant or ultimate ground of explanation or evaluation."

Flew:
1) (mathematics). A view pioneered by D. Hilbert: the only foundation necessary for mathematics is its formalization and the proof that the system produced is consistent.

Pragmatism

AHDEL:
1) *Philosophy*. "The theory, developed by Charles S. Peirce and William James, that the meaning of a proposition or course of action lies in its observable consequences, and that the sum of these consequences constitutes its meaning.
2) A method or tendency in the conduct of political affairs characterized by the rejection of theory and precedent, and by the use of practical means and expedients."

Angeles:
1) "Knowledge is derived from experience, experimental methods, and practical efforts."
2) "Knowledge must be used to solve the problems of everyday, practical affairs . . . and thinking must relate to practice and action."
3) The truth and meaning of ideas are asserted by their consequences.
4) "Truth is that which has practical value in our experience of life."
5) Truth changes and is tentative.

Flew:
"A label for a doctrine about meaning first made a philosophical term in 1878 by C. S. Peirce."

Naturalism

AHDEL:
1) Conformity to nature; factual or realistic representation, especially in art and literature.
2) *Philosophy*. The system of thought holding that all phenomena can be explained in terms of natural causes and laws, without attributing moral, spiritual, or supernatural significance to them.
3) *Theology*. The doctrine that all religious truths are derived from nature and natural causes and not from revelation.
4) Conduct or thought prompted by natural desires or instincts.

Angeles:
1) *Monistic:* Nature is the only reality.
2) *Antisupernaturalistic:* "All phenomena can be explained in terms of the inherent interrelationships of natural events. . . ."
3) *Proscientific:* (a) Natural phenomena can be explained by the methodology of the sciences, assuming the methodologies improve.
4) *Humanistic:* "Humans are one of the many (natural) manifestations of the universe . . ." [It follows naturalism (critical, ethical).]

Flew:
1) What is studied by the non-human and human sciences is all there is. There is no need for finding explanations for things outside the Universe. . . .
2) (in philosophical ethics), since G. E. Moore, the view "that value words are definable in terms of neutral statements of fact. . . ."

Materialism

AHDEL:
1) The opinion "that physical matter in its movements and modifications is the only reality." Thought, feeling, mind, and will is explainable by physical law. . . .
2) Physical well-being and worldly possessions constitute the greatest good and highest value in life.
3) Undue regard for worldly concerns. . . .

Angeles:
1) Nothing but matter in motion exists. "Mind is caused by material changes . . . and is completely dependent upon matter."
2) Purpose, awareness, intention, goals, meaning, direction, intelligence, willing, and striving are not characteristic of matter and the universe.
3) Nonmaterial entities such as spirits, ghosts, demons, angels do not exist. Consequently, there is no God or nothing supernatural in the universe. . . .
7) "Matter can be neither created nor destroyed.
8) No life, no mind, is immortal. . . .
11) Values do not exist in the universe independently of the activities of humans." [This definition is followed by definitions for: materialism (dialectical—Marx, Engels, mechanistic, reductive)]

Flew:
What exists is "either matter or entirely dependent on matter for its existence. The precise meaning and status of this doctrine are, however, far from clear."

John Curwen Observes Sarah Glover Teaching Music

Note. In Dickinson, P. (Ed.). (2010). *Bernarr Rainbow on music: Memoirs and selected writings*, pp. 134–136. The Boydell Press. Re-printed with permission by the Chair of the Trustees of the Rainbow Dickinson Trust.

A VISIT TO MISS GLOVER'S SCHOOL

John Curwen's own account published in the *Independent Magazine*, 1842, p. 240

This is an infant school at Norwich. It does not differ in its general aspect and arrangements from other infant schools. The daily employments of the children, their average age, and their appearance, correspond with what may be seen in most schools of a similar kind. But in one thing they are remarkably distinguished from all other schools that we have ever seen. These little children conduct their singing exercises with so much facility and delight, and, at the same time, with such accuracy both of time and tune, as to fill with astonishment all who hear them. Our readers will readily believe that this must be the case, when we tell them that, in the course of our visit, we heard the children sing canons in four, six and even in the eight parts, with great precision and beauty of execution. This was done from notes, without any instrument to lead them, and only in one case did the voices flatten, and in that case only by half-a-tone. To those who have been accustomed to the singing of young children, this will appear indeed astonishing, but we shall astonish them still more when we say, that the training which has produced such results does not occupy more than two hours in the week!—a length of time not greater than is given to singing exercises in every infant school in the land! Whence, then, arises the difference? From this cause—that, while in other schools, the time is loosely spent without plan or design, in Miss Glover's school the time is husbanded by a carefully arranged method. But this is not sufficient to explain all: it is necessary to add, that the method itself contains *more of true science*; and *less of technicality*; than any other method taught in England.

We will first describe the system as we saw it in operation, and then examine briefly its principles.

As we entered the room, the soft and regulated tone, and the sweet blending of the voices, such as to take not the ear by force, but steal on the senses as by some magic spell, assured us that music, real music, with all its subduing power, dwelt there.

On the gallery were seated all the younger children, with heads erect and shoulders back, singing (with the Sol-fa syllables), and as they sung, eagerly looking towards an upright board which stood at a little distance from the letters foot of the gallery. On this board were printed one above the other the initial letters of the Sol-fa syllables, showing much shorter distances between *Me* and *Fah* and between *Tè* and *Do* (the third and fourth, and seventh and eighth *of the scale*; for in this method *Do* is always the key-tone) than between the other notes. This *Musical Ladder*, as it is styled, corresponds with what we call the Modulator. By the side of the 'Ladder' stood a little monitor with a wand in her hand. She was pointing to the notes as the children sang them. The very movement of her wand was musical. She also held in charge with her other hand, a little infant, the youngest in the school, who could scarcely stand, but who nevertheless could sing. The children are taught to sing in this way, looking at the exact intervals as depicted on the Musical Ladder, until they enter the higher class of the school. This may be in the course of the six months, or in a much shorter time. We did not observe any distinct classification for the singing lessons; they are taken as part of the ordinary routine of the school. The children are thus rendered perfectly familiar with *an accurate pictorial representation of interval*; indeed they must carry a musical ladder in their mind's eye wherever they go; and by the correct association of mind thus established, they are well prepared for the next stage in their advancement.

This we had an opportunity of examining in another part of the room, where stood a class of twenty—the elder children in the school—having in their left hand the 'Sol-fa Tune Book', and in their right, short wands for the purpose of beating time.

The tune books were supported on a small instrument in the shape of a cross, with the longest bar extending beyond the book to the right-hand. Upon this projecting part of the 'book-holder,' as soon as the tune began, the loud beats of the measure were pretty sharply struck, while the soft beats were indicated by gentle touches of the wand on their left arm.

Miss Glover, the lady from whose invention and zealous patronage all these results have sprung, and whose Christian solicitude for the better interests of the children thus taught we have been thankful to witness, with a courtesy which we cannot too gratefully acknowledge, kindly exhibited to us every part of the method. The plan of procedure was in this wise: Supposing them about to sing the 14th canon, which is in eight parts, the teacher steps into the middle of the circle and announces 'fourteenth canon.' Immediately eight children hold up their wands, dividing the class into equal portions, so that each child may know which leader she is to follow. The chord of the keytone is then struck on a glass harmonicon, which is placed in the room for the purpose, and the canon begins. When the first division has sung the first measure, the monitor of the next division, giving a glance at those under her, which means 'follow me,' takes up the strain, beating time upon the book-holder and her arm. The rest of the division marked the time by *touching* with their wands the accent marks in their books. Thus round the class the growing harmony proceeds, until it swells out in the fullest chorus. Turning round we observed that the children on the gallery, by the help of a monitor and the musical ladder, were joining in the melody. Several pieces with words were also sung very beautifully, and on the following day Miss Glover very kindly exhibited to us, with a select class, her method of teaching the minor scale, and the manner in which the more advanced children were introduced, by easy steps, to the correct use of the old notation.

Sample Template for Organizing Coded Qualitative Data and Files

Date	File	Line	Speaker	Code	Talk
4–4–01	Glenwood 4–4–01	48–48	Anthony	MTR	I can't run a holiday concert in my current situation because 1) I can't insist that teachers do it, and 2) there's not enough room for everyone in the auditorium. But individual teachers or grade levels often do special programs.
4–4–01	Glenwood 4–4–11	50–54	OC	MTR	Anthony believes his current art and music teachers are "pretty neat people," especially his art teacher who does after school activities in the hallways and has a lot of student art work posted all over the school. These teachers are known as "specials" or "special area teachers."
4–4–01	Glenwood 4–4–11	55–57	Anthony	MTR	I like to, you know, go into the class when Tom is playing his guitar and join in, to give a positive feeling. I'm happy to see kids enjoying music.
11–30–01	Marcia 11–30–01	114–117	OC	MTR	I asked Marcia how she responded to a teacher who came into the room demanding a student. She said she "wouldn't tolerate it." I asked her what about teachers using music as a carrot—in other words keeping students out of music class as a punishment. I was very surprised when she said she would support teachers who did that.
10–16–01	Mike 10–16–01	31–32	OC	MTR	The music supervisor mentioned that "academic teachers" [his term] were "coverage teachers" (by grade and/or subject) and that their buildings would pay for subs when they went out for in-service training.

| 5–31–01 | Rob 5–31–01 | 2–8 | Rob | MTR | Sometimes they have grade level meetings um I'm not included in them. And—I get along with everybody around here. But—so I don't take it personally. It's just that we tend not to be included. And whenever we have been included . . . see, what they do, in here, is that they put together the music teachers, the art teachers, and the gym teachers, and we all sit together and say "what are we doing here" and we write down some issues that nobody reads. You know . . . and that's not right. |

Choices in Statistical Tests for Parametric and Non-Parametric Data

Comparisons are drawn from Table 37.1, "Choosing a statistical test" (graphpad.com/support/faqid/1790/), from Chapter 37 of Motulsky, H. (1995). *Intuitive biostatistics*. New York: Oxford University Press. See also Miksza & Elpus (2018, p. 276); and Russell (2018).

Note: **Bolded concepts and tests** are discussed in Chapters 10–12.

What your study is about	PARAMETRIC Measurement	NONPARAMETRIC Rank, Score, or Measurement
Describe one group	Mean, SD	Median
Quantify relationship between two variables	Pearson correlation (*r*)	Spearman correlation (*rs*)
Compare one group to a hypothetical value	One-sample *t* test	Wilcoxon test
Compare two unpaired groups	Unpaired (Independent samples) *t* test	Mann-Whitney test
Compare two paired groups	Paired (Dependent samples) *t* test	Wilcoxon test
Compare three or more unmatched groups	One-way *ANOVA*	Kruskal-Wallis test
Compare three or more matched groups	Repeated-measures ANOVA	Friedman test

About the Authors

Carol Frierson-Campbell teaches undergraduate and graduate methods courses in instrumental music education and research and coordinates the music education program at William Paterson University. Her scholarly interests include music education in marginalized communities, instrumental music education, and research pedagogy. In addition to co-authoring the second edition of this textbook, she recently served as lead editor for the volume *Sociological Thinking in Music Education: International Intersections* (Oxford University Press, 2022). Other projects include the edited 2-volume *Teaching Music in the Urban Classroom* (Rowman and Littlefield, 2006), and articles in *Action, Criticism, and Theory for Music Education*, *Music Education Research* and *Arts Education Policy Review*. During the 2015–2016 school year she served as Scholar in Residence at the Edward Said National Conservatory of Music in the occupied Palestinian Territories. Dr. F-C (as her students know her) also directs the WPU Music Fellows in partnership with the Paterson Music Project, providing music enrichment for children in Paterson, New Jersey.

Throughout her 20-year tenure at the University of North Texas College of Music and continuing since her 2002 retirement, **Hildegard C. Froehlich** has authored, co-authored, and/or edited 7 books and 10 book chapters and written numerous refereed and non-refereed articles and book reviews as well as proceedings of national and international conferences and symposia. She is perhaps best known for her textbooks: this one, which has its origin in *Research in Music Education: An Introduction to Systematic Inquiry* (Schirmer Books, 1987), co-authored with her late husband Edward Rainbow; and *Sociology for Music Teachers* (2nd edition, Routledge, 2017, co-authored with Gareth Dylan Smith; 1st edition, Prentice-Hall, 2007). In 2015, she published *A Social Theory for Music Education: Symbolic Interactionism in Music Learning and Teaching* (The Edwin Mellen Press). Along with her academic work, Hildegard has remained active musically for over 40 years by co-founding, directing, presiding over, and continuing to perform with the Chorus of the Denton Bach Society, a community-based, not-for-profit organization dedicated to the performance and study of classical choral repertoire.

Marie McCarthy is Professor of Music Education at the University of Michigan where she teaches courses on general music and a range of graduate seminars in music education. Her primary research focus is the transmission of music in historical contexts. She serves as Editor of the *Journal of Historical Research in Music Education* and Chair of the History Standing Committee of the International Society for Music Education (ISME). She is an Honorary Life Member of ISME, and of the Society for Music Education in Ireland.

Debbie Rohwer is Vice President for Planning, Chief of Staff, and Regents Professor of Music Education at the University of North Texas. She also directs and facilitates the Denton New Horizons Senior Citizen Band, which she initially organized in 1997, and she serves as past Chair of the Adult and Community Music Education Special Research Interest Group through NAfME. Dr. Rohwer's research on the topic of music learning with children and adults has been published extensively in national and international journals and books.

Index

Note: Page numbers in *italics* indicate a figure and page numbers in **bold** indicate a table on the corresponding page.